LEARNING TO BE A ~~SUPER~~ PRIMARY TEACHER

JONATHAN GLAZZARD

CRITICAL TEACHING

CORE KNOWLEDGE & UNDERSTANDING

First published in 2016 by Critical Publishing Ltd

British Library Cataloguing in Publication Data

A CIP record for this book is available from the British Library

ISBN: 978-1-910391-74-7

This book is also available in the following e-book formats:
MOBI: 978-1-910391-75-4
EPUB: 978-1-910391-76-1
Adobe ebook reader: 978-1-910391-77-8

Cover and text design by Greensplash Limited
Project Management by Out of House Publishing
Printed and bound in Great Britain by TJ International, Padstow

Critical Publishing

152 Chester Road
Northwich
CW8 4AL

www.criticalpublishing.com

CONTENTS

MEET THE AUTHOR

Jonathan Glazzard is Head of Academic Development at Leeds Trinity University. In this role he is responsible for the implementation of the learning, teaching and assessment strategy across all courses. He was awarded a National Teaching Fellowship in 2015 for having demonstrated an outstanding contribution to learning and teaching in higher education. Prior to undertaking his current role Jonathan was Head of Primary Initial Teacher Training courses at the University of Huddersfield. He is a qualified teacher and taught in primary schools before moving into higher education.

ACKNOWLEDGEMENTS

I would like to dedicate this book to all the trainee teachers and schools that I have worked with. Special thanks to my partner, Stuart, for all his support and patience.

INTRODUCTION

The recent government White Paper entitled *Educational Excellence Everywhere* makes it clear that education serves an agenda for social justice. It states:

An excellent education unlocks opportunity, helping children from all backgrounds to shape their own destiny. Wherever they live and whatever their background, ability or needs, every child and young person in this country deserves a world class education that allows them to reach their full potential and prepares them to succeed in adult life in modern Britain.

(DfE, 2016, para 1.2, p 5)

The key strategy for Initial Teacher Training (ITT) is to move to an increasingly school-led system for training teachers, while still retaining an important role for the best universities in the delivery of ITT. The award of Qualified Teacher Status will be replaced with a more challenging accreditation designed to raise the quality and status of the teaching profession, and accreditation will be awarded by schools rather than universities.

The White Paper states that '*One of the hallmarks of a mature profession is a body of evidence which sets out what works and what doesn't, and which develops and evolves over time*' (DfE, 2016, para 2.54, p 38). A new College of Teaching will be established to support the development of evidence-based practice. Concerns are also expressed in the White Paper that '*Despite decades of research showing its positive effects, systematic synthetic phonics had been disregarded by many schools, local authorities, and university education faculties*' (DfE, 2016, para 2.56, p 38).

This book does not address all of the challenges identified in the White Paper. Much of the text was written prior to the publication of the document, although it does promote an evidence-based approach to teaching by drawing on some of the latest research findings. The first chapter examines some of this research and excerpts of research are included in each chapter. The book also promotes the use of systematic approaches to synthetic phonics.

The book is structured so that it addresses some of the key recommendations in the Carter Review of 2015. In addressing these recommendations there are separate chapters on subject knowledge, planning and differentiation, child development, assessment, behaviour management, and special educational needs and/or disabilities. By focusing on these chapters the book is aligned with the current Teachers' Standards.

I hope you will gain valuable information from this text which will support your development as a beginning teacher. The White Paper will certainly challenge schools and ITT providers. The pace of change in both sectors in recent years has been relentless. It will take longer to ascertain whether the changes have a positive impact on the quality of teachers entering the profession and the quality of teaching in the classroom. Education has always been a political football but the pace of change in recent years has resulted in instability both in ITT and in schools.

In the midst of all the challenges you will inevitably face, my hope is that you will remember why you came into teaching. Most teachers enter the profession to make a difference to the life chances of children and young people. In short, to make a difference. Most teachers have a moral purpose which is underpinned by a commitment to social justice. I once met a teacher who had been teaching for 37 years. She told me that she had witnessed a plethora of policy changes during that time but despite these changes she was guided in her daily work by a commitment to some very clear and simple principles. I cannot recall all of them but they included the following: children are active learners; children develop at different rates; build on children's starting points; celebrate their achievements. This book might help to shape the development of your values in relation to education. Equally, your values will be shaped by the schools you work in, the mentors who guide you, your continuing professional development and your own research. This book does not have all the answers and in many cases there are no answers. Teaching is not black and white. There is no one way of doing things or even a 'right' way of doing things and what works with one learner or one class does not necessarily work with another. Teaching and learning are incredibly complex, but, in the words of the late Rita Pierson, they should bring joy! Keep an open mind. Question and learn from the practice you observe and maintain your interest. View yourself as a learner as well as a teacher and use this book as a starting point for that very exciting journey.

References

DfE (2016) *Educational Excellence Everywhere*. DfE.

1: USING RESEARCH

TEACHERS' STANDARDS

This chapter addresses the following Teachers' Standards:

Teachers' Standard 8: Fulfil wider professional responsibilities

Teachers must:

* *take responsibility for improving teaching through appropriate professional development, responding to advice and feedback from colleagues.*

In relation to this standard the term 'professional development' is interpreted broadly and includes teacher engagement with research and scholarship as well as access to courses, training, coaching and mentoring.

PROFESSIONAL LINKS

The *Carter Review of Initial Teacher Training* made the following recommendations:

Recommendation 1c: *Evidence-based teaching should be part of a framework for ITT content.*

Recommendation 6: *The Teachers' Standards should be amended to be more explicit about the importance of teachers taking an evidence-based approach.*

Recommendation 7: *A central portal of synthesised executive summaries, providing practical advice on research findings about effective teaching in different subjects and phases, should be developed. A future College of Teaching would be well placed to develop this.*

Recommendation 8: *ITT partnerships should make more systematic use of wider expertise outside university departments of education. There are many universities that are home to world-leading research and assessment organisations.*

(Carter, 2015, pp 8–9)

CHAPTER OBJECTIVES

* **What is this chapter about?**

In this chapter you will learn about:

1. the importance of evidence-based teaching – what works and how do we know?
2. some of the key research that underpins aspects of teaching.

* **Why is it important?**

Effective teaching is underpinned by research findings. Research helps us to understand the effectiveness of different teaching strategies, interventions and ways of working in the classroom. As a teacher it is important that the practices you implement in your classroom are evidence-based and informed by research. As a reflective teacher you have a responsibility to evaluate research and challenge it before applying it in the classroom. Research helps to demonstrate that teaching strategies have an impact and will make a difference to children's learning. Without research it is difficult to establish the effectiveness of particular teaching strategies and you could waste a lot of time implementing strategies which make little or no difference to children's learning.

The Carter Review stated that:

We believe it is critical that ITT should teach trainees why engaging with research is important and build an expectation and enthusiasm for teaching as an evidence-based profession. International evidence, including the RSA-BERA inquiry (British Educational Research Association (BERA), 2014), shows us that high-performing systems induct their teachers in the use, assessment and application of research findings.

(Carter, 2015, XVI, p 8)

Additionally,

Our findings suggest that sometimes ITT focuses on trainees conducting their own research, without necessarily teaching trainees the core skills of how to access, interpret and use research to inform classroom practice. It is important that trainees understand how to interpret educational theory and research in a critical way, so they are able to deal with contested issues.

(Carter, 2015, XVII, p 8)

Research findings can help to shape your educational values because they will help to inform your core beliefs about learning and teaching. During your ITT programme you will be introduced to seminal research findings on aspects of pedagogy such as assessment, feedback and early reading. Seminal research is research which has made a significant and often longstanding contribution to knowledge. It often informs current practice and is cited in books, journals and during teacher professional development sessions. However, as well as knowing seminal research it is also important that you keep up-to-date with the latest research findings on aspects of educational pedagogy. This will give you the confidence and knowledge to express your views to colleagues and to experiment with new approaches to teaching. Keeping up-to-date with current research findings will enable you to be a reflective teacher and it will keep you interested in teaching!

In this chapter, some key teaching methods and approaches are examined in relation to the current research to help you position your own teaching around the latest evidence. This chapter will also explore how you might access research and research summaries in order to keep up-to-date in your professional practice.

How to locate research

The starting point for you to access research is your ITT provider library. This may be a physical library which includes educational resources such as books and academic and professional journals. Your provider is also required to provide you with access to an electronic library. This will enable you to access online journals and electronic books as well as other resources such as newspaper articles. You will need to learn how to search electronic databases to help you locate research, and many providers now include this as part of the ITT induction process. You will need to learn which search words might yield the best results and then you will need to narrow the search by selecting various filters. General searches often produce several thousand sources so it is important to be as specific as you can when searching for material so that you can select sources from a narrower range.

Table 1.1 Useful websites where you can access research

Name of organisation	URL / web address
Department for Education	www.gov.uk/government/publications
The Sutton Trust	www.suttontrust.com/research/
National Association for Special Educational Needs	www.nasen.org.uk/resources/
The Reading Reform Foundation	www.rrf.org.uk/resources.html
The Joseph Rowntree Foundation	www.jrf.org.uk/publications

In addition to your electronic library, many sources are now freely available on the internet for you to access.

Subject associations and charities or interest groups may provide access to useful research via their individual websites. Google Scholar is also a useful search engine for finding research. It is important to bear in mind that just because something has been published, that alone does not ensure it is quality material. You should be sceptical about material that you access on the web, particularly if it has not been through a process of peer review. Peer review is a process which assures the quality of the research, which usually goes through a process of revision before it is published. When searching through your provider's online library you are well-advised to select the 'peer review' option which filters out any material which has not been subject to this.

As time is precious on any ITT programme you will not be able to read everything and you will not be expected to do so. To save time, many reports (particularly government reports) include an 'executive summary' of the publication at the front and it is usually sufficient to read this. Try to access the summaries of research findings rather than wasting valuable time reading whole studies.

Evidence-based teaching: phonics

This section demonstrates how you might approach looking at research and how you can use it to inform your practice. Specifically, it evaluates the effectiveness of synthetic phonics compared to analytic phonics. It presents the key research findings and offers a critical appraisal of this research.

During the last decade there has been a political focus which has highlighted the importance of systematic synthetic phonics in securing children's skills in word recognition. Successive governments in England have exerted pressure on schools to teach synthetic phonics and this has been regulated through various inspection frameworks. Additionally, inspections of initial teacher education in England have focused heavily on the extent to which training providers have ensured that all trainee teachers have thorough training in synthetic phonics. Publishers have developed commercial schemes for teaching synthetic phonics and high-profile individuals have developed consultancy work in this area. The political message is clear. Teachers have been told that synthetic phonics is the best way of teaching children to read. However, as critical, reflective teachers it is important to know that what you do in the classroom is substantiated by research evidence. You need to establish that what you are doing is likely to work and you need to be aware of other approaches if one strategy does not work with specific learners. Children are individuals. They learn in different ways and at different rates and one strategy will not necessarily suit all children.

Successive governments in England have, in recent decades, invested heavily in various educational initiatives. However, England lags behind other countries in terms of its performance in international education league tables. For example, in the Progress in International Reading Literacy Study (PIRLS) in 2011 there was a greater proportion of weaker readers in England than in many other high-achieving countries (Mullis et al, 2012). It would appear that the significant political investment has not always had the desired impact in terms of raising educational achievement.

It is important to critically examine the evidence from research findings to establish the effectiveness of different teaching strategies. In relation to the teaching of reading, the discipline of psychology is a good place to look for evidence. Teachers need a secure understanding of psychology to understand child development. Without this, it is difficult to plan for progression in learning or help children overcome misconceptions in their knowledge, skills and understanding. The next sections therefore examine the psychological research on different approaches to phonics before arriving at a synthesis.

Definitions

The term 'synthetic' is taken from the verb 'to synthesise'. Beginning readers are taught grapheme-phoneme correspondences and are taught to *blend* phonemes all through the word right from the outset in order to develop word reading skills (Johnston and Watson, 2007). They are also taught the reverse process of *segmenting* a spoken word into its constituent phonemes. These are then represented as graphemes for spelling. Letter sounds are learned at a rapid pace and the skills of blending and segmenting are taught from the start (Johnston and Watson, 2007). In contrast, analytic phonics introduces blending much later in the process. Children are taught to analyse the common phoneme in a set of words and individual phonemes are not pronounced in isolation (Strickland, 1998).

Evidence for synthetic phonics

The Rose Review in England (Rose, 2006) concluded that:

> *Having considered a wide range of evidence, the review has concluded that the case for systematic phonic work is overwhelming and much strengthened by a synthetic approach.*
>
> **(Rose, 2006, para 51, p 20)**

In this review, Rose recommended that synthetic phonics *'offers the best route to becoming skilled readers'* (p 19) and he argued that teachers should be required to teach synthetic phonics 'first' and 'fast'. This recommendation informed literacy policy in England and the content of initial teacher education courses.

Rose substantiated his claim by drawing on evidence from the Clackmannanshire research in Scotland (Watson and Johnston, 1998). The second experiment examined the performance of three groups of children who received interventions over a ten-week period. Each intervention lasted for 15 minutes twice a week. One group received sight vocabulary training, a second group received intervention in analytic phonics and a third group received intervention in synthetic phonics. The results led the researchers to conclude that synthetic phonics led to better reading, spelling and phonemic awareness gains than the other two approaches (Watson and Johnston, 1998).

A longitudinal study reported by Johnston and Watson (2005) has demonstrated that synthetic phonics is particularly effective for boys. This study reported that both boys and girls demonstrated substantial gains in word reading, spelling and comprehension which were sustained over time when taught through a synthetic phonics approach. However, the gain was larger for boys (Johnston and Watson, 2005). Additionally, the research found that synthetic phonics enabled children from areas of deprivation to overcome social disadvantage by demonstrating gains in reading and spelling which enabled these children to perform above their chronological age (Johnston and Watson, 2005). More recent research also supports these findings. For example, a study by Johnston et al (2011) compared the performance of ten-year-old boys and girls who had been taught to read by either synthetic or analytic phonics. The study found that the group taught by synthetic phonics had better spelling, word reading and comprehension than the group taught by analytic phonics. Additionally, the results demonstrated that the boys taught by synthetic phonics had better word reading, spelling and comprehension than the girls who had been taught by the same method.

However, the Clackmannanshire research (experiment 2 specifically) has received considerable criticism in the academic literature (Wyse and Goswami, 2008). The study lacked sufficient rigour in its design to establish whether the synthetic approach is superior to the analytic approach (Wyse and Goswami, 2008). Children in the analytic phonics group were taught fewer letters than children in the synthetic phonics group (Wyse and Styles, 2007) and the groups were given different amounts of teaching (Wyse and Styles, 2007). Additionally, the research design did not isolate the impact of additional treatment factors which might have contributed to the gains in reading, spelling and phonemic awareness (Ellis and Moss, 2014). For example, factors such as teacher effectiveness; parents' educational attainment; the quality of the literacy environment in the home; remedial help offered outside the intervention and other reading interventions which operated within the school were not controlled and therefore the evidence is insufficiently robust (Ellis and Moss, 2014). The study failed to report information about the time spent on phonics instruction outside the intervention, time spent on other reading activities and the contexts in which children were exposed to phonics (Ellis and Moss, 2014). Given these serious flaws in the reporting of the research and the design of the study Ellis and Moss concluded that:

> *The weakness of the research design, including the way the statistical data were analysed and reported, suggest it would be unwise to draw any clear conclusions for pedagogy or policy from this single study.*
>
> **(Ellis and Moss, 2014, p 249)**

Despite the methodological weaknesses of the Clackmannanshire research, Johnston and Watson (2005) concluded that *'synthetic phonics was a more effective approach to teaching reading, spelling and phonemic awareness than analytic phonics'* (p 351). However, as Wyse and Styles (2007, p 39) point out *'it is important that gains are shown for comprehension, not just for decoding and related skills'*. In the first experiment the reporting of the comprehension outcomes is ambiguous and in the second experiment the comprehension findings are not reported (Wyse and Styles, 2007). The subsequent longitudinal study published by Johnston and Watson (2005) reported gains in comprehension scores but there was no control group so it is not possible to attribute gains in comprehension to synthetic phonics (Wyse and Styles, 2007). Additionally, comprehension scores during the longitudinal study were assessed using different tests, thus invalidating any results.

Given the serious limitations of the research, it is questionable why Rose (2006) acknowledged the criticisms that were levelled against it but failed to take any of these into account. To launch a policy change on a lack of robust, empirical evidence was both hasty and naïve and not an adequate solution for addressing England's low position in the international literacy league tables.

EVALUATE

- *How robust is the evidence in support of the use of synthetic phonics? Explain your answer in as much detail as possible.*

Evidence for analytic phonics

Analytic phonics is often described as processing text by going from whole to part, rather than part to whole as is the case in synthetic phonics (Moustafa and Maldonado-Colon, 1998). It is a strategy which emphasises the use of larger grain sizes and the use of rime in reading by analogy.

Goswami (2005) has argued that synthetic phonics is highly effective in orthographically consistent languages. However, in languages such as English, which are not orthographically consistent, it is more difficult for children to use smaller grain sizes (ie phonemes) because the inconsistency is greater for smaller grapheme units than for larger grain sizes such as rimes (Goswami, 2005). Most languages use syllables with a simple consonant-vowel (CV) structure. However, in the English language most syllables have the following structures: CVC, CVCC or CCVC (Wyse and Goswami, 2008). In English, one grapheme can have multiple pronunciations, while in many other languages letters are consistently pronounced in the same way. Additionally, in English one phoneme can be represented by different graphemes while in most other languages a phoneme is always spelt in the same way.

The complexities of the English language inevitably mean that teaching phonics through small grain sizes will result in confusion for beginning readers when there is inconsistency in the sounds represented by these units in different words. Additionally, the inconsistencies transfer to spelling when one sound is represented by different graphemes in different words. Goswami (2005) argued that a developmental teaching sequence based on developing rhyming skills helps children to read by analogy and better suits the irregular orthography of English.

Research suggests that children code-switch from small to large grain sizes when learning English depending on the word they are reading (Brown and Deavers, 1999; Goswami et al, 2003). Some words have to be learned as whole units because they have *'no orthographic neighbours'* (Goswami, 2005, p 281). Other words, particularly CVC words, have consistent letter-phoneme recoding and the use of small grain sizes is an effective decoding strategy in these cases (Goswami, 2005). Some words contain rimes that are common to other words (*light/fight*) and therefore the use of rimes works particularly well in these cases. This suggests that analytic phonics has an important role to play in learning to read, given the orthographic inconsistencies of the English language.

EVALUATE

* *How robust is the evidence in support of the use of analytic phonics? Explain your answer in as much detail as possible.*

Evaluating the research evidence

According to Torgerson et al, *'There is currently no strong randomised controlled trial evidence that any one form of systematic phonics is more effective than any other'* (2006, p 49). Research evidence which is available is insufficient to allow for reliable judgements to be made about the efficiency of different approaches to systematic phonics instruction (Stuart, 2006). In countries where there are one-to-one mappings between letters and sounds (such as in Finland, Greece, Italy and Spain) there is evidence to suggest that synthetic phonics can be extremely effective (Landerl, 2000). However, the phonological complexity of the English language and the inconsistent spelling system mean that there is a need for direct instruction at levels other than the level of the phoneme in order to produce effective readers (Goswami, 2005; Wyse and Goswami, 2008). The inconsistency of English inhibits the automatic correspondences between graphemes and their phonemes (Goswami, 1999; Seymour et al, 2003) and thus it seems logical to suggest that beginning readers should be taught a range of grain sizes rather than focusing solely on the level of the phoneme.

There is now a considerable body of evidence to suggest that no one method of teaching children to read is superior to any other method (Landerl, 2000; Spencer and Hanley, 2003; Torgerson et al, 2006; Walton et al, 2001) and there is no empirical evidence to justify Rose's recommendation that the teaching of reading in England should rely on synthetic phonics. Much of his evidence was anecdotal (Wyse and Goswami, 2008) rather than empirical, and formulating policy on the basis of anecdotal accounts lacks sufficient rigour to justify its implementation.

Although the evidence on the most effective approach to teaching phonics is inconclusive, there is clear evidence that a systematic approach to phonics produces gains in word reading and spelling (Torgerson et al, 2006) irrespective of whether analytic or synthetic phonics is used. Walton et al (2001) concluded from their research that as long as tuition was systematic, then both approaches (synthetic or analytic) lead to similar gains and this finding is supported by a range of studies (Landerl, 2000; Spencer and Hanley, 2003; Torgerson et al, 2006; Walton et al, 2001).

CHALLENGE

* *Taking into account the research evidence presented above, do you think the evidence to support the implementation of a policy for synthetic phonics is sufficiently robust?*

APPLY

* *During your next period of school-based training, specifically observe children in Key Stage 2 who are struggling with the task of decoding print. It is likely that these learners have been taught a programme of synthetic phonics. What approaches are being used to support these learners to develop word recognition skills?*

Evidence-based teaching: models of reading development

In order to help you understand the importance of theory in informing educational practice this section examines two models of reading development. Given the current political emphasis on phonics in England, there is a need to examine the theoretical models which underpin reading development in order to establish whether phonics is sufficiently able to produce skilled readers.

The Simple View of Reading

The Simple View of Reading (SVR) was developed by Gough and Tunmer nearly 30 years ago (Gough and Tunmer, 1986). The model proposes that reading ability or reading comprehension (R) is the product of two components: decoding (D) and language comprehension (C). This is often represented by the formula $R = D \times C$. The model suggests that the two components are independent of each other and that each is necessary for successful reading (Gustafson et al, 2013). Thus, neither decoding nor language comprehension is sufficient in itself to produce skilled and effective reading. The model is represented below:

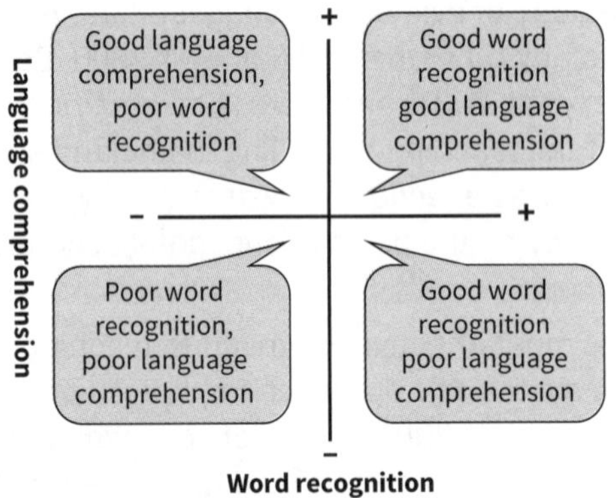

Figure 1.1 Simple View of Reading

The SVR as a model of reading development has strong academic support (Aaron, 1997; Catts et al, 2003; Kirby and Savage, 2008; Roberts and Scott, 2006) as well as support from policy makers in England. In 2006 Jim Rose recommended that *'the searchlights model should be reconstructed to take full account of word recognition and language comprehension as distinct processes related one to the other'* (Rose, 2006, p 70). The searchlights model had originally been adopted by the National Literacy Strategy (DfEE, 1998). The model promoted the use of multiple cues for reading unknown text. These included phonic, grammatical, graphic and contextual cues for tackling unfamiliar print. The model is represented below:

However, although this model emphasised that reading is a complex activity, it confounded the skills of word recognition and text comprehension by emphasising the use of text comprehension strategies for word recognition (Stuart et al, 2008).

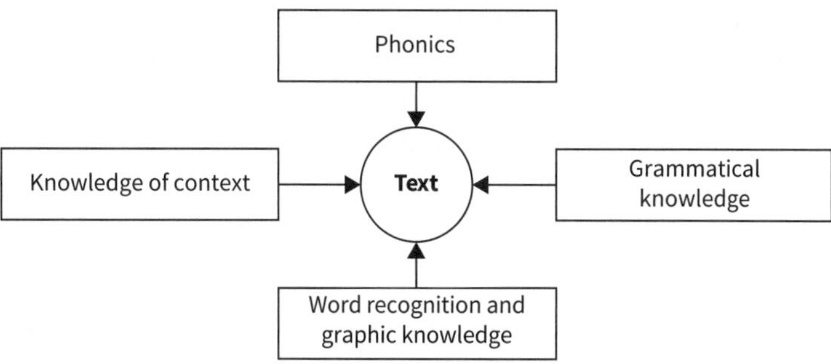

Figure 1.2 Searchlights model

In contrast to the searchlights model, the SVR emphasises the distinct role that word recognition and language comprehension make to reading development. Neither component is sufficient in isolation because each component makes a distinct contribution to reading ability (Gustafson et al, 2013). The combination of the two variables is a more effective predictor of reading ability than the contribution that each variable makes in isolation of the other (Gough and Tunmer, 1986; Joshi and Aaron, 2000). Several studies have demonstrated that different skills and abilities contribute to the development of comprehension and decoding, thus supporting their dissociation in reading development (Cutting and Scarborough, 2006; Kendeou et al, 2005, 2007; Muter et al, 2004). However, the assumption that decoding and language comprehension make independent contributions to reading development has been challenged more recently by Tunmer and Chapman (2012) who argued that one component of oral language comprehension (vocabulary) affects decoding.

However, the extent to which decoding and comprehension predict reading ability is dependent upon the level of reading skills. For children struggling as readers, decoding is a better predictor but comprehension is a better predictor to explain variance in reading ability among skilled readers (Hoover and Gough, 1990). The SVR is useful because it explains the variance in reading ability among individuals with reading difficulties. Thus, for individuals who struggle to read words accurately but are able to comprehend text this is due to deficiencies in word recognition (decoding). Children with dyslexia may fall into this quadrant. Some individuals are able to read words accurately and with fluency but they display limited understanding of the text. For these individuals the skill of word recognition (decoding) is established but the skill of comprehension is under-developed. They are described as hyperlexic. Many children with severe reading difficulties struggle in both aspects of word recognition and language comprehension. They can neither read words nor comprehend text.

Crucially, the model has direct practical implications for teachers (Kendeou et al, 2009). It enables teachers to assess which skill(s) may be responsible for reading difficulties and then to determine what type of intervention is necessary to remediate the difficulty (Savage, 2006). This is because the model clearly distinguishes between the skills of word recognition and language comprehension and therefore different approaches to teaching are required to develop each of these skills. Thus, if teachers know the cause of the reading failure, they are able to intervene more effectively. Studies demonstrate that children can perform differently in decoding and comprehension. A poor reader with good comprehension but poor decoding skills (as evidenced in studies by Adlof et al (2006) and Spooner et al (2004)) may benefit from a structured multi-sensory phonic intervention designed to develop automatic grapheme-phoneme correspondence and blending skills. A child with secure decoding but poor comprehension, as evidenced in several studies

(Cain, Oakhill and Lemmon, 2005; Nation, 2005; Stothard and Hulme, 1992), may benefit from a structured language intervention programme and increased exposure to oral language through a language development programme and exposure to a communication-rich environment, including opportunities for play, collaboration, speaking and listening. A child who displays poor word recognition and poor comprehension will benefit from structured intervention in both domains. Thus, the SVR supports both assessment and targeted intervention by separating the two fundamental components of reading.

EVALUATE

* *In what ways is the Simple View of Reading a useful model for teachers? Explain your answer.*

CHALLENGE

* *In what ways could it be argued that the Simple View of Reading over-simplifies the process of learning to read?*

Challenging the research evidence

Although the SVR is simple in the sense that it identifies only two components of reading (word recognition and language comprehension), the skills of decoding and comprehension are actually quite complex (Kirby and Savage, 2008; Tunmer and Greaney, 2010). The model thus risks over-simplifying the very complex skill of reading comprehension. The skill of decoding refers to the ability to quickly and with increasing automaticity *'derive a representation of the written, visual stimuli that gives access to adequate retrieval of information from the mental lexicon'* (Gustafson et al, 2013, p 293). Thus, the skill of decoding requires the retrieval of semantic information on the word level (Hoover and Gough, 1990). In dual-route models of word decoding, access to word meaning can be gained by *phonological decoding* or *visual-orthographic decoding* (Ellis and Young, 1988). As word recognition develops there is a gradual shift from phonological decoding to orthographic decoding (Gustafson et al, 2013) and skilled readers tend to use orthographic strategies rather than the phonological strategy which relies on grapheme-phoneme conversion (Ehri and Wilce, 1987). Additionally, Kirby and Savage (2008) argue that fluency as well as accuracy is important in decoding so this skill also needs to be developed. The danger of the SVR is that the model emphasises decoding as a key reading skill but fails to emphasise the importance of developing the sub-components of decoding which are essential in the development of decoding.

Likewise, the skill of comprehension is complex and can be sub-divided into sub-skills (Kirby and Savage, 2008). Comprehension involves several linguistic domains at the same time (Gustafson et al, 2013), including phonology, semantics, grammar and pragmatics. The SVR fails to recognise the development of linguistic comprehension within each of these domains. It is therefore unsurprising that some researchers have suggested more complex theories which sub-divide decoding and language comprehension into sub-components (for example, Velluntino et al, 2000, 2004).

APPLY

- *During your next period of school-based training identify learners who fall within each of the different quadrants of the SVR. Identify the specific intervention that each of them needs to improve their reading development.*

Ehri's model of reading development

Recent theories of reading development in alphabetic orthographies suggest that a critical stage of development in learning to read is the mastery of the skill of decoding (Stuart, Stainthorp and Snowling, 2008). This skill requires beginning readers to understand the relationship between graphemes and phonemes. Ehri's theory of reading development (Ehri, 1992, 1995) proposes four phases in the development of automatic word reading. These phases are termed: *pre-alphabetic; partial alphabetic; full alphabetic and consolidated alphabetic.*

In the pre-alphabetic phase children have not yet understood the relationship between phonemes and graphemes. At this phase their reading is dependent upon visual memory (Stuart, Stainthorp and Snowling, 2008). They may be able to read environmental print, especially if it appears with salient visual cues such as logos which use specific colours and fonts (Johnston and Watson, 2007). However, if the visual cues are removed children are generally unable to recognise the word (Johnston et al, 1996). Although there is some evidence to suggest that children use visual cues in words to aid word recognition (Ehri, 1992, 1995; Frith, 1985; Gough, 1993; Seymour and Elder, 1986), some researchers have suggested that the pre-alphabetic phase is not an essential phase in learning to read words (Jackson and Coltheart, 2001; Stuart and Coltheart, 1988).

In the partial alphabetic phase beginning readers are able to identify the initial and final phonemes in spoken words and they are able to make some connections between graphemes and their corresponding phonemes (Stuart, Stainthorp and Snowling, 2008). Their attempts at decoding are not always accurate at this phase but they are no longer arbitrary (Stuart, Stainthorp and Snowling, 2008). They are unable to decode print systematically throughout a word and they may make logical errors based on interpreting the initial and final phonemes correctly (Johnston and Watson, 2007).

At the full alphabetic stage letters are mapped sequentially onto sounds (Stuart, Stainthorp and Snowling, 2008) and therefore children are able to make connections between letters and sounds all the way through a word (Johnston and Watson, 2007). At this phase children have mastered the simple and complex alphabetic code and they are able to read phonetically regular words with accuracy. Once they have decoded a word accurately, children will start to automatically remember the word because at this phase children are establishing a sight vocabulary at the same time as developing proficiency in the skill of systematically decoding words.

In the consolidated alphabetic phase, children start to decode words on the basis of larger units of sound. These include morphemes, onsets and rimes. At this phase children are successful word readers; their decoding is becoming increasingly accurate and their reading is becoming more automatic and fluent (Stuart, Stainthorp and Snowling, 2008).

EVALUATE

- *How can Ehri's model of reading development inform practice in the classroom?*

Evaluating the research evidence

Ehri's model of reading development has practical relevance to teachers. It is a developmental model in that it identifies separate phases within developing the skill of word recognition and specifically blending. Teachers can use the phases to assess which point children have reached within their reading development and they can look to the subsequent phase to identify what skills the child needs to be developing next. Thus, the model can inform both teaching and assessment. The SVR fails to break down the skill of word recognition into distinct sub-phases and therefore is less informative to teachers in relation to how the skill of accurate word recognition develops. Ehri's model is also useful in terms of emphasising the important role that phonics plays in learning to read. The Rose Review (Rose, 2006) emphasised the importance of the alphabetic code as a body of knowledge that all children need to be taught and Ehri's theory of reading development underpins this approach to teaching reading.

CHALLENGE

- *What are the limitations of Ehri's model of reading development?*

Challenging the research evidence

However, Ehri's model falls somewhat short in neglecting the significant role that oral language comprehension plays in reading development. The SVR explicitly acknowledges that word recognition alone is insufficient to produce good readers. It has been argued that:

Vocabulary is one of the most consistent predictors of reading comprehension: children with good vocabularies understand texts better, and the predictive relationship between vocabulary and reading comprehension increases through the primary grades.

(Snow, 2002 and Torgerson et al, 1997 cited in Stuart et al, 2008, p 64)

Research suggests that although developing the skill of decoding makes the most significant contribution for children with reading difficulties (Gustafson et al, 2013), language comprehension is the most important predictor of reading comprehension for children with typical reading development (Gustafson et al, 2013; Hoover and Gough, 1990). Given this important finding, it is reasonable to suggest that although Ehri's model might more usefully support children with reading difficulties, it is unlikely to support those readers who are able to read words accurately and fluently but are, nevertheless, still struggling to comprehend text. The strength of the SVR is that it emphasises not only the importance of word recognition in reading development but also the crucial role that oral language comprehension plays in reading comprehension.

APPLY

* *During your next period of school-based training identify pupils in your class (or within your school) whose reading development appears to have arrested at the pre-alphabetic stage. What specific interventions do these learners need to improve their reading skills?*

Synthesis of the research

This section has described two models of reading development. It has explored the strengths and limitations of each model and compared and contrasted the models. Both models are useful in helping teachers to understand how children learn to read. Ehri's model provides a developmental framework to support teachers' understanding of the phases children progress through when developing the skill of word recognition. However, the model neglects the significant role that language comprehension plays in the process of learning to read. The SVR separates the two fundamental skills that contribute to reading comprehension (word recognition and language comprehension). The model usefully informs teachers that different kinds of teaching are necessary to develop each skill and the model helps teachers to understand what types of interventions are necessary to support reading development. However, the model fails to break down each of these skills into smaller sub-skills or phases of development that contribute to both word recognition and language comprehension. Ironically, the model fails to capture the complexity of the process of learning to read.

Given the strength of support for the role of oral language in the development of language comprehension and its subsequent role in reading comprehension, it seems logical to support Rose in arguing the need for practitioners to teach phonics within the context of a broad and rich language curriculum.

Evidence-based teaching: learning styles and multiple intelligences

This section discusses learning style theory and Gardner's theory of multiple intelligences. These theories have been influential to educational practice in recent years, offering potential solutions to educators in addressing issues of student disengagement and educational underachievement. This discussion explores both the strengths and limitations of each theory and concludes that there is insufficient convincing evidence to support their use in shaping pedagogy.

Learning style theory

Many teachers use the term *learning styles* uncritically as part of their day-to-day vocabulary. The theory assumes that students have a dominant channel (visual, auditory or kinaesthetic) through which they learn most effectively. Based on this premise it is assumed that if learning takes place using the dominant channel then learning will be more effective. The theory has direct practical importance for educators in that once a learning style has been assessed and identified through a learning style inventory then pedagogy can be adapted to enable the learner to learn through their dominant channel. There are numerous models (for example, Honey and Mumford, 2000; Kolb, 1984), each accompanied by an assessment which seeks to identify a dominant style based on an individual's responses to a series of questions about their learning behaviour. Each model has its own associated technical vocabulary (Coffield et al, 2004a, 2004b) and opposing categories, known as dichotomies.

EVALUATE

* *What do you think are the advantages and disadvantages of learning style theory?*

CHALLENGE

* *What are the limitations of learning style theory?*

Challenging the research evidence

A belief in the value of learning styles theory is evidently persistent, despite the prominence of critiques of this theory. One study found that an overwhelming majority of teachers across the world agreed that individuals learn better when they receive information in their preferred modality (Howard-Jones, 2014). Some writers have attempted to account for the popularity of learning style theory (Riener and Willingham, 2010), but there is clear psychological evidence that there are no benefits for learning from attempting to present information to learners in their preferred learning style (Geake, 2008; Howard-Jones, 2014; Pashler et al, 2009; Riener and Willingham, 2010). Coffield (2012) argues that *'In short, the research field of learning styles is theoretically incoherent and conceptually confused'* (p 220). There is an absence of an agreed theory or agreed technical vocabulary to underpin this theory and that essentially weakens the theory.

Supporters of learning style theory often present approaches to learning in the form of a pyramid which shows the percentages of information retained if content is introduced to students in different ways, for example, visually, auditorily or kinaesthetically. However, learning occurs when cognitive thinking is promoted (Willingham, 2008), cognitive thinking can be achieved by being 'active' or 'passive' and therefore this reduces the validity of learning style theory.

Research broadly supports direct instruction (Kirschner et al, 2006), rather than learners discovering things for themselves. Although motivation can be fostered by kinaesthetic approaches if teachers want students to learn new knowledge, ideas or strategies, they need to use direct teaching approaches. This research challenges constructivist learning theory, which partly underpins learning style theory.

It has been argued that research in the field of learning styles is incoherent and conceptually flawed (Coffield et al, 2004a, 2004b). This can be illustrated by the sheer number of dichotomies which the different models present and the overlap between them. Stan Ivie (2009) highlights how John Dewey rejected binaries (either/or thinking) which create false dichotomies and that in reality sharp distinctions do not exist, for example, activists/reflectors.

There is no agreed technical vocabulary and no agreed theory to underpin the dichotomies (Coffield et al, 2004a, 2004b). Additionally, learning style theory has become commercialised in recent times. The growth of the learning styles industry in recent years (Coffield et al, 2004a, 2004b) and the excessive number of models available serve to reduce

the credibility of learning style theory. Coffield (2012) argues that the existence of 70 learning style instruments demonstrates the disorganised nature of this field of enquiry. In the absence of an agreed model or agreed vocabulary, this creates confusion among educators who are responsible for meeting the needs of their students.

APPLY

* *There are many learning style questionnaires on the internet. Locate one of these and use it to assess your own learning style. Follow the instructions on the questionnaire.*

Limitations of learning style questionnaires

Learning styles are assigned on the basis of an individual completing a test in which they are required to make generalisations about how they might respond to specific challenges. However, individuals may not be able to assign a category to their behaviour; they may give responses which are socially desirable and they may feel constrained by the predetermined format of the test (Coffield et al, 2004a, 2004b). Coffield (2012), in his critique of learning style inventories, argues that context largely shapes how we behave. As individuals respond to various challenges throughout a day they will be required to use a range of learning styles and this undermines a theory which suggests that there is a dominant learning style.

The statements on learning style questionnaires are often decontextualised. A good example of this is presented by Sternberg using the following example: *When faced with a problem, I like to solve it in a traditional way* (Sternberg, 1999). When faced with this statement the reader has to be able to make a response based on the limited range of information given. Using this example to illustrate the problem of decontextualisation, it is not clear what type of problem is being referred to in this statement. Additionally, there is no reference to the context in which the problem has manifested itself. The context can largely influence how people respond to problems. For example, problems in the workplace may be addressed in very different ways to problems which occur within friendships, relationships or other social groups. Some problems can be addressed individually while it may be more effective to address other problems collectively. However, the statement assumes that the problem should be addressed by an individual rather than a larger collective. It is not clear to the reader what is meant by a 'traditional' response to a problem and it could be argued that some problems necessitate an innovative response rather than a 'traditional' response (Coffield et al, 2004a, 2004b). Far too much is left to interpretation and the reader is left to make a choice from a pre-determined list on the basis of this interpretation. Although it is highly unlikely that there will be one way of solving a problem, the question nevertheless implies that this is the case. These arguments weaken the credibility of learning style theory.

It is important for students know how to enhance their learning by developing a repertoire of approaches (Coffield et al, 2004a, 2004b) because students need to use different learning styles to complete different kinds of tasks. Additionally, effective learners use a range of styles of learning rather than relying predominantly on one dominant learning style. According to Coffield et al (2004a, 2004b) there is no substantial evidence that matching learning styles to tasks (matching hypothesis) increases educational attainment. In fact, evidence from empirical studies of matching is contradictory (Coffield et al, 2004a,

2004b); therefore, it would be unwise to base pedagogical decisions upon research evidence which is inconclusive.

Coffield et al (2004a; 2004b) argue that learning styles can artificially restrict students' learning experience by limiting the channels through which learning takes place. Learning style theory also leads to the assumption that learners have a fixed style of learning which cannot be changed (Coffield et al, 2004a, 2004b). This is an unwise assumption for both educators and students because it limits the opportunities for learning.

According to Garner (2000) there is confusion as to whether Kolb is arguing for learning style traits (which are stable) or states (which are flexible). This lack of clarity in articulating a theory undermines its credibility. It has also been argued that Kolb lacks clarity on whether his theory actually promotes learning styles or four stages of learning (Bergsteiner et al, 2010). Additionally, Kolb's model fails to differentiate between primary and secondary learning processes; it fails to differentiate between learning activities and typologies of learning; and it ignores certain learning constructs (Bergsteiner et al, 2010). However, in contrast there is a substantial body of literature which has emphasised the usefulness of Kolb's theory (Abbey et al, 1985; Kruzich et al, 1986; Nulty and Barrett, 1996; Raschick et al, 1998).

Bjork and Bjork (2011) refer to one common assumption on which learning style theory is based. Learning style theory assumes that keeping learning constant and predictable will improve later retention. However, they found that varying the types of task that learners complete and varying the learning context in fact improves retention of knowledge and skills.

Evidence-based teaching: multiple intelligences

Charles Darwin was the first psychologist to measure intelligence directly, and during the early twentieth century prominent psychologists developed a series of tests designed to measure intelligence (Binet and Simon, 1916; Spearman, 1927; Terman, 1916; Thurstone, 1938). However, despite these early advances in measuring intelligence, the work of Gardner later in the twentieth century (Gardner, 1975, 1979, 1982) began to challenge traditional views of intellect, which had emphasised how specific aspects of brain functioning were part of a single *'semiotic function'* (Gardner and Hatch, 1989, p 5). Research in the latter part of the twentieth century suggested that the human mind was modular and that distinct psychological processes were evident when dealing with different kinds of mental functions (Gardner and Wolf, 1983; Gardner, Howard and Perkins, 1974). Traditional intelligence, aptitude and achievement tests had over-emphasised logical and linguistic capacities (Gardner and Hatch, 1989). However logical-mathematical and linguistic symbolisation were (and to a certain extent still are) predominant forms of symbol use in schools which marginalise those students who are unable to demonstrate achievements in these domains.

IQ testing is one way of measuring general intelligence. Although the value of these tests has been disputed in the academic literature (Strydom and Du Plessis, 2000), other academic commentators have pointed out that they provide a useful indication of a child's general cognitive abilities (Nettelbeck and Wilson, 2005). Despite these differences in opinion there is now a consensus that intelligence represents an *'ability to understand complex ideas, to adapt effectively to the environment, to learn from experience, [and] to engage in various forms of reasoning to overcome obstacles by taking thought'* (Neisser et al, 1996, p 77). However, theorists (Gardner, 1983, 1999) envisaged cognitive abilities as several forms of intelligence which are unrelated rather than viewing general intelligence as an indication of cognitive ability.

Gardner was concerned that this narrow measure of intelligence failed to recognise that human activity involves other varieties of symbol use. Gardner developed a broader definition of intelligence which included problem-solving and practical forms of intelligence. He saw the human intelligences as relatively autonomous, meaning that one was not dependent on the other. In collaboration with his colleagues, Gardner carried out a systematic review of the literature on human intelligence. They examined the cognitive capacities of typically developing individuals as well as those of prodigies, atypically developing individuals and savants. They found that individuals differ in their intelligence profiles and that there was no inevitable correlation between any two intelligences. Multiple intelligences theory was introduced by Gardner in his book *Frames of Mind* (1983). Gardner initially concluded that there were seven intelligences (linguistic; logical-mathematical; musical; spatial; bodily-kinaesthetic; intrapersonal; interpersonal) and in 1995 he added an eighth intelligence – naturalistic. The assumption of the theory is that the intelligences are independent of each other and that individuals often demonstrate an uneven profile in that some intelligences will be greater than others.

Standard intelligence tests demonstrate a bias towards logical and linguistic skills. The assessment of intelligence using these tests is carried out artificially by removing a child from the social context in which learning takes place. In contrast, assessment of multiple intelligences is not decontextualised and takes place within a familiar social and cultural context (Gardner and Hatch, 1989), thus making the assessment more naturalistic. Almeida (2010) has argued that standard intelligence tests used in psychology are not significantly different to those used a century ago. This is despite advances in socioconstructivist learning theory, which has emphasised the importance of social and cultural factors in the learning process and the role of talk in promoting learning. Despite these developments within learning theory, a psychometric approach to testing intelligence is still the dominant approach (Almeida, 2010). The psychometric tests present items in an abstract manner and terminology is often vague and generalised.

Gardner's work on intelligence presents an alternative to the dominant psychometric approaches. Assessment of intelligence takes place within classroom contexts and therefore the assessment has better ecological validity than standard psychometric tests (Almeida, 2010). Intelligence relates to the ability to undertake a wide variety of problem-solving tasks, the ability to think in an abstract manner and an ability to infer relationships, thus highlighting the multi-dimensional nature of intelligence (Almeida, 2010). In addition, different individuals pursue different goals and therefore it seems logical to argue that there are many different types of intelligence (White, 2006).

EVALUATE

* *What are the advantages and disadvantages of learning style theory?*

CHALLENGE

* *What are the criticisms of multiple intelligence theory?*

Challenging the research evidence

According to John White:

Putting children into boxes that have not been proved to exist may end up restricting the education they receive, leading teachers to overly rigid views of individual pupils' potentialities, and, what is worse, a new type of stereotyping.

(White, 2005, p 9)

Multiple intelligence theory has been rejected outright by researchers that support psychometric approaches to measuring intelligence (Brand, 1996; Sternberg, 1983), with some claiming that Gardner's intelligences are styles of cognition rather than intelligences per se (Morgan, 1992).

Although Gardner has emphasised that separate intelligences work largely independently, most activities tend to draw on several intelligences (Klein, 1997). Nettelbeck and Wilson (2005) emphasise that Gardner's separate intelligences overlap rather than exist independently. For example, Klein (1997) highlights that conversation draws on both interpersonal and linguistic intelligences. Although Gardner has emphasised that pairs of intelligence may overlap or be correlated in some way, this weakens his claim for categorising the intelligences as distinct entities. If intelligence systems work together in practice, then this could in fact support the notion of one general intelligence and that abilities in specific areas are merely components of this intelligence.

Although Gardner cites examples of geniuses, many of these geniuses excel in more than one domain and within a subset of a domain rather than demonstrating high performance throughout a domain (Klein, 1997). Additionally, many geniuses do not fit the categories of Gardner's intelligence and given that geniuses are rare, these examples are unhelpful as a basis for educational practice (Klein, 1997). This weakens Gardner's work. For example, Gardner discusses savants; individuals who do one thing very well. However, Klein challenges this by pointing out that these individuals do not usually excel across a whole domain (Klein, 1997). Klein uses the example of hyperlexic autistic readers who can decode print well but have poor comprehension – therefore, they do not have high linguistic intelligence. Children with dyslexia may have good listening comprehension or oracy skills while at the same time have poor phonological skills. Therefore, dyslexics do not necessarily demonstrate a weakness across the entire domain of linguistic intelligence. Some pupils may have particular strengths in solving calculations but demonstrate poor spatial awareness, thus demonstrating an uneven profile across the domain of logical-mathematical intelligence.

Furthermore, Gardner's model relates achievement in specific areas to intelligence, in contrast to traditional views of intelligence which focus on cognitive thought processes. However, the linking of intelligence to achievement is problematic because it suggests that this achievement will have relative stability over time (Klein, 1997). However, achievements can decline over a period of time, particularly if skills are not practised. In contrast, cognitive thought processes have relative stability over time. This raises questions about whether intelligence should be defined on the basis of specific abilities, skills and talents rather than on the basis of an individual's cognitive thought processes.

A significant limitation of Gardner's theory is that students who score low in a specific intelligence might avoid activities that draw on this intelligence even though they might learn through perseverance (Covington, 1992; Palmquist and Young, 1992). Additionally, children might choose to disengage with activities which they find challenging (Klein, 1997). Klein

(1997) emphasises that reliable methods for assessing the different intelligences in Gardner's theory have not been established and that the categories are too broad to be useful.

Gardner fails to specify the evidence which supports each intelligence and therefore multiple intelligence theory lacks empirical support (Waterhouse, 2006). He fails to provide a set of sub-components which can be tested for each intelligence (Waterhouse, 2006). The various intelligences are described by general characteristics rather than specific components and this has prevented researchers from conducting rigorous tests to explore the validity of his theory (Waterhouse, 2006). He assumed that the theory required no empirical validation because it is based on a synthesis of research findings. However, multiple intelligence theory merely assumes the validity of the intelligences because there is no rigorous way of actually testing these (Waterhouse, 2006).

APPLY

* *Look at Gardner's intelligences. Discuss with a colleague whether you have a dominant intelligence and support your answer with examples.*

Applying the research evidence

Gardner's theory has several important applications: these include planning schemes of work which span all the intelligences; providing intervention programmes in areas of weakness or enrichment programmes in areas of strength for learners with special educational needs or gifted students (Klein, 1997). In addition, the theory challenges those schools which currently over-emphasise logical-mathematical and linguistic knowledge to adapt the adopted pedagogical approaches so that the different intelligences are reflected in models of curriculum delivery.

Synthesis

Coffield et al (2004a; 2004b) argue that research evidence on formative assessment (Black and Wiliam, 1998) is academically robust. Therefore, it would be better for educators to concentrate on developing this aspect of their pedagogy rather than focusing on learning style theory which has no agreed theoretical base and no robust assessment procedure to underpin the various models. Learner feedback is critical in promoting learning by accelerating achievement (Black and Wiliam, 1998) but there is no biological or educational justification for dividing learners into learning-style groups. Theories of multiple intelligence also lack empirical justification because there is no agreed tool for measuring intelligence within each domain. Additionally, learners are unlikely to excel across a whole domain and are more likely to demonstrate strengths in specific aspects within a domain. Different tasks require different abilities and therefore it seems illogical to group learners using artificial constructs. Both theories categorise learners either on the basis of learning style or intelligence; these categories place restrictions on students which can be detrimental to learning. Effective learners use a range of different styles of learning and abilities in different tasks and therefore it seems more logical for educators to ensure that they use a wide range of pedagogical approaches which enable students to use a variety of channels of learning.

Evidence-based teaching: discovery learning

Now that you understand how to evaluate research findings systematically, try to read, evaluate and challenge the following specific piece of research on *discovery learning*. Discovery learning is an approach through which learners discover key ideas for themselves without exposure to direct teaching methods. Enthusiasm for discovery learning is not supported by research evidence, which broadly favours direct approaches to teaching (Kirschner et al, 2006). Although learners do need to build new understanding on what they already know, if teachers want students to learn new ideas, knowledge or skills, they need to use direct teaching approaches.

READ

- *Using your ITT provider electronic library, access the following research:*

  Kirschner, P A, Sweller, J, and Clark, R E (2006) Why minimal guidance during instruction does not work: An analysis of the failure of constructivist, discovery, problem-based, experiential, and inquiry-based teaching. Educational Psychologist, 41(2): 75–86.

EVALUATE

- *What arguments do the authors put forward to support the claims they have made?*
- *Do the authors consider sufficiently contrasting perspectives? Explain your answer.*
- *To what extent is this research supported or contested by constructivist and behaviourist theories of learning?*

CHALLENGE

- *Are the arguments put forward by the authors sufficiently supported by evidence from experimental studies?*
- *Are there any weaknesses in the assertions that have been made?*

APPLY

- *When you are undertaking school-based training, divide your learners into two groups. Teach an aspect of the curriculum through experiential learning to one group. Teach the same aspect of the curriculum through direct teaching to the other group. Assess the learning of both groups on the same day after one week. Which method do you think was the most effective and why? What other factors might have contributed to the results?*

Evidence-based teaching: grouping

Evidence on the effects of grouping by ability suggests that it makes very little difference to student achievement (Higgins et al, 2013). Although it is claimed that ability grouping can allow teachers to target pupils' specific needs, it can also create an exaggerated sense of within-group homogeneity and between-group heterogeneity in the teacher's mind (Stipek, 2010). This can result in teachers failing to respond to children's individual needs by assuming that all learners within a group have the same needs. Ability grouping can also result in teachers going too fast with the high-ability groups and too slow with those in low-ability groups.

READ

* *Access the Sutton Trust toolkit using the following link:*
  www.educationendowmentfoundation.org.uk/toolkitDownload the full version of the toolkit. Open the document and find the section on 'setting or streaming'.

EVALUATE

* *How robust is the evidence that is presented? Explain your answer.*

CHALLENGE

* *Search for research that challenges the findings in the toolkit.*

APPLY

* *During your school-based training observe classes taught both in ability and mixed-ability groups. Which approach do you think was most effective and why?*

Evidence-based teaching: reading for pleasure

The Department for Education (DfE) is currently promoting the importance of reading for pleasure. Given the significant political focus on phonics in recent years, it would not be surprising if some schools focused less on encouraging children to read for pleasure. Evidence suggests that the majority of children in England reported that they do enjoy reading (Clark and Rumbold, 2006). In 2010, 22 per cent of children reported that they enjoyed reading very much; 27 per cent said they enjoyed it quite a lot; 39 per cent said they enjoyed it quite a bit, and 12 per cent reported that they did not enjoy reading at all (Clark, 2011). Compared to international evidence, children in England report that they read less frequently for pleasure outside of school than children in many other countries (Twist et al, 2007). Evidence consistently demonstrates that children enjoy reading less as they get older (Clark and Douglas 2011; Clark and Osborne, 2008; Topping, 2010). However, there is evidence to suggest that while the frequency with which young people read declines with age, the length of time for which they read when they do read increases with age (Clark, 2011). Several studies have indicated that boys enjoy reading less than girls and that children from working-class backgrounds read less for enjoyment than children from middle and upper social classes (Clark and Douglas, 2011; Clark and Rumbold, 2006). Additionally, evidence has shown children from Asian backgrounds have more positive attitudes to reading and read more frequently than children from White, mixed or Black backgrounds (Clark and Douglas, 2011).

Research increasingly indicates that a growing number of children do not read for pleasure (Clark and Rumbold, 2006). Between 2000 and 2009, on average across Organisation for Economic Cooperation and Development (OECD) countries the percentage of children who report reading for enjoyment daily dropped by five percentage points (OECD, 2010). This is supported by evidence from PIRLS 2006 (Twist et al, 2007), which found that attitudes towards reading had declined among children.

The DfE published a report in 2012 entitled *Research Evidence on Reading for Pleasure* (DfE, 2012), which summarised key research findings. These included the following.

* Reading for pleasure enhances educational achievement and attainment as well as personal development (Clark and Rumbold, 2006).
* There is a positive relationship between frequency and enjoyment of reading and attainment (Clark, 2011; Clark and Douglas, 2011).
* Reading enjoyment has a greater impact on children's educational success than their family's socio-economic background (OECD, 2002).
* There is a positive link between positive dispositions towards reading and achieving highly on reading assessments (Twist et al, 2007).
* Regularly reading stories or novels outside of school is associated with higher achievement in reading assessments (Mullis et al, 2007; PISA, 2009).
* International evidence also supports these findings; US research reports that independent reading is the best predictor of reading achievement (Anderson, Wilson and Fielding, 1988).
* Reading for pleasure has a positive impact on children's social and emotional development (Clark and Rumbold, 2006).
* Other benefits of reading for pleasure include: text comprehension and knowledge of grammar, positive reading attitudes, pleasure in reading in later life, increased general knowledge (Clark and Rumbold, 2006).

(research cited in DfE, 2012, p 4)

READ

* *Read the DfE review on reading for pleasure using the following link: www.gov.uk/government/uploads/system/uploads/attachment_data/file/284286/reading_for_pleasure.pdf.*

EVALUATE

* *Does the research evidence appear to be sufficiently robust? Explain your answer.*

CHALLENGE

* *Select one finding from this review of research and find counterevidence that challenges it.*

APPLY

* *During your next period of school-based training, find out what your school is doing to promote reading for pleasure. Make a note of the strategies that the school has implemented.*

Evidence-based teaching: deployment of support staff

The largest and most in-depth study ever carried out on the use and impact of teaching assistant (TA) support in everyday classroom environments is the multi-method DISS project. Unlike previous studies, it linked what TAs actually do in classrooms to effects on pupil progress. The DISS project critically examined the relationship between TA support and the academic progress of 8200 pupils. It put forward a coherent explanation for the *negative relationship* found on the basis of careful analyses of multiple forms of data collected in classrooms.

READ

* *Read the DISS project. You can find it using the following link: www.ioe.ac.uk/diss_research_summary.pdf.*

EVALUATE

* *Is the evidence presented in the research sufficiently robust? Explain your findings.*

CHALLENGE

* *Find some research which offers a contrasting perspective to that which is offered in the DISS project.*

APPLY

* *During your school-based training, observe carefully how teaching assistants are deployed across school during lessons. Carry out a learning walk which focuses on teaching assistant deployment across the school. Note down instances of effective practice where teaching assistants were positively impacting on pupils' progress and independence. Were there any examples of ineffective practice?*

Evidence-based teaching: assessment, marking and feedback

Black and Wiliam (1998) identified the following practices as those which yield the largest gains in achievement for learners:

* use of classroom discussions, classroom tasks and homework to determine the current state of student learning/understanding, with action taken to improve learning/correct misunderstandings;
* provision of descriptive feedback, with guidance on how to improve, during the learning;
* development of student self- and peer-assessment skills.

READ

* *Using your ITT provider's electronic library access the following research: Black, P and Wiliam, D (2010) Raising standards through classroom assessment. Kappan Classic, 92(1): 81–91.*

EVALUATE

* *Does the evidence presented in the research appear to be sufficiently robust? Explain your answer.*

CHALLENGE

* *Search for research findings with contrasting perspectives.*

APPLY

* *During your school-based training, conduct a marking scrutiny by looking at samples of children's books.*

- *Is the feedback specifically linked to the success criteria?*
- *Is there specific, positive feedback in relation to the success criteria?*
- *Are targets consistently identified?*
- *Is there evidence that learners are engaging with the feedback by responding to targets?*
- *Is there evidence that feedback and specifically target setting is enabling learners to make progress?*

Evidence-based teaching: active learning

Active approaches to teaching and learning have been promoted in education for many years. Research now suggests that the promotion of thinking is far more critical to effective learning and that thinking can be promoted by learners being active or passive (Coe et al, 2014).

EVALUATE

* *What are the advantages and disadvantages of active learning?*
* *To what extent is the notion of active learning supported by learning theory?*
* *Which learning theory underpins passive learning?*

CHALLENGE

* *Drawing on your own experience, can you think of times when the use of active learning has been particularly effective?*

APPLY

* *During your school-based training observe the use of active or passive approaches to learning in lessons. How do learners respond to these different approaches? Did you find any evidence of learning gains using passive approaches?*

Learning retention: evidence from cognitive psychology

Researchers in cognitive psychology have investigated the nature of learning, the conditions under which it occurs and the role of memory in this process. A useful summary can be found in Bransford et al (2000). Research suggests that some approaches that may appear to make learning harder in the short term, and less satisfying for learners, actually result in better long-term retention.

Emphasising the difference between short-term performance and long-term learning, Bjork and Bjork (2011) call these *desirable difficulties*, and give four specific examples.

1. Varying the Conditions of Practice: Varying the learning context, types of task or practice, rather than keeping them constant and predictable, improves later retention, even though it makes learning harder in the short term.
2. Spacing Study or Practice Sessions: The same amount of time spent reviewing or practising leads to much greater long-term retention if it is spread out, with gaps in between to allow forgetting. This 'is

one of the most general and robust effects from across the entire history of experimental research on learning and memory' (Bjork and Bjork, 2011, p 59).

3. Interleaving versus Blocking Instruction on Separate To-Be-Learned Tasks: Learning in a single block can create better immediate performance and higher confidence, but interleaving with other tasks or topics leads to better long-term retention and transfer of skills.
4. Generation Effects and Using Tests (Rather Than Presentations) as Learning Events: Having to generate an answer or procedure, or having to retrieve information – even if no feedback is given – leads to better long-term recall than simply studying, though not necessarily in the short term. Testing can also support self-monitoring and focus subsequent study more effectively. 'Basically, any time that you, as a learner, look up an answer or have somebody tell or show you something that you could, drawing on current cues and your past knowledge, generate instead, you rob yourself of a powerful learning opportunity' (Bjork and Bjork, 2011, p 61).

(cited in Coe et al, 2014, p 17)

The dynamic model of educational effectiveness

The dynamic model of educational effectiveness (Creemers and Kyriakides, 2006) identifies 21 effective teaching practices. These are grouped under eight headings, cited in Coe et al (2014, p 16).

Orientation

(a) Providing the objectives for which a specific task/lesson/series of lessons take(s) place.

(b) Challenging students to identify the reason why an activity is taking place in the lesson.

Structuring

(a) Beginning with overviews and/or review of objectives.

(b) Outlining the content to be covered and signalling transitions between lesson parts.

(c) Drawing attention to and reviewing main ideas.

Questioning

(a) Raising different types of questions (i.e., process and product) at appropriate difficulty level.

(b) Giving time for students to respond.

(c) Dealing with student responses.

Application

(a) Using seatwork or small-group tasks in order to provide needed practice and application opportunities.

(b) Using application tasks as starting points for the next step of teaching and learning.

The classroom as a learning environment

(a) Establishing on-task behaviour through the interactions they promote (i.e., teacher–student and student–student interactions).

(b) Dealing with classroom disorder and student competition through establishing rules, persuading students to respect them and using the rules.

Time management

(a) Organising the classroom environment.

(b) Maximising engagement rates.

Assessment

(a) Using appropriate techniques to collect data on student knowledge and skills.

(b) Analysing data in order to identify student needs and report the results to students and parents.

(c) Teachers evaluating their own practices.

EVALUATE

* *Evaluate the model by identifying its strengths and limitations. Are there any elements of effective teaching that are missing from the model?*

CHALLENGE

* *Ofsted no longer look for a model of teaching. In what ways can models such as the one described limit creativity in the classroom?*

APPLY

* *Plan a lesson to address the elements of this model.*

Evidence-based teaching: use of praise

Praise for students may be seen as affirmational and positive, but several studies suggest that the wrong kinds of praise can be detrimental to learning. Studies on this aspect include those by Dweck (1999) and Hattie and Timperley (2007). Stipek (2010) argues that praise that is meant to protect the self-esteem of low-ability students actually conveys a message of the teacher's low expectations. Children whose failure was responded to using sympathy were more likely to attribute their failure to lack of ability than those who were presented with anger. This results in learned helplessness.

EVALUATE

* *What are the advantages and disadvantages of praise?*

CHALLENGE

* *In relation to your professional experience in schools, can you think of instances in which the use of praise was particularly effective?*

APPLY

* *During school-based training, observe the use of praise in different classrooms. Note down the dialogue that took place during the episode of praise on sticky notes. Use one sticky note per episode. Afterwards, sort the sticky notes into specific praise categories, for example, 'empty praise' and 'specific descriptive praise'.*

Critical reflections

This chapter has introduced you to the role of educational research in teaching. It has introduced some fundamental research which might inform your teaching and provided opportunities for you to evaluate research findings. The extent to which you are able to use research outcomes to inform your practice will be dependent on a variety of factors, including the educational policy drivers set by central government as well as the policies in individual schools. The pressure upon schools and teachers to raise standards in recent years has resulted in prescriptive *top-down* approaches to learning and teaching. Examples include the literacy and numeracy strategies which were introduced during the late 1990s and still leave their legacy in primary schools today. The danger of implementing prescriptive approaches is that they are not underpinned by educational research. It is important to go back to the research to be able to argue with conviction about what works and which approach will have the best impact on student achievement. Implementing an educational approach because you have been told to do so is not sound educational practice.

KEY READINGS

Classic:

Petty, G (2014) *Evidence-Based Teaching: A Practical Approach.* 2nd ed. Oxford: Oxford University Press.

Contemporary:

Bell, M (2014) *Classroom Teaching That Works: A Practical Guide to Using Evidence-based Teaching Methods*. Amazon Media EU S.à r.l: Amazon Digital Services, Inc.

Hattie, J and Timperley, H (2007) The power of feedback. *Review of Educational Research*, 77(1): 81–112.

References

Aaron, P G (1997) A component-based approach to the diagnosis and treatment of reading disabilities, in Ericson, B and Ronnberg, J (eds) *Reading Disability and Its Treatment*, EMIR, Report No. 2. Norrkoping: Eve Malmquist Institute for Reading, Linkoping University, pp 37–66.

Abbey, D S, Hunt, D E and Weiser, J C (1985) Variations on a theme by Kolb: A new perspective for understanding counseling and supervision. *The Counseling Psychologist*, 13: 477–501.

Adlof, S M, Catts, H W and Little, T D (2006) Should the Simple View of Reading include a fluency component? *Reading and Writing*, 19: 933–58.

Almeida, P (2010) Questioning patterns, questioning profiles and teaching strategies in secondary education. *International Journal of Learning*, 17(1): 587–600.

Anderson, R C, Wilson, P T and Fielding, L G (1988) Growth in reading and how children spend their time outside of school. *Reading Research Quarterly*, 23(3): 285–303. [online] Available

at: www.ideals.illinois.edu/bitstream/handle/2142/18003/ctrstreadtechrepv01986i00389_opt.pdf?sequence=1 (accessed 15 May 2016).

Bergsteiner, H, Avery, G C and Neumann, R (2010) Kolb's experiential learning model: Critique from a modelling perspective. *Studies in Continuing Education*, 32(1): 29–46.

Binet, A and Simon, T (1916) *The Development of Intelligence in Children* (E. Kit, Trans.). Baltimore, MD: Williams & Wilkins.

Bjork, E L and Bjork, R A (2011) Making things hard on yourself, but in a good way: Creating desirable difficulties to enhance learning, in Gernsbacher, M A, Pew, R W, Hough, L M and Pomerantz, J R (eds) *Psychology and the Real World: Essays Illustrating Fundamental Contributions to Society*. New York: Worth Publishers, pp. 56–64.

Black, P J and Wiliam, D (1998) *Inside the Black Box: Raising Standards through Classroom Attainment*. London: King's College London.

Brand, C (1996) *The G Factor: General Intelligence and Its Implications*. New York: John Wiley.

Bransford, J D, Brown, A L and Cocking, R R (2000). *How People Learn: Brain, Mind, Experience, and School: Expanded Edition*. Washington, DC: National Academy Press. [online] Available at: www.colorado.edu/MCDB/LearningBiology/readings/How-people-learn.pdf (accessed 20 June 2016).

Brown, G D A and Deavers, R P (1999) Units of analysis in nonword reading: Evidence from children and adults. *Journal of Experimental Child Psychology*, 73(3): 208–42.

Cain, K, Oakhill, J V and Lemmon, K (2005) The relation between children's reading comprehension level and their comprehension of idioms. *Journal of Experimental Child Psychology*, 90: 65–87.

Carter, A (2015) *Review of Initial Teacher Training*. London: DfE.

Catts, H W, Hogan, T P and Fey, M E (2003) Sub-grouping poor readers on the basis of individual differences in reading-related abilities. *Journal of Learning Disabilities*, 36(3): 151–64.

Clark, C (2011) *Setting the Baseline: The National Literacy Trust's First Annual Survey into Reading – 2010*. London: National Literacy Trust.

Clark, C and Douglas, J (2011) *Young People's Reading and Writing: An In-depth Study Focusing on Enjoyment, Behaviour, Attitudes and Attainmen*. London: National Literacy Trust.

Clark, C and Osborne, S (2008) *How Does Age Relate to Pupils' Perceptions of Themselves as Readers?* London: National Literacy Trust.

Clark, C and Rumbold, K (2006) *Reading for Pleasure: A Research Overview*. London: National Literacy Trust.

Coe, R, Aloisi, C, Higgins, S T and Major L E (2014) *What Makes Great Teaching? Review of the Underpinning Research*. London: The Sutton Trust.

Coffield, F (2012) Learning styles: Unreliable, invalid and impractical and yet still widely used, in Adey, P and Dillon, J (eds) *Bad Education: Debunking Myths in Education*. Maidenhead: Open University Press, pp 215–30.

Coffield, F J, Moseley, D V, Hall, E and Ecclestone, K (2004a) *Should We Be Using Learning Styles? What Research Has to Say to Practice*. London: Learning and Skills Research Centre/University of Newcastle upon Tyne.

Coffield, F J, Moseley, D V, Hall, E and Ecclestone, K (2004b) *Learning Styles and Pedagogy in Post-16 Learning: A Systematic and Critical Review*. London: Learning and Skills Research Centre/University of Newcastle upon Tyne.

Covington, M (1992) *Making the Grade: A Self-worth Perspective on Motivation and School Reform*. Cambridge, M.A: Cambridge University Press.

Creemers, B P M and Kyriakides, L (2006). Critical analysis of the current approaches to modelling educational effectiveness: The importance of establishing a dynamic model. *School Effectiveness and School Improvement*, 17: 347–66. [online] Available at: www.rug.nl/staff/b.p.m.creemers/paper_on_the_dynamic_model_at_sesi.pdf (accessed 20 June 2016).

Cutting, L E and Scarborough, H S (2006) Prediction of reading comprehension: Relative contributions of word recognition, language proficiency and other cognitive skills can depend on how comprehension is measured. *Scientific Studies of Reading*, 10: 277–99.

DfE (2012) *Research Evidence on Reading for Pleasure*. London: DfE.

DfEE (1998) *The National Literacy Strategy: Framework for Teaching*. London: DfEE.

Dweck, C S (1999) Caution – praise can be dangerous. *American Educator*, Spring 1999: 4–9. [online] Available at: www.aft.org/pdfs/americaneducator/spring1999/PraiseSpring99.pdf (accessed 20 June 2016).

Ehri, L C (1992) Reconceptualising the development of sight word reading and its relationship to recording, in Gough, P B, Ehri, I D, Treiman, R (eds) *Reading Acquisition*. Hillsdale, NJ: Erlbaum, pp 107–44.

Ehri, L C (1995) Phases of development in learning to read words by sight. *Journal of Research in Reading*, 18: 116–25.

Ehri, L C and Wilce, L S (1987) Cipher versus cue reading: An experiment in decoding acquisition. *Journal of Educational Psychology*, 79: 3–13.

Ellis, A and Young, A (1988) *Human Cognition Neuropsychology*. London: Lawrence Erlbaum.

Ellis, S and Moss, G (2014) Ethics, education policy and research: The phonics question reconsidered. *British Educational Research Journal*, 40,(2): 241–60.

Frith, U (1985) Beneath the surface of developmental dyslexia, in Patterson, K E, Marshall, J C and Coltheart, M (eds) *Surface Dyslexia: Neuropsychological and Cognitive Studies of Phonological Reading*. London: Erlbaum, pp 301–30.

Gardner, H (1975) *The Shattered Mind*. New York: Knopf.

Gardner, H (1979) Developmental psychology after Piaget: An approach in terms of symbolisation. *Human Development*, 15: 570–80.

Gardner, H (1982) *Art, Mind and Brain*. New York: Basic Books.

Gardner, H (1983), *Frames of Mind: The Theory of Multiple Intelligences*, New York: Basic Books.

Gardner, H (1999) *Intelligence Reframed*. New York: Basic Books.

Gardner, H and Hatch, T (1989) Multiple intelligences go to school: Educational implications of the theory of multiple intelligences. *Educational Researcher*, 18(8): 4–9.

Gardner, H and Wolf, D (1983) Waves and streams of symbolisation, in Rogers, D R and Sloboda, J A (eds) *The Acquisition of Symbolic Skills*. London: Plenum, pp 19–42.

Gardner, H, Howard, V and Perkins, D (1974) Symbol systems: A philosophical, psychological and educational investigation, in Olson, D (ed) *Media and Symbols*. Chicago: University of Chicago Press, pp 37–55.

Garner, I (2000) Problems and inconsistencies with Kolb's learning styles. *Educational Psychology*, 20(3): 341–48.

Geake, J (2008) Neuromythologies in education. *Educational Research*, 50(2): 123–33.

Goswami, U (1999) Causal connections in beginning reading: The importance of rhyme. *Journal of Research in Reading*, 22: 217–40.

Goswami, U (2005) Synthetic phonics and learning to read: A cross-language perspective. *Educational Psychology in Practice*, 21(4): 273–82.

Goswami, U, Ziegler, J C, Dalton, L and Schneider, W (2003) Non-word reading across orthographies: How flexible is the choice of reading units? *Applied Psycholinguistics*, 24: 235–47.

Gough, P B (1993) The beginning of decoding. *Reading and Writing*, 5: 181–92.

Gough, P B and Tunmer, W E (1986) Decoding, reading and reading disability. *Remedial and Special Education*, 7(1): 6–10.

Gustafson, S, Samuelsson, C, Johansson, E and Wallmann, J (2013) How simple is the Simple View of Reading? *Scandinavian Journal of Educational Research*, 57(3): 292–308.

Higgins, S, Katsipataki, M, Kokotsaki, D, Coleman, R, Major, L E and Coe, R (2013) *The Sutton Trust-Education Endowment Foundation Teaching and Learning Toolkit. London: Education Endowment Foundation*. [online] Available at: www.educationendowmentfoundation.org.uk/toolkit (accessed 20 June 2016).

Honey, P and Mumford, A (2000) *The Learning Styles Helper's Guide*. Maidenhead: Peter Honey Publications Ltd.

Hoover, W A and Gough, P B (1990) The Simple View of Reading: Reading and writing. *An Interdisciplinary Journal*, 2: 127–60.

Howard-Jones, P A (2014) Evolutionary perspectives on mind, brain and education. *Mind, Brain, and Education*, 8(1): 21–33.

Ivie, S (2009) Learning styles: Humpty dumpty revisited. *Erudit*, 44(2): 177–92.

Jackson, N E and Coltheart, M (2001) *Roots to Reading: Success and Failure*. New York: Psychology Press.

Johnston, R and Watson, J (2005) *The Effects of Synthetic Phonics Teaching on Reading and Spelling Attainment: A Seven-Year Longitudinal Study*. Edinburgh, SEED.

Johnston, R and Watson, J (2007) *Teaching Synthetic Phonics*. Exeter: Learning Matters.

Johnston, R, McGeown, S and Watson, J (2011) Long-term effects of synthetic phonics versus analytic phonics teaching on the reading and spelling ability of 10-year-old boys and girls. *Reading and Writing*, 25: 1365–84.

Johnston, R S, Anderson, M and Holligan, C (1996) Knowledge of the alphabet and explicit awareness of phonemes in pre-readers: The nature of the relationship. *Reading and Writing*, 8: 217–34.

Joshi, R M and Aaron, P G (2000) The component model of reading: simple view of reading made a little more complex. *Reading Psychology*, 21: 85–97.

Kendeou, P, Lynch, J S, van den Broek, P, Espin, C A, White, M J, and Kremer, K E (2005) Developing successful readers: Building early comprehension skills through television viewing and listening. *Early Childhood Education Journal*, 33: 91–98.

Kendeou, P, Savage, R and van den Broek, P (2009) Revisiting the simple view of reading. *British Journal of Educational Psychology*, 79(2): 353–70.

Kendeou, P, van den Broek, P, White, M and Lynch, J (2007) Pre-school and early elementary comprehension: Skill development and strategy interventions, in McNamara, D S (ed), *Reading Comprehension Strategies: Theories, Interventions and Technologies*. Mahwah, NJ: Erlbaum, pp 27–45.

Kirby, J and Savage, R S (2008) Can the simple view deal with the complexities of reading? *Literacy*, 42(2): 75–82.

Kirschner, P A, Sweller, J and Clark, R (2006) Why minimal guidance during instruction does not work: An analysis of the failure of constructivist, discovery, problem-based, experiential and inquiry-based teaching. *Educational Psychologist*, 41: 75–86.

Klein, P D (1997) Multiplying the problems of intelligence by eight: A critique of Gardner's theory. *Canadian Journal of Education*, 22(4): 377–94.

Kolb, D A (1984) *Experiential Learning: Experience as the Source of Learning and Development*. Englewood Cliffs, New Jersey: Prentice Hall.

Kruzich, J M, Friesen, B J and Van Soest, D (1986) Assessment of student and faculty learning styles: Research and application. *Journal of Social Work Education*, 3: 22–30.

Landerl, K (2000) Influences of orthographic consistency and reading instruction on the development of nonword reading skills. *European Journal of Psychology of Education*, 15: 239–57.

Morgan, H (1992) An analysis of Gardner's theory of multiple intelligence. Paper presented at the Annual Meeting of the Eastern Educational Research Association, ERIC document reproduction service No ED 360 088.

Moustafa, M and Maldonado-Colon, E (1998) Whole-to-parts phonics instruction: Building on what children know to help them know more. *The Reading Teacher*, 52: 448–58.

Mullis, I V S, Martin, M O, Foy, P and Drucker, K T (2012) *PIRLS 2011 International Results in Reading*. Chestnut Hill, MA: Boston College, TIMSS & PIRLS International Study Center. [online]. Available at: http://timssandpirls.bc.edu/pirls2011/reports/international-results-pirls.html (accessed 11 December 2012).

Mullis, I V S, Martin, M O, Kennedy, A M and Foy, P (2007) Students' reading attitudes, self-concept, and out-of-school activities, in *PIRLS 2006 International Report: IEA's Progress in International Reading Literacy Study in Primary Schools in 40 Countries*. Chestnut Hill, MA: Boston College, TIMSS & PIRLS International Study Center, Lynch School of Education. [online] Available at: http://timss.bc.edu/PDF/P06_IR_Ch4.pdf (accessed 15 May 2016).

Muter, V, Hulme, C, Snowling, M J and Stevenson, J (2004) Phonemes, rimes, vocabulary and grammatical skills as foundations of early reading development: Evidence from a longitudinal study. *Developmental Psychology*, 40: 665–81.

Nation, K (2005) Children's reading comprehension difficulties, in Snowling, M and Hulme, C (eds) *The Science of Reading: A Handbook*. Oxford: Blackwell, pp 248–66.

Neisser, U, Boodoo, G, Bouchard, T J, Boykin, A W, Brody, N, Ceci, S J, Halpern, D F, Lochlin, J C, Perloff, R, Sternberg, R J, and Urbina, S (1996) Intelligence: Knowns and unknowns. *American Psychologist*, 51: 77–101.

Nettlebeck, T and Wilson, C (2005) Intelligence and IQ: What teachers should know. *Educational Psychology: An International Journal of Experimental Educational Psychology*, 25(6): 609–30.

Nulty, D D and Barrett, M A (1996) Transitions in students' learning styles. *Studies in Higher Education*, 21(3): 333–45.

OECD (2002) *Reading for Change Performance and Engagement Across Countries: Results from PISA 2000*. Paris: OECD.

Palmquist, M and Young, R (1992) The notion of giftedness and student expectations about writing. *Written Communication*, 9: 137–68.

Pashler, H, McDaniel, M, Rohrer, D and Bjork, R (2009) Learning styles: Concepts and evidence. *Psychological Science in the Public Interest*, 9(3): 105–19.

PISA (2009) *Results: Executive Summary. Figure 1: Comparing Countries' and Economies' Performance.* [online] Available at: www.oecd.org/pisa/46643496.pdf (accessed 15 May 2016).

Raschick, M, Maypole, D E and Day, P A (1998) Improving field education through Kolb's learning theory. *Journal of Social Work Education*, 34(1): 31–42.

Riener, C and Willingham, D (2010) The myth of learning styles. *Change: The Magazine of Higher Learning*, 42: 32–35.

Roberts, J A and Scott, K A (2006) The simple view of reading: Assessment and intervention. *Topics in Language Disorders*, 26: 127–43.

Rose, J (2006) *Independent Review of the Teaching of Early Reading*. Nottingham: DfES Publications.

Savage, R (2006) Reading comprehension is not always the product of nonsense-word decoding and linguistic comprehension: Evidence from teenagers who are extremely poor readers. *Scientific Studies of Reading*, 10(2): 143–64.

Seymour, P H K and Elder, L (1986) Beginning reading without phonology. *Cognitive Neuropsychology*, 1: 1–36.

Seymour, P H K, Aro, M and Erskine, J M (2003) Foundation literacy acquisition in European orthographies. *British Journal of Psychology*, 94: 143–74.

Snow, C E (2002) Reading for understanding: Toward a research and developmental program in reading comprehension (Rand ReadingStudy Group). [online] Available at: www.rand.org/publications/MR/MR1465?MR1465.pdf

Spearman, C (1927). *The Abilities of Man*. London: MacMillan.

Spencer, L H and Hanley, J R (2003) Effects of orthographic transparency on reading and phoneme awareness in children learning to read in Wales. *British Journal of Psychology*, 94(1): 1–28.

Spooner, A L R, Baddeley, A D and Gathercole, S E (2004) Can reading and comprehension be separated in the Neale analysis of reading ability? *British Journal of Educational Psychology*, 74: 187–204.

Sternberg, R J (1983) How much gall is too much gall? A review of *Frames of Mind: The Theory of Multiple Intelligences*. *Contemporary Education Review*, 2: 215–24.

Sternberg, R J (1999) *Thinking Styles*. Cambridge: Cambridge University Press.

Stipek, D (2010) *How Do Teachers' Expectations Affect Student Learning?* [online] Available at: www.education.com/reference/article/teachers-expectations-affect-learning/ (accessed 20 June 2016).

Stothard, S E and Hulme, C (1992) Reading comprehension difficulties in children: The role of language comprehension and working memory skills. *Reading and Writing*, 4: 245–56.

Strickland, D S (1998) *Teaching Phonics Today: A Primer for Educators*. Newark, DE: International Reading Association.

Strydom, J and Du Plessis, S (2000) *IQ test: Where does it come from and what does it measure?* cited in Nettlebeck, T and Wilson, C (2005) Intelligence and IQ: What teachers should know. *Educational Psychology: An International Journal of Experimental Educational Psychology*, 25(6): 609–30.

Stuart, M (2006) Teaching reading: Why start with systematic phonics teaching? *The Psychology of Education Review*, 30(2): 6–17.

Stuart, M and Coltheart, M (1988) Does reading develop in a sequence of stages? *Cognition*, 30: 139–81.

Stuart, M, Stainthorp, R and Snowling, M (2008) Literacy as a complex activity: Deconstructing the simple view of reading. *Literacy*, 42(2): 59–66.

Terman, L M (1916) *The Measurement of Intelligence: An Explanation of and a Complete Guide for the use of the Stanford Revision and Extension of the Binet-Simon Intelligence Scale*. Boston: Houghton Mifflin.

Thurstone, L L (1938). *Primary Mental Abilities*. Psychometric Monographs, No.1. Chicago: University of Chicago Press.

Topping, K J (2010) *What Kids are Reading: The Book-reading Habits of Students in British Schools, 2010*. London: Renaissance Learning UK.

Torgerson, C J, Brooks, G and Hall, J (2006) *A Systematic Review of the Research Literature on the Use of Phonics in the Teaching of Reading and Spelling*. London: DfES.

Torgesen, J K, Wagner, R W, Rashotte, C A, Burgess, S and Hecht, S (1997) Contributions of phonological awareness and rapid automatic naming ability to the growth of word reading skills in second- to fifth-grade children. *Scientific Studies of Reading*, 1: 161–85.

Tunmer, W and Greaney, K (2010) Defining dyslexia. *Journal of Learning Disabilities*, 43: 229–43.

Tunmer, W E and Chapman, J W, (2012) The simple view of reading redux: Vocabulary knowledge and the independent components hypothesis. *Journal of Learning Disabilities*, 45(5): 453–66.

Twist, L, Schagan, I and Hogson, C (2007) *Progress in International Reading Literacy Study (PIRLS): Reader and Reading National Report for England 2006*. Slough: NFER and DCSF.

Vellutino, F R, Scanlon, D M and Lyon, G R (2000) Differentiating between difficult-to remediate and readily remediated poor readers: More evidence against the IQ achievement discrepancy definition of reading disability. *Journal of Learning Disabilities*, 33: 223–38.

Vellutino, F R, Fletcher, J M, Snowling, M J and Scanlon, D (2004) Specific reading disability (dyslexia): What have we learned in the past four decades? *Journal of Child Psychology and Psychiatry*, 45: 2–40.

Vellutino, F R, Tunmer, W E, Jaccard, J and Chen, S (2007) Components of reading ability: Multivariate evidence for a convergent skills model of reading development. *Scientific Studies of Reading*, 11: 3–32.

Walton, P D, Bowden, M E, Kurtz, S L and Angus, M (2001) Evaluation of a rime-based reading program with Shuswap and Heiltsuk First Nations prereaders. *Reading and Writing*, 14: 229–64.

Waterhouse, L (2006) Inadequate evidence for multiple intelligences, Mozart effect and emotional intelligence theories. *Educational Psychologist*, 41(4): 247–55.

Watson, J E and Johnston, R S (1998) Accelerating reading attainment: The effectiveness of synthetic phonics. *Interchange*, 57. Edinburgh: SOEID.

White, J (2005) *The Myth of Howard Gardner's Multiple Intelligences*. London: ioelife, Institute of Education.

White, J (2006) *Intelligence, Destiny and Education: The Ideological Roots of Intelligence Testing*. London: Routledge.

Willingham, D (2008) *Learning Styles Don't Exist*. Video available online at: www.youtube.com/watch?v=sIv9rz2NTUk (accessed 26 December 2014).

Wyse, D and Goswami, U (2008) Synthetic phonics and the teaching of reading. *British Educational Research Journal*, 34(6): 691–710.

Wyse, D and Styles, M (2007) Synthetic phonics and the teaching of reading: The debate surrounding England's 'Rose Report'. *Literacy*, 41(1): 35–42.

2: SUBJECT KNOWLEDGE AND PEDAGOGY

TEACHERS' STANDARDS

This chapter addresses the following Teachers' Standards:

Teachers' Standard 3: Demonstrate good subject and curriculum knowledge

Teachers must:

* *have a secure knowledge of the relevant subject(s) and curriculum areas, foster and maintain pupils' interest in the subject, and address misunderstandings;*
* *demonstrate a critical understanding of developments in the subject and curriculum areas, and promote the value of scholarship;*
* *demonstrate an understanding of and take responsibility for promoting high standards of literacy, articulacy and the correct use of standard English, whatever the teacher's specialist subject;*
* *if teaching early reading, demonstrate a clear understanding of systematic synthetic phonics;*
* *if teaching early mathematics, demonstrate a clear understanding of appropriate teaching strategies.*

PROFESSIONAL LINKS

The *Carter Review of Initial Teacher Training* stated that:

XI. Evidence suggests that a high level of subject expertise is a characteristic of good teaching (Coe and others, 2014). We have found that the most effective courses address gaps and misconceptions in trainees' core subject knowledge. This is important for both primary and secondary courses and across all subjects.

XII. Across all subjects and phases we have found variability in the way subject knowledge is addressed. Given the importance of subject knowledge for good teaching, this is not satisfactory.

XIII. Overall, we have been pleased to see the majority of ITT programmes are preparing trainees to teach the new national curriculum. However, we are concerned about a significant minority of courses where it appears programmes have not been updated to reflect changes.

XIV. There are some particular challenges for subject knowledge development – the breadth of the subject knowledge primary teachers need to teach the new curriculum, for example, may be difficult to cover, especially within a one-year programme. We believe there is a number of ways that providers and the system could build in extra opportunities for the development of subject knowledge.

XV. Teachers who understand the way pupils approach different subjects, understand the thinking behind pupils' methods and can identify common misconceptions are more likely to have a positive impact on pupil outcomes (Sadler and others, 2013 and Hill and others, 2005). We believe ITT should address subject-specific issues including phases of progression within the subject, links between subjects as well as common misconceptions and how to address these. This is important for both primary and secondary programmes. Both trainers and mentors should have a strong grasp of subject-specific pedagogy. However, there are important areas of content on subject-specific pedagogy that are not addressed on all courses.

(Carter, 2015, pp 7–8)

The review made the following recommendations:

Recommendation 1a: *Subject knowledge development should be part of a future framework for ITT content.*

Recommendation 1b: *Issues in subject-specific pedagogy should be part of a framework for ITT content.*

Recommendation 2: *All ITT partnerships should:*

- *I.* rigorously audit, track and systematically improve trainees' subject knowledge throughout the programme;
- *II.* ensure that changes to the curriculum and exam syllabi are embedded in ITT programmes;
- *III.* ensure that trainees have access to high quality subject expertise;
- *IV.* ensure that trainees have opportunities to learn with others training in the same subject.

Recommendation 3: *Schools should include subject knowledge as an essential element of professional development.*

Recommendation 4: *The DfE should make funded in-service subject knowledge enhancement courses available for primary teachers to access as professional development.*

Recommendation 5: *Universities should explore offering "bridge to ITT" modules in the final years of their subject degrees for students who are considering ITT programmes.*

(Carter, 2015)

CHAPTER OBJECTIVES

* What is this chapter about?

This chapter aims to develop your subject knowledge by introducing you to the progression within subjects. It also introduces you to common pupil misconceptions within specific subjects. The chapter focuses on developing your pedagogical subject knowledge. This means that it will develop your knowledge of how to teach the subjects of the national curriculum. In addressing different subjects, this chapter takes each subject in turn and examines the associated issues. When reading through the chapter, it may feel as though the subjects are disconnected. In reality highly effective teachers encourage pupils to make links between the subjects by applying the learning from one subject to another. It is important that you remember that there are connections between subjects and that you make the links between various subjects in your planning. However, presenting each subject separately helps you to focus on the subject-specific knowledge and skills which make subjects distinct. It is only after pupils have developed subject-specific knowledge and skills that they can then apply the learning from one subject to another.

This chapter does not introduce you to all the subject-specific content. Your ITT provider will rigorously audit and track the development of your subject knowledge throughout your training. It is your responsibility to identify your areas of strength and weakness and to ensure that your subject knowledge is at least good in all subject areas by the end of your training. You will need to develop your subject knowledge through your own research and through working with mentors in school. Your mentors should provide you with opportunities to develop both your subject-specific and subject pedagogical knowledge through high quality mentoring and subject-specific feedback on your teaching. The best mentors will set you subject-specific targets which help you to develop your subject knowledge for primary teaching. You also need to observe outstanding teachers teaching outstanding lessons. This will help you to develop your subject knowledge. Your training course should be well-designed so that it provides you with subject-specific input. There should be good coherence between central training by your provider and the training you receive in school. This will ensure that you get the opportunity to put your training into practice.

✱ Why is it important?

This chapter is important because research suggests that good subject knowledge is critical to securing good outcomes for learners. With good subject knowledge you will be able to teach with confidence, answer pupils' questions and address pupils' misconceptions. Good subject knowledge will enable you to identify the next steps in learning so that you are able to move children's learning forward. It will also enable you to take learning back a stage if your learners are developing misconceptions. In order to do this, you need to understand the phases of progression within specific subjects. Understanding phases of progression will also enable you to differentiate your teaching more effectively because you will be able to pinpoint more precisely which 'phase' a child is working in within a specific subject.

Aspects of subject knowledge

Evans et al (2008) identified the following aspects of teacher subject-knowledge:

Subject knowledge per se

- the key concepts, language, skills and topics that define the subject or curriculum area;
- progression in the subject or curriculum area as defined by the national curriculum and other national expectations;
- the relevance of the subject or curriculum area and why aspects of the subject or curriculum area are taught;
- the connections across subjects or curriculum areas, including literacy, numeracy and ICT across the curriculum;
- the relationships within the subject or curriculum area;
- assessment of pupils' achievement in the subject or curriculum area.

Pedagogical subject knowledge

- a range of teaching skills and strategies to promote pupils' learning in the subject including behaviour management and those proposed by the national strategies;
- the ability to plan lessons and sequences of lessons that are matched to pupils' needs, including opportunities for learning through homework;

- the ability to make use of a range of resources including ICT skills in the assessment of pupils' learning and the ability to use the information to plan for teaching which meets pupils' needs;
- the ability to make a subject accessible to pupils at different stages in their learning and development and to provide a supportive learning environment;
- the ability to reflect on and improve teaching and learning;
- high expectations of all pupils and skills in working to overcome barriers to their learning?

Knowledge of pupils' development

- how pupils' learning in the subject is affected by developmental, social, religious, ethnic, cultural and linguistic influences;
- the range of ways in which pupils learn;
- how pupils develop as learners within the subject;
- how the subject and curriculum area needs to be adapted to meet pupils' individual needs and contexts;
- how parents and carers contribute to their children's learning and development?

Attitudes

- the inclusion, achievement and well-being of all pupils;
- towards the subject or the curriculum area and for teaching it;
- being creative in developing learning opportunities for all pupils;
- continuing professional development within the subject or curriculum area;
- working as part of a team, learning from others and contributing to the learning community.

(Evans et al, 2008)

When each of these aspects is working together rather than in isolation, this creates optimum conditions for the development of strong subject knowledge for teaching.

EVIDENCE-BASED TEACHING

According to Coe et al (2014, p 19):

targeting support for teachers at particular areas where their understanding or their knowledge of student misconceptions is weak may be a promising strategy, a claim that is supported by reviews of the impact of teacher professional development in these areas (Timperley et al, 2007; Blank and de las Alas, 2009).

EVALUATE

- *What are the benefits of undertaking professional development in weaker areas of subject knowledge?*
- *What other aspects of teaching are important apart from subject knowledge?*

CHALLENGE

- *Discuss the commonly held view that teachers just need to be one step ahead of children.*

The view presupposes that there is no point in learning everything at the point of training and that it is best to research subject knowledge at the point when it is needed.

APPLY

- *Complete your subject audits that you will have been given at the start of your training. In what areas do you have strong and weak subject knowledge?*

Subject-specific terminology in English

The glossaries in the national curriculum English framework provide examples of spelling rules and definitions of subject-specific terms with examples. You need to audit your own subject knowledge in relation to the spelling rules and the subject-specific terminology. The appendices of the national curriculum also provide an overview of the phonic knowledge that you need to know and examples of spelling that children need to learn. You need to make sure that you are confident with all of these aspects of the national curriculum. It is not appropriate to repeat here all of the subject knowledge content that is specified in the appendices of the English strand of the national curriculum. You are advised to read the national curriculum carefully and to use it to support the development of your subject knowledge.

IN PRACTICE

When you are in school, meet with the subject leader for English. Find out if the school follows various schemes for teaching phonics, guided reading, grammar, spelling and punctuation. If so, spend some time familiarising yourself with these schemes.

Progression in mathematics

A good starting point to developing your mathematical subject knowledge is to read thoroughly the mathematics strand of the national curriculum. In order to teach mathematics effectively throughout the primary school, you will need to have good mathematical subject knowledge in the following areas: addition and subtraction; multiplication and division; fractions, decimals and percentages; position and direction; geometry; measurement; number and place value; statistics; ratio and proportion. In each of these areas you will need to be able to understand the mathematical content right through to Year 6 in order to demonstrate that you have achieved Teaching Standard 3. Your mental arithmetic skills will also need to be at least good. All of these areas are specified clearly in the national curriculum so you need to become really familiar with this document.

It is critical that you understand progression within each strand of learning in primary mathematics. This is because a clear understanding of progression will enable you to identify pupils' next steps in learning, thus you will be able to advance their mathematical knowledge, understanding and skills. Additionally, understanding progression will enable you to take learning back a stage if children are demonstrating misconceptions. The national curriculum mixes all of the mathematical strands together under each year group and thus it is not helpful for identifying progression within a single strand of mathematics. By isolating each strand and then identifying what needs to be taught within a strand from Year 1 to Year 6 you will be able to identify the progression within a strand of mathematics

much more clearly. The following example outlines progression sequences within two strands of mathematics.

Strand: progression in geometry

Year 1

Pupils should be taught to:

* recognise and name common 2-D and 3-D shapes, including:
  - 2-D shapes (for example, rectangles [including squares], circles and triangles);
  - 3-D shapes (for example, cuboids [including cubes], pyramids and spheres).

Year 2

Pupils should be taught to:

* identify and describe the properties of 2-D shapes, including the number of sides and symmetry in a vertical line;
* identify and describe the properties of 3-D shapes, including the number of edges, vertices and faces;
* identify 2-D shapes on the surface of 3-D shapes, [for example, a circle on a cylinder and a triangle on a pyramid];
* compare and sort common 2-D and 3-D shapes and everyday objects.

Year 3

Pupils should be taught to:

* draw 2-D shapes and make 3-D shapes using modelling materials; recognise 3-D shapes in different orientations and describe them;
* recognise angles as a property of shape or a description of a turn;
* identify right angles, recognise that two right angles make a half-turn, three make three quarters of a turn and four a complete turn; identify whether angles are greater than or less than a right angle;
* identify horizontal and vertical lines and pairs of perpendicular and parallel lines.

Year 4

Pupils should be taught to:

* compare and classify geometric shapes, including quadrilaterals and triangles, based on their properties and sizes;
* identify acute and obtuse angles and compare and order angles up to two right angles by size;
* identify lines of symmetry in 2-D shapes presented in different orientations;
* complete a simple symmetric figure with respect to a specific line of symmetry.

Year 5

Pupils should be taught to:

* identify 3-D shapes, including cubes and other cuboids, from 2-D representations;
* know angles are measured in degrees: estimate and compare acute, obtuse and reflex angles;

* draw given angles, and measure them in degrees (°);
* identify:
  - angles at a point and one whole turn (total 360°)
  - angles at a point on a straight line and ½ a turn (total 180°)
  - other multiples of 90°
* use the properties of rectangles to deduce related facts and find missing lengths and angles;
* distinguish between regular and irregular polygons based on reasoning about equal sides and angles.

Year 6

Pupils should be taught to:

* draw 2-D shapes using given dimensions and angles;
* recognise, describe and build simple 3-D shapes, including making nets;
* compare and classify geometric shapes based on their properties and sizes and find unknown angles in any triangles, quadrilaterals, and regular polygons;
* illustrate and name parts of circles, including radius, diameter and circumference and know that the diameter is twice the radius;
* recognise angles where they meet at a point, are on a straight line, or are vertically opposite, and find missing angles.

(Herts for Learning – Teaching and Learning)

Strand: progression in number and place value

Year 1

Pupils should be taught to:

* count to and across 100, forwards and backwards, beginning with 0 or 1, or from any given number;
* count, read and write numbers to 100 in numerals; count in multiples of twos, fives and tens;
* given a number, identify one more and one less;
* identify and represent numbers using objects and pictorial representations including the number line, and use the language of: equal to, more than, less than (fewer), most, least;
* read and write numbers from 1 to 20 in numerals and words.

Year 2

Pupils should be taught to:

* count in steps of 2, 3, and 5 from 0, and in tens from any number, forward or backward;
* recognise the place value of each digit in a two-digit number (tens, ones);
* identify, represent and estimate numbers using different representations, including the number line;
* compare and order numbers from 0 up to 100; use <, > and = signs;
* read and write numbers to at least 100 in numerals and in words;
* use place value and number facts to solve problems.

Year 3

Pupils should be taught to:

* count from 0 in multiples of 4, 8, 50 and 100; find 10 or 100 more or less than a given number;
* recognise the place value of each digit in a three-digit number (hundreds, tens, ones);
* compare and order numbers up to 1000;
* identify, represent and estimate numbers using different representations;
* read and write numbers up to 1000 in numerals and in words;
* solve number problems and practical problems involving these ideas.

Year 4

Pupils should be taught to:

* count in multiples of 6, 7, 9, 25 and 1000;
* find 1000 more or less than a given number;
* count backwards through zero to include negative numbers;
* recognise the place value of each digit in a four-digit number (thousands, hundreds, tens, and ones);
* order and compare numbers beyond 1000;
* identify, represent and estimate numbers using different representations;
* round any number to the nearest 10, 100 or 1000;
* solve number and practical problems that involve all of the above and with increasingly large positive numbers;
* read Roman numerals to 100 (I to C) and know that over time, the numeral system changed to include the concept of zero and place value.

Year 5

Pupils should be taught to:

* read, write, order and compare numbers to at least 1,000,000 and determine the value of each digit;
* count forwards or backwards in steps of powers of 10 for any given number up to 1,000,000;
* interpret negative numbers in context, count forwards and backwards with positive and negative whole numbers through zero;
* round any number up to 1,000,000 to the nearest 10, 100, 1000, 10,000 and 100,000;
* solve number problems and practical problems that involve all of the above;
* read Roman numerals to 1000 (M) and recognise years written in Roman numerals.

Year 6

Pupils should be taught to:

* read, write, order and compare numbers up to 10,000,000 and determine the value of each digit;
* round any whole number to a required degree of accuracy;

- use negative numbers in context, and calculate intervals across zero;
- solve number and practical problems that involve all of the above.

(Herts for Learning – Teaching and Learning)

It is important that children are given opportunities to develop mastery of specific mathematical concepts before you move them on to higher level objectives. This means that you need to provide your learners with opportunities to apply the mathematical skills they have been learning to varying contexts. One way of doing this is to give them plenty of opportunities to solve problems using the mathematical skill they have been taught. There is little point in children knowing that $7 + 3 = 10$ unless they also know that 7p + 3p = 10p. Transferring the context from number to money in this example helps the children to deepen their understanding. They might be able to recognise simple two- and three-dimensional shapes when these are presented to them using plastic shapes. However, to deepen this learning they need to be able to identify these same shapes in the environment on buildings, signs, furniture and packaging. This ability to transfer learning from one context to another deepens the learning. Children might know that the number 17 is made up of one ten and seven ones (units). However, to deepen their understanding of the concept of place value they need to know that 17p is made up of one 10p plus seven 1p coins.

Children's misconceptions in mathematics

It is important that you are aware of common children's misconceptions in mathematics. If you understand the common misconceptions that pupils have in mathematics you will be able to plan your lessons so that you can specifically address these misconceptions in your teaching. There are many misconceptions that pupils make and whole books have now been produced to help you research this. It is not possible to cover them all here. Examples include:

Misconception 1

Objective: Find a difference by counting up from the smaller to the larger number.

Misconception: Counts up unreliably by counting the starting number to get one too many in the answer.

Misconception 2

Objective: Ordering decimals

Order these numbers, smallest first: 21.2, 1.112, 3.1, 11.4, 0.2112.

Child's answer: 3.1, 11.2, 21.2, 1.112, 0.2112.

This child has relied on a common generalisation that, 'the larger the number of digits, the larger the size of the number'.

Misconception 3

Objective: Understand the operation of addition

$\_ + 6 = 10$

When pupils are faced with problems such as the above, they see two numbers and add them (eg $6 + 10 = 16$) instead of reading it as a sentence.

IN PRACTICE

When you next go into school talk to the subject leader for mathematics. Is there a plan in the school which identifies progression within the strands of mathematics from Year 1 to Year 6?

Subject knowledge in science

The following list identifies the subject knowledge that you need to teach science at Key Stage 1 and Key Stage 2. The national curriculum emphasises the importance of children working scientifically so that scientific knowledge is developed through the process of scientific investigation. Thus, you need to provide your learners with opportunities to develop scientific knowledge and understanding through investigation. They will develop key scientific skills such as planning investigative work, predicting, comparing, observing, measuring, recording, presenting data and drawing conclusions through scientific investigation. Additionally, they will use data to give explanations and they will learn to communicate their findings through scientific investigation. They will start to understand the importance of fair testing.

Working scientifically helps children to understand the scientific process. However, it is not necessary to teach all of these skills in one go. Scientific skills should be taught systematically. This allows you to focus specific lessons on developing specific skills. One lesson, for example, might focus on predicting and another lesson might focus on fair testing. Eventually, when children have been taught all the skills they can start to combine them so that by the time they reach Year 5 or Year 6 they are able to follow the whole scientific process.

Just like in mathematics, children develop many misconceptions in scientific understanding. If you are aware of these misconceptions, you can plan your teaching so that you are able to address these very explicitly. Examples include:

- children often think that magnets are attracted to objects because they have magical properties or that a magic glue makes them stick;
- children sometimes say that there is no gravity on the moon, or that things will float away on the moon because there is no air to hold them down;
- children often describe dissolving as disappearing and say that the salt or sugar has disappeared. They often confuse the terms melting and dissolving;
- children often think that all solids are heavy and they struggle to understand that sugar and salt are solids because they can be poured like liquids;
- children may think that a material is a fabric;
- some children do not see trees as plants because they associate the word 'plant' with something small. They see a tree as a tree! They may not associate carrots and potatoes with the word 'plant' as they see these as vegetables.

There are many scientific misconceptions and it is not possible to list all of them here. However, these examples illustrate the need to research into children's scientific misconceptions for the topics you are teaching. This will enable you to address these as part of your lesson content. It is also important that your subject knowledge in science is good so that you do not transmit any scientific misconceptions to your learners!

Audit your own subject knowledge in science against each of the teaching topics listed in the national curriculum (www.gov.uk/government/publications/national-curriculum-in-england-science-programmes-of-study). Which aspects are you secure in and which require further development? Do you know the common scientific misconceptions that children develop in each of these categories?

* Working scientifically
* Plants
* Animals (including humans)
* Everyday materials
* Seasonal changes
* Living things and their habitats
* Light
* Forces and magnets
* Sound
* Electricity
* Earth and space
* Evolution and inheritance
* Important knowledge

CRITICAL QUESTIONS

* *Is it better to address children's scientific and mathematical misconceptions as you teach topics or to accept that misconceptions arise due to the stage of development and therefore the associated level of understanding that children have reached?*
* *Would it be better to address misconceptions when children are developmentally ready to accommodate new understanding?*

Subject knowledge in history

The importance of historical enquiry cannot be overstated. The most effective learning in history takes place when children develop historical knowledge and understanding through gleaning information from source materials. Source materials could include historical artefacts, photographs, diaries, letters, visits to museums, posters, pictures and film. Sources can be primary sources or secondary sources. Through interacting with source materials and becoming 'history detectives', children can start to ask questions about the past. Teaching history through role-play/drama is a powerful way of learning about the past.

The starting point for learning about the passage of time and changes over time is to start with children's own history. Simple timelines using photographs of themselves at different ages is a really effective way of demonstrating the process of change over time. Developmentally, it makes sense for children to understand their own history before they start to understand changes in their own lives and their family. Following this, they can start to learn about famous figures such as Queen Victoria.

At Key Stage 1, in order to confidently teach the history national curriculum you need to:

* know about changes in society within living memory;
* know about events beyond living memory that are significant nationally or globally (for example, the Great Fire of London, the first aeroplane flight or events commemorated through festivals or anniversaries);
* know about the lives of significant individuals in the past who have contributed to national and international achievements. Some should be used to compare aspects of life in different periods (for example, Elizabeth I and Queen Victoria, Christopher Columbus and Neil Armstrong, William Caxton and Tim Berners-Lee, Pieter Bruegel the Elder and L S Lowry, Rosa Parks and Emily Davison, Mary Seacole and/or Florence Nightingale and Edith Cavell);
* know about significant historical events, people and places in their own locality;
* understand progression in understanding chronology.

At Key Stage 2, in order to confidently teach the history national curriculum you need to:

* know about changes in Britain from the Stone Age to the Iron Age, eg hunters and early farmers; bronze age, religion, technology and travel; Iron Age hill forts, tribal kingdoms, farming, art and culture;
* know about the Roman Empire and its impact on Britain;
* know about settlement in Britain by Anglo-Saxons and Scots;
* know about the Viking and Anglo-Saxon struggle for the UK to the time of Edward the Confessor;
* know about the history of the local area in which you are working;
* know about a theme or aspect of British history that extends pupils' knowledge beyond 1066, eg the first railways or the Battle of Britain;
* know about the achievements of the earliest civilisation, eg Ancient Egypt;
* know about Ancient Greece;
* know about a non-European society that provides contact with British history, eg Mayan civilisation.

In order to teach history effectively you need to understand the difference between a primary and a secondary source. In addition, you need to understand how to use source material for historical enquiry.

CRITICAL QUESTIONS

* *The national curriculum focuses on British history. Do you agree with this?*
* *Do you think the content in Key Stage 1 is appropriate taking into account children's stage of development?*
* *Do you think the balance between content and skills is right in the national curriculum?*

Subject knowledge in geography

Geography knowledge is not fixed because the world is continually changing. The following geographical concepts are embedded in the national curriculum:

* **Space:** the location of geographical features and regions;
* **Place:** the study of places involves knowing the geographical features which exist, what a place is like and how it is changing;
* **Scale:** the 'zoom lens' that enables us to view places from global to local levels.

So, when planning geography lessons or sequences of lessons you need to ensure that you are clear about which of these concepts you are teaching. Developing a sense of place – such as, for example, a sensory exploration of a 'rainforest' – only becomes geography when you begin to understand its location and links with other places both globally and locally. Combining the concepts adds depth and supports a deeper understanding of people, places and environments.

Geographical enquiry

Geographical enquiry is central to effective geography teaching. Geographical enquiry is a process of active investigation in which pupils are fully engaged. Enquiry work should include open-ended activities in which you provide opportunities for pupils to find things out for themselves as well as more teacher-led activities where you will want to make clear teaching points to children. Enquiry involves answering questions, problem-solving, identifying issues and finding solutions, through providing an appropriate range of teaching and learning experiences.

Effective geographical enquiry provides opportunities for children to develop both geographical skills (eg observation) and geographical knowledge. Through geographical enquiry you can select suitable content and appropriate geographical questions in order to tackle an issue or theme in a distinctly geographical way. This approach can work at different scales in the classroom as well being used to frame one lesson or a whole unit of work.

Selecting localities

The national curriculum refers to areas of different scales and some specific places such as North and South America. A **local-scale study** is the area in which people live their everyday lives. For primary school pupils this is usually their immediate local environment such as where they live and play or where they go to school. It may also include places they visit with parents on a frequent basis. In contrast, a **geographical region** is generally a large area of land with distinguishing geographical, ecological, cultural or political features that make it different from other areas. A geographical region may exist within one country or be spread over several countries.

You may have always taught a study based on countries such as India or Africa at Key Stage 2. You can still teach these countries but the Americas are a statutory component of the new national curriculum. At Key Stage 1 you can teach about any contrasting non-European country. At Key Stage 2 you are also required to teach about resources, such as food, energy, and trade links; and key aspects of physical geography such as rivers, mountains, volcanoes and climate zones. You can select the countries that you feel are most appropriate for teaching children about these aspects.

The Americas are a vast place to teach about. Start by developing pupils' core geographical knowledge. This includes knowing the location and names of the North and South American continents and their make-up in terms of countries, regions, key cities and physical features. Then, drawing on the idea of a 'zoom lens' it is then possible to study specific places in more depth, making comparisons between them. For example, you might go on to study the significance of the Amazon rainforest or the topicality of Brazil and look at specific places within those regions at a local scale. Starting wide and then focusing the study down is a useful approach to planning a sequence of lessons.

Fieldwork

Fieldwork is statutory for all key stages and ideally should be done at least once every year by every year group. In Key Stage 1 you might focus on the school grounds and the immediate locality of the school, ie the area that can be reached by walking. In Key Stage 2 pupils might investigate the wider locality in which they live. Pupils from different year groups might visit the same place, for example, the local high street, but adopt a different focus or enquiry.

According to the Geographical Association the following broad 'dimensions' of progress – what it means to 'get better' at geography – can be helpful when thinking about both planning and assessment:

* moving outwards from the familiar to the less familiar;
* acquiring greater fluency with 'world knowledge';
* working with increasingly complex and/or abstract ideas and generalisations;
* using data that becomes more multivariate;
* investigating people-environment relations;
* applying geographical thinking to new contexts and situations;
* becoming more precise (in language, ideas, skills), and making distinctions;
* becoming more comfortable with 'grey areas' where answers are not so clear cut;
* connecting information and ideas, and building (not just receiving) new knowledge;
* drawing on increasing breadth of content and contexts;
* understanding the importance of perspective, recognising a range of values and views.

(www.geography.org.uk/news/2014nationalcurriculum/primaryprogress/)

Checking your geography subject knowledge

The following checklist will help you to assess your own geographical subject knowledge in relation to the national curriculum:

Can you:

* name and locate the world's seven continents;
* name and locate the world's five oceans;
* name, locate and identify the characteristics of the four countries of the United Kingdom;
* name, locate and identify the capital cities of the United Kingdom and their characteristics;
* name, locate and identify the seas surrounding the United Kingdom and their characteristics;
* locate the world's countries focusing on Europe;
* locate Russia;
* locate North and South America;
* identify physical and human characteristics of countries and major cities;
* name and locate counties of the United Kingdom;
* name and locate cities of the United Kingdom.

It is very important that you do not reinforce stereotypes in your teaching. Not all people who live in Africa are poor and not everyone who lives in England is rich! Some people in places such as India and Africa live in very expensive houses and are far richer than many people in England. Be careful not to present countries in 'tragic' and disrespectful ways.

Subject knowledge in music

The following checklist will help you to assess your own geographical subject knowledge in relation to the national curriculum:

Do you understand the following terms?

pitch; duration; dynamics; tempo; timbre; texture; musical notation

Also do you know about:

* the history of music;
* the work of a great composer;
* the work of a great musician;
* music drawn from different traditions?

You need to teach your pupils key musical terminology, so in order to be able to do this you need to understand the terminology yourself. Music Express has produced a useful glossary of key musical terms. These are listed below:

Accompaniment: The underlying sounds used to support a melody line.

Acoustic: See *Playing methods*.

Arrangement: A new version of an existing piece of music.

Arrhythmic: See *Free.*

Beat/pulse: Beat and pulse are used synonymously to refer to the regular heartbeat of the music – the 'steady beat'.

Body percussion: Sounds which can be made using parts of the body, eg clapping, tapping knees, etc.

Call and response: A style of music in which a leader sings or plays a short melody (the call) and a chorus of singers/players respond with an answering short melody (the response).

Chord: Two or more notes played at the same time.

Conductor: The person elected to lead a group of singers or instrumentalists.

Crescendo: Getting louder.

Dimensions/elements: The inter-related building blocks of music (formerly referred to in the English national curriculum as elements): duration, dynamics, pitch, structure, tempo, texture, and timbre.

Diminuendo: Getting quieter.

Dot notation: A simple form of Western staff notation. Dots are placed in height and distance relation to each other to indicate pitch and duration.

Drone: A sound or sounds played constantly throughout all or part of a piece of music as an accompaniment.

Duet: A song or piece of music for two parts of equal importance.

Duration: The word used in music to refer to the length of a sound or silence.

Dynamics/volume: The loudness of the music, usually described in terms of loud/quiet.

Elements: See *Dimensions.*

Free/arrhythmic: Music which has no discernible steady beat.

Glissando A slide up or down from one musical note to another, in the manner of a rapid, sliding scale.

Graphic notation: A form of notation in which the composer freely invents symbols which give an impression of sound.

Graphic score: A score in which musical intention is recorded by means of graphic symbols.

Improvisation: A piece of music which is created spontaneously.

Improvise: To invent music as you go along.

Leap: The space between two musical notes which is greater than a step (see *Step movement*).

Major: One of the most common types of eight-note musical scale. Often described as having a happy sound (see also *Minor*).

Melodic phrase/phrase: A small unit of a melody, often corresponding to a line of a song.

Melody: A tune.

Metre: The grouping of beats into twos, threes, fours, etc. For instance, in waltz music the beats are grouped in threes, whereas in march music they are grouped in twos or fours.

Minor: One of the most common types of eight-note musical scale. Often described as having a sad sound (see also *Major*).

Notations: Ways of writing music down – examples include graphic notation and staff notation.

Ostinato (plural ostinatos/ostinati): A short rhythmic or melodic pattern which is repeated over and over.

Phrase: See *Melodic phrase.*

Pictorial symbols: A simple form of notation in which a picture is used to represent a sound, eg car picture = motor sounds.

Pitch: Refers to the complete range of sounds in a piece of music from the lowest to the highest.

Pitch movement: The steps and leaps by which a melody moves up and down in pitch.

Pizzicato: The technique of playing a string instrument, eg violin, by plucking the strings rather than playing them with the bow.

Playing methods: Acoustic (non-electronic) sounds are made by shaking, scraping, tapping or blowing a soundmaker.

Pulse: See *Beat.*

Rest: A silence.

Rhythm: Patterns of long and short sounds played within a steady beat.

Rhythmical: Music which is underpinned by a steady beat.

Rhythm pattern: A short section of rhythm.

Score: A written representation of music designed to record a composer's intention.

Solo: A piece of music for one singer or instrumentalist.

Soundmaker: Any sound source used as a musical instrument.

Step movement: Notes of a melody which move stepwise up or down.

Structure: Most music is underpinned by a structure which may be as simple as beginning, middle and end.

Symbol: Any written representation of a sound.

Tempo (plural tempi): The speed at which music is performed, usually described in terms of fast/slow.

Texture: Layers of sound, such as those created by a melody accompanied by a drum beat.

Timbre: All instruments, including voices, have a particular sound quality which is referred to as timbre, eg squeaky.

Tremolo: The rapid repetition of notes, producing a quavering effect. It can either be on one note or between two notes.

Tuned percussion: Percussion instruments which make sounds with a defined pitch, eg glockenspiel.

Untuned percussion: Percussion instruments which make sounds of indefinite pitch, eg hand drum.

Volume: See *Dynamics*.

(www.musicexpress.co.uk/extras/glossary)

Subject knowledge in art and design

Like all other curriculum areas, art and design has its own vocabulary which makes it a distinct subject. You need to understand this terminology in order to teach it well. The following definitions cover the terminology in the national curriculum and have been taken from the following website: www.bbc.co.uk/education/subjects/zn3rkqt.

Are you familiar with the following concepts in art which are embedded into the national curriculum?

Colour; pattern; texture; line; form; space; tint; shade.

Are you familiar with the historical and cultural development of specific art forms and the work of great artists, architects and designers? You will need to make sure that you are in order to teach the national curriculum. You will also need to understand progression across the year groups in specific strands of art such as drawing, painting, printing, sculpture, and progression in these areas from Key Stage 1 to Key Stage 2.

Line: Line is the path left by a moving point. For example, a pencil or a brush dipped in paint. A line can take many forms. It can be horizontal, diagonal or curved. It can also change over its length, starting off curved and ending up horizontal.

Shape: A shape is an area enclosed by a line. It could be just an outline or it could be shaded in. Shapes can be either **geometric**, like a circle, square or triangle, or **irregular**.

Form: Form is a **three dimensional shape**, such as a cube, sphere or cone.

Sculpture and 3D design are about creating forms. In 2D artworks, tone and perspective can be used to create an illusion of form.

Tone: This refers to the lightness or darkness of something. This could be a shade or how dark or light a colour appears.

Tones are created by the way light falls on a 3D object. The parts of the object on which the light is strongest are called **highlights** and the darker areas are called **shadows**. There will a range of tones in between the highlights and shadows.

Texture: This is to do with the **surface quality** of something, the way something feels or looks like it feels. There are two types of texture: actual texture and visual texture.

Actual texture really exists, so you can feel it or touch it. You can create actual texture in an artwork by changing the surface, such as sticking different fabrics onto a canvas. Combining different material techniques can create interesting textures.

Visual texture is created using marks to represent actual texture. It gives the illusion of a texture or surface but if you touched it, it would be smooth. You can create visual texture by using different lines, shapes, colours or tones. Think about how different marks can be used to show texture.

Pattern: A design that is created by repeating lines, shapes, tones or colours. The design used to create a pattern is often referred to as a **motif**. Motifs can be simple shapes or complex arrangements. Patterns can be manufactured, like a design on fabric, or natural, such as the markings on animal fur.

Colour: Red, yellow and blue are **primary colours**, which means they can't be mixed using any other colours. In theory, all other colours can be mixed from these three colours.

Two primary colours mixed together make a **secondary colour**.

Subject knowledge in physical education

In order to confidently teach physical education across Key Stages 1 and 2 you will need to understand how to teach:

* throwing and catching;
* balancing;
* stretching;
* jumping;
* games (including competitive games);
* tactics for attacking and defending;
* athletics;
* teach outdoor and adventurous activities;
* dance.

In each of these aspects you will need to have a clear understanding of progression across the year groups and progression from Key Stage 1 to Key Stage 2.

CRITICAL QUESTION

* *What do you think about the focus on teaching competitive sports?*

Subject knowledge in computing

To teach the computing curriculum across Key Stage 1 and Key Stage 2 you will need to:

* understand algorithms;
* understand the uses of technology beyond school;
* understand how to teach e-safety;
* design, write and debug programs;
* use logical reasoning to predict the behaviour of simple programs;
* use technology to create, organise, store, manipulate and retrieve digital content;
* use sequence, selection and repetition in programs, including control technology;
* use blogging and use discussion boards;

* use the interactive whiteboard (including creating resources) within school;
* use tablet technology to support teaching and learning;
* use search engines;
* design and create a range of programs, systems and content, including collecting, analysing, evaluating and presenting data and information;
* understand computer networks, including the internet;
* use video conferencing to support teaching and learning;
* use a variety of programs to support teaching and learning, including word processing and graphic design programs;
* combine a variety of software.

Subject knowledge in languages

Modern languages are not statutory at Key Stage 1 although many schools teach a language other than English at Key Stage 1. If you do not speak a language, do not panic. There is time during your training to learn a modern language to a level where you will be able to teach it with confidence. Children need to be able to:

* listen attentively to spoken language and show understanding by joining in and responding;
* explore the patterns and sounds of language through songs and rhymes and link the spelling, sound and meaning of words;
* engage in conversations; ask and answer questions; express opinions and respond to those of others; seek clarification and help;
* speak in sentences, using familiar vocabulary, phrases and basic language structures;
* develop accurate pronunciation and intonation so that others understand when they are reading aloud or using familiar words and phrases;
* present ideas and information orally to a range of audiences;
* read carefully and show understanding of words, phrases and simple writing;
* appreciate stories, songs, poems and rhymes in the language;
* broaden their vocabulary and develop their ability to understand new words that are introduced into familiar written material, including through using a dictionary;
* write phrases from memory, and adapt these to create new sentences, to express ideas clearly;
* describe people, places, things and actions orally and in writing;
* understand basic grammar appropriate to the language being studied, including (where relevant): feminine, masculine and neuter forms and the conjugation of high-frequency verbs; key features and patterns of the language; how to apply these, for instance, to build sentences; and how these differ from or are similar to English.

It is important that you do all you can to bring the language to life. You should use objects, puppets, software on the computer, paired conversations and small group conversations to facilitate active engagement in learning. Teaching should focus on developing children's skills in communicating in the language with a focus on correct pronunciation. You therefore need to plan lessons so that there is an appropriate balance of listening, speaking and writing in the language. The national curriculum aims to develop pupils' proficiency in one language.

CRITICAL QUESTIONS

- *What are the advantages of learning a language in Key Stage 1?*
- *What are the disadvantages of learning a language in Key Stage 1?*

Subject knowledge in religious education

Religious education is not part of the national curriculum but it is nevertheless a statutory subject. Schools follow a locally agreed syllabus which determines the content to be taught. As a basis for developing your subject knowledge you must make sure that you have good knowledge of the six major world religions. These are: *Christianity; Buddhism; Hinduism; Islam; Judaism; Sikhism.*

For each religion you need to know about special places and objects associated with that religion, places of worship, celebrations, beliefs, authority and ways of life for those who follow that religion. It is important that you maintain a neutral stance when teaching religious education. Thus, you should focus on teaching religious education as a body of knowledge (ie what are the beliefs and practices of the religion) rather than making any judgement on those beliefs and practices. The best way to express this is to use the term *Hindu's believe...* rather than presenting those beliefs as facts.

Try to bring the subject to life so that pupils remain motivated. This can be done through visits to places of worship or by bringing representatives of the faith into the classroom to talk to children about the faith. Most schools celebrate major festivals such as Diwali using a range of approaches such as cooking, food tasting, music and dance. The best way for children to learn about a religion is to learn it through enquiry (similar to the approaches I have recommended for science and history). Thus, pupils can learn about religions through interacting with religious artefacts, photographs, special clothing, stories and so on. They should be taught to remain respectful of all faiths and they need to understand that different people have different beliefs.

Progression in design and technology

The Design and Technology Association has developed a framework to help teachers to understand progression in strands of learning in design and technology, covering the following areas:

- designing;
- making skills;
- evaluating;
- technical knowledge;
- cooking and nutrition.

Visit www.data.org.uk/media/1128/progression-framework-ks1-ks2.pdf and read the full list, then have a look at the critical questions below.

CRITICAL QUESTIONS

* *How might you use this progression framework to differentiate your teaching?*
* *How useful is this progression framework to teachers who teach specific year groups?*

EXTENDED THINKING

* *Do you agree that the primary national curriculum is too heavy in content? Explain your answer.*
* *Do you think the content in the primary national curriculum is appropriate and relevant for children in the twenty-first century?*
* *The national curriculum specifies the knowledge, understanding and skills that children need for life in twenty-first century society. However, given the pace of technological advancement in the last 20 years we cannot predict what skills children will need in the future. Given the fact that workers of the future are likely to need creativity as well as knowledge, do you think the national curriculum is fit for purpose?*

EVIDENCE-BASED TEACHING

According to Coe et al (2014, p 44):

The evidence to support the inclusion of content knowledge in a model of teaching effectiveness is strong, at least in curriculum areas such as maths, literacy and science. Different forms of content knowledge are required. As well as a strong, connected understanding of the material being taught, teachers must also understand the ways students think about the content, be able to evaluate the thinking behind non-standard methods, and identify typical misconceptions students have.

EVALUATE

* *Which type of subject knowledge is more important – pedagogical subject knowledge (knowledge of how to teach a subject) or subject knowledge per se (knowledge of the subject content)?*

CHALLENGE

* *In what ways should your role as a teacher extend beyond a purely transmission role where knowledge is imparted to learners? How can you encourage learners to take greater responsibility for their own learning? How can you utilise the fact that technological advances mean knowledge is much more easily accessible?*

APPLY

* *In school observe lessons to identify how teachers address pupils' misconceptions in specific subjects.*

EXTENDED THINKING

* *Is the role of a curriculum to prepare children to be workers of the future? Explain your answer.*

TECHNOLOGY

Subject associations are a really valuable resource to support the development of your subject knowledge. Much of the material is freely available or you may choose to become a member of an association for a small fee. This will enable you to access additional resources.

Examples of subject associations include:

- *The Association for Science Education: www.ase.org.uk/home/*
- *The Geographical Association: www.geography.org.uk/*
- *The Historical Association: www.history.org.uk/*
- *Mathematical Association: www.m-a.org.uk/primary-maths*
- *United Kingdom Literacy Association: https://ukla.org/*
- *Design and Technology Association: www.data.org.uk/*

Critical reflections

The breadth of the primary national curriculum is sometimes overwhelming. You cannot be expected to know and understand everything before you teach it and teachers are certainly not walking encyclopaedias or fountains of knowledge. The key point that I want to make is that you have a responsibility to ensure that your subject knowledge is good at the point when you teach something. This will require some commitment on your part to research the subject matter and children's likely misconceptions before you teach it. Thorough planning and preparation will ensure that you are able to teach subject content with confidence. If you are unsure about specific national curriculum content or are unsure about how to teach it, do not be afraid to talk to your mentors in school or appropriate subject leaders. No-one will expect you to be an expert in everything, especially given the curriculum breadth you are required to teach. However, you will be expected to be proactive in researching information and talking to colleagues before you teach some content to your pupils.

KEY READINGS

Classic:

Pollard, A (2014) *Reflective Teaching in Schools*. 4th ed. London: Bloomsbury Publishing Plc.

Contemporary:

Hansen, A (ed) (2014) *Children's Errors in Mathematics*. Exeter: Learning Matters.

Haylock, D (2014) *Mathematics Explained for Primary Teachers*. 5th ed. London: Sage.

Medwell, J, Wray, D, Moore, G and Griffiths, V (2014) *Primary English: Knowledge and Understanding*. 7th ed. London: Learning Matters.

References

BBC Bitesize (n.d.) Art & design: Elements of ar-t. [online] Available at: www.bbc.co.uk/education/subjects/zyg4d2p (accessed 20 June 2016).

Carter, A (2015) *Review of Initial Teacher Training*. London: DfE.

Coe, R, Aloisi, C, Higgins, S T and Major, L E (2014) *What Makes Great Teaching? Review of the Underpinning Research*. London: The Sutton Trust.

Data.org.uk (n.d) Design and technology progression framework: Key Stages 1 and 2. [online] Available at: www.data.org.uk/media/1128/progression-framework-ks1-ks2.pdf (accessed 15 May 2016).

Evans, A, Hawksley, F, Holland, M and Caillau, I (2008) Improving subject knowledge and subject pedagogic knowledge in employment-based secondary initial teacher training in England. [online] Available at: http://shura.shu.ac.uk/187/1/fulltext.pdf (accessed 16 April 2016).

Geographical Association (n.d.) Planning for progress at primary with the 2014 national curriculum. [online] Available at: http://geography.org.uk/news/2014nationalcurriculum/primaryprogress/ (accessed 15 May 2016).

Herts for Learning – Teaching and Learning (n.d.) [online] Available at: www.thegrid.org.uk/learning/maths/ks1-2/nat_curriculum/index.shtml (accessed 15 May 2016).

Music Express Online (n.d.) Don't know your Timbre from your Timbrel? Fear not – help is at hand. [online] Available at: www.musicexpress.co.uk/extras/glossary (accessed 15 May 2016).

3: SUBJECT KNOWLEDGE IN ENGLISH

TEACHERS' STANDARDS

This chapter addresses the following Teachers' Standard:

Teachers' Standard 3: Demonstrate good subject and curriculum knowledge

Teachers must:

* *have a secure knowledge of the relevant subject(s) and curriculum areas, foster and maintain pupils' interest in the subject, and address misunderstandings;*
* *demonstrate a critical understanding of developments in the subject and curriculum areas, and promote the value of scholarship;*
* *demonstrate an understanding of and take responsibility for promoting high standards of literacy, articulacy and the correct use of standard English, whatever the teacher's specialist subject.*

PROFESSIONAL LINKS

The *Carter Review of Initial Teacher Training* stated that:

XI. Evidence suggests that a high level of subject expertise is a characteristic of good teaching (Coe and others, 2014). We have found that the most effective courses address gaps and misconceptions in trainees' core subject knowledge. This is important for both primary and secondary courses and across all subjects.

XII. Across all subjects and phases we have found variability in the way subject knowledge is addressed. Given the importance of subject knowledge for good teaching, this is not satisfactory.

XIII. Overall, we have been pleased to see the majority of ITT programmes are preparing trainees to teach the new national curriculum. However, we are concerned about a significant minority of courses where it appears programmes have not been updated to reflect changes.

(Carter, 2015, pp 7–8)

The review made the following recommendations for ITT courses:

Recommendation 1a: *Subject knowledge development should be part of a future framework for ITT content.*

Recommendation 2: *All ITT partnerships should:*

I. rigorously audit, track and systematically improve trainees' subject knowledge throughout the programme;
II. ensure that changes to the curriculum and exam syllabi are embedded in ITT programmes;
III. ensure that trainees have access to high quality subject expertise;
IV. ensure that trainees have opportunities to learn with others training in the same subject.

(Carter, 2015, p 7)

The recently published government White Paper for education states that:

Despite decades of research showing its positive effects, systematic synthetic phonics had been disregarded by many schools, local authorities, and university education faculties. Growing support within the teaching profession led to a number of new synthetic phonics reading schemes. In 2012, we introduced the phonics reading check at the end of Year 1 and three years on, the proportion of 6-year-olds achieving the expected standard in the check has risen by 19 percentage points to 77%, equivalent to 120,000 more children on track to become excellent readers.

(DfE, 2016, para 2.56, p 38)

The government continues to demonstrate a strong allegiance to systematic synthetic phonics and to the phonics check for pupils in Year 1.

CHAPTER OBJECTIVES

* **What is this chapter about?**

This chapter introduces you to the key elements of English in the national curriculum. The purpose of the chapter is to support the development of your own subject and pedagogical knowledge.

* **Why is it important?**

Despite the achievement stated above, far too many children do not reach the expected standards in reading and writing by the end of primary school (DfE, 2016). The new national curriculum sets out exacting expectations for every year group in order to drive up standards in English. There is greater focus on grammar, spelling and punctuation, reading for enjoyment and the use of correct registers of communication. These changes will help to raise attainment in English. The challenging expectations place an onus on teacher training providers to ensure that future teachers have the knowledge and skills required to teach the full breadth of the national curriculum.

In view of the expectations in the national curriculum and the messages in both the Carter Review (Carter, 2015) and the White Paper (DfE, 2016), it is essential that you leave your ITT programme with good subject knowledge in English. Your ITT provider has a responsibility to ensure that the programme design provides sufficient opportunity for trainees to develop good subject knowledge. However, given that some programmes are only a year in duration and many are now school-based, the training provider will not be able to teach you everything you need to know. You therefore have a responsibility to ensure that you are developing good subject knowledge through processes such as auditing, self-testing and personal research. This chapter cannot address all the elements of English as outlined in the national curriculum. It covers key areas of spoken language, reading and writing but you will need to read it in conjunction with the national curriculum framework.

Spoken language

Spoken language and the development of pupils' listening skills should be embedded throughout all subjects of the national curriculum as a tool for promoting learning. The skills of developing good spoken language should be taught within English lessons and then applied across the full breadth of the curriculum. You cannot assume that children will start their primary education with accurate spoken language and good listening skills. Even if these skills are secure, they may not know how spoken language should be adjusted to take into account the audience and the social setting. You may hear children and parents speaking to each other in ways which are inappropriate and children may continue to use casual forms of communication with teachers and other adults in school if parents have not explicitly explained to children that the way they communicate with adults must differ from the way they communicate with each other. If teachers fail to address this issue then children will enter the adult world without adequate knowledge of the fact that communication must be adjusted to take into account the audience, topic of conversation, purpose and location.

Good spoken language provides the foundations for reading and writing development. Children who cannot speak in sentences will find it difficult to write in sentences. Exposing children to a rich language environment will support the development of children's linguistic awareness, linguistic comprehension and phonological awareness. Linguistic awareness is the ability to develop a wide repertoire of language. Linguistic comprehension is the ability to understand the meanings of words. Phonological awareness is the ability to tune into sound (eg picking up on rhyme and alliteration) and to detect sounds of varying grain sizes (whole words, syllables, rimes). It is a critical skill for subsequent development of phonemic awareness. Phonemic awareness refers to the ability to hear the smallest sounds within a word. Listening and attention is a pre-requisite skill for both phonological and phonemic awareness, both of which are critical to reading development. Children who are unable to listen attentively will find it difficult to hear sounds of different grain sizes and this will affect reading development.

Developing good spoken language and being a good listener are essential for subsequent success in the adult world. Effective communication is a necessary requirement for dealing with social encounters in both formal and informal settings. Children born into socially deprived environments may start school with under-developed language and communication skills and it is critical that early intervention and support is provided to improve this aspect of development.

Registers for effective communication

The ability to alter spoken language according to audience, topic, purpose and location is known as *register*. The way we speak to others fundamentally depends on:

- ***who*** we are speaking to;
- ***what*** is being talked about;
- ***why*** the conversation is taking place;
- ***where*** the conversation is taking place.

Most adults know that it is important to select and use *appropriate registers* for effective communication. To illustrate this, think about the way you converse with your friends during a social occasion. You probably would not converse in the same way with your doctor or university lecturer. You may adopt a more formal approach when you speak to those in more powerful positions. If you met someone for the first time in a formal situation such as a job interview, you would not use an informal style of communication with them because this would be completely inappropriate and you would probably not secure the position for which you had applied. Now think about the way in which you communicate with your parents. You would probably not communicate with your parents in the same way that you would speak with a friend. There are unspoken rules to communication and you will have picked many of these up subconsciously during your lives without explicitly being taught them.

Static register

This is a 'frozen register' in that there are very specific, fixed ways of speaking in certain situations. An example of this is the way in which communication is played out during legal proceedings. Specific words and phrases are spoken in very specific ways by the judge, solicitors and the jury. When the Lord's Prayer is spoken it is done so in a very specific way. The style of the communication is fixed in these situations and the wording does not alter.

Formal register

A formal register is used in specific formal contexts. In a graduation ceremony the chancellor or vice-chancellor of the university or other official representatives will speak in quite a formal way to the audience. In religious ceremonies faith leaders will speak formally to their congregations. This form of communication tends to be impersonal and is adopted during speeches, presentations, announcements and sermons. It is a form of communication which is used between strangers.

Consultative register

This is a standard form of communication normally used in professional discourse. It is the way in which a doctor and patient or teacher and student should speak to each other. It might also be used in counsellor/client relationships. This form of communication is used when there is an expert/novice relationship between the two people who are holding the conversation. There is an element of formality and professionalism but the dialogue is often friendly but professional.

Casual register

This form of communication is the form that takes place between friends. It is often informal and is characterised by the use of slang, vulgarities, frequent interruptions or colloquialisms. This form of communication is often evident in letters to friends or written communications on social networking sites. It may be characterised by a 'group language' where members of a social group share a particular style of social language.

Intimate register

This is a private language mainly reserved for close family members or people who are intimate. It is a highly informal language which is private and known only to two people or a social group and it may include verbal and non-verbal forms of communication.

Various registers of communication differ in their complexities and the regularity of syntax and grammar. The formal register, for example, may be characterised by spoken language which is grammatically accurate. In contrast, communication in the casual register may be characterised by grammatically incorrect spoken language. It is important to note that register is not associated with the speaker but rather with the social and professional contexts in which the conversations take place. You will vary your register depending upon who you are speaking to, and judges, faith leaders, chancellors and vice-chancellors will certainly use a casual register when speaking to their friends or family members or even an intimate register when speaking to their partners!

Teaching children about register

It is important that very young children are taught that they should vary the way they speak according to who they are speaking to. Some of the children that you teach will come from families in which parents use a more consultative register. This is quite important, particularly for very young children because they need to learn that there is an expert/novice relationship between them and their parents. Sometimes parents and children may jump from using a consultative register to using a casual register and the intimate register may be used from time to time. The register will vary depending on the context, ie the situation, the topic of conversation and the location of that communication. As children get older, particularly as children reach adolescence, parents may start to adopt a more casual register. Many adolescents can cope with this well and they recognise the boundaries that exist between them and their parents. However, some children may exploit this and use it as an opportunity to minimise power differentials between the parent and the child.

Some children may start school having only ever been exposed to a casual register. Their conversations may be characterised by colloquialisms, slang and vulgarities. These children will need to be explicitly taught about the rules of communication. School is a professional context. Children come to school to learn from their teachers and other adults. They do not come to school to form friendships with these adults. They need to be taught that there is a specific way of conversing with adults and that this will differ from the way that they communicate with their friends, for example, when they are out in the playground or when they play with their friends in different social contexts. Fundamentally, children need to be taught that they will speak differently in the classroom, even to their peers, compared to the ways in which they speak to their peers in the playground because the formality of the classroom and its purpose necessitates different forms of communication. They need to be taught that even if they alter the way they speak to their peers depending on whether they are out in the playground or in the classroom, the way in which they converse with their teachers and other adults in school should always be consistent, ie using a consultative register.

If children do not learn to use different registers of speech for different purposes in different contexts, then they are at a fundamental disadvantage when they leave school and enter the world of work. They might not keep a job for very long if they use a casual or intimate register with their boss, for example. They need to learn that there is a more formal way of communicating with strangers who are in more powerful positions compared to the casual and informal conversations that they have with their friends. You would not speak to the Queen in the same way as you speak to a friend and children need to recognise this from the very beginning of their education, otherwise they will get into bad habits.

Modelling register

Adults in school need to model communicating effectively with each other. Schools are professional, working environments so adults need to converse with each other using a consultative register. When you next go into school observe the way adults communicate with each other:

* Are they polite to each other?
* Do they listen to each other?
* Do they maintain eye contact?
* Do they wait for the person who is speaking to finish before responding?
* Do they wait their turn or do they 'butt in' to conversations?

As a teacher you are a role model of communication. You therefore need to consider the way you interact with all adults in school and parents. Your communications with parents should be professional using a consultative register. They should not take place using a casual register. Next, take some time to observe the way in which adults interact with children in conversations. Do they communicate using Standard English or do they slip into a casual register by using colloquialisms, incorrect grammar and slang? Observe the way that adults interact with children in the classroom and in the playground. Is the consultative register consistently being applied or do adults slip into using the casual register in more informal situations? Observe the register that is being used in assemblies. Is there evidence that a more formal register is being used in this context?

Rules for communication

Generally, pupils and teachers in school should use a professional discourse which indicates the nature of the expert/novice relationship. Additionally, within the classroom context pupils should speak to each other using a consultative register because they are in a formal setting. Establishing some simple rules for communication in the classroom with your pupils will act as a useful frame of reference. These could include the following.

* Wait your turn if someone is speaking to the person you want to talk to.
* Start your conversation with a polite word such as 'please' or 'excuse me', then say something.
* Allow the person you have spoken to give a response.
* Look at the person who is speaking and listen to what they are saying.
* At the end of the conversation thank the person for talking to you.

These can be adjusted depending on the age of the pupils but having clear rules helps to demonstrate high expectations and it gives the pupils a framework to follow to support their spoken language.

Use of Standard English

It should be noted that Standard English is not limited to a specific accent and it covers most registers. The aim of the national curriculum is for all children to use Standard

English in both spoken and written language. As a trainee teacher you will need to make a conscious effort to speak and write in correct Standard English when you are in school. If your mentor identifies a weakness in your spoken or written language, try not to feel that they are personally attacking you. After all, it is important to remember that communicating in Standard English is part of the Teachers' Standards. This is because you are a role model and children will copy what you say and write. It is not about altering your accent and it is certainly not about speaking using a posh voice. It is a matter of making sure that your grammar is correct when you are speaking. Common mistakes include:

- *'Who is sat quietly on the mat?'* rather than *'Who is sitting quietly on the mat?'*
- *'You have done it lovely'* rather than *'You have done lovely work!'* (Brien, 2012).
- *'I am stood next to the door'* rather than *'I am standing next to the door'*.

Although it is accepted that people alternate between Standard and non-Standard English depending on who they are speaking to and the particular context in which the conversation takes place, Standard English tends to be used in formal situations where clarity of expression is required. Children also need to be able to write in Standard English; therefore, it follows that if children are unable to speak in Standard English their written expression may also be affected. It is important to correct children when they use non-Standard English in situations which require the use of Standard English. However, this must be addressed sensitively in order to protect the child's self-concept. One way of doing this sensitively without directly correcting pupils is to rephrase what they have said to you by providing them with the correct model of Standard English.

Discussions

Very young children can be supported in having discussions in a range of ways. These include discussions:

- about texts they have listened to or read;
- about how to solve a problem;
- about their ideas for a story;
- in role-play/drama;
- which arise as part of a collaborative activity, for example, in mathematics or science.

This is not an exhaustive list but it is important to point out that discussions should take place across the full breadth of the curriculum and not just in English. They should be explicitly planned into lessons so that pupils have opportunities to talk about their learning. Good learners collaborate through high quality discussion. Some teachers may be reluctant to plan discussion tasks in mathematics, science, history and other subjects because of the lack of recorded evidence which they may feel is necessary. However, it is important to remember that Ofsted inspectors look for evidence of learning taking place in lessons, not just evidence of written outputs that children produce and much learning arises from discussions. Discussion as an approach to learning and teaching reflects a socio-constructivist model of learning and the work of Vygotsky (1978) who argued that children learn through social interaction and the use of language. You might need to start with organising children in pairs to undertake paired discussion in the initial stages and then gradually increase the size of the groups. You need to teach the pupils the rules of discussion. These include:

* making eye contact with the speaker;
* everybody having a turn at speaking;
* one person speaking at a time;
* speaking in a clear voice;
* using appropriate vocabulary;
* being clear about what you mean and supporting what you say with evidence;
* using the language of reasoning, eg *I think*, *because*, *therefore*;
* responding to the other speaker;
* using questions to clarify understanding;
* making extended contributions;
* using facial expressions and gestures.

Debates

Very young children can be taught the rules of a good debate. Within the context of a debate there are usually two contrasting viewpoints. Children will initially need to be supported through the process of taking part in a debate but once they are familiar with the process and rules then they can gradually take increasing ownership of their own debates. The following structure might help you:

* Introduce the debate, particularly the two opposing views.
* Divide pupils into two groups. One group will discuss arguments *for* and the other group will discuss arguments *against*.
* Give the pupils thinking time to orally rehearse what they are going to say.
* Allow them to plan their responses and teach them how to make notes to support their talk.
* Allow one group to speak and put forward their arguments while the other group listen to them.
* Allow the other group to speak, putting forward the contrasting arguments.
* Resolve the debate by having a class vote and synthesise by concluding that *most people in class X think...*

The ability to participate in debate and respect the opinions of others, even when we disagree, is one of the essential attributes of an educated and civilised human being. It is imperative to teach children that different people have different opinions but that we should respect people's viewpoints even if we do not agree with them. It is important to set some ground rules. These include:

* not interrupting others when they are speaking;
* not ridiculing the opinions of others;
* listening to what others have to say;
* being prepared to change your viewpoint if someone convinces you that your viewpoint needs to change;
* stating a reason for your opinions.

These can be phrased in child-friendly terms and you can remind the children about these rules at the start of the lesson. A good debate cannot be rushed and the children need thinking time and time to talk through and orally rehearse their ideas. The quality of the lesson will largely be determined by the quality of the debate which takes place; the richness of the discussion; the quality of the arguments being put forward; and children's participation, immersion and obsession in the debate.

You can use children's fiction and non-fiction texts as a stimulus for debate. Traditional stories can result in some effective debates including:

- Did Jack do the right thing by selling the cow? (Yes/No)
- Was the Wolf telling the truth in the True Story of the Three Little Pigs? (Yes/No)
- Did Goldilocks do the right thing by breaking into the Bear's house? (Yes/No)

You also need to think about how debates can then be integrated across the curriculum. Examples include:

- Was it right that children had to work down the mines in Victorian times? (history)
- Should we only be allowed to have one car per family? (geography)
- Should farmers sell their land for house building? (geography)
- Should animals be kept in zoos? (science)

CRITICAL QUESTIONS

- *Should children in Key Stage 1 debate controversial issues in society? Explain your answer as fully as possible.*
- *How will you teach children to handle conflicting opinions?*
- *How can you link debate into class themes or topics?*
- *When organising a debate, should children be forced to take a standpoint with which they disagree?*
- *How will you organise the pupils into the groups for and against?*
- *What additional debates could you introduce in those subjects mentioned above?*

Reading development

The Simple View of Reading

The Simple View of Reading (Gough and Tunmer, 1986) identifies the two components of reading:

- recognising and decoding printed words;
- linguistic comprehension – the ability to understand spoken language.

Children will almost certainly struggle to understand the texts they listen to and read if they do not understand and have a wide repertoire of *spoken language*. Children will also find it difficult to understand the printed or spoken word if they do not understand the vocabulary they are reading or hearing. However, if children are unable to read the printed word then this will impact detrimentally on their understanding of the texts they read.

The Simple View of Reading demonstrates that *both* linguistic comprehension and word recognition are essential to good reading development. Research has demonstrated how separate measures of word recognition (decoding) and linguistic comprehension together give a good account of how well children can read (Johnston and Watson, 2007). Thus, measures of decoding (D) and linguistic comprehension (C) together help to predict children's abilities in *reading comprehension ability* (R) or ($R = D \times C$) (Johnston and Watson, 2007, p 26). Children need to be able to read the words on a page as well as being able to understand them to comprehend what they are reading. Both elements are important in developing good reading comprehension and each element needs to be assessed separately in order to determine whether children require intervention within a specific domain. Each element requires a different kind of teaching but teachers fundamentally need to focus on both aspects in order to give children the best chance of becoming good readers.

A good reader is not simply a good decoder. Children cannot read well if they do not understand what they are reading. However, as stated above, without good decoding skills children will not be able to understand what they are reading. It is therefore critical that teachers in the Early Years Foundation Stage and in Year 1 place greater emphasis on developing children's skills in decoding. Once this skill is secure and children are fluent in word recognition, teachers will then be able to place greater emphasis on developing their understanding of texts. However, it is important to emphasise that I am not suggesting a linear relationship between word recognition and language comprehension. You should not focus exclusively on developing children's skills in decoding before you move onto developing their skills in comprehension. Both skills should be developed concurrently but there will be greater emphasis initially on decoding in order to develop children's fluency in reading.

You need to ensure that as well as focusing on decoding (sounding out and blending) children have opportunities to further develop their language. They need to learn language through being immersed in rich language and social contexts and they need to have opportunities to listen and respond to a wide range of stories, poems and non-fiction texts. The skill of word recognition needs to be taught within a rich language context so that all the time children are being flooded with language. As children focus on decoding texts, it is important that you talk to them about the text that they are reading so that they understand it. You can do this by:

- engaging them in dialogue about the illustrations;
- asking them questions about the text;
- relating the text to their own experiences;
- asking them to predict what might happen next;
- talking to them about the characters.

Initially, children need to focus their energies on sounding out and blending phonemes to read words. Your role, as well as supporting them with blending, is to ensure that they understand what they are reading through engaging them in dialogue about the text. You might initially have to do more work than the pupils do in terms of comprehension because they will be focusing on decoding. Once word recognition is secure and fluent, you should place more emphasis on the children being able to answer your questions about the text through:

- answering questions where the answer can be directly extracted from the text;
- making predictions;

* making inferences;
* giving a response to the text;
* encouraging the children to *read as a writer* (see below).

The more children read, the better their linguistic comprehension will be. Introducing children to a wider range of books, poetry and non-fiction texts will extend their exposure to language. This will have a positive impact on their reading comprehension ability. Additionally, children's skills in decoding print will improve with the more practice they have through reading.

As a teacher it is critical for you to understand the reasons which underpin poor achievement in reading. Children's reading development could be impeded because their skills in decoding are not secure, even though they may have good linguistic comprehension. These pupils require additional support in decoding print through access to a multi-sensory phonics programme.

In contrast, some children may be good decoders but have poor linguistic comprehension. Their reading comprehension skills will not improve unless their language comprehension improves and consequently these pupils may well need access to a language intervention programme. These pupils attack print well but they may not understand the meaning of the words they are reading.

A child who has both poor linguistic comprehension and poor decoding skills may need a language intervention programme and a phonics intervention. They need support to improve their skills in both domains because reading comprehension ability is the product of both.

Effective readers are those who have well-developed language comprehension and fluent word recognition skills. The national curriculum (DfE, 2013) is clear in its expectation that children should start to move away from sounding out and blending as soon as possible so that an over-reliance on decoding does not inhibit their understanding of the texts they are reading. You therefore need to teach children to decode quickly and accurately. Once they have been exposed to a word several times, they need to develop the skill of saying the word quickly and automatically so that they do not 'lose the thread' of what they are reading.

CRITICAL QUESTIONS

* *How will you use the Simple View of Reading to identify the needs of poor readers?*
* *How will you decide which type of intervention is appropriate for your poor readers?*
* *How will you monitor the effectiveness of any interventions you implement?*

Additionally, the Simple View of Reading helps teachers to recognise that developing pupils' skills in each domain requires different *types* of teaching. The national curriculum is explicit that word recognition skills should be taught through access to a systematic phonics programme in which phonic knowledge is developed progressively by following a clearly structured approach to introducing the alphabetic code. Historically, there was once a view that decoding printed words was largely unimportant (Goodman, 1973) because it was thought that skilled readers did not need to read all the words on a page. At the time it was considered that it was more important to understand the meaning of the text from the context rather than reading every word accurately. However, research evidence has now demonstrated that guessing words from the context is what *unskilled* readers do (Johnston and Watson, 2007). Children will make greater progress in reading if they have a strategy for working out unfamiliar words (Johnston and Watson, 2007). Although some children are able to recognise words as whole word shapes by committing them to memory, this approach does not help children to read words which they encounter in texts that they have not seen before. The phonics approach, in contrast, provides children with a strategy for working out unfamiliar words. Once word recognition becomes automatic, children are then able to focus to a greater extent on the skill of linguistic comprehension.

CRITICAL QUESTIONS

- *What type of teaching is needed to develop pupils' skills in word recognition?*
- *What type of teaching is needed to develop pupils' skills in linguistic comprehension?*

As a trainee teacher it is important that you understand how children develop as readers. Understanding models of reading development will help you to identify what stages children have reached in their reading development and what their next steps are. This will help you to plan suitable learning opportunities to advance their reading development. However, the problem with developmental frameworks is that they over-simplify the learning process when in reality learning is quite complex. Learning to read is a complex process but once it is mastered we read with automaticity and make it look simple.

To illustrate the process of achieving automaticity, let us think carefully about the process of learning to drive a car. There are many skills to master when learning to drive: changing gear at the right time; holding the car on the biting point; accelerating; decelerating; indicating to make a turn and so on. When we first learn to drive we have to think consciously about every process step by step. We often cannot see the 'big picture' (where we are going) because we are focusing on changing the gear, pressing the clutch or accelerator pedal or indicating left or right. It is the same when children are first learning to read. They have to focus on several skills: sounding out the phonemes; blending phonemes together to read words; moving across a line of text from left to right; moving onto the next line and so on. It is hardly surprising that they lose the meaning of the text when they are focusing on all the technical aspects of reading; we can help them to keep a sense of the text by engaging them in dialogue about it. Once these skills become embedded and automatic, children can then focus less on them, leaving them more 'brain space' to focus on the plot, the characters and the description.

Ehri's model (Ehri, 2005) of sight word reading is well-established and encompasses the thinking of major theorists. In examining children's reading development Ehri found that children progress through four phases of reading development. These are summarised below.

Pre-alphabetic phase

Ehri found that very young children rely on visual cues to help them read words. At this phase, children are very aware of print in their environment. They can read logos (such as Cadbury's or Coca-Cola) because they learn to recognise the word within the context in which they normally see it. They draw on cues such as colours, shapes and sizes of letters

to help them to recognise words which they see in the environment. If these cues are removed, then children cannot generally recognise the word when it is presented in normal print (Johnston et al, 1996).

Partial alphabetic phase

At this phase, children start to use their knowledge of the alphabet to attempt to read words although they do not work all the way through the phonemes in a word from left to right (Johnston and Watson, 2007). They may overly focus on the initial phoneme within a word, for example by reading *bin* as *boy*. They are making use of some phonic knowledge at this phase but often it results in inaccurate word reading. Poor readers tend to arrest in their reading development at this phase (Romani et al, 2005) and these pupils often benefit from access to a multi-sensory phonics programme taught at a much slower pace than traditional synthetic phonics programmes. Very able poor readers such as those with dyslexia may adopt a visual rather than alphabetic approach to reading (Johnston and Morrison, 2007). In view of Ehri's model of reading development, all pupils whose development is arrested at this phase need further support to help them master the alphabetic code and its application in reading.

Full alphabetic phase

In the full alphabetic phase children are able to make connections between the letters and phonemes all the way through a word. When presented with the letters t-a-p at this phase a child can say the corresponding phonemes in sequence to read *tap*. As children start to develop knowledge of *digraphs* (two letters representing one sound), they can sound out words such as *throat* by saying and blending the phonemes represented by the corresponding graphemes from left to right through the word, in this instance th-r-oa-t.

Consolidated alphabetic phase

At this phase, children start to recognise morphemes (units of meaning), for example, by combining them to read whole words. Children also start to recognise rimes within words rather than needing to break words down into smaller graphemes. They then start to use their knowledge of rimes to read words by analogy.

Phonological and phonemic awareness

Phonological awareness is the ability to identify syllables, onsets and rimes within words. Children with good phonological awareness are able to identify rhyming strings. They can hear the 'at' sound in *cat* and are able to substitute onsets to go in front of the rime to generate new words (*rat/sat/mat/bat*). They are able to identify the odd one out in a series of rhyming words and they are able to hear syllabic divisions within words. Bradley and Bryant (1983) reported a strong correlation between children's ability to recognise rhyme and their subsequent development as good readers. This illustrates the importance of immersing children in rhyme from a very early age through access to nursery rhymes, rhyming games and rhyming stories.

Phonemic awareness is the ability to perceive and manipulate the phonemes in *spoken* words (Johnston and Watson, 2007). A child with good phonemic awareness would be able to tell you that *mat* has three sounds (m-a-t) and that *coat* also has three sounds (c-oa-t).

Children with good phonemic awareness are able to hear the sounds in a *spoken* word in the correct sequence from left to right all through the word.

Enunciation of phonemes

In synthetic phonics you should always use the pure sound (or soft sound) by pronouncing it without the 'schwa': this is an extra sound or unstressed vowel which is sometimes added onto phonemes. It is very easy to add an 'uh' sound to the end of phonemes. For example, 'c' in the word *cat* should not be pronounced '*cuh*'. Pronouncing the sound clearly and precisely will make the process of blending sounds together much easier.

Smallest meaningful units of sound

In synthetic phonics words are broken down into the smallest meaningful units of sound as follows:

Table 3.1 Breaking down words

flag	f/l/a/g
grass	g/r/a/ss
boat	b/oa/t
crisp	c/r/i/s/p
spray	s/p/r/ay
duck	d/u/ck
snail	s/n/ai/l
string	s/t/r/i/n/g
chop	ch/o/p (ch is a *consonant digraph)*

This means that consonant blends such as bl/cl/cr/dr/sp are not taught because they can be broken down further into their separate sounds. Instead, they are taught as *adjacent consonants* (two consonants which make two separate sounds). Teaching consonant blends was common in analytic phonics where pupils were once taught using onset and rime (for example, *br-ush*).

Sound buttons

To encourage children to focus on each separate grapheme in a word and its corresponding phoneme, the use of sound buttons can support children in the early stages of learning to read with the process of blending. Examples are shown in Table 3.2:

Table 3.2 Examples of sound buttons

d	**o**	**g**	
.	.	.	
s	**t**	**o**	**p**
.	.	.	.
c	**o**	**a**	**t**
.	—	.	

EVIDENCE-BASED TEACHING

The type of phonics being taught

The Independent Review of the Teaching of Early Reading (Rose, 2006) advocated the *synthetic* approach to phonics as *'the best and most direct route'* (2006, p 4) into early reading. The approach emphasises the importance of teaching children to blend phonemes all through the word for reading and additionally emphasises blending as the prime approach to reading. It is taught at a rapid pace and the process of blending is applied to the text almost from the very start of the programme after enough *grapheme-phoneme correspondences* have been taught to build words. In contrast, *analytic phonics* focuses on introducing children to word families (dog/fog/log/jog) with a focus on the *rime*. Using their knowledge of rimes, children can then learn to read words by inference without reading all the way through the word. The grapheme-phoneme correspondences are introduced at a slower pace and blending phonemes for reading is introduced much later than in synthetic phonics programmes. There is an over-emphasis of the initial phonemes within words and on reading words initially rather than blending all through the word and the phonemes which are introduced tend to appear at the beginning of words.

The evidence which underpins synthetic phonics is compelling (Johnston and Watson, 2004) and has demonstrated that children taught using synthetic phonics made better progress in their reading compared to children taught using analytic phonics.

EVALUATE

* *What are the arguments for and against teaching children to read through phonics?*

CHALLENGE

Wyse and Goswami (2008) have questioned the evidence which underpins the claims made about synthetic phonics. It could be argued that a knowledge of rimes is particularly important because it is more efficient to break words down into onset and rimes (c-at) rather than into smaller phonemes (c-a-t). Additionally, it is logical to argue that if children can recognise the word *boat* because of their ability to identify the rime *oat* then they will also be able to read *goat*, *coat*, *throat* and *float*.

APPLY

In school observe a phonics lesson.

* *What type of phonics are children being taught?*
* *Discuss with the teacher what impact the phonics teaching is having on the children's skills in decoding.*

The alphabetic code

In English we represent the sounds of spoken words by letters and the alphabetic code shows the graphemes which represent each sound of speech. Various versions of the English alphabetic code are available and it is recommended that you display an alphabetic code chart in your classroom so that children begin to associate each of the sounds of speech with their corresponding graphemes.

The simple alphabetic code

In the simple alphabetic code children are introduced to one grapheme (letter or group of letters) for each sound of speech. Although there are 26 letters of the alphabet, there are not enough letters to represent all the sounds of speech (phonemes). This means that letters are grouped into twos (digraphs) or threes (trigraphs) to represent all the sounds of speech. In the simple code each phoneme is represented by one spelling variation which may be one letter or two or more letters. There are 40+ phonemes in the English language and each one is represented by a spelling variation (or grapheme).

The complex alphabetic code

In the complex code children are introduced to the different spelling variations (graphemes) that represent a sound of speech. Thus, the sound /ue/ can be represented by oo (*spoon*), ew (*flew*), u-e (*tune*) or ue (*true*). Additionally, one grapheme can represent various phonemes. For example, the grapheme 'ch' represents different sounds as in *church*, *champagne* and *chemist*.

Key concepts which you must understand

Concept 1: Sounds (phonemes) are represented by letters (graphemes)

English is an alphabetic language – unlike Chinese, for example, where whole words are represented by characters.

Concept 2: A phoneme can be represented by one letter (grapheme) or by a group of two or more letters

For example, (*th*, *igh*, *ear*)

Concept 3: The same sound (phoneme) can be represented (spelled) more than one way

***c**at*

***k**ite*

***ch**emist*

Concept 4: The same grapheme (spelling) may represent more than one phoneme

*dr**ea**m – d**ea**f*

*fr**own** – bl**own***

*f**ie**ld – tr**ie**d*

Concept 5: The split vowel digraph

In the word ***name***, the **a-e** grapheme represents one unit of sound which is enunciated as /ay/. Therefore, this word is decoded as /n/ay/m/.

In the word ***pine*** the **i-e** grapheme represents the sound /igh/ so this word is decoded as /p/ie/n.

EXTENDED THINKING

- *The Year 1 phonics screening check is an assessment of decoding skills rather than reading skills. Why has the government brought this check into Year 1? To what extent does it serve as an accountability tool for schools and teachers?*

Exception words

The national curriculum (DfE, 2013) refers to 'exception words'. These are words which have an unusual correspondence between the spelling and the sound. An example of an exception word would be *said* because the sound in the middle of the word is /e/ although this sound is represented by the letters *ai*. The phonics scheme that your school uses will identify the different exception words that need to be taught at specific phases. When teaching children to read exception words, it is logical to draw their attention to the part of the word that is tricky because this will help them later with spelling these words.

Decoding and encoding

When pupils *decode* text they translate the graphemes into sounds and merge (blend) these sounds together all the way through the word in sequence in order to read the target word. When pupils *encode* or *segment* a word they translate the spoken word into symbols (Brien, 2012) by identifying the constituent phonemes that make up the word and translating these into the corresponding graphemes either through writing or selecting the appropriate symbols. Decoding and encoding (blending and segmenting, respectively) are reversible processes.

Decodable texts

The national curriculum (DfE, 2013) explicitly states that pupils should read books which are closely matched to their developing phonic knowledge. This gives pupils the best chance of successfully decoding print. Even if the words presented in the text are unfamiliar pupils should, theoretically at least, have the necessary phonic knowledge to be able to successfully tackle the print in the text through sounding out the phonemes and blending them together to identify the target word. However, Rose (2006) was clear that pupils also need access to a rich language and literacy curriculum, which includes having access to a wide range of stories, poems, rhymes and non-fiction texts. This will help pupils to develop a love of reading because they should be able to make choices about which texts they wish to read.

CRITICAL QUESTIONS

* *What are the advantages of decodable texts?*
* *What are the disadvantages of decodable texts?*
* *Can you find any literature to support your arguments?*

Morphology

A word's morphology is its internal make-up or structure. Morphology links the study of words with the study of grammar because morphemes, the smallest units of meaning in words, can indicate meaning and may also indicate how a word functions in a sentence (Medwell, 2014, p 61).

Table 3.3 Elements of a word's structure

Root word	The form of a word after all affixes are removed that can stand alone, eg *help* is the root word in *helpful*
Prefix	A prefix is added at the beginning of a word in order to turn it into another word, eg *overtake, disappear*
Suffix	A suffix is added at the end of a word. Suffixes have two functions: they can either create new words, eg *thoughtless* or change the function of the word, eg *beauty* (noun) – *beautiful* (adjective). Unlike root words, suffixes cannot stand on their own as complete words.

At this point it is helpful to define and consider the three possible elements of a word's structure, as shown in Table 3.3.

In English there are two types of morphemes:

Free morphemes: these are 'stand-alone' words and can be content words such as nouns, main verbs and adjectives or function words such as determiners, conjunctions and prepositions.

Bound morphemes: these cannot exist in isolation and are almost exclusively prefixes and suffixes

Prefixes are generally more easily understood as they only have one possible function and that is to create new words. However, suffixes can cause more problems because the reader needs to identify not only a new word, but often a new function in a sentence. Some suffixes are derivational morphemes and change the grammatical category of a word:

* Change a noun into an adjective, eg *beauty – beautiful.*
* Change an adjective into a noun, eg *fearless – fearlessness.*
* Change a verb into a noun, eg *promote – promoter.*
* Create verbs – *orchestrate.*
* Create adverbs – *happily.*

Complicated isn't it? Now consider inflectional morphemes which assign a particular grammatical property to the word. They act as markers to indicate:

* tense, eg *walk – walked*;
* comparison. eg *big – biggest*;
* number, eg *car – cars*;
* possession, eg *John – John's.*

All of this morphological knowledge is demanded as you move from teaching Key Stage 1 to Key Stage 2 and it is important to make sure that the children don't just see morphology as adding to the beginnings or ends of words – they need to understand what they are doing.

Phrasing

A phrase is more than just a group of words; it is a group of words that have a unified function in a sentence. Each phrase carries meaning. Children need to identify the words that *go together* and you need to show them. An activity as simple as cutting a sentence

into phrases and asking the child to read each phrase individually and identify its meaning will support a child's understanding of how to identify which words go together. So which words do go together?

Noun phrase: this is a phrase that tells us the 'who' or 'what' of a sentence, eg

Who: *the big dog/the big hairy dog/the big hairy brown dog*

Adverbial phrase: this is a phrase that tells us the 'when', 'where' or 'how' of a sentence, eg

When: *at midnight/at midnight yesterday evening*

Where: *along the moonlit path/along the moonlit path behind the palace*

How: *very excitedly*

If you then add a verb – 'ran' you have the whole sentence: *At midnight yesterday evening, the big hairy dog ran, very excitedly, along the moonlit path behind the palace.*

Good phrasing supports both word recognition and comprehension. Always encourage children with poor fluency to read aloud and listen to themselves – only then will they hear when it doesn't sound right and make sense.

Reading with expression

Expression is a word full of meaning and complexity. When you ask a child to read with expression, what are you asking them to focus on? When you model reading with expression to what are you asking them to listen?

Expression refers to prosody – the rhythm of speech. This rhythm is made up of a number of features.

You will come to know that the amount of correct expression indicates how much the reader comprehends in the text.

Table 3.4 Features of rhythm

Intonation (the use of pitch)	This relates to the rise and fall of the voice. It can distinguish the difference between a statement and a question.
Stress	This is the degree or emphasis given to a sound or syllable. In a word it can distinguish between a noun or a verb, eg in the word *permit* if you stress the first syllable it is a noun, but if you stress the second syllable it becomes a verb: permit/permit Strong stressed syllables can also convey the meaning of a sentence. The meaning and implications changes depending on where the stress is located: HARRY kicked the ball. (not Fred) Harry KICKED the ball. (not threw) Harry kicked the BALL. (not my head)
Tone	The tone of the voice expresses emotion, eg anger, sarcasm, apology.

Flow, accuracy and expression are the key elements of fluency. The more fluently a child reads, the more they comprehend – the more they comprehend, the more fluent they become. It is vital that you teach for fluency from the beginning with even the most novice of reader. What the child knows and has control over should be read smoothly and at speed. Don't accept slow word-by-word reading on texts that are within the child's control. They need to hear themselves as good readers and to achieve this you need to teach fluency through books with which they are familiar. Use texts that the child has already shown they can decode so that all of their focus can be on fluency and comprehension. This will speed up their processing and they will more readily apply their skills of accurate word reading and fluency on new texts.

There is one more word that is crucial to consider if a child is to become a fluent reader: *confidence*. A lack of confidence in anything, whether that be playing a particular sport or singing in public, leads to being tentative, actions may become disjointed and ultimately you may just give up. Giving up cannot be an option in learning to read and yet many children, even in Key Stage 1, can be heard saying 'I can't read'. To be confident a child must taste success and to achieve success it is your job to offer texts that are within their control. This is not a case of giving the children texts that are *too easy* – a text is only *too easy* when it ceases to have any challenge. Returning to the idea of familiar books, you can see that you are offering the child a *new* challenge when they use an already decoded text to develop fluency. They will begin to hear themselves as good readers and will become motivated and confident to broaden the range of texts that they read. Confidence is also linked to enjoyment – if a child is good at something, they will enjoy it and seek to do more. Be careful as a teacher that you don't inadvertently remove the 'positive' from reading.

Reading comprehension

Brien (2012) identifies four different levels of comprehension. These are:

1. **Literal comprehension:** the ability to extract straightforward information from the text;
2. **Inferential comprehension:** the ability to search for clues in the text by reading between the lines;
3. **Evaluative comprehension:** the ability to understand what may be around and beyond the text;
4. **Appreciative comprehension:** the ability to understand the qualities of the text.

This list demonstrates how comprehension skills gradually increase in complexity, with literal comprehension being the lowest level of comprehension. Comprehension in fiction should provide pupils with opportunities to explore unusual vocabulary and phrasing, imagery and the evocation of emotions (Brien, 2012).

The national curriculum from Year 1 states that pupils should check that the text makes sense to them as they read and self-correct when what they have read does not fit in with their syntactic or semantic knowledge. These terms are summarised below:

* **Syntactic knowledge:** the structure or grammatical correctness of a sentence such as word order;
* **Semantic knowledge:** the meaning of the text and whether it makes sense to the reader based on their prior knowledge.

A sentence could be structurally or grammatically incorrect (syntax) but still have meaning. Many readers use their knowledge of syntax and semantic knowledge when reading to self-correct and to check that what they have read is accurate. The context in which the word in written (syntax and semantics) can give information about whether the word has been read accurately.

Children also need to look at the **graphical features** of text (word length, shape) to check their reading accuracy.

Using your knowledge of syntax, semantics and graphical knowledge, you can ask pupils the following questions when reading:

- Does it sound right?
- Does it make sense?
- Does it look right?

Children can self-correct their responses to a word if they have read a word incorrectly and through accurate word recognition they will develop a better understanding of the text.

CRITICAL QUESTIONS

- *Should comprehension strategies be used for word recognition as described above?*
- *What are the advantages of using knowledge of syntax and semantics for word recognition?*
- *What are the disadvantages?*
- *Do skilled readers self-correct through knowledge of the context in which the word is written or is this an attribute of poor readers?*

Reading comprehension strategies

Reading as a writer

Effective readers are able to *read as a writer*. As they read texts they are able to consider:

- why the author may have chosen to use certain vocabulary;
- why the author has added emphasis to certain words, for example, through the use of capitalisation;
- why the author has used specific punctuation;
- how the author has used grammar at the word, sentence or text level.

Understanding why the author has made certain decisions when composing texts will help children to think more clearly about the impact they are trying to make on the reader when they produce their own writing (*writing as a reader*). However, before children are able to write like this, they need to consider how authors have used language to create an effect as they read texts created by others. Both processes, *reading as a writer* and *writing as a reader*, are therefore connected. Effective readers will be able to discuss the choices that authors have made when constructing texts and the impact this makes on the reader.

Teaching children to read as a writer can be a focus during shared and guided reading sessions. When you plan these lessons you will need to carefully consider the questions you need to ask children to develop this level of comprehension. Questions could include:

- Can you spot any adjectives?
- Why do you think the author used adjectives to describe the setting for this story?
- How do these adjectives help you as a reader?
- Why do you think the author has used an exclamation mark at the end of that sentence?

* Why do you think the author decided to write that word in capital letters?
* Can you spot any adverbs?
* Why do you think the author has used adverbs? How do they help you as a reader?
* Why has the author used sub-headings in this text?
* Can you spot any pronouns in this text? Why do you think the author has used pronouns?

These questions can be extended as children's comprehension develops. Challenging questions could include:

* Why do you think the author has used subordination?
* Why has the author used expanded noun phrases?
* Why do you think the author has used a question?

The focus is on developing children's understanding of what impact the author is trying to create on the reader when they make decisions about choice of grammar, presentation or punctuation. Children will only have a partial understanding of a text unless they are able to put themselves in the shoes of the author and consider the relationship between the text and the reader.

Reading pictures

Long before pupils start to read the printed word, teachers can start to develop their comprehension skills through supporting them in 'reading' pictures. The purpose of this is to develop their comprehension of a picture through the use of guided questioning. You might ask questions such as:

* Where is this? *Focus on the setting.*
* What can you see in the picture? *Focus on the identification of nouns.*
* What is happening? What are they doing? *Focus on the event[s].*
* Why might this be happening? *Early stages of developing inference.*

You can begin this process by just using one picture initially. You can then extend this by presenting pupils with a series of pictures which represent the setting, characters and events from a story. You can then ask them to talk through the story with you orally.

As children then start to read books it is important to ask them to use the pictures to support their comprehension of the story. After they have read the text you can then ask them questions about the pictures to support their understanding. Sometimes the pictures completely support the text. However, in some texts the illustrations extend the story further. It is important that children know that the illustrations are important in supporting their understanding of the text. I do not advocate the children using picture cues as a word recognition strategy but I do support the use of illustrations to facilitate children's understanding of the text.

Developing familiarity with texts

Children's understanding of a text will improve with greater familiarity of the text. In the Early Years Foundation Stage and in Key Stage 1, pupils need to be provided with opportunities to develop their familiarity with texts. The better they know a text, the more

they will understand it. Developing familiarity with stories helps children to understand the sequence of events and the characters in the text. You need to use a range of activities to develop familiarity. These include:

* developing role play-areas around the text;
* introducing interactive story displays (table-top displays) which include props from the story to support pupils in re-enacting the story;
* the use of audio stories;
* opportunities to investigate the story through drama;
* the use of film/digital clips;
* oral recounts of the story using the storyteller's chair;
* opportunities to represent story characters using a range of artistic media.

Book introductions

Book introductions are important in terms of setting the context. Usually it is common practice for teachers to spend time discussing aspects of the book such as the cover, title, name of the author, name of the illustrator and the blurb. It is good practice to 'walk through' the book with the children before they read it. This will give them an opportunity to look at the illustrations and gain a sense of the text. You can use this as an opportunity to draw their attention to specific new vocabulary which is included in the text and to draw their attention to any structural or presentational features of the text. Spending time on these initial activities will make the tasks of word recognition and comprehension easier for children.

Building memory

Children need good memories to be able to recall the sequence of events in a story. Through the use of some simple activities you can support the development of children's memories. *Kym's Game* is a traditional game which helps to train the memory. In this game pupils are presented with a set of objects on a tray. They are asked to look at these objects and remember the items. The pupils then close their eyes and one item is removed. They are then asked to open their eyes and identify that item. You can make this game more or less complicated by increasing or decreasing the number of items on the tray or by removing more than one item.

Retelling stories

Early reading comprehension starts with children being able to re-tell a story. To support young children in this process, they need to develop familiarity with some well-known stories and they need to hear them time and time again. Children love hearing a story several times and very often they have a favourite story which they like to hear. Familiarity with stories will help children when they come to retelling them. If they know a story really well then retelling it will not be too much of a challenge.

Some ways of developing familiarity with stories include:

* listening to a story several times;
* listening to a story using a range of digital media as well as text;

* using puppets to re-enact stories they have heard;
* making collages or paintings of characters from stories;
* creating a role-play area which enables children to re-enact the story;
* making masks of characters so that children can re-enact the story;
* creating a storyteller's chair so that children can orally retell the story.

Sequencing events

To develop children's understanding of sequencing events from stories you can use a washing line. Colour photocopy and laminate some illustrations from the story. These could include:

* an illustration of the setting;
* illustrations to show key events from the story;
* an illustration of the ending.

The illustrations can be pegged onto the washing line and arranged in the wrong order. You can ask the pupils to help you to arrange the illustrations in the correct order to assess their understanding of the story. The number of events selected could be increased or reduced depending on the abilities of the children and you could position vocabulary in between the illustrations to develop their understanding of time (*first*, *next*, *then*, *after that*, *finally*).

To maximise participation and to get a more accurate assessment of children's sequencing skills children could work in pairs to do this activity without the aid of a washing line. You would simply provide them with smaller laminated illustrations and ask them to order them on a timeline or a story map. Sequencing activities can also be carried out on the interactive whiteboard. Children are presented with the pictures or text of the story depending on their abilities and they can move these around into the correct positions on the board.

Making predictions

Asking children to make predictions about what might happen next in a story is an obvious way of assessing their understanding of the text they are reading or listening to. You can do this by reaching a specific point in a story and asking them to talk through with a response partner what they think might happen next. When children become skilled in making oral predictions, you can ask them to write down predictions on sticky notes and you can collect these and use them as a focus for discussion.

Questioning

Asking questions about texts enables you to assess children's understanding and extend their thinking. You can ask a range of questions. These might include:

* **literal questions:** these are usually closed questions which require children to recall facts from texts;
* **inferential or deductive questions:** these require children to give a response by piecing together information which is in the text. The answers to these questions will not be directly stated in the text. Children will be expected to 'read between the lines' to give a suitable response;
* **evaluative questions:** these questions require children to evaluate the text (what did you think about this story or poem?).

Examples of questions could include:

- Who is the most important character in this story?
- What do we know about the setting?
- Why has the writer used this word or this punctuation?
- What do you see in your mind as you read this?
- What is the effect of the use of rhyme in this poem or story?
- How can we find the information quickly in this text?
- Why has the author used diagrams to support the text?
- What sort of character is X?

Bloom's Taxonomy (Bloom et al, 1956) provides a useful hierarchical framework for planning higher-order questioning which promotes thinking. The stages of the model can help you to plan increasingly challenging questions to cater for the needs of more-able learners. The examples below illustrate how the model could be applied to reading comprehension:

Knowledge: Recall questions (literal comprehension: *Who? What? Where? When? How?)*

Comprehension: Questions which require to explain something.

Application: *What other examples are there in the text of X?*

Analysis: Close reference to the text to substantiate something: *What is the evidence in the text for X?*

Synthesis: *How could we improve this story?*

Evaluation: *What did you think about this story? What was your favourite part of this story and why? How does this story compare to other stories?*

Encouraging children to ask their own questions about texts they read or listen to is a powerful way of getting children to engage closely with texts.

Good readers ask themselves questions before, during and after reading. These may be questions seeking information or clarification, or questions that express doubt or disagreement. Successful readers interact with the text. Again, the skill of questioning must be modelled. As explored in Chapter 5 this is first achieved by posing questions to the children that they must become 'detectives' to answer. Don't leave your questions about the text only until after reading, give the children a purpose to begin reading. Set them a quest, whether that be selecting words and phrases that capture the reader's interest and imagination, or identifying characters' feelings, thoughts and motives from their actions.

Understanding the purpose for reading is at the heart of engaging with a text and being able to truly comprehend what is read. As they become more independent in Key Stage 2 the children need to be able to evaluate the reading task they are undertaking. This is where the questioning begins and is very much linked to prediction. If you know the purpose, then you can tell whether you are being successful. If you can identify the structure of the text, then you begin to understand how information is organised and what kind of meaning you are searching for, whether that be literal, inferential or evaluative. Questions the reader must ask themselves are:

- What is it about? (Earthquakes)
- What kind of reading is it? (Explanation)
- Why am I reading this? (To find out the causes of earthquakes)
- How long will it take me to read? (Can I skim and scan?)

As you can see, comprehension is as much about asking questions as it is answering them. The more we generate our own 'wonderings' and then seek the answers, the more independent and successful we become as readers. The richest learning comes from answering our own questions. I am more likely to recognise a question about 'authorial intent' if I can generate my own. To give this 'detective work' purpose, it is important that these questions are directed towards a text that we have some ownership of or commitment to. Stand-alone comprehension exercises on random extracts may give some practice in answering specific question types, but it is more likely that the children will engage with a text they are currently reading (eg that is being shared in a guided reading session). While they are developing my own questioning skills they need to have some prior knowledge of the text. As with all good teaching you should start with 'the known' – let the child generate questions around a familiar story first. They can then apply this skill to new and more complicated texts.

A reminder: earlier in this chapter I identified the three main types of comprehension questions: Literal, Inferential and Evaluative.

Literal: the answer is right there in the text and can be 'lifted' directly from it.

Inferential: the answer requires the reader to read 'between the lines' and make their own connections. As they infer they use deduction and interpretation.

Evaluative: the answer requires the reader to make a judgement or choice and justify these. This includes 'reading like a writer' and identifying the author's intentions regarding what they are trying to communicate and how they use structure and language to achieve this.

Consider the following text and examples of questions that might be asked:

Goldilocks arrived at the Three Bears' house as the sun rose over the hill. The door was unlocked and so she carefully lifted the latch and entered.

> **Literal question:** Whose house was it? (The Three Bears')
>
> **Inferential question:** What time of day was it? (Early morning)
>
> **Evaluative:** Should Goldilocks have entered the house?

From an early age children are able to answer these types of questions as they are guided by an 'expert other' (Vygotsky, 1978), but in Key Stage 2 the focus is again on independence and so the children need frequent opportunities to practise and hone their questioning skills. The following activities not only give them these opportunities, but also give you as the teacher the possibility for ongoing assessment.

Other reading comprehension strategies

The following strategies may support you in developing children's understanding of texts:

* **Visualisation:** *What picture do you now have in your head about the Giant in Jack and the Beanstalk? What picture do you have in your head of the forest in Red Riding Hood?*
* **Drawing:** *Draw a picture of the setting for this story now that you have listened to the author's description of the setting.*
* **Story maps:** Ask children to plan out the events of a story in sequence onto a story map after they have listened to it.

* **Sequencing and rearranging:** Present children with a jumbled-up story and ask them to re-order it into the correct sequence. Present children with jumbled-up text for instructions, recounts or non-chronological reports and ask them to organise the text into the appropriate sequence or position. In the case of non-chronological reports, they will need to organise the various pieces of information under the correct sub-headings.
* **Summarising:** Read to a certain point in a text and then stop and ask the children to summarise the text up to this point. Being able to see the 'big picture' is a vital comprehension skill. Summarising is all about tracking down the main idea in a text and then being able to express it both verbally and in writing. This is not a skill that children find easy and you will have to give them plenty of opportunities to use their own words to shorten a piece of text so that they include only the essential information. If I was to ask you what the 'main idea' in *Goldilocks and the Three Bears* was, how would you answer? Children will go into detail about porridge and broken chairs, but in reality it is ultimately a tale about a young girl who breaks into a house and is caught in the act.
* **Drawing characters:** Present children with a large outline of a character from a story and ask them to write words on the outline to describe the character. On the inside of the outline they can be asked to write words to describe the character's personality, and on the exterior of the outline they can be asked to write words to describe the character's appearance.
* **Text highlighting:** Ask pupils to go through a piece of text and highlight all the words and phrases which tell them something about a character or setting.
* **Character ranking:** Ask children to rank characters from the kindest to the meanest in a story.
* **Writing a blurb:** Ask children to write their own blurb for a story they have listened to. This will enable you to check that they have understood the story.
* **Solving problems:** Read a story but stop at a point where a character faces a problem or dilemma. Ask the children for suggestions for how this problem might be solved and pool ideas together. Stop at key points of the story and ask them to tell you what they would do if they were characters in the story?
* **Best bit:** Ask them to tell you which bit was the funniest/scariest/best/worst and why.
* **Building vocabulary:** Build banks of new words that children encounter in texts and display these along with synonyms.
* **Meet the author:** Ask the children to think of questions that they would like to ask the author about the text. You could become the author of the text and using hot seating the children could be encouraged to ask you questions about the text. Once this process has been modelled, you could ask the children to take on the role of being the author.

Inference

Inferential comprehension refers to the ability to piece together pieces of given information in order to answer a question where the answer cannot be directly extracted from the text. It is similar to doing detective work in that it involves searching for clues in the text. Asking inferential questions is a higher form of questioning than literal questions where the answers are obvious in the text. It involves reading between the lines. The ability of pupils to make inferences on the basis of what is being said or done in a text is now an expectation of Year 1 pupils in the national curriculum. In the past teachers may have focused on developing pupils' literal comprehension at this stage, due to the emphasis on developing skills in decoding print. Developing inferential comprehension is a skill which you will need to model to the children, particularly in Year 1. You will need to demonstrate how to combine several pieces of information in a text to make an inference and you will need to explain that the answers might not be in the text but that the clues are there to help them find the answers. Once you have modelled being a reading detective by finding the clues and making inferences you will then be able to support the children in developing this skill through guided and individual reading sessions.

Reading for pleasure

The national curriculum states that:

All pupils must be encouraged to read widely across both fiction and non-fiction to develop their knowledge of themselves and the world in which they live, to establish an appreciation and love of reading, and to gain knowledge across the curriculum. Reading widely and often increases pupils' vocabulary because they encounter words they would rarely hear or use in everyday speech. Reading also feeds pupils' imagination and opens up a treasure-house of wonder and joy for curious young minds.

(DfE, 2013, p 14)

Michael Rosen, former Children's Laureate recently commented that:

We're talking about reading for pleasure, but what an odd thing to have to campaign for. It's kind of like saying 'Let's campaign for air, or for nice soup'. You read, you have a good time. That should be the end of it.

(Michael Rosen, Hay Festival, 2014)

However, reading for pleasure has unfortunately become a luxury that many teachers cannot afford to invest time into. The pressures of a prescriptive national curriculum, school inspections, statutory assessment tests and league tables have resulted in a paradoxical situation in which schools and teachers find reading for pleasure difficult to justify.

Gaining pleasure from an activity makes that activity worthwhile and easy to justify in educational terms. However, children gain a great deal more than pleasure if they choose to read widely. Avid readers *are* able to increase their own knowledge rapidly as well as broadening their vocabularies and imaginations. Reading increases intelligence. Additionally, more practice in reading leads to improvements in writing abilities as well as reading because children begin to internalise the essential skills of spelling, grammar and punctuation. As they start to read widely, children begin to absorb the conventions of expression and they are able to use these ideas in their own work.

The All-Party Parliamentary Group for Education stated that:

The active encouragement of reading for pleasure should be a core part of every child's curriculum entitlement because extensive reading and exposure to a wide range of texts make a huge contribution to students' educational achievement.

(All-Party Parliamentary Group on Education, 2011)

The new national curriculum (DfE, 2013) is now much less prescriptive than the former national curriculum. There is now more freedom for teachers to tailor the curriculum

to meet the needs of their pupils and there is no prescribed model of teaching. Some teachers in some schools are still pinioned by the shackles of the National Literacy Strategy (DfEE, 1998) which introduced the literacy hour into primary schools. Lessons were compartmentalised and tightly structured and there was no time for children to hear or read whole texts or to write extensively. This led to practices such as teachers reading extracts of texts to pupils to fulfil specific objectives.

An example of this approach would be a teacher reading an extract of a story setting to a class, with a specific focus on identifying adjectives to describe nouns. The pupils would not hear the whole story but would focus on identifying the adjectives in the text. This approach reduces English to a technical exercise rather than promoting reading for pleasure. To gain real pleasure children need to be transported into a story. They need to be engaged. They need to be completely absorbed into the events. They need to visualise themselves in the text. They need to be able to see the events unfolding in front of them as if they are there in the story. They need to share the feelings of suspense, excitement, joy, sadness and pain that the characters are experiencing. A good story absorbs the reader or listener through the power of evocative language. An extract from a text will not create this same sense of engagement because the reader or listener needs to share the full journey with the characters.

EVIDENCE-BASED TEACHING

Key trends from academic research

The DfE published a report in 2012 entitled *Research Evidence on Reading for Pleasure* (DfE, 2012) which summarised key research findings. These included:

* *Reading for pleasure enhances educational achievement and attainment as well as personal development (Clark and Rumbold, 2006).*
* *There is a positive relationship between frequency and enjoyment of reading and attainment (Clark 2011; Clark and Douglas 2011).*
* *Reading enjoyment has a greater impact on children's educational success than their family's socio-economic background (OECD, 2002).*
* *There is a positive link between positive dispositions towards reading and scoring highly on reading assessments (Twist et al, 2007).*
* *Regularly reading stories or novels outside of school is associated with higher achievement in reading assessments (Mullis et al, 2007; PISA, 2009).*
* *International evidence also supports these findings; US research reports that independent reading is the best predictor of reading achievement (Anderson et al, 1988).*
* *Reading for pleasure has a positive impact on children's social and emotional development (Clark and Rumbold, 2006).*
* *Other benefits to reading for pleasure include: text comprehension and knowledge of grammar; positive reading attitudes; pleasure in reading in later life; increased general knowledge (Clark and Rumbold, 2006).*

(research cited in DfE, 2012)

EVALUATE

- *Why do you think children in England read less for pleasure compared to other countries?*

CHALLENGE

- *If reading for pleasure enhances children's social and emotional development, what might the impact be on the social and emotional development of children who read stories with violence or aggression in them?*

APPLY

- *How would you develop a reading area in your classroom? What texts would you include? How might you promote links between reading and writing in this area?*

IN PRACTICE

- *In school observe how reading for pleasure is being promoted. Is there a whole school policy on reading for pleasure?*

CRITICAL QUESTIONS

- *Why do you think reading for pleasure has a greater impact on attainment than social background?*
- *Think back to your own experiences as a child in primary school. Can you recall how it felt to listen to a really good story? Did you have story time?*
- *When was the last time you were absorbed in something that you read?*
- *What are the barriers which prevent you from reading for pleasure?*
- *How might these be overcome?*
- *How many children's books can you list from memory?*
- *How many children's authors can you name?*
- *How familiar are you with the work of these authors?*
- *What do you like to read?*
- *When and where do you like to read?*
- *Have you observed opportunities for children to read for pleasure during your placement experiences?*

The following research findings are taken from *Research Evidence on Reading for Pleasure* (DfE, 2012).

Evidence suggests that the majority of children reported that they do enjoy reading (Clark and Rumbold, 2006). In 2010, 22 per cent of children reported that they enjoyed reading very much; 27 per cent said they enjoyed it quite a lot; 39 per cent said they enjoyed it quite a bit, and 12 per cent reported that they did not enjoy reading at all (Clark, 2011). Compared to international evidence, children in England report that they read less frequently for pleasure outside of school than children in many other countries (Twist et al, 2007). Evidence consistently demonstrates that children enjoy reading less as they get older (Clark and Douglas 2011; Clark and Osborne, 2008; Topping, 2010). However, there is evidence to suggest that while the frequency with which young people read declines with age, the length for which they read when they do read increases with age (Clark, 2011).

Several studies have indicated that boys enjoy reading less than girls and that children from working-class backgrounds read less for enjoyment than children from middle and upper social classes (Clark and Douglas, 2011; Clark and Rumbold, 2006). Additionally, evidence has shown that children from Asian backgrounds have more positive attitudes to reading and read more frequently than children from White, mixed or Black backgrounds (Clark and Douglas, 2011).

Research increasingly indicates that a growing number of children do not read for pleasure (Clark and Rumbold, 2006). Between 2000 and 2009, on average across OECD countries the percentage of children who report reading for enjoyment daily dropped by five percentage points (OECD, 2010). This is supported by evidence from Mullis et al (2007) (Twist et al, 2007), which found that attitudes towards reading had declined among children.

CRITICAL QUESTIONS

* *Why do you think that children from lower socio-economic backgrounds read less for pleasure than children from more privileged social classes?*
* *How would you explain the differences in reading attitudes between the different ethnic groups?*
* *How would you explain the differences in reading attitudes between boys and girls?*

IN PRACTICE

During school-based training find out how schools promote reading for pleasure. Is there a whole school approach to reading for pleasure? Look at the reading areas. Are there a range of texts in reading areas to appeal to different interests and do the texts reflect aspects of social and cultural diversity? Do children have access to a school library and if so are they allowed to take books home? Does the school have a policy for rewarding children who read for pleasure?

Spelling

Applying phonics knowledge to spelling

The national curriculum (DfE, 2013) states that children must be taught to read through the use of a systematic phonics programme. Through a systematic approach, children will be introduced to the sounds (phonemes) made by single letters, digraphs and trigraphs and they will be introduced to the complex alphabetic code. They will use their phonic knowledge to read words (blending) by enunciating the sounds that the graphemes make within a word, saying these in sequence all the way through a word and combining them to read the target word. They also need to use their phonic knowledge for spelling. This process is called segmenting or encoding. During the process of encoding pupils hear each of the separate sounds (phonemes) within a spoken word and then they select or write the appropriate symbols to represent these sounds. The processes are reversible and should be taught consecutively within phonics lessons. The use of a *phoneme frame* may initially support pupils to segment words. In a phoneme frame pupils write each grapheme in a separate box as follows:

d	o	g
g	oa	t
l	igh	t

f	l	a	g

The process of using a phoneme frame will act as a scaffold by helping children to focus on the number of sounds they can hear within a word. The process can be broken down as follows:

* Listen to the spoken word.
* Use your fingers to count the phonemes you can hear in the word.
* Which phoneme can you hear first? Write down/select the grapheme that represents this phoneme.
* Which phoneme can you hear next? Write down/select the grapheme that represents this phoneme.
* Repeat the above process until you have written down or selected all of the graphemes that represent each phoneme in the word.

Initially it is important to give the pupils words to spell which are within the scope of their existing phonic knowledge. For example, you would not ask pupils to spell the word *boil* if you have not taught the /oi/ grapheme-phoneme correspondence. Once pupils have applied their phonic knowledge to spell a word several times, the physical act of practising the spelling several times will mean that the spelling becomes more automatic. They may soon be able to spell it without hearing the sounds in the words. However, some pupils take longer to reach the stage of spelling words automatically and a multisensory approach might be necessary. To make your spelling lessons more memorable, you could consider using the following approaches and you should be able to add your own ideas to this list:

* writing words in different coloured sand;
* writing words in glitter;
* writing words in salt;
* writing words in cornflour mix;
* building words on magnetic boards using magnetic letters;
* using chunky chalks in the playground to write words on the floor;
* asking pupils to trace over each letter of a word where each letter has been made out of sandpaper;
* asking them to close their eyes and to visualise the word and to tell you the letters that they can see in the word;
* writing words on slate boards using chalk;
* printing words using foam letters and paints;
* stamping letters out of malleable media (such as play dough) to make words;
* using water pistols to write words outside on the floor with water;
* asking pupils to write words on paper using white wax crayons and asking them to paint over the page to reveal the word they have written.

Multisensory approaches to teaching spelling work effectively for all children. However, it is important that the process of segmenting words into their constituent sounds and representing these as graphemes is a process which is reinforced in all writing that children do, not just the writing they produce in the phonics lesson. When you model writing in front of the whole class (shared writing), ask the pupils to help you to segment words which are phonically regular. Reinforce the process of segmentation during guided writing and encourage pupils to apply this skill during their independent writing. Reading should be taught alongside spelling and pupils need to understand that they can read back the words they have spelt. Pupils will start to spell many words in a phonetically plausible way once they master the skill of segmenting. You need to praise them for their attempts even when they spell an exception word using their phonic knowledge (for example, they might spell *said* as *sed*). You should accept this up to the point where you have taught them the correct spelling. After this point you should correct misspellings because the correct spellings have been introduced to the pupils.

Spelling rules

The national curriculum (DfE, 2013) includes statutory rules and guidance to support the teaching of spelling and this is set out in Appendix 1 in the English strand of the primary national curriculum. Children generally can read more words than they can spell. Once they have been introduced to the alternative spelling variations of the graphemes in the complex alphabetic code, children then need to make decisions in their spelling about which graphemes to use in words (for example, whether to write *leaf* or *leef*). Those children with a good memory may be able to remember which graphemes to use and as children's reading develops they will absorb the spellings of words less consciously through their reading. A multi-sensory approach to spelling, as described above, will help children to remember which graphemes to use in words because through this approach the correct spelling is reinforced visually, auditorily and kinaesthetically.

You need to teach the spelling rules explicitly and I recommend the following approach:

Revisit: Revisit specific spelling rules that children have previously been taught, for example, by focusing on those rules which the pupils find tricky.

Teach: Introduce the new rule by modelling how the rule works. You might want to show how the rule is applied to two or three words.

Practise: Give the children time to investigate the spelling rule, perhaps by organising them into pairs and asking them to apply the rule to other words. You might want them to find exceptions to the rule.

Apply: Give the children a sentence to write which requires them to apply the rule.

You need to bear in mind that just because children have been taught a rule does not mean that they will automatically apply that rule in their own independent writing. Children may be able to apply the rule within the spelling lesson but they may forget the rule when it comes to their own writing. If the children have been taught a rule, you should make a specific point about this when you provide them with feedback. Perhaps you could remind them of the rule and then give them further opportunities to apply it.

Using phonic knowledge and spelling, although closely related, are different skills. The first is about making good phonetic choices, while the second is about developing an understanding of rules and conventions that can be generalised across many words. Spelling a word as it sounds is not always a reliable strategy, particularly as the child's vocabulary becomes broader. Many words have the same pronunciation, but different spellings, while many others have the same spelling but different pronunciation. Remember:

* in the complex alphabetic code one phoneme can be represented by different graphemes;
* in the complex alphabetic code one grapheme can represent more than one phoneme.

Don't make spelling a guessing game. It is important to share conventions with the children. It is your job to make learning as easy as possible. Consider the following:

* English words do not end in the letter 'v' unless they are abbreviations (rev.) Therefore, if the last sound is 'v' add an 'e' – *live, above, love*.
* When an 'o' sound follows the letter 'w' it is frequently spelt with the letter 'a' – *wander, wallet, wash*.
* An 'or' sound before an 'l' is frequently spelt with the letter 'a' – *all, ball, call, always*.
* An 'ee' sound at the end of a word is usually spelt with 'y' – *funny, lazy, mouldy*. Similarly, when choosing between 'oi' and 'oy' it is worth noting that words in English do not end in 'oi' and so the spelling would be 'oy', *eg enjoy*.
* When adding the prefix 'in' (meaning 'not') to a word it is important to consider the letter that the root word begins with:
  - in words beginning with 'l', 'in' becomes 'il', eg *illegal*;
  - in words beginning with 'm' or 'p', 'in' becomes 'im', eg *immortal*;
  - in words beginning with 'r', 'in' becomes 'ir', eg *irregular*.

Spelling by analogy

Teaching children to spell words by analogy can sometimes be useful. This strategy draws on children's knowledge of rime. For example, if pupils can spell *goat* because they recognise the rime /oat/ they are likely to be able to spell *coat* and even *throat* but this strategy will not work for spelling *note*.

CRITICAL QUESTION

* *Spelling words by analogy does not fit with a systematic synthetic phonics approach to spelling (described above) in which words are broken down into the smallest units of sound. However, I do not believe that one strategy works for all pupils. Do you agree?*

Mnemonics

These provide a way of spelling more difficult words such as:

* *necessary* – one collar and two sleeves;
* *because* – big elephants can always understand small elephants;
* *separate* – there is *a rat* in sep*arat*e;
* *said* – Sally-Anne is dancing.

Dictionaries

Dictionaries are a useful resource to support children with their independent writing. Pupils can use them to locate spellings of words or definitions and this will reduce the pressure on you by breaking their dependency on you to provide the spellings. I recommend starting with simple picture dictionaries because the picture cue helps children to locate the word. As they progress they will need to be taught explicitly how dictionaries work because the dictionaries become more complex. You will need to teach them how to locate words in a dictionary using their knowledge of alphabetic ordering. Initially, this can be taught by teaching them how to locate words using the first letter only. More-able children can progress onto ordering words by the second or third letter so you can give them words beginning with the same initial letter but with different subsequent letters and ask them to put the words in order. Children need experience of ordering words firstly by the first letter, then the second and third letters and so on. They also need experience of locating words in dictionaries. They need to be taught these skills in the daily literacy lesson and then they need opportunities to apply these skills when they are writing independently. The transference of this skill may not be automatic so the skill of using dictionaries may need to be further reinforced in guided reading sessions. Children should also be taught how to use electronic dictionaries and simple electronic spell checkers. Alphabet mats on tables to show alphabetic order are also a useful resource.

Independent usage of dictionaries continues to be a focus of the national curriculum in Key Stage 2 and it is important to give children opportunities to become fluent readers of dictionaries. They need to understand how they work and when they should be used. You need to encourage the children to use their knowledge of the different options for spelling sounds and that they should continue their efforts to locate words when their initial search has been unsuccessful, for example, the child who tries to look up *grieve* under *gree* needs to be reminded to consider other possibilities.

Although dictionaries can support independence, they can be overused and break the flow of writing. You don't want what MacKay describes as an *'almost neurotic preoccupation with accuracy that can kill a lesson'* (MacKay, 2005). Encourage the children to underline uncertain spellings and return to checking them in a dictionary at the end of the lesson or section of writing. Again, spelling checkers are useful tools if the first attempt at spelling the word was logical and reasonably close to the target; however, if this is not the case then the child may be offered inappropriate suggestions. They need to be prepared to question whether the pronunciation of the given word matches the one they are attempting to spell.

Thesaurus

There are a number of good reasons for learning how to use a thesaurus and these should be shared with the children:

* By exploring synonyms, the child can avoid repetition in their writing.
* They can find the word that 'best' expresses an idea.
* Vocabulary can be enriched and developed.

However, the use of these language tools should always be accompanied with a caution and again the children need to be taught how to use them appropriately. They need to understand the following two points:

* Not all synonyms are equal – they do not all mean exactly the same thing.
* A *big* word is not always the *best* word.

Lots of work around 'shades of meaning' will allow the children to identify which words are appropriate and carry the meaning that will allow their reader to both visualise the picture they are painting with words and indeed to decide whether they empathise or not with the event or character being described. Consider these two sentences and the choice of words: The chubby baby gurgled/The corpulent baby snickered.

CRITICAL QUESTIONS

* *How do these two sentences paint different pictures of the character?*
* *Why is it important for children to explore how their choice of words impact on their reader and what activities might you introduce for them to explore 'shades of meaning'?*

Spelling common exception words

Children will be introduced to exception words as part of their systematic phonics programme and they will be expected to learn to read and spell these words. The stage a pupil has reached within a phonics programme may affect whether a word is classed as an exception word or not. For example, in the very early stages of a phonics programme the word *light* may be classed as an exception word. However, later in the programme pupils will be introduced to the grapheme-phoneme correspondence /igh/ and then this word is then phonically decodable. Some words are not phonically regular (for example, words such as *the*, *people*, *said*). These words cannot be spelt effectively using a phonics approach. You can teach the spellings of these words using approaches such as look, say, cover, write, check or mnemonics although pupils may partially be able to use their phonic knowledge to spell the parts of the word which are phonically regular. These exception words should be displayed in the classroom on word walls, word banks or on word mats for pupils to access independently.

Spelling through syllables

Words such as *pocket*, *rabbit*, *carrot* and *thunder* each have two syllables. You can teach pupils to clap the syllables and to use their phonic knowledge to spell each syllable in turn. They can then combine the spellings of the syllables to make the whole word.

Prefixes and suffixes

Prefixes and suffixes that pupils must be taught are identified in Appendix 1 of the national curriculum. These should be displayed in the classroom along with their root words. You can model the correct spelling by representing the prefix (or suffix) and root word in a different colour.

Look, cover, write, check

This approach relies on a strong visual memory. The process works in the following way:

Look: children look at the word carefully, memorise it and say it.

Cover: children cover the word.

Write: children write the word from memory.

Check: children check their spelling attempt against the word.

CRITICAL QUESTIONS

* *What are the advantages and disadvantages of this approach?*
* *What are the arguments for and against spelling tests?*
* *Do you agree that teachers should accept phonically plausible attempts at spelling?*
* *Should teachers display children's work if there are spelling errors in it?*
* *Should children in Year 1 and Year 2 be asked to re-draft their writing so that the spelling is accurate? What the arguments for and against this?*
* *Why do pupils with dyslexia struggle with spelling? Research into this.*
* *How can teachers support pupils with dyslexia to improve their spelling? Research into this.*

Homophones and near-homophones

A homophone is a word which has the same pronunciation as another word but has a different meaning and may differ in spelling. Examples include:

be/bee;

blue/blew;

sun/son;

there/their/they're;

hear/here;

night/knight;

see/sea;

bare/bear.

Pupils need to be taught the difference in meaning between the different homophones. Near-homophones have a very similar pronunciation, for example, *quiet/quite* or *one/won*. Think about how you could teach homophones in an inspiring way.

Contractions

In contractions the apostrophe is placed where a letter or letters are omitted when writing in a shortened form. Examples include *can't* (cannot), *didn't* (did not) and *I'll* (I will). Care should be taken with *its* and *it's*, for example:

It is snowing [It's snowing]

It has been snowing [It's been snowing]

However, *it's* is never used for the possessive.

CRITICAL QUESTION

* *Should children be taught to use contractions in their writing given that students in universities are normally not allowed to use contractions in academic writing?*

Possessive apostrophe

Pupils in Year 2 need to be taught the rules about apostrophe use for singular nouns. In the case of singular nouns, the apostrophe is placed before the 's'. For example, *the girl's pencil case, the boy's shoe*. This will need discrete teaching and it will need to be reinforced through:

* shared and guided reading;
* marking and feedback on children's work;
* discrete lessons;
* highlighting possessive apostrophes in texts;
* sorting apostrophe use in words into correct and incorrect use.

Dictation

Regular dictation will improve the practice children get with spelling and handwriting. Daily dictation will also improve their confidence. I suggest that you choose sentences or captions which are within the scope of children's existing phonic knowledge. You can also include exception words that children have been taught. Once you have dictated the sentence and given the children time to write it, show them the correct model of how to write the sentence so that they can self-assess their writing. Ask the children to record their attempts using:

* chalks on chalk boards;
* small whiteboards and dry wipe marker pens;
* writing using coloured pencils;
* writing on coloured or textured paper;
* writing with crayon.

CRITICAL QUESTION

* *What are the arguments for and against dictation?*

Multisensory approaches

Children initially must master the hand movements necessary to form each letter. Initially these may be gross motor movements and with practice children should be then encouraged to refine these same movements. When teaching letter formation, the following steps will support you:

* **Look:** the teacher models the formation of a large letter on the board. Interactive white boards are not ideal for this purpose as the alignment is often inaccurate.
* **Trace:** the child traces over the letter repeatedly while also articulating the sound. Avoid tracing over dotted letters as children may focus on joining the dots and this will impede the flow of the letter formation.
* **Copy:** the child copies the letter repeatedly while also articulating the sound.

* **Write from memory:** the model is removed and the child practices the formation of the letter.
* **Eyes shut:** the child writes the letter from memory with their eyes shut to commit the letter formation to memory.

Letter formation should be practised using a variety of materials, including tracing in salt, sand and glitter, writing in the air, writing on each other's backs, tracing on hessian and silk or writing with water. It may be necessary to manipulate the child's hand to support letter formation. Initially the focus is on the child developing the correct movement for forming each letter. As the child progresses they can be introduced to track lines which will help them to focus on proportion, ascenders and descenders.

Many pupils find the task of writing challenging because in the early stages of learning to write they have not yet reached the stage of automaticity. Children often have brilliant ideas which they are able to articulate very effectively. However, beginning writers cannot simply focus on recording their ideas on paper and developing them further into powerful texts which engage the reader. This is because pupils also have to consciously think about aspects such as spelling, handwriting and punctuation at the same time as developing *ideas* and this can slow down the process of composition. As pupils develop automaticity in applying the skills of spelling, handwriting and punctuation they can then focus their attention more sharply on developing ideas which draw the reader into the text. They can then start to consider the use of vocabulary, grammar and punctuation to create powerful effects.

We want children to see themselves as writers and authors of their own work. In order to develop children's confidence in writing it is important that their attempts at writing are valued. As a trainee teacher you need to ensure that you give children credit for their *ideas* even when their spelling, handwriting and punctuation require attention. Although it is important that these aspects are addressed systematically over time through high quality teaching and clear target setting, great authors are all able to use writing as a tool to make a connection with the reader. Caulley (2008) emphasises the importance of writing stories which give the reader a *'sense that the action is unfolding in front of them – that the reader is part of the scene. The reader hears the conversation, sees the gestures, and follows the actions of the characters'* (p 429). Ideas and the use of vocabulary, grammar and punctuation *for effect* are important in writing because they help the writer to make this significant connection with the reader. If children are to view themselves as authors, they need to be able to recognise that great ideas and writing for effect are essential ingredients of powerful texts.

The next sections will introduce you to some fundamental principles of teaching early composition. It will not address everything you need to know about teaching writing but it will provide you with a basis for underpinning your approach to teaching writing.

Developing children as writers

Oral rehearsal

In the early stages of becoming writers, children need to be supported to orally rehearse their ideas before they write. Some pupils do not speak in sentences and if children are unable to *say* a sentence then they will almost certainly find it impossible to *write* a sentence. In the Early Years Foundation Stage and in Year 1 you need to model this process to children because they are unlikely to use oral rehearsal automatically. When you model the process of writing a sentence to young children, the following steps will help you to address this very systematically:

* **Think it:** Explicitly model the thinking of a sentence;
* **Say it:** Say the sentence out loud;
* **Count the words:** Count the number of words in the sentence;
* **Write it:** Write the sentence word by word;
* **Read it aloud:** Does it make sense? Can I improve it?
* **Check it:** Have I got the correct number of words? Have I got a capital letter at the start of my sentence? Have I got a space between each word? Have I got a full stop at the end of my sentence?

If children observe you following this process, then they will gradually start to use this in their own writing. There is a clear expectation in the national curriculum (DfE, 2013) that pupils in Year 1 should be writing in sentences and this process will help them to achieve this. Many pupils start to write something without fully thinking through the sentence they are attempting to write before they write it. You need to encourage them to 'lock the sentence into their head' and say it out loud before they write it. This process should be repeated for every sentence that children attempt to write so that they get into the habit of using a systematic approach to support them in their writing.

Some pupils in your class may not be writing in sentences. These pupils will need extra support, particularly in Year 1, to support them to achieve this. The process above can also be adapted for children who are developmentally working at the stage of writing captions rather than sentences. However, do remember that a caption is a collection of words rather than a sentence so it does not need a capital letter and a full stop.

The process of oral rehearsal can be developed further as pupils become more confident at writing longer texts. Pupils should be given thinking time to think through their ideas before they start to compose any form of writing. The best authors spend time thinking before actually writing anything down. Great writing cannot be rushed and it evolves over time. Once they have thought through their ideas, pupils should then be encouraged to plan their writing using a systematic approach. More information about planning writing is included later in this chapter.

Once pupils have had thinking time and planning time they should then be given an opportunity to orally rehearse their ideas with a response partner. Working with their response partner they can then build on their initial ideas to improve them. They can annotate their plans accordingly to demonstrate the changes that have been made to the original ideas. Obtaining feedback from their peers in this way is important because the best writing is often produced through a process of collaboration rather than in isolation. Peers can be a valuable source of advice to a writer. They can suggest ideas which will make the writing more interesting and exciting and they can give the author an insight into how the reader might respond to the writing before the text has actually been written. They can suggest to the author better words to use and ways of improving the presentation and layout. In the case of writing narratives, a response partner can provide feedback on the characters, the build-up, climax, resolution or ending and this can help to improve the story. You need to teach your pupils that the best authors are like *magpies* who steal ideas from other people to make their writing better.

The process described above takes time. If you want pupils to produce good quality writing, then you cannot expect this to happen within the space of a one-hour lesson. You need to think of teaching composition more in terms of a sequence of lessons; each lesson builds progressively on the previous lesson so that at the end of the unit of work pupils have a quality piece of writing which they can be proud of. Generating good ideas is not a process which should be rushed. Many great authors spend months or even years producing a text which they are happy with and children need to be taught that their best ideas might take time to develop.

Contexts and purposes for writing

Setting up a context for writing is perhaps one of the most important things that you need to do. Without a context for writing, children have no clear purpose for writing and the writing task is disconnected to other learning that is taking place in the classroom. The Ofsted report *Moving English Forward: Action to Raise Standards in English* (Ofsted, 2012) highlighted some of the weaknesses in the teaching of writing. These include:

* too few opportunities for pupils to complete extended writing;
* too little time in lessons to complete writing tasks;
* too little emphasis on creative and imaginative tasks;
* too little emphasis on the teaching of editing and redrafting;
* too little choice for pupils in the topics for writing;
* too few real audiences and purposes for writing.

(Ofsted, 2012, p 25–26)

Additionally, the report states that:

Teachers need to ensure that English in classrooms integrates tasks and purposes related to the 'real world' beyond school, and includes real audiences, contexts and purposes.

(Ofsted, 2012, para 142, p 53)

The contexts for writing in Year 1 or Year 2 could emerge from a class topic or theme, texts that children are reading or real situations in the school or in the community. Creating contexts for writing will also provide you with opportunities to make writing purposeful and link the teaching of writing to other aspects of the curriculum. Your ability to create a context for writing will largely depend on your own creative thinking. However, if you do it well you will be able to hook children into learning. A good hook will ignite children's enthusiasm for writing and they will soon be immersed and even obsessed about what they are writing. Getting children obsessed about writing is what you should be aiming to achieve in your lessons. You need to get them to want to write in the first place and then they need to sustain their engagement until they have achieved a good quality outcome.

Getting children obsessed about learning is a characteristic of outstanding teaching. This is evident when children are not simply attentive in lessons but when they are truly engrossed in the task they are doing. Attentive pupils can equal passive learners. As a trainee teacher you need to think carefully about how you will immerse your learners in a writing task to the point where they do not want to stop writing. Creating contexts and giving children clear purposes for writing is certainly a step in the right direction and therefore a significant amount of thought needs to go into the planning of lessons. Great teachers spend as much time (if not more time) thinking through their lessons as they do writing detailed lesson plans. Time spent thinking is time well spent if it results in lessons which are set in context and ignite children's interests.

There is no correct model of how a writing lesson should be structured. There is no right way of teaching and no correct way of structuring a lesson. You should not aim to be a carbon copy of your mentor. Develop your own style of teaching and your own educational values and beliefs. Focus on inspiring your learners by hooking them into writing. Make the writing task relevant to them and set it in context. Talk less in lessons and give them more time on task to develop their ideas. Encourage them to collaborate and persevere even when they find writing difficult. Focus on supporting them to take pride in their work and allow them opportunities to revisit it to make it better. Give them 'tools for learning' to help them to work independently. These could include:

- working walls which display good models of text types and vocabulary;
- alphabet mats;
- dictionaries;
- a shoulder partner;
- a writing journal.

Give your learners different audiences for writing. The audience for a piece of writing is often the teacher but you need to encourage them to write to different people. Examples could include:

- writing stories, poems or non-fiction texts for the school library for others to read;
- writing a letter to the headteacher about an issue in the school;
- writing a letter to the local council about a community issue;
- creating persuasive posters to encourage parents to attend a school event;
- writing poems and displaying them around the school grounds for others to read;
- writing something for the school blog.

Scaffolding creativity in narrative writing

Some pupils find it difficult to compose a story from scratch. This is because teachers sometimes ask them to compose stories before they have had the opportunity to build up their knowledge of well-known stories. Good authors read widely and through reading a range of texts they build up a large repertoire of ideas for their own writing. In the Early Years Foundation Stage and in Year 1 children need to initially be introduced to well-known stories. They need to be given various opportunities to re-tell these stories and they need to consolidate their understanding of these stories through role-play, drama and other creative opportunities. At this age pupils need opportunities to listen to digital versions of stories and to explore re-enacting stories using puppets. Once pupils have become familiar with well-known stories, they will start to re-tell these stories orally and to internalise the story language used in these texts. This vocabulary should then start to appear in their writing.

Once familiarity has been established with well-known stories you can teach children to adapt these by making some small changes to the original text. This could include:

* changing the setting where the story takes place;
* substituting one character for another;
* changing an event;
* changing the ending;
* adding in new events;
* changing the title.

You can teach children to work within the framework of the original text but by making a change the story becomes their story. However, the original story acts as a scaffold so that pupils are not expected to create a story from nothing.

As pupils develop their confidence in adapting stories by creating new settings, characters, events or endings, they will gradually develop the ability to invent their own stories. However, even at this stage children are not creating a story from nothing. They will have read and listened to a wide range of stories. They will have developed a bank of ideas and vocabulary in their writing journals and they will be able to orally rehearse their ideas with their peers.

Editing writing

Great authors never produce a perfect piece of writing the first time. They re-read their work, edit it and make it better and this is a process which we need to teach pupils. The national curriculum (DfE, 2013) states that pupils in Year 2 must be taught to:

* evaluate their writing with the teacher and other pupils;
* re-read their writing to check that it makes sense;
* proofread their writing to check for errors in spelling, grammar and punctuation;
* read aloud what they have written with appropriate intonation to make the meaning clear.

This process of editing writing is a process which you must model to pupils, particularly during shared writing with the whole class. After the pupils have helped you to compose a class text, you can ask them to re-read it to check firstly for sense and secondly for accuracy in spelling, grammar and punctuation. You can then involve the pupils in making decisions about how to make the writing even better, for example, by adding in additional descriptive vocabulary.

Writing poetry

There is an emphasis in the national curriculum on teaching children to recite poetry by heart from Year 1 but children are not expected to write poetry until Year 2. The processes described above for narrative texts should also support you in teaching poetry. Pupils need opportunities to listen to and read a range of different types of poetry. They need to be given opportunities to learn poems by heart and to perform them. Once children are familiar with poetry they should be given opportunities to adapt existing poems and rhymes by altering some of the words. This will enable them to create their own version of a poem within an existing framework. Once pupils have had opportunities to adapt poems they should be taught how to create their own poems.

Different types of poems have their own structural and language features; you need to model these to pupils through processes such as shared writing. Children should not be asked to write an acrostic poem unless they have had opportunities to read acrostic poetry and the opportunity to contribute to creating a class acrostic poem. Modelling clearly plays a very important role in all teaching because children cannot be expected to produce high quality work unless they have seen good examples and been given opportunities to create these as a class or in smaller groups.

Children's knowledge of noun phrases (for example, *the blue butterfly*) for description and specification, tense, adjectives and adverbs can all be used to create effects in poetry. Children need to explore the world through all of their senses using first-hand experiences. A poem about a season will be far richer if children have been given opportunities to observe, touch, hear, taste and smell things that specifically relate to that season. Exploring the world through senses is a powerful way of generating descriptive vocabulary. Once this vocabulary has been generated, children can then use it to write simple poems.

In addition to exploring the real world through senses, children can explore the imagined world through role-play, drama and technology. Immersive space technology enables children to explore settings which they would otherwise not be able to. Through pop-up mini-immersive spaces or large immersive spaces which fill a school hall or classroom, children can be taken into places such as space, deserts, rainforests, beaches and so on. A drama lesson within an immersive space can provide a stimulus for a poetry lesson or a lesson on writing a story setting. If we expose children to rich experiences such as these prior to writing, the quality of their work will be far superior. This is because they will have experienced the sights, sounds and even smells of that setting before we ask them to write about this in a poem.

Vocabulary, grammar and punctuation

The national curriculum (DfE, 2013) identifies very specific statutory content which must be taught in each year group in relation to grammar (word, sentence and text level) and punctuation. In Year 1 pupils need to be introduced to the effects of adding prefixes and suffixes onto words and they need to understand the meaning of specific terminology including *verb*, *clause* and *pronoun*. In Year 2 pupils need to understand terminology including *noun*, *noun phrase*, *adverb*, *tenses* and teachers need to teach pupils about conjunctions. These terms are explained in the glossary in the national curriculum.

The aim of developing children's knowledge of grammar and punctuation for effect is for pupils to produce more sophisticated writing which makes an impact on the reader. Although pupils will need discrete lessons on adverbs, verbs, nouns, noun phrases, adjectives and so on, you will also need to draw attention to the ways in which writers use grammar and punctuation in their texts during shared and guided reading sessions. When grammar and punctuation are taught within context, pupils are then able to see how writers have specifically used it to create a more profound effect on the reader. This is known as *reading as a writer.* This process focuses on encouraging children to think carefully about the impact the writer is trying to have on the reader through the choice of specific vocabulary and punctuation.

CRITICAL QUESTIONS

- *What are the arguments for and against teaching grammar through decontexualised grammar exercises?*
- *What are the arguments for and against teaching punctuation through decontexualised punctuation exercises?*
- *Should punctuation and grammar only be taught in the context of texts?*

Grammar for writing

Word classes

There are many word classes: nouns, verbs, adjectives, adverbs, pronouns, prepositions, determiners and conjunctions. There is not space here to look at them all in detail and you must review your own understanding of these terms. However, it is important to consider two vital points when exploring word classes with children. The first point is that the function of words is not fixed and can change according to how they are used and placed within a sentence. Consider the word *fast* and its function in the following sentences:

* *The family observed the fast* (noun).
* *The fast car sped along the motorway* (adjective).
* *I fast during the religious festival* (verb).
* *He moved very fast across the open ground* (adverb).

The second point is that it is not enough for children to learn the definitions of these words – many children can tell you, for example, that an adverb 'adds more information to the verb', but do they understand that it can tell you how, where or when an action took place? Understanding is crucial if the children are to apply and extend their own usage in their writing.

Grammar at sentence level

Children are taught that a sentence is a group of words that go together to make sense of an individual thought or idea – a set of words that is complete in itself. But what does this actually mean? Within a sentence there are smaller chunks of sense:

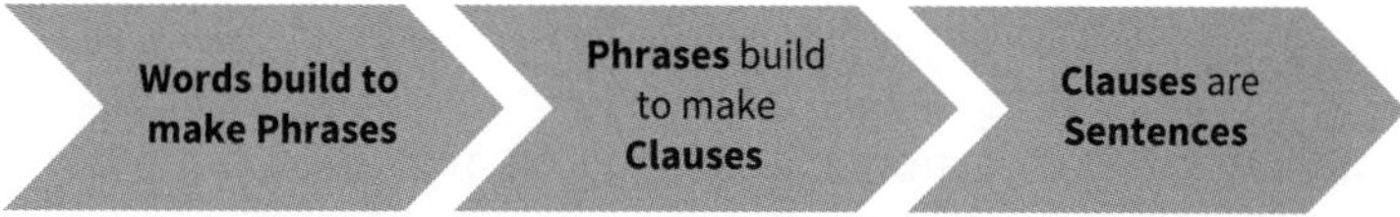
Words build to make Phrases
Phrases build to make Clauses
Clauses are Sentences

Phrases were considered earlier in this chapter, in particular, the adverbial phrase which is particularly powerful in adding impact to early writing. Consider the previous case study on adverbs and the detail they add to the how, where and when of a message. Now turn your attention to the term *clause*. A clause contains a subject and a verb, for example, *She fled*. In its simplest form this is a sentence – it is a main clause and a simple sentence consists of one main clause that can stand alone and make sense. There are three types of sentences that children must identify and use: *simple*, *compound* and *complex*. These will be defined in the following section, but first see if you can identify which of these three types of sentences this is:

At midnight on Friday, the young girl fled from the royal ball, rather tearfully, along the moonlit path in front of the castle.

This is a *simple sentence*; although it may be quite complicated, in that it has three adverbial phrases, it is not grammatically complex. As long as there is only one verb (*fled*) there is only one clause. In this case the child has constructed an effective simple sentence. It is the construction of this message and the choices made that you need to explore. The emphasis here is on construction and grammar. Children are often put off writing by the actual act of writing itself – too much, too soon. If they are learning about the correct and most effective use of grammar it should be an exercise in co-construction where you take on the role of scribe in the early stages. They are busy developing their understanding of word modification and the control of sentence structure.

When constructing sentences with children you should begin by orally composing and modifying sentences through question and answer activities as you record the children's ideas.

Example

Begin with the simplest of sentences:

The cat walked.

T: *Can you give an adjective to describe the cat?*

C: *The fat cat walked.*

T: *How did the fat cat walk?* (adverb)

C: *Slowly the fat cat walked.*

T: *Where did the fat cat slowly walk?* (adverbial phrase)

C: *Slowly the fat cat walked up the hill.*

T: *Can you think of a more powerful verb?* (word modification)

C: *Slowly the fat cat meandered up the hill.*

T: *When did the fat cat meander up the hill?* (adverbial phrase)

C: *At midnight, the fat cat slowly meandered up the hill.*

Compound sentences

A compound sentence has two or more clauses joined by *and*, *or*, *but* or *so*. The clauses are of equal weight and are all main clauses, for example:

The boy sang. The girl danced.

Each of these is a main clause (a simple sentence) and can stand independently. However, depending on the conjunction chosen, the meaning of the sentence can change:

The boy sang and the girl danced.

The boy sang but the girl danced.

The boy sang so the girl danced.

Again, I suggest that the use of conjunctions when exploring the construction of a compound sentence be explored physically with cut-up sentences before the task of applying this new knowledge to writing.

Complex sentences

Although many children in Key Stage 1 will be writing complex sentences, it is in Key Stage 2 that the terminology of main and subordinate clauses needs to be introduced and understood. A complex sentence consists of one main clause and one or more subordinate clauses.

* A **main clause**, when removed from a sentence, makes sense on its own.
* A **subordinate clause**, when removed from a sentence, will not make sense on its own. It needs the main clause to make sense. It begins with a subordinate conjunction (eg *after*, *when*, *since*, *because*, *although*) or a relative pronoun (eg *that*, *which*, *whose*, *who*). It contains both a subject and a verb, but does not form a complete sentence. Instead, it adds additional information to the main clause.

Example

Subordinate clauses can go before or after the main clause:

<u>When the dog barked</u>, the baby woke up.

The baby woke up <u>when the dog barked</u>.

Or it may be embedded within the main clause:

The dog, <u>which was called Rover</u>, ran through the park.

There are different types of subordinate clauses, including relative, conditional and non-finite. You might want to review your own subject knowledge around these terms, but the important learning for the children at this point is to be able to identify main and subordinate clauses within complex sentences. Can they identify the most important part of the sentence (the main clause), or which part can be left out but still leave the sentence making sense (the subordinate clause)? Again, this is your opportunity to model this exploration for the whole class or group.

Punctuation

"Let's eat, grandma", exclaimed Little Red Riding Hood, taking the biscuits from her basket.

"No, let's eat grandma", cried the wolf.

It is amazing how one little black mark on a page, in this case a comma, can change the whole meaning of a sentence and possibly even save lives!

Punctuation is important and children need to understand how to use it accurately and effectively. It is all about awareness of grammatical chunks. Children first learn to demarcate simple sentences with capital letters and full stops. But as their sentences become more complicated and complex, they must learn how to demarcate the breaks between phrases, clauses and words, to distinguish speech and add emphasis to their thoughts and ideas.

There are many punctuation marks and again you must review your own subject knowledge of what they are and how they are used. In this chapter I am concerned with emphasising the need to engage children in purposeful investigation that can make the study of punctuation fun. They need to realise that punctuation is an art, not a science (Medwell et al, 2014), because as you have seen a sentence can often be punctuated in different ways.

Text cohesion and coherence

Cohesion is the 'glue' that sticks sentences together. Children learn to 'glue' words together, using correct grammar and punctuation, to form meaningful sentences. They then learn how to put sentences together to form paragraphs and to put paragraphs together to form whole texts. Again this needs to be taught and modelled – cutting texts up and asking them to order them is a simple way of drawing their attention to how they are linked.

However, the text must also be coherent, which means that it must be logical, well organised and easy to read and understand by its audience. Coherence, therefore, is very much related to 'writing as a reader'. A writer needs to 'pull in' their audience and make them want to carry on reading – it's about creating a 'page turner'. The focus here is on impact and effect, on making choices that enrich the writing and allow it to flow.

Varying sentence types

Although children in Key Stage 2 need to be able to write complex sentences, they also need to understand that too many 'complicated' sentences can make their writing difficult to follow. They must learn to vary their sentences and choose the most effective for the task in hand. A long sentence is not always the best sentence. For example, if you consider 'adventure stories' tension is often introduced by short, sharp sentences:

A door slammed. David froze.

Different sentence types are used, such as questions, to cast doubt into the reader's mind:

What was that?

Repetition is employed to give the impression of danger approaching:

He heard steps. Steps that were coming closer. Steps that echoed through the long, dark corridor behind him.

Paragraphing

Paragraphing becomes important as texts become longer and more detailed. The correct use of paragraphs show that a writer knows how to 'break text up'. It is important that children understand the reasons for starting new paragraphs and don't simply see them as a 'clump' of sentences and think that after a certain number of sentences it must be time for a new paragraph.

EXTENDED THINKING

- *Should spelling, punctuation and grammar be taught in a de-contextualised way? Explain your answer.*
- *What are your views on grammar, spelling and punctuation tests in primary school?*

TECHNOLOGY

You can bring English to life through a variety of software packages to support the development of phonics, reading and writing. Spoken language can also be developed through video-conferencing. Mobile technology can be used to encourage children to read and write.

Critical reflections

This chapter has focused on enhancing your subject and pedagogical knowledge in spoken language, reading and writing. The national curriculum has increased the expectations for children in English and this requires you to ensure that your subject knowledge is well-developed. While it is important that you understand the subject-specific terminology, it is essential that you engender in children a passion for reading and writing. If you lack

enthusiasm in reading and writing, then you will find it difficult to inspire children to be readers and writers. As a teacher you should embrace reading and writing for pleasure and you should transmit this enthusiasm to children. Although the rules of grammar and punctuation need to be taught, teach them in context so that pupils are encouraged to use grammar and punctuation for effect in their writing. This will improve the quality of their writing. Enthusing children about spoken language reading and writing is one of the most important things that teachers can aim to achieve in primary schools.

KEY READINGS

Classic:

Rose, J (2006) *Independent Review in the Teaching of Early Reading: Final Report*. Nottingham: DfES.

Contemporary:

Medwell et al (2014) *Primary English: Theory & Practice*. 7th ed. London: Learning Matters Ltd: Sage.

References

All-Party Parliamentary Group for Education (2011) *Report of the Inquiry into Overcoming the Barriers to Literacy*. [online] Availabe at: www.educationengland.org.uk/documents/pdfs/2011-appge-literacy-report.pdf (accessed 15 May 2016).

Anderson, R C, Wilson, P T and Fielding, L G (1988) Growth in reading and how children spend their time outside of school. *Reading Research Quarterly*, 23(3): 285–303. [online] Available at: www.ideals.illinois.edu/bitstream/handle/2142/18003/ctrstreadtechrepv01986i00389_opt.pdf?sequence=1 (accessed 20 June 2016).

Bloom, B S (ed) Engelhart, M D, Furst, E J, Hill, W H and Krathwohl, D R (1956) *Taxonomy of Educational Objectives: The Classification of Educational Goals. Handbook 1: Cognitive Domain*. New York: David McKay.

Bradley, L and Bryant, P (1983) Categorising sounds and learning to read: A causal connection. *Nature*, 301: 419–21.

Brien, J (2012) *Teaching Primary English.* London: Sage.

Carter, A (2015) *Review of Initial Teacher Training*. London: DfE.

Caulley, D N (2008) Making qualitative research reports less boring: The techniques of writing creative non-fiction. *Qualitative Inquiry*, 14(3): 424–49.

Clark, C (2011) *Setting the Baseline: The National Literacy Trust's First Annual Survey into Reading – 2010*. London: National Literacy Trust.

Clark, C and Douglas, J (2011) *Young People's Reading and Writing: An In-depth Study Focusing on Enjoyment, Behaviour, Attitudes and Attainment*. London: National Literacy Trust.

Clark, C and Osborne, S (2008) *How Does Age Relate to Pupils' Perceptions of Themselves as Readers?* London: National Literacy Trust.

Clark, C and Rumbold, K (2006) *Reading for Pleasure: A Research Overview*. London: National Literacy Trust.

DfE (2012) *Research Evidence on Reading for Pleasure*. London: DfE.

DfE (2013) *The National Curriculum in England: Key Stages 1 and 2 Framework Document*. London: DfE.

DfE (2016) *Educational Excellence Everywhere*. [online] Available at: www.gov.uk/government/uploads/system/uploads/attachment_data/file/508447/Educational_Excellence_Everywhere.pdf (accessed 15 May 2016).

Ehri, L C (2005) Development of sight word reading: phases and findings, in Snowling, M J and Hulme, C (eds) *The Science of Reading: A Handbook*. Oxford: Blackwell, pp.135–54.

Goodman, K S (1973) The 13th easy way to make learning to read difficult: A reaction to Gleitman and Rozin. *Reading Research Quarterly*, 8: 484–93.

Gough, P B and Tunmer, W E (1986) Decoding, reading and reading disability. *Remedial Special Education*, 7: 6–10.

Johnston, R S and Watson, J E (2004) Accelerating the development of reading, spelling and phonemic awareness skills in initial readers. *Reading and Writing*, 17: 327–57.

Johnston, R and Watson, J (2007) *Teaching Synthetic Phonics*. Exeter: Learning Matters.

Johnston, R S and Morrison, M (2007) Towards a resolution of inconsistencies in the phonological deficit theory of reading disorders: Phonological reading difficulties are more severe in high IQ poor readers. *Journal of Learning Disabilities*, 40: 66–79.

Johnston, R S, Anderson, M and Holligan, C (1996) Knowledge of the alphabet and explicit awareness of phonemes in pre-readers: The nature of the relationship. *Reading and Writing*, 8: 217–34.

MacKay, N (2005) *Removing Dyslexia as a Barrier to Achievement: The Dyslexia Friendly School Toolkit*. Wakefield, SEN Marketing.

Medwell et al (2014) *Primary English: Theory & Practice*. 7th ed. London: Learning Matters Ltd.

Mullis, I V S, Martin, M O, Kennedy, A M and Foy, P (2007) Students' reading attitudes, self-concept, and out-of-school activities, in *PIRLS 2006 International Report: IEA's Progress in International Reading Literacy Study in Primary Schools in 40 Countries*. Chestnut Hill, MA: Boston College, TIMSS & PIRLS International Study Center, Lynch School of Education. [online] Available at: http://timss.bc.edu/PDF/P06_IR_Ch4.pdf (accessed 20 June 2016).

OECD (2002) *Reading for Change: Performance and Engagement Across Countries – Results from PISA 2000*. Paris: OECD.

Office for Standards in Education (Ofsted) (2012) *Moving English Forward: Action to Raise Standards in English*. London: Ofsted.

PISA (2009) Results: Executive Summary. Figure 1: Comparing Countries' and Economies' Performance. [online] Available at: www.oecd.org/pisa/46643496.pdf (accessed 15 May 2016).

Romani, C, Olson, A, Di Betta, A M (2005) Spelling disorders, in Snowling, M J and Hulme, C (eds) *The Science of Reading: A Handbook*. Malden, MA: Blackwell Publishing Ltd, pp 431–48.

Rose, J (2006) *Independent Review in the Teaching of Early Reading: Final Report*. Nottingham: DfES.

The Telegraph (2014) Michael Rosen: 'Children are no longer encouraged to read for pleasure'. [online] Available at: www.telegraph.co.uk/culture/hay-festival/10852437/Michael-Rosen-Children-are-no-longer-encouraged-to-read-for-pleasure.html (accessed 15 May 2016).

Topping, K J (2010) *What Kids are Reading: The Book-reading Habits of Students in British Schools, 2010*. London: Renaissance Learning UK.

Twist, L, Schagan, I and Hogson, C (2007) *Progress in International Reading Literacy Study (PIRLS): Reader and Reading National Report for England 2006*. Slough: NFER and DCSF.

Vygotsky, L (1978) *Mind in Society*. London and Cambridge, MA: Harvard University Press.

Wyse, D and Goswami, U (2008) Synthetic phonics and the teaching of reading. *British Educational Research Journal*, 34(6): 691–710.

4: SUBJECT KNOWLEDGE IN MATHEMATICS

TEACHERS' STANDARDS

This chapter addresses the following Teachers' Standards:

Teachers' Standard 3 Demonstrate good subject and curriculum knowledge

Teachers must:

* *have a secure knowledge of the relevant subject(s) and curriculum areas, foster and maintain pupils' interest in the subject, and address misunderstandings;*
* *demonstrate a critical understanding of developments in the subject and curriculum areas, and promote the value of scholarship;*
* *demonstrate an understanding of and take responsibility for promoting high standards of literacy, articulacy and the correct use of standard English, whatever the teacher's specialist subject;*
* *if teaching early reading, demonstrate a clear understanding of systematic synthetic phonics;*
* *if teaching early mathematics, demonstrate a clear understanding of appropriate teaching strategies.*

PROFESSIONAL LINKS

The *Carter Review of Initial Teacher Training* stated that:

XI. Evidence suggests that a high level of subject expertise is a characteristic of good teaching (Coe and others, 2014). We have found that the most effective courses address gaps and misconceptions in trainees' core subject knowledge. This is important for both primary and secondary courses and across all subjects.

XV. Teachers who understand the way pupils approach different subjects, understand the thinking behind pupils' methods and can identify common misconceptions are more likely to have a positive impact on pupil outcomes (Sadler and others, 2013 and Hill and others, 2005). We believe ITT should address subject-specific issues including phases of progression within the subject, links between subjects as well as common misconceptions and how to address these. This is important for both primary and secondary programmes. Both trainers and mentors should have a strong grasp of subject-specific pedagogy. However, there are important areas of content on subject-specific pedagogy that are not addressed on all courses.

(Carter, 2015, pp 7–8)

The review made the following recommendations:

Recommendation 1a: *Subject knowledge development should be part of a future framework for ITT content.*

Recommendation 1b: *Issues in subject-specific pedagogy should be part of a framework for ITT content.*

Recommendation 2: *All ITT partnerships should:*

1. rigorously audit, track and systematically improve trainees' subject knowledge throughout the programme;

II. ensure that changes to the curriculum and exam syllabi are embedded in ITT programmes;

III. ensure that trainees have access to high quality subject expertise;

IV. ensure that trainees have opportunities to learn with others training in the same subject.

Recommendation 3: *Schools should include subject knowledge as an essential element of professional development.*

Recommendation 4: *The DfE should make funded in-service subject knowledge enhancement courses available for primary teachers to access as professional development.*

Recommendation 5: *Universities should explore offering "bridge to ITT" modules in the final years of their subject degrees for students who are considering ITT programmes.*

(Carter, 2015)

CHAPTER OBJECTIVES

* **What is this chapter about?**

This chapter mainly focuses on developing your understanding of how to teach calculations. It does this through presenting an example of a whole school policy on calculations.

* **Why is it important?**

Although there are other areas of mathematics that you need to be familiar with, a secure understanding of how to teach calculations is essential and many other areas of mathematics depend on this.

Addition

The emphasis throughout primary school, but especially at Key Stage 1, is on visual, auditory and kinaesthetic (concrete) approaches before moving on to more abstract strategies using informal methods and jottings. Addition would be taught as combining two sets (or more) by counting on.

Expected at the end of Foundation Stage

Children are encouraged to develop a mental picture of the number system in their heads to use for calculation. They develop ways of recording calculations using pictures.

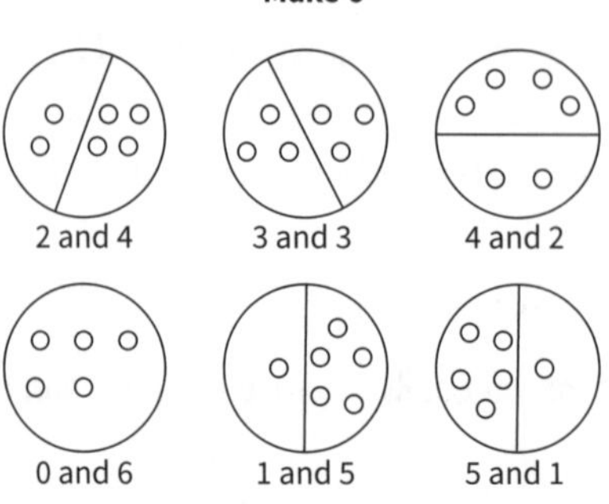

Count all: (3 + 5) Count out three counters and then five counters and then find the total by counting all the counters.

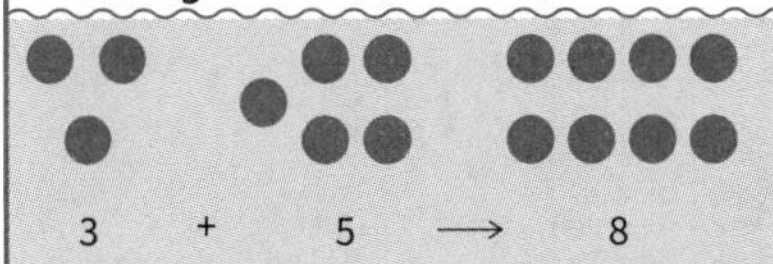

Count on from the first number: Put the first number, 3, in your head and then count on 5 more.

'3' 4 5 6 7 8

Expected at the end of Year 1

Count on from the larger number: Understand that addition can be done in any order.

Building on the methods taught in the Foundation Stage, the children will use fingers and a number line to find the answer.

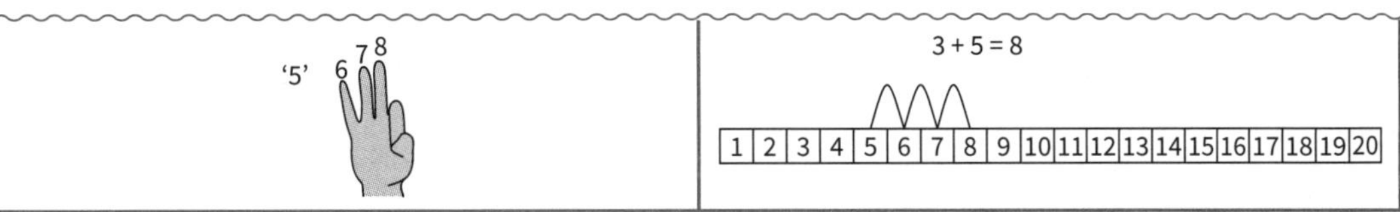

Using a hundred square: In Year 1 children begin to use a hundred square and become more confident with larger numbers and the number system. Using a hundred square the children can add 1s as they do using a number line. A hundred square is also ideal when adding ten to a number.

32 + 7 = 39

1	2	3	4	5	6	7	8	9	10
11	12	13	14	15	16	17	18	19	20
21	22	23	24	25	26	27	28	29	30
31	32	33	34	35	36	37	38	39	40
41	42	43	44	45	46	47	48	49	50
51	52	53	54	55	56	57	58	59	60
61	62	63	64	65	66	67	68	69	70
71	72	73	74	75	76	77	78	79	80
82	82	83	84	85	86	87	88	89	90
91	92	93	94	95	96	97	98	99	100

24 + 10 = 34

1	2	3	4	5	6	7	8	9	10
11	12	13	14	15	16	17	18	19	20
21	22	23	24	25	26	27	28	29	30
31	32	33	34	35	36	37	38	39	40
41	42	43	44	45	46	47	48	49	50
51	52	53	54	55	56	57	58	59	60
61	62	63	64	65	66	67	68	69	70
71	72	73	74	75	76	77	78	79	80
82	82	83	84	85	86	87	88	89	90
91	92	93	94	95	96	97	98	99	100

Expected at the end of Year 2

Using a hundred square to add two two-digit numbers: Once the children are confident with partitioning numbers they are then taught to add two two-digit numbers and this would firstly be taught using a hundred square.

Addition in columns for preparation of formal written methods: This is taught by partitioning the numbers and recording in columns so place value is supported. This prepares for the formal written methods in Year 3. To begin with, this is taught practically using Base Ten Dienes to add units first and then tens.

35 + 23 =

35 + 20 + 3 = 58

1	2	3	4	5	6	7	8	9	10
11	12	13	14	15	16	17	18	19	20
21	22	23	24	25	26	27	28	29	30
31	32	33	34	35	36	37	38	39	40
41	42	43	44	45	46	47	48	49	50
51	52	53	54	55	56	57	58	59	60
61	62	63	64	65	66	67	68	69	70
71	72	73	74	75	76	77	78	79	80
82	82	83	84	85	86	87	88	89	90
91	92	93	94	95	96	97	98	99	100

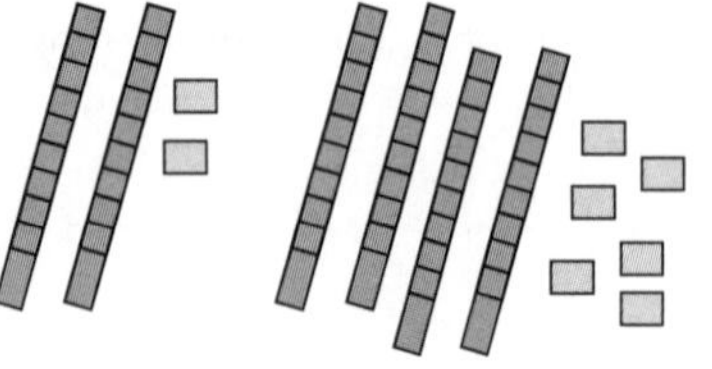

						T			U				
2	2	+	4	6	=	2	0	+	2				
						4	0	+	6				
						6	0	+	8		=	6	8

Expected at the end of Year 3

Formal written method of column addition: It is expected at the end of Year 3 children will be able to add with up to three digits, using formal written methods using column addition. This is taught practically at first to embed the understanding of place value. Then it is taught practically alongside recording using a formal written method. Firstly, we start with adding two two-digit numbers.

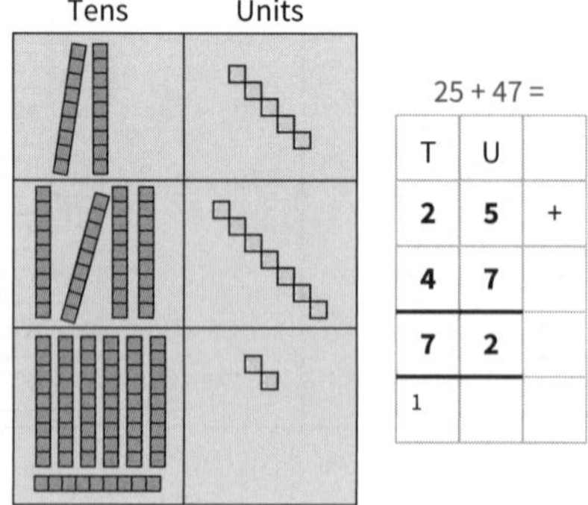

25 + 47 =

T	U	
2	**5**	+
4	**7**	
7	**2**	
1		

Script:

Remember to always write T and U above the correct column. <u>Always</u> add the units first. The + sign goes at the right-hand side alongside the top number.

Adding units: 5 + 7 =12. We can't put the 12 in the units column because 5 + 7 is more than 10. So, we **take** the 10 out and **give** it to the tens. So the 2 units are left which can go in the units column between the equal lines. **Adding tens:** Remind the children they are now dealing with the tens. So we have 20 + 40 plus 1 more 10, which equals 70. How many tens is that? 7 tens. So 7 goes in the answer box between the equal lines.

Formal written method of column addition: At the end of Year 3 it is expected that the children will be able to add numbers up to three digits, using formal written methods of column addition; again, this will be taught practically at first.

H	T	U	
4	2	9	+
1	4	3	
5	7	2	
	1		

Script:

Remember to always write H, T and U above the correct column. Always add the units first. The + sign goes at the right-hand side alongside the top number.

Adding units: 9 + 3 =12. I can't put the 12 in the units column because 9 + 3 is more than 10. So, we **take** the 10 out and **give** it to the tens. I write this under the equal lines in the tens column to add later. So 2 units are left which can go in the units column. Write this between the two equal lines.

Adding tens: Remind the children they are now dealing with the tens. I have 20 + 40 plus 1 more 10, which equals 70. How many tens is that? 7 tens. So 7 goes in the answer box between the two equal lines.

Adding hundreds: Remind the children they are now dealing with the hundreds. I have 400 + 100, which equals 500. How many hundreds is that? 5 hundreds so 5 goes in the answer box between the two equals lines.

Expected at the end of Year 4

Formal written method of column addition: In Year 4 it is expected the children will be able to add up to four digits using the formal written methods of column addition. This will build on the progress made in Year 3 and if needed it would still be taught practically.

Th	H	T	U	
3	6	9	5	+
2	5	4	3	
6	2	3	8	
1	1			

Script:

Remember to always write Th, H, T and U above the correct column. Always add the units first. The + sign goes at the right-hand side alongside the top number.

Same as previous for adding TU.

Adding hundreds: Remind the children they are now dealing with the hundreds. So, 600 + 500 plus one more hundred, which equals 1200. How many hundreds is that? 12 hundreds, so because it's larger than 10 hundreds we **take** the 1000 out and **give** it to the thousands. I put the 1 thousand underneath the answer box in the thousand column. So the 2 hundreds which are left can go in the answer box between the equal lines.

Adding thousands: Remind the children they are dealing with the thousands. So, 3000 + 2000 plus one more thousand, which equals 6000. How many thousands is that? 6 thousands, so 6 goes in the answer box.

Expected at the end of Year 5

Formal written method of column addition: At the end of Year 5 it is expected that the children will be able to add whole numbers with more than four digits, using formal written methods.

Tth	Th	H	T	U	
2	6	4	2	9	+
1	0	8	4	3	
3	7	2	7	2	
	1		1		

Formal written method of column addition: Once the children are confident with these written methods, they will be taught how to use this column method with decimals, including money. Again, where needed, this would be taught practically at first.

	U	T	H	+
£	1 •	3	6	
£	4 •	0	5	
£	5 •	4	1	
	1	1		

Script:

This is just the same as the examples above. You still start adding the digits in the right-hand column, in this case the hundredths. Notice how again the columns have been labelled to support with place value.

Expected at the end of Year 6

By Year 6 it is expected that children should be able to use the formal written methods of column addition so an emphasis is placed on using and applying these methods to solve problems.

Other examples of how the column method may be used:

+				
	3	6	9	5
		5	4	3
	4	2	3	8
	1	1		

1 •	3	6	9
4 •	0	5	3
5 •	4	2	2
	1	1	

CRITICAL QUESTION

- *Is it more important that children follow the steps or rules of addition to arrive at the correct answer or that children understand the addition strategies?*

Subtraction

The emphasis throughout school, but especially at Key Stage 1, is on visual, auditory and kinaesthetic (concrete) approaches before moving onto more abstract strategies using informal methods and jottings. Subtraction may be taught as 'take away' or by 'finding the difference'.

Expected at the end of the Foundation Stage

Children are encouraged to develop a mental picture of the number system in their heads to use for calculation. They develop ways of recording calculations using pictures.

Unlike addition, subtraction cannot be done in any order (18 – 7 is not the same as 7 – 18). Usually the largest number must come first.

Partitioning sets and learning number facts: For example, pairs that make 8, 9, 10 and knowing that 12 is made up of 5 and 7.

Counting back/take away/reduction: Use number lines, bead strings and practical resources to support calculation. Teachers *demonstrate* the use of the number line to count back in ones.

Expected at the end of Year 1

The number line should also be used to show that 13 – 5 means the 'difference between 13 and 5' or 'the difference between 5 and 13' and how many jumps they are apart.

Using a hundred square: In Year 1 children begin to use a hundred square and become more confident with larger numbers and the number system. Using a hundred square the children can subtract 1s as they do using a number line. A hundred square is also ideal when subtracting ten from a number by moving up one space from the starting number.

Expected at the end of Year 2

Using a hundred square to subtract two two-digit numbers: Once the children are confident with partitioning numbers they are then taught to subtract two two-digit numbers and this would firstly be taught using a hundred square by partitioning the number into tens and units.

$$54 - 22 = 32$$

First, start at the largest number (54) and take away the tens by moving up two spaces on the hundred square, building on the work in Year 1. Then take away the units.

1	2	3	4	5	6	7	8	9	10
11	12	13	14	15	16	17	18	19	20
21	22	23	24	25	26	27	28	29	30
31	32	33	34	35	36	37	38	39	40
41	42	43	44	45	46	47	48	49	50
51	52	53	54	55	56	57	58	59	60
61	62	63	64	65	66	67	68	69	70
71	72	73	74	75	76	77	78	79	80
82	82	83	84	85	86	87	88	89	90
91	92	93	94	95	96	97	98	99	100

Subtraction in columns for preparation of formal written methods: This is taught by recording in columns so place value is supported and this prepares for the formal written methods taught in Year 3. To begin with, this is taught practically using Base Ten Dienes to subtract units first and then subtract tens.

Once children have shown understanding of presenting their work using a column method, they may be taught the vertical subtraction formal written method, as in Year 3. They would firstly be taught to subtract two two-digit numbers as in Year 3.

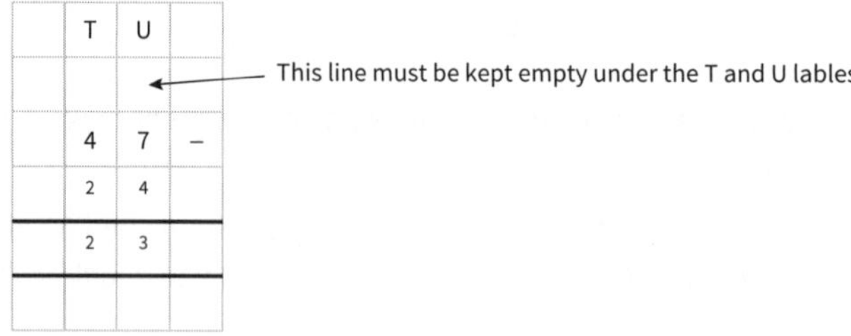

Expected at the end of Year 3

Formal written method of column subtraction: This is taught practically at first to embed the understanding of place value. Then it is taught practically alongside recording in a formal written method. At the end of Year 3 it is expected that the children will be able to subtract numbers up to three digits, using formal written methods of column subtraction. Firstly, we start with subtracting two two-digit numbers.

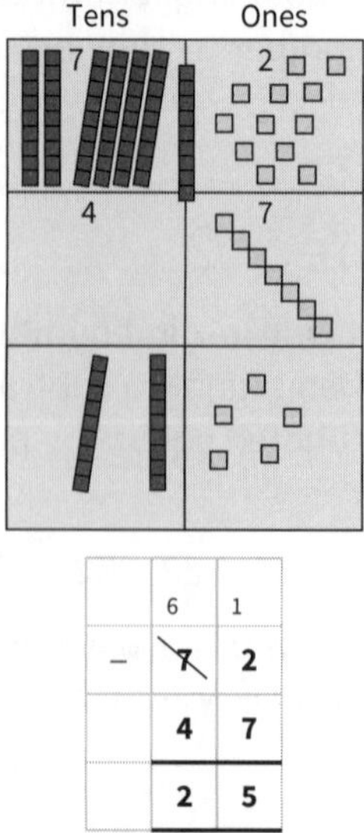

Script:

Remember to always write T and U above the correct column. Always subtract the units first. The – sign goes at the right-hand side alongside the top number.

Subtracting the units: 2 – 7 =. **I have** 2 and I want to take away 7. I can't do this so I need to **take** a 10 from the tens and **give** it to the units. I cross out the tens and write the new number above the tens. So I now **have** 6 tens. Write the 1 ten above the 2 units so the calculation is now **I have** 12 and I want to take away 7. I can do this calculation and the answer is 5. I write this under the units column between the equals lines.

Subtracting the tens: 60 – 40 **=. I have** 60 and I want to take away 40. This I can do and the answer is 20. So I have 2 tens and I write the 2 under the tens column between the equals lines.

Formal written method of column subtraction:

H	T	U	
	7	1	
5	~~**8**~~	**2**	–
3	**4**	**7**	
2	**3**	**5**	

At the end of Year 3 it is expected that children will subtract numbers up to three digits, using formal written methods of column subtraction; again, this will be taught practically first.

Script:

Remember to always write H, T and U above the correct column. Always subtract the units first. The – sign goes at the right-hand side alongside the top number.

Subtracting the units: 2 – 7 =. **I have** 2 and I want to take away 7. I can't do this so I need to **take** a 10 from the tens and **give** it to the units. I cross out the tens and write the new number above the tens. I now **have** 7 tens. Write the 1 ten above the 2 units so the calculation is now I have 12 and I want to take away 7. I can do this calculation and the answer is 5. I write this under the units column between the equals lines.

Subtracting the tens: 70 – 40 **=.** I **have** 70 and I want to take away 40. This I can do and the answer is 30. So I **have** 3 tens and I write the 3 under the tens column between the equals lines.

Subtracting the hundreds: 500 – 300 =. I **have** 500 and I want to take away 300. This I can do and the answer is 200. So I have 2 hundreds so I write the 2 under the hundreds column between the equals line. The answer is 235.

Expected at the end of Year 4

Formal written method of column subtraction: In Year 4 it is expected that the children will subtract up to four digits using the formal written methods of column subtraction. This would be built on the progress made in Year 3 and if needed it would still be taught practically.

Script:

Th	H	T	U	
	3	1	6	
~~4~~	**2**	~~7~~	**3**	–
1	**6**	**4**	**5**	
6	**6**	**2**	**8**	

Remember to always write Th, H, T and U above the correct column. Always subtract the units first. The – sign goes at the right-hand side alongside the top number.

Subtracting the units: 3 – 5 =. I **have** 3 and I want to take away 5. I can't do this so I need to **take** a 10 from the tens column and **give** it to the units. I cross out the tens and write the new number above the tens. So I now have 6 tens. Write the 1 ten above the 3 units so the calculation is now I **have** 13 and I want to take away 5. I can do this calculation and the answer is 8. I write this under the units column between the equals lines.

Subtracting the tens: 60 – 40 **=.** I **have** 60 and I want to take away 40. This I can do and the answer is 20. So I have 2 tens and I write the 2 under the tens column between the equals lines.

Subtracting the hundreds: 200 – 600 =. I **have** 200 and I want to take away 600. I can't do this so I need to **take** a 1000 from the thousand column and **give** it to the hundreds. I cross out the thousand and write the new number above the hundreds. So I now have 3 thousands. Write the 1 thousand above the 2 hundreds so the calculation is now I **have** 12 hundreds and I want to take away 6 hundreds. I can now do this calculation and the answer is 600. So I have 6 hundreds and I write 6 under the hundreds column between the equals line.

Subtracting the thousands: 3000 – 1000 =. Remember, this is now 3000 because I took one thousand and gave it to the hundreds. So, I **have** 3000 and I want to take away 1000. I can do this and the answer is 2000. So I have 2 thousands and I write this under the thousands column between the equals line.

Expected at the end of Year 5

Formal written method of column subtraction: At the end of Year 5 it is expected that the children will be able to subtract whole numbers with more than four digits, using formal written methods.

Formal written method of column subtraction: Once the children are confident with these written methods they will be taught how to use this column method with decimals, including money. Again, where needed, this would be taught practically first.

	U	t	h	
		3	1	
£	3 •	~~4~~	2	-
£	2 •	2	9	
£	1 •	2	3	

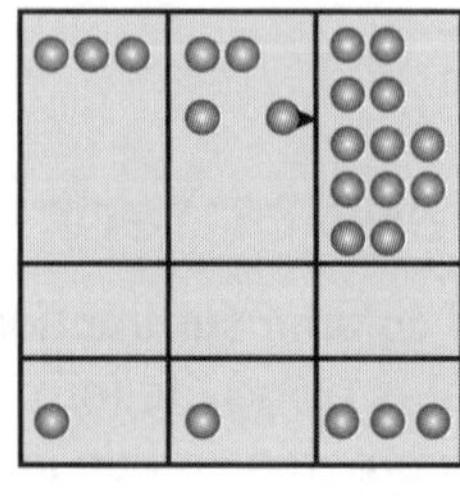

Expected at the end of Year 6

By Year 6 it is expected that children should be able to use the formal written methods of column subtraction so an emphasis is placed on using and applying these methods to solve problems.

CRITICAL QUESTION

* *Is it more important that children follow the steps or rules of subtraction to arrive at the correct answer or that children understand the subtraction strategies?*

Multiplication

Expected at the end of the Foundation Stage

Children will experience equal groups of objects and will count in 2s and 10s and begin to count in 5s. They will work on practical problem-solving activities involving equal sets or groups using apparatus. They will develop their understanding of multiplication and use jottings to support calculation.

Expected at the end of Year 1

Counting in equal steps: Building on from the work in the Foundation Stage, the children will continue to work on counting in equal steps in 2s, 5s and 10s. Some children will do this visually or practically to begin with so they see it as grouping objects.

Doubling numbers: Children begin to see that doubling numbers involves having two 'lots of' the same number and this begins to link with repeated addition.

Expected at the end of Year 2

In Year 2 the children continue to build on their knowledge of counting in 2s, 5s and 10s to recall and use multiplication facts. To begin with, this is taught as repeated addition. An array may also be used as a visual aid to understand that multiplication can be answered in any order.

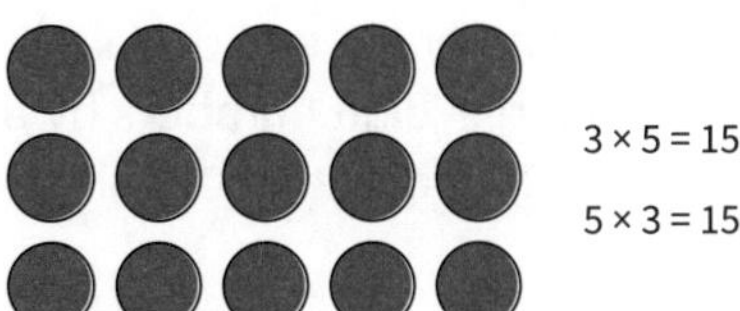

Partitioning: By the end of Year 2 some children will be ready to partition a multiplication to answer mentally. They will be encouraged to make jottings to support their working.

By encouraging children to organise their jottings vertically, this supports the work in addition and subtraction. It should be stressed to the children the importance of setting their work out correctly.

1	7	×	3					
1	0	×	3	=	3	0	+	
	7	×	3	=	2	1		
					5	**1**		

Expected at the end of Year 3

Formal written methods of multiplication: By the end of Year 3 it is expected that children will be able to calculate multiplication statements for the tables they know, including for two-digit numbers times one-digit numbers using formal written methods. Children are expected to know multiplication facts for 3, 4 and 8 multiplication tables.

H	T	U	
	3	7	×
		4	
1	**4**	**8**	
	2		

Script:

Remember to always write H, T and U above the correct column. Always multiply the units first. The x sign goes at the right-hand side alongside the top number.

Multiplying the units: 7 lots of 4 = 28. I have 28. I know I can't put 28 units in the units column so I take my tens out and give them to the tens column. Write the 2 just below the answer box in the tens column. Now I put the 8 units between the equals lines in the unit column.

Multiplying the tens: 30 lots of 4 = 120. *If the children can't tell you what 30 lots of 4 are, call it 3 x 4. Explain that this equals 12 but it is 12 lots of 10, which equals 120.*

I now have my other 2 tens to add on, which gives me 140. I now take the 100 out, which leaves me 4 tens so 4 can go in the tens column between the equal lines. The 100 goes in the hundreds column.

Expected at the end of Year 4

Formal written method of multiplication: By the end of Year 4 it is expected that children will be able to multiply two-digit and three-digit numbers by a one-digit using the formal written method. Children are expected to recall all multiplication facts for multiplication tables up to 12 × 12.

Example: Multiplying a three-digit number by a one-digit number.

	Th	H	T	U	
	2	7	4	1	×
				6	
1	**6**	**4**	**4**	**6**	
		2			

Script:

Remember to always write H, T and U above the correct column. Always multiply the units first. The x sign goes at the right-hand side alongside the top number.

Multiplying the units: 2 lots of 7 = 14. I have 14. I know I can't put 14 units in the units column so I take my tens out and give them to the tens column. Put the 1 ten just below the answer box in the tens column. Now I put the 4 units between the equals lines in the unit column.

Multiplying the tens: 40 lots of 7 = 280. *If the children can't tell you what 40 lots of 7 are, call it 4 × 7. Explain that this equals 28 but it is 28 lots of 10, which equals 280.*

I now have my other ten to add on, which gives me 290. I now take the hundreds out, which leaves me 9 tens, so 9 can go in the tens column between the equal lines. The 200 goes in the hundred column just below the answer box in the hundred column.

Multiplying the hundreds: 300 lots of 7 = 2100. If the children can't tell you what 300 lots of 7 are, *call it 3 × 7. Explain that this equals 21 but it is 21 lots of 100, which equals 2100.*

I now have my other hundreds to add on, which gives me 2300. I now take the thousands out, which leaves me with 3 hundreds so 3 can go in the hundreds column between the equal lines. The 2000 goes in the thousand column.

Expected at the end of Year 5

Formal written method of multiplication: By the end of Year 5 it is expected that children will be able to multiply up to four digits by a one or two-digit number using a formal written method, including long multiplication for two-digit numbers.

Example: Multiplying a four-digit number by a one-digit number.

	Th	H	T	U	
	2	7	4	1	×
				6	
1	**6**	**4**	**4**	**6**	
		2			

Script:

Remember to always write Th, H, T and U above the correct column. Always multiply the units first. The x sign goes at the right-hand side alongside the top number.

Multiplying the units: 1 lot of 6 = 6. I have 6 units. I put the 6 units between the equals lines in the unit column.

Multiplying the tens: 40 lots of 6 = 240. *If the children can't tell you what 40 lots of 6 are, call it 4 × 6. Explain that this equals 24 but it is 24 lots of 10, which equals 240.*

I now take the hundreds out, which leaves me 4 tens, so 4 can go in the tens column between the equal lines. The 200 goes in the hundred column just below the answer box in the hundred column.

Multiplying the hundreds: 700 lots of 6 = 4200. *If the children can't tell you what 700 lots of 6 are, call it 7 × 6. Explain that this equals 42 but it is 42 lots of 100, which equals 4200.*

I now have my other 2 hundreds to add on, which gives me 4400. I now take the thousands out, which leaves me with 4 hundreds, so 4 can go in the hundreds column between the equal lines. The 4000 goes in the thousand column just below the answer box in the hundred column.

Multiplying the thousands: 2000 lots of 6 = 12000. *If the children can't tell you what 2000 lots of 6 are, call it 2×6. Explain that this equals 12 but it is 12 lots of 1000, which equals 12000.*

I now have my other 4 thousands to add on, which gives me 16000. I now take the tens of thousands out, which leaves me with 6 thousands, so 6 can go in the thousands column between the equal lines. The 10000 goes in the tens of thousands column.

Expected at the end of Years 5 and 6

Formal written method of long multiplication: In Year 5 children are expected to multiply a four-digit number by a two-digit number using long multiplication. This is then consolidated in Year 6.

Multiply a two-digit number by a two-digit number:

	Th	H	T	U						
			2	3	×					
			1	4						
			9	2		2	3	×	4	
		2	3	0		2	3	×	1	0
		3	2	2						
		1	1							

Script:

Remember to always write Th, H, T and U above the correct column. Always multiply the units first. The x sign goes at the right-hand side alongside the top number. Always start with multiplying the top number by the units of the bottom number first.

Multiplying the units of the top number by the units of the bottom number: 3 lots of 4 = 12. I have 12. I know I can't put 12 units in the units column so I take my tens out and give them to the tens column. I put the 1 ten just below the answer box in the tens column. Now I put the 2 units under the unit digits.

Multiplying the tens of the top number by the units of the bottom number: 20 lots of 4 = 80. *If the children can't tell you what 20 lots of 4 are, call it 2×4. Explain that this equals 8 but it is 8 lots of 10, which equals 80.*

Now I must add the ten I have put under the equal lines in the tens column. So this equals 90. I cross out the ten I have added. I have 9 tens so 9 goes in the tens column under the tens digits.

Now multiply the top number by the tens of the bottom number.

Multiplying the tens of the bottom number by the units of the top number: Before I do any multiplying I add a zero in the next row in the units column as I am not dealing with the units. This is called a place holder.

10 lots of 3 = 30: I now have 3 tens so this goes in the tens column in the next row.

Multiplying the tens of the bottom number by the tens of the top number: 10 lots of 20 = 200. As this answer is now 2 hundreds, 2 goes in the hundreds column.

Now we have completed the multiplications, we now need to add our two answers using the standard written method.

Formal written method of long multiplication: Multiply a four-digit number by a two-digit number.

		Th	H	T	U								
		6	5	2	3	×							
				2	5								
	3	2	6	1	5		6	5	2	3	×	5	
1	3	0	4	6	0		6	5	2	3	×	2	0
1	6	3	0	7	5								
	1	~~12~~	~~1~~	~~1~~									

Script:

Remember to always write Th, H, T and U above the correct column. <u>Always</u> multiply the units first. The x sign goes at the right-hand side alongside the top number.

Steps to Success:

1. Always start multiplying the top number by the units of the bottom number.
2. Multiply the unit of the bottom number by each of the top digits, recording below the line.
3. Remember to cross out any additional digits that need adding on as you go along.
4. Once each top digit has been multiplied by the bottom unit, begin multiplying the tens digit of the bottom number by each digit of the top number.
5. <u>Always</u> write a zero as a place holder before you begin multiplying the bottom tens digit by any of the digits in the top number.
6. Once all multiplications have been completed, add the two answers together using the standard column method of addition.

Write the answer between the two lines at the bottom of the long multiplication.

CRITICAL QUESTION

* *Is it more important that children follow the steps of long multiplication to arrive at the correct answer or that children understand the mathematical processes they are undertaking?*

Division

Multiplication and division are concepts which start to be developed in the Foundation Stage, and continue to be built on throughout the child's school life. The connection between multiplication and division must be emphasised from the start, and constantly reinforced.

Division has two aspects, sharing and grouping, which are conceptually very different, although numerically they give the same 'answer'.

For division to be meaningful, it is often best introduced within a context.

The written methods build on the children's understanding of mental methods, based on place value and partitioning.

Expected at the end of the Foundation Stage

Children will understand equal groups and share items out in play and problem solving. They will count in 2s and 10s and later in 5s.

Children will develop their understanding of division and use jottings to support calculation.

Sharing

Example: 15 marbles shared equally between 5 children

Some thoughts on division at Key Stage 1 and Key Stage 2

Consider the following simple word problems, all of which are easily accessible to children in Key Stage 1 and Key Stage 2:

I bake 13 buns. I want to share them equally between my 4 children. How many buns will each child get?

I have £13.00 to share equally between my 4 children. How much money will each child get?

I buy some marbles. There are 13 in a packet. I want to share them equally between my 4 children. What happens now? (The children come up with some wonderful suggestions, and this, of course, leads to the important question of how many more packets we need to buy before we can share equally.)

I am having a party for 13 people. I need paper plates which come in packets of 4. How many packets must I buy?

I made 13 fancy decorations. They have to be packed in strong boxes, with 4 in each box, to keep them safe. How many boxes can I fill?

Clearly, all these problems can be represented using the same number sentence, despite their very different 'answers'. Children need to know from the start that there are these choices to be made, and to ask themselves, *What sort of answer am I looking for, and what units am I working in?* This can be expressed as what am I *counting in? Am I counting in packets, children, buns or what?*

Expected at the end of Year 1

In Year 1 the teaching of division is built on the practical work in the Foundation Stage. The children will use concrete objects and pictorial representations and arrays with the support of the teacher.

Describing an array

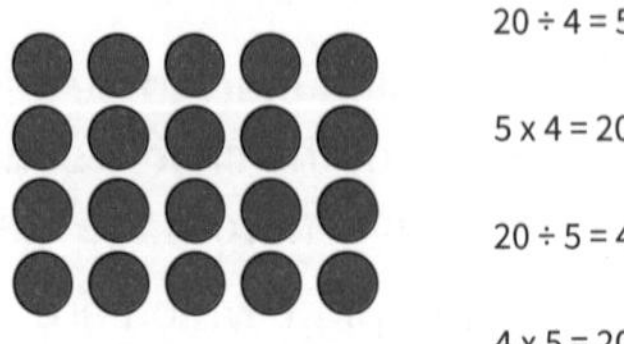

Division by sharing

Example: Share a pizza equally between four people. Cut the pizza in quarters. How many pieces are there?

Division by grouping

Example: 15 marbles put into groups of 3.

Expected at the end of Year 2

In Year 2 the children use division with the multiplication facts they can recall. It is expected that they will be able to recall multiplication and division facts for the 2, 5 and 10 multiplication tables. It is expected that by the end of Year 2 children will be able to calculate mathematical statements for division and write them using ÷ and =.

To encourage this, talk through what the calculation means. This would be done in context with the question. Always encourage the children to check their answer.

Example questions

Do 5 lots of 3 make 15?

What is 15 divided by 3?

How many lots of 3 can I take out of 15?

Expected at the end of Year 3

Formal written method of short division: By the end of Year 3 it is expected that children will be able to calculate division statements using the multiplication tables they know, including for two-digit numbers divided by one-digit numbers using formal written methods.

It would be expected that the children will be reminded of the 'talk through' taught in Year 2 so that they fully understand the mathematical statement.

Remember to use the words *How many lots of?*

Partitioning: This method would be used to divide mentally, for example, 39 ÷ 3

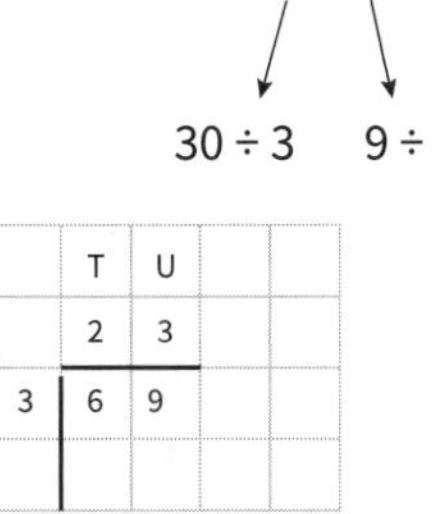

Script:

Remember to always write T and U above the correct column.

Working with the tens first: How many lots of 3 can I take out of 6? The answer is 2. I write 2 in the box above 6.

Working with the units: How many lots of 3 can I take out of 9? The answer is 3. I write 3 in the box above 9.

Some children may be able to do this easily so should be taught this method to the next level.

Working with remainders

	T	U	
	2	4	
3	**7**	**12**	

Remember to use the words *How many lots of?*

Script:

Remember to always write T and U above the correct column.

Working with the tens first: How many lots of 3 can I take out of 7? The answer is 2. Write 2 in the box above 7. I know 2 lots of 3 is 6 so I have 1 ten left over so that goes into the units column. I show this by writing a small 1 next to the 2 to read 12.

Working with the units: How many lots of 3 can I take out of 12? (1 ten plus 2 units) The answer is 4. There are 4 lots of 3 in 12 so I write 4 in the box above the 12.

Expected at the end of Year 4

Formal written methods of short division: By the end of Year 4 it is expected that children will be able to divide two-digit and three-digit numbers by a one-digit number using formal written methods.

Script:

Example: for 318 ÷ 6 =

Remember to always write H, T and U above the correct column.

Working with the hundreds first: How many lots of 6 can I take out of 3? The answer is 0. If the children wish they can write a faint 0 in the box above the three. Or if they prefer they can leave it empty to read the next number as 31.

Working with the tens: How many lots of 6 can I take out of 31? The answer is 5. I write 5 in the box above 1. I know 5 lots of 6 are 30 so I have 1 ten left over so that goes into the units column. I show this by writing a small 1 next to the 8 to read 18.

Working with the units: How many lots of 6 can I take out of 18? (1 ten plus 8 units) The answer is 3. There are 3 lots of 6 in 18 so I write 3 in the box above the 18.

Some children may be able to do this easily so should be taught this method to the next level using remainders.

Script:

Example: 852 ÷ 7 =

Remember to always write H, T and U above the correct column.

Working with the hundreds first: How many lots of 7 can I take out of 8? The answer is 1. Write 1 in the box above 8. I know 1 lots of 7 is 7 so I have 1 hundred left over so that goes into the tens column. I show this by writing a small 1 next to the 5 to read 15.

Working with the tens: How many lots of 7 can I take out of 15? The answer is 2. Write 2 in the box above 15. I know 2 lots of 7 are 14 so I have 1 ten left over so that goes into the units column. I show this by writing a small 1 next to the 2 to read 12.

Working with the units: How many lots of 7 can I take out of 12? The answer is 1. There is 1 lot of 7 in 12 so I write 1 in the box above the 12. 1 lot of 7 is 7 so that means I have 5 left over. We call this a remainder and write it at the end of our answer as a r5.

Expected at the end of Year 5

Formal written methods of short division: By the end of Year 5 it is expected that children will be able to divide numbers up to four digits by a one-digit number using the formal written method of short division and interpret remainders appropriately for the context.

Script:

Example: 1449 ÷ 4 =

Remember to always write Th, H, T and U above the correct column.

Working with the thousands first: How many lots of 4 can I take out of 1? The answer is 0. If the children wish they can write a faint 0 in the box above the 1. Or if they prefer, they can leave it empty to read the next number as 14.

Working with the hundreds: How many lots of 4 can I take out of 14? The answer is 3. Write 3 in the box above 4. I know 3 lots of 4 are 12 so I have 2 hundreds left over so that goes into the tens column. I show this by writing a small 2 next to the 4 to read 24.

Working with the tens: How many lots of 4 can I take out of 24? The answer is 6. Write 6 in the box above 24.

Working with the units: How many lots of 4 can I take out of 9? The answer is 2. Write 2 in the box above the 9. 2 lots of 4 are 8 so that means I have 1 left over. We call this a remainder and write it at the end of our answer as a r1.

When the children are working in the context of money or measures they will be taught to put the decimal point followed by 00. This is so the children understand the remainder in the context of the question.

Example: £1449 ÷ 4

Use the script from above. Then follow this for working with the units, tenths and hundredths.

Working with the units: How many lots of 4 can I take out of 9? The answer is 2. Write 2 in the box above the 9. I know 2 lots of 4 are 8 so I have 1 unit left over. This goes in the tenths column. I show this by writing a small 1 next to the 0 to read 10.

Working with the tenths: How many lots of 4 can I take out of 10? The answer is 2. Write 2 in the answer box above the 0. 2 lots of 4 are 8 so that means I have 2 tenths left over so that goes into the hundredths column. I show this by writing a small 2 next to the 0 to read 20.

Working with the hundredths: How many lots of 4 can I take out of 20? The answer is 5. Write 5 in the answer box above the 0.

Expected at the end of Year 6

By the end of Year 6 it is expected that children will be able to divide numbers by a two-digit number using the formal written method of short division where appropriate, interpreting remainders according to the context. It is suggested that children use the short division for dividing up to 12. This would be the same as the Year 5 example.

Formal written methods of long division: It is expected at the end of Year 6 that the children will be able to divide numbers up to four digits by a two-digit whole number using the formal written method of long division, and interpret remainders as whole number remainders, fractions or by rounding, as appropriate for the context.

Script:

Example: 2468 ÷ 15

Remember to always write Th, H, T and U above the correct column.

Working with the thousands first: How many lots of 15 can I take out of 2? The answer is 0. If the children wish they can write a faint 0 in the box above the 0. Or if they prefer, they can leave it empty to read the next number as 24.

Working with the hundreds: How many lots of 15 can I take out of 24? The answer is 1. (15 with 9 left over.) Write 1 in the box above 4 in the hundreds column. Write 15 under the 24 and subtract 15 from 24 and the answer is 9. Write this in the hundreds column under the 5.

Working with the tens: Bring the 6 tens down next to the 9 remaining hundreds. How many lots of 15 can I take out of 96? The answer is 6. (90 with 6 left over.) Write 6 in the box above the 6 in the tens column. Write 90 under the 96 and subtract 90 from the 96. The answer is 6. Write this in the tens column under the 0.

Working with the units: Bring the 8 units down next to the 6 remaining tens. How many lots of 15 can I take out of 68? The answer is 4 (60 with 8 left over.) Write 4 in the box above the 8 in the units column. 4 lots of 15 are 60 so that means I have 8 left over. I call this a remainder and write it at the end of our answer as a r8.

IN PRACTICE

Ask the mathematics subject leader for a copy of the school's calculation policy and compare it with the policy presented in this chapter.

CRITICAL QUESTION

* *Is it more important that children follow the steps of long division to arrive at the correct answer or that children understand the mathematical processes they are undertaking?*

Progression in primary mathematics

The Hertfordshire Grid for Learning has produced some useful progression frameworks to demonstrate what progression looks like in the strands of mathematics. These can be accessed from the following website: www.thegrid.org.uk/learning/maths/ks1-2/nat_curriculum/index.shtml.

EXTENDED THINKING

* *Mathematics is a subject which is often right or wrong. However, mathematical investigations allow children the opportunity to explore multiple solutions to a problem. Is it more important that children understand mathematics as a process or that they arrive at the correct answers? Explain your response.*

IN PRACTICE

Find out whether progression frameworks in strands of mathematics are used in your school to aid planning.

EXTENDED THINKING

- *In a technological world of computers and calculators, how important is it that children are able to use pencil and paper methods for solving calculations?*

EVIDENCE-BASED TEACHING

Research has discovered 21 teaching practices, grouped under eight headings, which are associated with gains in student outcomes. These include the following:

1. **Orientation:** (a) Providing the objectives for which a specific task/lesson/series of lessons take(s) place. (b) Challenging students to identify the reason why an activity is taking place in the lesson.
2. **Structuring:** (a) Beginning with overviews and/or review of objectives. (b) Outlining the content to be covered and signalling transitions between lesson parts. (c) Drawing attention to and reviewing main ideas.
3. **Questioning:** (a) Raising different types of questions (ie, process and product) at appropriate difficulty level. (b) Giving time for students to respond. (c) Dealing with student responses.
4. **Teaching/ modelling:** (a) Encouraging students to use problem-solving strategies presented by the teacher or other classmates. (b) Inviting students to develop strategies. (c) Promoting the idea of modelling.
5. **Application:** (a) Using seatwork or small-group tasks in order to provide needed practice and application opportunities. (b) Using application tasks as starting points for the next step of teaching and learning.
6. **The classroom as a learning environment:** (a) Establishing on-task behaviour through the interactions they promote (ie, teacher–student and student–student interactions). (b) Dealing with classroom disorder and student competition through establishing rules, persuading students to respect them and using the rules.
7. **Management of time:** (a) Organising the classroom environment. (b) Maximising engagement rates.
8. **Assessment:** (a) Using appropriate techniques to collect data on student knowledge and skills. (b) Analysing data in order to identify student needs and report the results to students and parents. (c) Teachers evaluating their own practices.

(Creemers and Kyriakides, 2006, cited in Coe et al, 2014, p 6)

EVALUATE

- *How useful is this framework as a tool to support your practice? Explain your answer.*

CHALLENGE

- *What are the limitations of objectives-led teaching?*
- *What are the limitations of modelling as a teaching strategy?*

APPLY

- *Apply this framework to a mathematics lesson that you plan. What elements of the framework have you addressed in the plan?*

TECHNOLOGY

While there is an abundance of resources on the internet to support your mathematics teaching, it is important not to underestimate the importance of helping pupils to understand that mathematics is all around them in the environment. The environment is a rich resource for teaching many mathematical concepts, including shape, geometry, measures and statistics. Ensure that you relate your mathematics teaching to the real world as much as possible.

Critical reflections

This chapter has introduced you to some key strategies for teaching mathematical calculations. The expectations on children in the mathematics national curriculum are high and you will need to consider carefully how you challenge children to achieve these expectations while, at the same time, protecting their self-esteem. You will need to ensure that your own subject knowledge is good by thoroughly researching topics before you teach them. It is important that children have access to practical resources to support their mathematical understanding and these should only be removed when children are ready to process mathematics in a more abstract way. To motivate your learners, you will need to approach your mathematics teaching with confidence and enthusiasm and you will need to address children's mathematical misconceptions in a sensitive way.

KEY READINGS

Classic:

Cockcroft, W H (1982) *Mathematics Counts: Report of the Committee of Inquiry into the Teaching of Mathematics in Schools*. [online] Available at: www.educationengland.org.uk/documents/cockcroft/cockcroft1982.html (accessed 20 June 2016).

Contemporary:

Hansen, A (2014) *Children's Errors in Mathematics*. Exeter: Learning Matters.

Haylock, D and Manning, R (2014) *Mathematics Explained for Primary Teachers.* London: Sage.

References

Carter, A (2015) *Review of Initial Teacher Training*. London: DfE.

Creemers, B P M and Kyriakides, L (2006) Critical analysis of the current approaches to modelling educational effectiveness: The importance of establishing a dynamic model. *School Effectiveness and School Improvement*, 17: 347–66. [online] Available at: http://esf.ric.si/Data/Sites/2/literatura/Critical_analysis...pdf (accessed 20 June 2016).

5: CHILD DEVELOPMENT

TEACHERS' STANDARDS

This chapter addresses the following Teachers' Standards:

Teachers' Standard 5: Adapt teaching to respond to the strengths and needs of all pupils

Teachers must:

* *demonstrate an awareness of the physical, social and intellectual development of children, and know how to adapt teaching to support pupils' education at different stages of development.*

PROFESSIONAL LINKS

The *Carter Review of Initial Teacher Training* made the following recommendation:

Recommendation 1e: *Child and adolescent development should be included within a framework for ITT content.*

(Carter, 2015)

CHAPTER OBJECTIVES

* **What is this chapter about?**

This chapter addresses general theories of child development as well as subject-specific aspects of child development. It examines children's development within language, reading, writing and mathematics. This chapter makes clear the relationship between theories and classroom practice. It addresses aspects of child development which have direct applications to classroom practice.

* **Why is it important?**

Without a secure understanding of subject-specific child development, you will not be able to provide your learners with practice which is developmentally appropriate. A good knowledge of stages of development will help you to identify next steps in learning and this will inform both planning and teaching. Additionally, this knowledge will help you to understand the underpinning foundations of knowledge, skills and understanding. This will enable you to take the learning back to a previous stage of development in order to provide teaching which is in line with children's development. A knowledge of child development will help you to understand sequences of progression within strands of learning, which is critical for effective teaching.

ITT courses have often over-emphasised the theoretical aspects of child development at the expense of the practical applications. Both theory and practice are equally important but theory will help you to provide a rationale for your practice. If you cannot articulate the theory which underpins the various approaches to teaching then you will find it difficult to explain why you do what you do in your teaching. This chapter provides you with the relevant theoretical underpinning knowledge but it makes explicit the practical implications that are borne out of theory.

Language and communication development

Oral language development is rooted in the early sounds and interactions of babies. Children will develop communication skills at different rates and as a practitioner you play a fundamental role in facilitating the development of these skills. Children need to confidently use language to communicate before they will be able to write. Children's language can be developed through interactions with adults and each other. You can support the development of these skills in a range of ways. These must include:

- spending time talking to and having conversations with babies and children;
- providing rich play-based learning that will facilitate social interaction and communication and using these as opportunities to extend children's language and communication;
- seizing opportunities for sustained shared thinking;
- developing a language and communication-rich enabling environment;
- identifying children's needs in relation to language and communication and planning to support subsequent development in relation to these;
- modelling speaking in complete sentences;
- providing children with opportunities to ask their own questions.

Poor language and communication disadvantages children, frequently resulting in low achievement in literacy. Children who are able to articulate a sentence are better prepared to write in sentences. Children who can develop oral narratives will subsequently be able to transfer these skills to producing written narratives. Children with broader experiences of language will have a wider range of vocabulary to draw upon in their writing. Varied, rich, stimulating and meaningful experiences underpin subsequent successes in writing. Children are able to draw on such experiences as they develop as writers. Some children will be immersed in rich language and communication experiences in their formative years. However, some children may be raised in language impoverished environments which inevitably impede their development in language, communication and literacy. These children will require your expertise to support and enhance their development.

You cannot assume that children's speech, language and communication skills will develop automatically. As a teacher you play a fundamental role in supporting the development of these skills through your interactions with children and through creating an enabling learning environment which supports the development of language, talk and communication. Communication and language skills are the basis for children to subsequently become good readers and writers. It is essential that you have some understanding of typical levels of development so that you can identify children who need further support. Although children are unique individuals and develop at their own rates, benchmarking their development against typical development will enable you to identify those children who may be struggling, thus enabling you to provide targeted intervention to groups and individuals.

The Communication Trust (2011) provided some useful benchmarks for communication development and you can also refer to the Development Matters guidance in the Early Years Foundation Stage to help you identify what stages children have reached.

By **six months** babies usually:

- *make sounds, including crying, gurgling and babbling to themselves and others;*
- *make noises to get your attention;*

* *watch your face when you talk to them;*
* *get excited when they hear voices, perhaps by kicking, waving their arms or making noises;*
* *smile and laugh when other people laugh;*
* *make sounds back when talked to.*

(The Communication Trust, 2011)

You can facilitate communication in babies by getting down to their level so that they can see your face. Talking to them and singing songs and rhymes are basic activities that should engender a response in babies. Using facial expressions and leaving gaps in your conversations to enable them to give a response are also useful strategies for facilitating communication.

By **one year of age** children use a wider range of communication strategies. At this age they may point to get your attention and they begin to understand simple words, especially if these are accompanied with a gesture. At this age babies can usually:

* *recognise the names of familiar objects;*
* *take turns in 'conversations' through babbling back to an adult;*
* *babble strings of sounds;*
* *say simple words.*

(The Communication Trust, 2011)

By the **age of 18 months** babies will usually attempt to talk using a limited number of words. These words will be words that they have heard in the home. Some of the words may not be pronounced correctly and after they have spoken a word adults can repeat it back to them so they can hear the correct articulation. It is at this age when children usually begin to understand simple phrases and they can usually recognise a wider range of objects than they are able to name. Extending children's vocabulary at this age is vital so when children point to objects it is important to tell them the correct name of the object. As a teacher you need to model correct spoken English so you will need to use the correct words for objects. However, you will also need to bear in mind that parents may have introduced children to alternative 'baby' words and they will need to unlearn these.

By the **age of two** children usually have a greater vocabulary. They understand and use more words and they use and understand a wider repertoire of short phrases. Children often understand more than they can say. Typically, children at the age of two can:

* *use 50 or more single words;*
* *use short phrases;*
* *ask simple questions;*
* *understand between 200–500 words;*
* *understand simple questions;*
* *enjoy pretend play;*
* *become frustrated when they are unable to make themselves understood.*

(The Communication Trust, 2011)

Adults can extend their language development by using adjectives to describe simple nouns. Playing with children and extending their vocabulary and sharing books are essential activities for extending children's language and communication.

At the **age of three** children will:

* *use up to 300 words, including nouns and adjectives;*
* *use simple verbs;*
* *use simple prepositions;*
* *string four or five words together to say simple captions;*
* *ask questions;*
* *have clearer speech;*
* *understand longer instructions and questions;*
* *be able to have conversations.*

(The Communication Trust, 2011)

Children may have specific difficulties with the pronunciation of sounds such as 'sh', 'ch' and 'th' and they may miss sounds off the beginning of words. The most effective way of addressing this is to repeat back what they have said using the correct enunciations of the phonemes. It is at this stage where adults should be engaging children in extended conversations. Children may not speak in full sentences at the age of three. Rather than correcting them, it is better to repeat back what they have said using full sentences so that their self-concepts are not damaged.

By the **age of four** children are usually able to:

* *say many more words, phrases and sentences;*
* *use longer sentences and link sentences;*
* *use clearer speech;*
* *describe past events that they have experienced;*
* *listen to longer stories and answer simple questions about them;*
* *use number, colour and time-related words;*
* *enjoy imaginative play.*

(The Communication Trust, 2011)

By the **age of five** children will usually:

* *take turns in much longer conversations;*
* *use correct sentences when speaking;*
* *understand the meanings of words;*
* *retell short stories in sequence;*
* *use most sounds of speech;*
* *enjoy listening to stories, songs and rhymes;*
* *understand spoken instructions;*
* *use talk to take on different roles in imaginative play;*
* *use talk to solve problems and organise thinking and activities;*
* *understand words such as first, next, last and simple prepositions.*

(The Communication Trust, 2011)

CRITICAL QUESTIONS

* *What is the impact of language impoverished environments on children's language and literacy development?*
* *What impact might technology have on the use of language and communication in the home environment?*

Supporting children with speech, language and communication difficulties

As a teacher you must acknowledge that all children will have attained varying levels in their speech, language and communication skills. You must initially be aware of the differences between speech, language and communication. The Communication Trust (2011) provides useful definitions of these terms:

Speech *refers to speaking in a clear voice ... without hesitating too much or without repeating words... and being able to make sounds ... clearly.*

Language *refers to talking and understanding, joining words together into sentences... knowing the right words to explain what you mean.*

Communication *refers to how we interact with others, using language or gestures in different ways, for example to have a conversation or give directions. It is also being able to understand other people's points of view and understanding body language and facial expressions.*

(The Communication Trust, 2011)

You must remember that children communicate in a range of different ways. These may include both verbal and non-verbal forms of communication. Non-verbal communication should be valued and may include simple eye contact, gesturing or children leading you to show you objects and places.

Children may encounter difficulties in either one or more of these aspects. Through careful assessments you must initially identify the specific difficulties that children are experiencing. It is only by doing so that you will be able to offer them appropriate support.

You need to consider the ways in which you can create a communication-friendly environment to support and enhance children's language development. You will need to attend to the following aspects which include:

* developing areas where children can engage in conversation without the distraction of noise;
* the consideration of space which provides children with a chance to focus on and enjoy communication without additional distractions;
* the provision of visual cues such as visual timetables, labels using pictures and words, stimulus displays and interactive displays which include labels and captions, and communication books to facilitate picture exchange communication.

Adults play a fundamental role in supporting the development of children's speech, language and communication skills. As children engage in learning you should seize opportunities to extend children's language. As you interact with children you should scaffold their language development by introducing them to new words and phrases, as well as technical vocabulary. Additionally, as you plan for adult-directed teaching it is essential that you identify new vocabulary on your lesson plans. The development of vocabulary must be considered in all aspects of learning. However, you must be aware that an introduction to new vocabulary does not necessarily result in children automatically understanding and using it. Children may need to be introduced to vocabulary several times within a relevant context before they will even start to use it independently. Displaying new vocabulary is also a useful way of consolidating meaning. For example, a representation of a triangle alongside a written label can help children to make an association between a word and its meaning.

You will have responsibility for identifying children who encounter speech, language and communication difficulties. Some children will have already been referred to external agencies, while others may have been referred and discharged due to lack of parental support. Other children may not have been identified at all. Should you have any concerns about specific children and the specific support they require, you are advised to discuss this with the Special Educational Needs Coordinator. However, you may find the following strategies helpful:

- simplifying language and using short chunks of language to communicate meaning;
- slowing down your speech;
- ensuring that the majority of the vocabulary you use is within the child's understanding;
- providing children with thinking time to process what has been communicated to them;
- encouraging them to echo what has been said to them;
- ensuring that a child is looking at you as you speak to them and vice versa;
- explaining in advance the information that children will be required to recall;
- supporting your explanations with visual cues, including pictures, objects diagrams and gestures;
- demonstrating learning in tandem with your explanations; for example, when naming the parts of a flowering plant, you would ensure that as you identify each part you also refer to these parts on a real plant;
- affording children time to communicate their needs and explanations without rushing them or anticipating and responding before they have had time to finish speaking. Children who stammer should not be interrupted because this may damage their confidence and impair their willingness to communicate;
- resisting the temptation to correct children as they speak. It is advisable to repeat what they have communicated, including the correct model of spoken language, after the child has finished speaking;
- rewarding children with praise for their attempts to communicate.

You cannot assume that all children will have enjoyed and adopted good communication skills. Adults around them may not have been good role models and it is your responsibility to identify this and then ensure that this becomes a focus for the child's development. The rules of communication need to be taught and modelled in one-to-one interactions with you and other colleagues. Once children become confident communicators in this context, you can then extend their experiences by engaging them in opportunities to communicate with their peers on a one-to-one basis. This would be followed by communication in groups and eventually as part of the whole class. Children need to be taught explicitly the rules of communication. These include:

- good listening skills;
- allowing the speaker to finish before responding to them;

* taking turns in conversation;
* developing the skills of negotiation;
* considering the effect and impact of their communications.

The Early Years Foundation Stage Guidance (DfE, 2012) provides a broad developmental framework for extending children's communication and language. You can refer to this document to support you in assessing the development of individual children as well as identifying their next developmental steps which you will then need to support. This document also provides guidance to support you in developing an enabling learning environment. A fundamental aspect of such an environment is for you to ensure that you consistently model the use of correct standard spoken English, including the use of grammar. As a teacher you are a role model of standard spoken English. The standard of your own spoken and written forms of English must be exemplary. This is a current key focus in education and is embedded in the Teacher's Standards (DfE, 2012). It does not refer to regional accents, which are to be celebrated. You must be able to clearly distinguish between grammar, pronunciation and accent. You can speak using correct standard English with any accent.

CRITICAL QUESTIONS

* *Does language and vocabulary need to be taught or is it something which children internalise naturally? Explain your answer.*
* *How can teachers encourage children with limited or no verbal communication skills to communicate?*

The early stages of reading development: pre-reading skills

Emergent reading

Children develop an awareness of environmental print from a very early age. They are surrounded by signs, logos and notices and they quickly begin to associate these with meaning. Their awareness of print gradually expands as they are exposed to magazines, newspapers and books in the home environment. Children who are raised in a literate home environment are more likely to become good readers. Some children, unfortunately, are brought up in print impoverished environments and this can have detrimental effects on their subsequent reading development.

Palaiologou (2010) discusses how children move from being naïve readers to more expert readers. Initially children may 'read' the pictures, but later in their development they start to pay more attention to the text. In the emergent stage of reading, the crucial foundations for subsequent reading development are laid. Children start to understand that books are different to toys and very young babies enjoy sharing picture books with adults. It is never too early to instil a respect for books in children. Books have a clear purpose and should be valued and enjoyed. Storing them separately, while also making them accessible, will facilitate an early love of literature.

As children develop they begin to understand how books work. It is at this stage that children will start to interact with books through turning the pages, pointing to pictures and naming objects. As their participation increases they will gradually enjoy listening to and joining in with stories. Children enjoy repetitive texts and this facilitates their participation in storytelling. Gradually they will be able to retell stories, recognise and name familiar characters and re-enact scenes from stories. They will begin to develop their own stories using pictures as a stimulus. Developing an attractive book area will engender a love of books in children. This should include:

- predictable texts;
- counting books;
- rhyming texts;
- non-fiction texts;
- traditional tales;
- cumulative tales;
- nursery rhymes;
- big books;
- story sacks;
- puppets;
- story CDs;
- books produced by children.

Young children are attracted to the illustrations on the front of books and glean a great deal of information, relating to the content of the book, from these illustrations. For this reason, it is recommended that books are displayed with the front covers clearly visible.

Concepts about print

Children will begin to develop a more in-depth understanding of text within the emergent stage of reading. Marie Clay used the term 'concepts about print' to indicate the level of knowledge and understanding that children need to acquire before they are able to become good readers. These concepts provide the necessary foundations for subsequent reading development and include:

- understanding directionality – text is read from left to right and top to bottom;
- identifying letters;
- identifying words;
- naming punctuation;
- understanding the function of punctuation;
- understanding book orientation;
- identifying the front and back cover;
- identifying the title;
- identifying the spine;
- understanding that it is the print that communicates the meaning;
- recognising inverted print;

* recognising when letters are transposed in words;
* identifying anagrams;
* understanding that correct word ordering results in meaning;
* understanding the concept of first and last;
* understanding the difference between upper and lower case letters.

These concepts about print are an intrinsic part of assessing children's development in reading. As children read, in a variety of contexts, including shared, guided and individual reading, you must take the opportunity to focus carefully on the concepts they understand as well as those which need to be developed. It is too easy to overlook these basic concepts which are fundamental to becoming an effective reader.

As children's phonemic knowledge develops they will start to blend phonemes to decode words. It is at this stage that children's comprehension may be impeded. As children focus on the smallest units of sound within words, they may not internalise the meaning of the text. However, it is important to remember that decoding is a time limited strategy. It unlocks the door to word recognition and once acquired children will be able to focus more on reading for meaning. Certainly, without decoding skills children will not be able to understand text. The Simple View of Reading demonstrates that the skills of word recognition and those of language comprehension should be developed concurrently, even though the emphasis in the early stages of development should be on developing the skill of word recognition. Consequently, while children are focusing on decoding, you need to ensure that the development of their comprehension skills is not neglected. Strategies for developing reading comprehension will be explored later in this chapter.

It is at the emergent stage of reading that children start to interact with books and develop their interest in literature. In the early stages of emergent reading, children can often be observed pretending to read, drawing on their experiences of sharing books with adults as well as their knowledge of the concepts of print. This should be encouraged and valued. You should also provide children with opportunities to share books with one another.

CRITICAL QUESTIONS

* *How can you use concepts about print to support children's reading development?*
* *How important is the development of emergent reading skills?*

Development of auditory and phonological awareness

Before children develop their skills in phonemic awareness, they need to develop the skill of sound discrimination. Children will find it difficult to discriminate between phonemes if they are unable to discriminate between everyday sounds. The skills of auditory awareness (hearing sounds) and auditory discrimination (distinguishing between sounds) are crucial foundations for subsequent reading development.

The starting point for developing auditory skills is to focus on developing the skill of auditory attention. Children need to be able to identify when they hear an everyday sound by signalling that they have heard it. They need to be able to identify where sounds are coming from by pointing to the location of the sound. Once the skill of auditory attention is established, children need to be able to discriminate between everyday sounds. Although sounds can be grouped into broader categories (such as *animal* sounds or the sounds of *traffic*), they essentially need to be able to hear the differences between everyday sounds. Thus, children need to be able to distinguish between the sound of a car, motorbike, aeroplane, train, bicycle and so on. They need to be able to distinguish between the sounds made by various animals (pig, cow, dog, cat, sheep etc). Additionally, they need to be able to sort sounds into various categories (long/short sounds; high/low sounds). If children are able to discriminate between everyday sounds at an early stage in their development, they will find it easier to discriminate between phonemes at a later point in their development.

In addition to developing the skill of sound discrimination through exposure to everyday sounds, instrumental sound discrimination can be developed through simple activities using musical instruments. Children can identify the sounds of different musical instruments and they can categorise instrumental sounds into long and short sounds or high and low sounds. They can also explore different sounds through body percussion activities by experimenting with different sounds that their bodies can make.

Although much of this does not resemble 'reading' in the traditional sense, sound discrimination lays the foundations for subsequent phonemic awareness and phoneme discrimination. Children will struggle to discriminate between smaller units of sound (phonemes) if they cannot discriminate between everyday sounds. In developing the skill of phoneme discrimination, it is useful to consider this from a developmental perspective. Most phonics programmes immediately focus on encouraging children to hear and discriminate between sounds at the level of the phoneme from the start of the programme. However, from a developmental perspective this does not make sense. Developmentally, it is logical for children to identify and discriminate between larger 'chunks' of sound before being introduced to the smallest 'chunks' of sound. By asking them to immediately process sound at the level of the phoneme, phonics schemes do not take into account the fact that there is a developmental sequence which leads towards children working at the level of the phoneme. This sequence has been summarised in the following sections.

CRITICAL QUESTION

* *Why is general sound discrimination an important stage of development before the skill of phoneme discrimination?*

Compound word blending and segmenting

Children need the skill of blending to process words at the phoneme level. This is the skill of enunciating all the phonemes in order throughout a word and merging them together to read the target word. For writing, children also need the skill of segmenting. This is the skill of hearing the separate phonemes in a given word and representing these as graphemes for writing.

Before we ask children to blend sounds at the level of the phoneme (*d-o-g* to represent *dog*) or to segment words into constituent phonemes (segmenting *sun* into the phonemes *s-u-n*), a developmental perspective focuses on introducing *auditory* blending and segmenting at the whole word level.

Compound word auditory blending and segmenting is a good starting point for this. A compound word is a word made up of two discrete words. Thus, the word *hairbrush* is made up of *hair* and *brush*. Children find it relatively straightforward to blend *hair* and *brush* to produce the target word *hairbrush*. They often find it easy to segment *hairbrush* into the two constituent words *hair* and *brush.* Developing children's confidence in compound word blending and segmenting is a good starting point for developing the skills of blending and segmenting.

Developmentally, it is easier for children to process whole words than it is to process the smallest units of sound within a word. There are many compound words on which children can practise the skills of blending and segmenting. Examples include: *toothpaste*, *hotdog*, *sunshine*, *raindrop*, *bookcase* and you will be able to think of many others.

CRITICAL QUESTIONS

- *How might you draw on your understanding of compound word blending to support a child who has specific difficulties with blending at the syllable level?*
- *Do children who struggle with phoneme blending necessarily need more phonics? Explain your answer.*

Syllable blending and segmenting

Once children have mastered the skill of compound word auditory blending and segmenting at the whole word level, a developmental perspective focuses on developing these two skills with smaller sound units. The next meaningful sound level after whole words is the level of the syllable. Children can blend syllables together to generate whole words (auditory blending) and they can separate a whole word into the constituent syllables (auditory segmenting). It is easier to blend the syllables *win/dow* rather than blend the phonemes *w/i/n/d/ow* because there are fewer units of sound to process. Additionally, it is easier to blend *sun/flow/er* (syllable level) rather than *s/u/n/f/l/ow/er* (phoneme level). An effective way of teaching syllable segmentation is to encourage children to clap out the syllables in words.

CRITICAL QUESTION

- *How might you draw on your understanding of syllable blending to support a child who has specific difficulties with blending at the level of onset and rime?*

Onset and rime blending and segmenting

Once children have mastered the skill of syllable blending and segmenting, the next meaningful units of sound are the onsets and rimes within a word. The onset is the part of the word that comes before the vowel. The rime is the part of the word that includes the vowel and the rest of the word. Thus, in the word *boat* 'b' is the onset and 'oat' is the rime. When the word is separated into its onset and rime it can be represented as *b-oat.* From a developmental perspective, it is easier to blend the onset and rime rather than blending at the level of the phoneme because there are fewer units of sound to process. In the example given, it is easier to blend *b-oat* (two sound units) than blending three separate phonemes (*b-oa-t*). Developmentally, children are still processing sound at an auditory level at this stage.

In the early stages of reading development, children's memories are not fully developed. If children blend at the level of the phoneme they are required to hold a greater number of sound units in their memories before processing them. However, if they blend at the level of onset and rime, they only need to hold two sound units in their memories. In earlier stages of memory development, blending at the level of onset and rime is developmentally appropriate because there are fewer sound units to both retrieve from the memory and process.

CRITICAL QUESTION

* *How might you draw on your understanding of onset and rime blending to support a child who has specific difficulties with blending at the level of the phoneme?*

Phoneme blending and segmenting

From a developmental perspective, it is necessary to develop the memory to the point where children are able to memorise the sequence of multiple units of sound for the skill of phoneme blending. Once children are secure with auditory onset and rime blending and segmenting, it is developmentally appropriate to introduce them to phonemes. Thus, a child progresses from blending the phonemes *c-at* to blending *c-a-t*. After they have become proficient with processing larger units of sound, they can start to process sound at the phoneme level. A phoneme is the smallest meaningful unit of sound in a word. The skills which have been developed up to this point have been developed through an auditory approach. Children can now begin to practise the skill of auditory blending and segmenting at the phoneme level before introducing them to phoneme blending for reading and segmenting at the level of the phoneme for writing. Some children will struggle with phoneme blending and segmenting and may need further consolidation with onset and rime or syllable blending and segmenting before they work on phoneme blending and segmenting.

CRITICAL QUESTIONS

* *Many phonics schemes introduce auditory blending and segmenting at the level of the phoneme right from the start. Do you think this is appropriate? Explain your answer.*
* *Given the phonic irregularity of the English language is it better to teach children to process sound at the level of the phoneme or the level of the rime? Explain your answer.*

Rhyme awareness

Children who can hear rhyme at a very early age are likely to go on to become good readers. This is because children who can hear rhyme have good phonological awareness. They are able to 'tune into sound' and they are able to identify similarities and differences between the sounds they hear. Children with poor rhyme awareness are at risk of becoming poor readers. They need further exposure to rhyme through the use of rhyming stories, songs and rhyming games. This will help to develop their phonological awareness.

Rhyme awareness can be approached using a developmental perspective. Children progress from having no awareness of rhyme to some awareness of it. They subsequently start to detect rhyme (ie identify two rhyming words out of a set) before being able to generate rhyme (ie generate a different rhyming word from a string of rhyming words).

Odd one out or *rhyme identification* activities are useful ways of developing awareness of rhyme. This can initially be approached by presenting children with objects, before progressing onto miniature objects, photographs, line drawings and silhouettes.

CRITICAL QUESTIONS

* *Why is rhyme important in reading development?*
* *What might you do to support children who struggle to tune into rhyme?*

Development of visual attention

As well as auditory skills, children need good visual skills to be able to read. They also need a visual memory because they need to be able to hold graphemes in their memory and associate these with the correct phoneme. The development of visual memory can be addressed developmentally by focusing initially on developing the skill of visual attention. A child could be presented with an object such as an apple and asked to touch it. They might also be asked to point to the object or direct their eye-gaze towards it. Without the skill of visual attention, children will find it difficult to focus on looking at graphemes at a later stage when they start to learn phonics.

Development of visual discrimination

Once visual attention is secure, children subsequently need to develop the skill of visual discrimination. At a later point in their development, when they come to the task of reading they will be expected to discriminate between different graphemes that are represented on a page. They will find this difficult to do if the skill of visual discrimination is not established.

The starting point for developing the skill of visual discrimination is to present children with two objects such as a toy car and a toy bus. The child might be asked to point to the car and then the bus. The position of the objects could be swapped to provide additional challenge. This task can be made more complex by introducing children to more objects before asking them to identify one specific object.

Once visual discrimination is secure using objects, children can then be asked to visually discriminate between a set of photographs. This is more challenging because photographs are more abstract than objects. The skill of visual discrimination can then be developed using line drawings and silhouettes; this introduces children to increasing degrees of abstraction.

In developing the skill of visual discrimination, children can be introduced to *odd one out* activities. Initially this could be done through objects. Children could be presented with four objects, three of which are the same and one of which is different. They could be asked to identify the 'odd one out' from the set. The skill can then be developed by progressing to the use of photographs, line drawings and silhouettes, which are more abstract.

The skill of visual discrimination can be developed in many other ways. In mathematics children can be asked to sort plastic shapes into colours, then into shapes, sizes and properties. They might be asked to match two like objects. Teachers often think of these activities as mathematical tasks. While they do develop mathematical skills, they also develop the skill of visual discrimination which underpins reading development. Activities such as jigsaws develop not only motor skills but also skills in visual discrimination. We do not tend to think of jigsaws as a 'reading' activity but tend to focus on the role that jigsaws can play in developing children's physical development. However, one task can cut across many different areas of learning in the early years and therefore it is important to be able to identify the cross-curricular links.

Many areas of continuous provision in the early years provide children with silhouette outlines so that they can match objects to the outline silhouette. Often teachers provide silhouettes so that children know where to position objects. It aids their independence because they know where resources are kept and it helps them to tidy away their resources. However, providing children with silhouettes presents an opportunity to develop the skill of visual discrimination using abstract resources. Although such tasks are rarely considered as 'reading' activities, they provide children with an opportunity to develop their pre-reading skills and should therefore be considered as crucial in children's reading development.

CRITICAL QUESTIONS

- *Why is visual discrimination important in reading development?*
- *Look through the Early Years Foundation Stage framework. Is visual discrimination embedded within it as a key skill to be taught?*

Development of visual memory

Children need visual skills to become good readers. Although it is important to focus on the development of auditory skills, it is equally important to focus on the development of visual memory to enable children to retrieve visual information from their memory store. When a child is introduced to the letter shape 's' (grapheme), they will be taught the corresponding phoneme that this grapheme represents. This is often referred to as a grapheme-phoneme correspondence. The child is then expected to commit the grapheme to their memory, which enables them to select the appropriate grapheme in response to the corresponding phoneme.

Often insufficient consideration is given to development of visual memory. It is too easy to introduce children to visual information and to expect them to retrieve this without considering visual memory from a developmental perspective. Some children automatically have good visual memories. They receive visual information and are able to retrieve this with relative ease. However, many children have under-developed visual memories and this can impede progress when learning to read.

A starting point for developing visual memory is to use objects. Children can be presented with a series of objects which are randomly arranged. The objects are then covered and the child is asked to recall the objects that they have just seen. Another way of developing this skill is to present children with a familiar object such as a toy snowman. The snowman is dressed with a hat, scarf, sunglasses and gloves. The child is asked to remember what the snowman is wearing. The snowman is then hidden behind a screen and one item

of clothing is removed. The snowman is then presented again and the child is asked to identify the item of clothing that has been removed. In this way you can train children to develop a visual memory. You can make the task easier or more difficult by reducing or increasing the number of objects they are required to remember.

CRITICAL QUESTIONS

* *Why is visual memory important in reading development?*
* *Look through the Early Years Foundation Stage framework. Is development of visual memory embedded within it as a key skill to be taught?*

Development of visual sequential memory

Learning to read through a phonics approach is a time-limited skill. If children have to constantly sound out words, then this will reduce fluency and make reading an extremely laborious task. The aim of teaching reading is to develop children's automaticity in recognising printed words on a page. To achieve this aim, children require a visual sequential memory. They remember the specific order of the letters within a word; this enables them to say the word quickly and automatically. The development of a visual sequential memory will help them to remember the order of letters within a word, thus enabling them to match a printed word on a page to the same word in their visual memory. Children also need to develop a visual sequential memory for writing. When they learn to write a word, they have to remember the order of the letters within a word in order to spell the word correctly.

The use of objects is a good starting point for developing a visual sequential memory. A child could be introduced to two objects which are presented in a line. The objects could then be covered with a cloth and the child could be asked to identify the objects starting from the object on the left. The number of objects could gradually be increased as children's visual sequential memories develop. When the objects are covered with a cloth, the child is asked to remember the objects and their order, moving through from left to right.

CRITICAL QUESTIONS

* *Why is visual sequential memory important in reading development?*
* *Look through the Early Years Foundation Stage framework. Is visual sequential memory embedded within it as a key skill to be taught?*

Theories of reading development

Theories of reading development help us to understand more clearly how children learn to recognise the printed word. Ehri's model of reading development (Ehri, 1995) demonstrates how children progress through a series of phases to become confident readers. The phases are briefly summarised on pages 72–73.

IN PRACTICE

In school carry out a one-to-one reading conference with specific children. Try to identify what phase children are operating at within Ehri's model. Once you have identified this for each child, think about how you will support them to move on to the next phase.

Supporting children with reading difficulties

While working with children, you will quickly identify those who have reading difficulties. Doing so is simply discovering the tip of the iceberg. Children will encounter difficulties in their reading for many different reasons and it is your responsibility to quickly identify exactly what these difficulties are to enable you to address them effectively. Using the Simple View of Reading as an assessment tool is an effective way of identifying where the difficulty lies. Children experience problems with word recognition (blending/sight vocabulary) or with language comprehension, or both of these skills. Once you have identified the difficulty encountered by a child, you are then able to focus on planning appropriate interventions to address the challenge. When assessing children's reading it is essential that you consider the following aspects:

- phonological awareness: awareness of rhyme, alliteration, rhythm and syllables;
- an awareness of onset and rime;
- identifying a variety of units of sound within words which are precursors to subsequent phonemic awareness;
- phonemic awareness: the ability to identify and manipulate the phonemes in spoken words in sequence. This includes the ability to make grapheme-phoneme correspondences as well as blending and segmenting;
- sight word recognition: this includes sight recognition of tricky words;
- concepts about print: these include, orientation of the book; understanding that print rather than pictures carry the message; direction of the print; line sequence; page sequence; the function of punctuation; and an understanding of frequently used vocabulary, including *beginning*, *middle* and *end*;
- an inability to distinguish between similar graphemes, which could include *d* and *b* or *g* and *q*;
- an ability to decode print but an inability to understand its meaning.

A highly kinaesthetic approach to enable children to develop the skills of grapheme-phoneme correspondence, as well as the skills for blending and segmenting, is recommended. Be aware that some children may not be ready for developing phonemic awareness because the building blocks for doing so may not be in place. In this instance you should focus on further developing children's phonological awareness or general sound discrimination skills.

Before children can become confident and effective readers they must have mastered the alphabetic code. This can be more challenging for some children than others and it will be necessary for you to recognise this and set the pace accordingly. Drawing on the work of Broomfield and Combley (2003), I support their approach for introducing children to grapheme-phoneme correspondences. The basic approach includes the following steps:

- **see:** children need to see both upper and lower case versions of the letter and to understand that both these letters share the same sound;

- **hear:** children need to hear the sound which corresponds with the grapheme they are learning. Children must also be able to identify a sound in various positions in different words. An example of this is to identify the 'p' sound in the spoken words *pig*, *cap*, *happy*: They must note whether the sound comes at the beginning, middle or end of the word;
- **say:** children must say the sound. To support them in doing so, the sound must be articulated correctly by the teacher;
- **write:** children should be able to write the grapheme, using a range of media and multi-sensory approaches.

As children begin to make grapheme-phoneme correspondences they can be introduced to blending and segmenting. Again, multi-sensory approaches should be employed. These could include introducing children to writing in glitter, in the air or with water. Children who are encountering ongoing problems with reading will need to overlearn grapheme-phoneme correspondences. Broomfield and Combley (2003) recommend daily routines which are familiar to children, including a pack of reading cards with which they practise grapheme-phoneme correspondences every day. Each reading card should include:

- upper and lower case versions of the letter on the front of the card;
- a word containing a clear example of the letter-sound link and a corresponding picture on the back of the card. For example, *sun*/s/ with a picture of the sun.

The picture is used as a cue for the child to identify the word and then the target sound. Because children use these cards every day their skills confidence will develop and they will develop automatic recognition of grapheme-phoneme correspondence. It is important that children do not experience a sense of failure. This can be avoided by ensuring that when they encounter difficulties with a specific grapheme-phoneme correspondence, this is included within a group of known grapheme-phoneme correspondences. Once children have developed a bank of known grapheme-phoneme correspondences, these can be used in games such as *Snap*. It is important that children see and hear the phoneme and then trace the corresponding grapheme at the same time as saying the phoneme. This multi-sensory approach will deeply embed the learning.

Once a child has developed grapheme-phoneme correspondence in relation to the full alphabet, it can be helpful to present the alphabet to them as an arc. On a daily basis they can, initially, be asked to remove a given grapheme from the arc and place it underneath the alphabet arc. Once they can confidently achieve this for all graphemes you can then engage them in selecting the graphemes to build words below the alphabet arc. Each day you will focus on a specific grapheme. This will be placed in the centre of the arc and remain there throughout the lesson. All word building must relate to this grapheme. For example, if the target grapheme is 'g' the child could be asked to add further graphemes to build the words: *got*, *rag*, *again*, *gift*, *flag* and *grin*. Ensure that the target words given to children are always within their phonic knowledge.

Paired reading with the teacher as well as with peers can develop children's confidence with reading. A text can be shared between two people and used in a range of ways which may include: taking turns to read a page of the text while both are following the text; the more confident reader beginning to read the text and the other child indicating when they feel confident enough to take over the role as reader. The children may also wish to read together at the same time.

There are several other interventions available to support children who are encountering difficulties with reading. An example of this is Reading Recovery. Be mindful of using an intervention that appropriately meets the needs of the child you are supporting. Delivering many of these interventions requires training and it is essential that you ensure that interventions are delivered by trained colleagues only.

You should carefully consider your choice of texts and match these carefully to the needs and interests of each child. Simple texts are usually suitable for young children. However, an older child may need to develop similar skills to his younger peers but would clearly not enjoy reading the same text. Choosing simple texts to meet the learning needs of older children requires very careful consideration. The wrong text choice can quickly result in an older child becoming disengaged with reading.

Writing development

Over twenty years ago, Nicholls et al (1989) produced a theoretical framework for the stages of development in writing. The levels within this framework do not relate to national curriculum levels of achievement but the model is a useful framework which will help you to understand how children's writing develops. The stages in the model are summarised in the table below:

Table 5.1 A model of writing development (adapted from Nicholls et al, 1989)

Stage of development in writing	Characteristics of children's writing	What you can do to support children's development
Level 1: Orientation towards writing	* Scribble text – exploring the possibilities of mark-making implements. * Scribble which incorporates invented symbols. * Scribble and drawings. * Scribbles/drawings and recognisable letters and numbers. * Whole words incorporated into scribbles/drawings or random letters.	* Value children's attempts at writing and encourage them to read it to you. * Focus on helping the children to understand the difference between a word and a picture. * Observe children writing to see if they can control the writing implement; work from left to right; leave spaces between words; write some high-frequency words and use knowledge of grapheme-phoneme correspondences to write simple words, focusing on use of initial sound. Use observations to inform planning.
Level 2: Early text making	* Writing which children can read to the teacher. This writing includes some conventional letters.	* Model segmentation during shared writing. * Model spacing between words. * Model letter formation. * Teach a bank of sight words and ask children to practise writing these. * Develop understanding of a sentence.

(*Continued*)

Table 5.1 (Continued)

Stage of development in writing	Characteristics of children's writing	What you can do to support children's development
Level 3: Initial independent writing	* Simple texts which can be partly read by others. * Ability to organise words into sentences. * Ability to spell some familiar words using knowledge of sound and sight recognition.	* Model uses of punctuation in shared reading and writing. * Model linking sentences in shared reading and writing. * Extend repertoire of spellings.
Level 4: Associate writing	* Accurate and fluent texts. * Use of punctuation. * Use of conventional spelling patterns. * Ability to link sentences.	* Model the features of different text types. * In shared and guided reading, expose children to different genres. * In shared writing, model composition of different text types. * Teach complex sentences.
Beyond level 4	* Texts using the structural and language features of different genres. * More complex sentences.	* Model the process of drafting, editing, re-drafting.

Emergent writing

Children must acquire controlled gross motor skills as a pre-requisite to the fine motor skills needed to become effective writers. It is essential that you assess the development of each child's gross motor skills and engage them in activities to further develop these as is necessary. Ensure that such activities are enjoyable and provide children with a range of opportunities to practise their gross motor movements. These activities could include:

* the use of ribbon sticks using one hand – most children will select their dominant hand;
* the use of ribbon sticks using two hands;
* using broad brushes and paints to make marks using one hand and then two hands;
* using chunky chalks to make marks;
* making patterns in the air with one hand, then two hands, then with a finger – patterns could be free movements in response to music and then could become more refined using shapes;
* using sticks or fingers to make marks in sand, glitter, soil or gravel.

Once children are using controlled gross motor movements you can now begin to focus on developing their fine motor skills. Initially you must not be pressurised into rushing the children into using pencils and paper to make marks, although these should be available. Fine motor skills can be developed, for example, using tweezers in a range of sizes to pick up objects of various sizes. Children can be gradually introduced to manipulating and building with simple construction materials with smaller components. Threading various sized beads onto laces is also another excellent way of developing fine motor skills.

Children need to be introduced to a wide range of mark-making materials and they need opportunities to explore how to use these. You should work alongside children to model the ways in which the different mark-making tools can be used. Children's exposure to these tools will lead to them developing greater control in the use of them.

During the emergent stage of writing many children start to view themselves as 'writers'. This should be encouraged and celebrated. Children do not follow a clear developmental path as they learn to write. You may see many but not all of the following characteristics in children's early attempts as 'writers':

* random marks;
* simple drawings, showing increasing control;
* combination of drawings and marks and/or recognisable graphemes;
* repeated patterns;
* attempts to copy features of writing they have seen, including lists and lines of writing;
* the appearance of recognisable but random letters or graphemes;
* letters from their own names;
* an emerging ability to produce graphemes and articulate the corresponding phoneme;
* inconsistent letter formation and mixed upper and lower case letters;
* children's attempts to 'read' what they have written and ascribe meaning to their marks;
* a developing understanding that in English print is written and read from left to right and top to bottom.

At this stage you need to work alongside children to model the different purposes for writing. All areas of provision in the setting should offer opportunities for children to mark-make and write and your role in scaffolding these skills cannot be overstated. Children need to see you as a writer and you need to demonstrate the purposes of writing within different contexts. At this stage children are clearly 'writers' and it is your responsibility to further develop these skills. Children's attempts at mark-making provide evidence of their development in writing. When you are in school you should collect and carefully analyse the independent writing that children have produced and use this as a basis for planning the next steps in learning for each child.

Children will continue to benefit from working alongside adults to further develop their skills as writers. These should include:

* effectively holding a writing implement;
* writing their own name using upper and lower case letters appropriately;
* learning to form letters correctly.

Emergent writing is the foundation for developing children's self-concept and confidence about being a writer. It is vital that their development is nurtured and celebrated. Much damage can be done if children's early attempts at writing are devalued. Disregarding children's early independent attempts to write can have significant and long-lasting effects on their subsequent attitudes towards writing.

Writing words and labels

As children become more competent and develop their understanding of phoneme-grapheme correspondence, opportunities should be created for them to write simple regular words. If they are supported and encouraged they should be able to make more phonetically plausible attempts at more complex words. It is at this stage that you

should be able to create purposes to enable them to apply these newly acquired skills. A purposeful 'in-road' into encouraging children to write words at this stage of their development is to introduce labels. There must be a clear purpose for the labels which could include:

- labelling objects for an interactive display;
- labelling classroom resources;
- labelling models that they have made;
- scientific labels relating to materials – shiny, dull, wood, metal, plastic etc.

It is important to draw children's attention to labels on display in the learning environment so that they begin to develop an awareness of their purpose.

Phonics lessons will have introduced the children to some exception words. These are the only words that need to be displayed and accessible to the children. They should be encouraged to make phonetically plausible attempts to write and read all other words. Encouraging them to do so will offer you an invaluable insight into children's achievements and future learning needs.

Children's attempts at writing words will vary enormously. Some may write single letters. Others will write groups of letters and some letters may be omitted. These attempts will enable you to assess each child's ability to hear the order of the phonemes in each word and to offer targeted support in this area.

Writing captions

The learning environment should include simple captions which convey meaning to the children and wherever possible should be derived from the children's current phonic knowledge. Again, children's attention must be drawn to these captions. They should not be seen as wallpaper and their meaning and purpose must be clear. Children need to see adults writing captions. This can be achieved through shared writing as well as working alongside children. Displays of children's work relating to current learning often provide an effective stimulus for writing captions. Ideas from the children should be encouraged and the caption should initially be written by the practitioner with the children as a shared writing opportunity.

Phonics lessons provide an opportunity for children to write simple captions created and spoken by you. These should relate directly to the focus of the lesson.

Children's independent attempts at writing captions should be encouraged. They will independently write captions in the mark-making area as well as other areas of provision. Additionally, children might write captions for classroom displays or class books. They also enjoy adding captions to their own drawings.

Writing a sentence

Initially you will have to model a process which will support children in writing a simple sentence. This can be done through shared writing and you may find the following steps helpful:

Think it – model thinking of a sentence in your head.

Say it – say the sentence out loud several times and ask the children to check for meaning.

Write it – encourage the children to support you in writing the words in the correct order.

Read it – to check that the written sentence matches the spoken sentence.

In shared writing, children's contributions to the writing process should be sought. Children can be challenged to think of their own sentence and you can scribe this with their support. You can dictate simple sentences during your phonics lessons and challenge children to make attempts at writing them down. These sentences must relate to the stage of the alphabetic code that has been taught.

Some children may struggle to develop their understanding of a sentence needing to make sense. To support them in developing this understanding you can support them in reading a simple sentence. You can then present the same sentence to them as single words which they must then re-order. It is a useful activity to demonstrate that when the words are in the wrong order no meaning can be derived from the sentence.

Sentences should be displayed in the learning environment and there should always be opportunities for children to write independently. With plenty of opportunities for children to develop their early writing skills through guided and shared writing, they should begin to develop the confidence to write simple sentences independently. These attempts should be valued and they will also provide you with an assessment opportunity to identify their next steps. These next steps will become a focus for guided and shared work in the immediate future. Children need to be involved in assessing their own sentences against clear success criteria. These may include leaving spaces between each word in a sentence, demarcating sentences with a capital letter and a full stop, and ensuring that the sentence makes sense. Success criteria will vary from child to child and many children will not be able to focus on more than one criterion at a time. Children should be reminded about their personal writing targets before they start to write and they should be given the opportunity to evaluate their work against these. You should praise the child's attempts and feedback should be focused and relate to the success criteria. You should then communicate 'next steps' to the children.

Supporting children with writing difficulties

I have often found that children apply their phonic knowledge and skills to reading before they apply them to writing. Therefore, writing may develop at a slower pace to reading. To address this discrepancy children must have access to a structured writing programme. This can effectively be devised by the teacher to support them in developing the confidence and skills to apply their phonic knowledge to the writing process. You may find the following strategies helpful in supporting children to develop the confidence and ability to apply their phonic knowledge in writing:

- modelling of the writing process through shared writing opportunities;
- engaging children in dictation activities matched to the child's phonic knowledge: through the process of dictation children can write words, captions and sentences;
- engaging them in regular opportunities to segment words into their constituent graphemes through multi-sensory approaches: writing in sand, salt and glitter;
- planning explicit teaching of the spelling of exception words: this could include introducing children to the strategy of looking at the exception word, tracing over the letters with highlighters, chalks or the finger, copying the word and finally writing it from memory. You will need to engage the children

in further opportunities to read and write the exception word. You should also make the spelling of the word a focus and address any misspellings of it in the children's independent writing only after it has been taught. As the children read you should also draw their attention to the word as it appears within text;

* accessing alphabet mats: to support the children's independent writing;
* accessing exception word mats: to support the children's independent writing;
* drawing on interests and experiences to ensure that they have a clear context and purpose for writing;
* supporting children with sentence structure: reassembling single words to create a sentence. This supports children in understanding the sense of a sentence through 'unjumbling sentences';
* engaging them in oral rehearsal before writing;
* introducing clear writing frames will support children who are familiar with a range of genres but require support and guidance on the structural and language features of each genre. Mind maps and planning templates are useful resources.

Before writing children must have had prior experiences on which they can draw. They must be familiar with a range of children's literature. Broad experiences of literature will provide them with a good foundation for taking and then adapting what they have heard, experienced and read. Drama is an effective tool for engaging children in experiencing text and cross-curricular work. Children can draw upon the ideas they have developed in drama lessons and use these in their own written work. It is important that you provide all children with positive feedback about their written work in order to engender a positive self-concept. Feedback should be focused and developmental by focusing on one specific target that the child should address in future work. Subsequent progress should be monitored against this target. In this way small steps become big strides in a child's development.

Development in spelling

Henderson (1985) has established a theory of development which suggests that children move through a sequence of phases as they develop their skills in spelling. Initially children's development in spelling is pre-phonetic and is characterised by simple mark-making. Children then progress through a semi-phonetic phase where they represent some of the phonemes within words with the corresponding graphemes. Children progress to the phonetic stage where simple consonant-vowel-consonant words are written correctly but they do not yet understand all spelling patterns. During the more advanced stages of spelling development in this model, children start to develop an understanding of larger units of sound within words as well as understanding prefixes, suffixes and the ability to apply more complex spelling rules.

Behaviourist theories

Behaviourist theory is based on the principle of reward and sanction. The premise is that if learners are rewarded for good behaviour they will be likely to repeat it. If learners are sanctioned for poor behaviour they will be unlikely to repeat it. B F Skinner is one of the most well-known behaviourist theorists. The theory assumes that educators can condition learners into adopting specific types of desirable behaviour and through punishments it is possible to eradicate unwanted behaviour.

The use of praise in the classroom is based on behaviourist theory. However, as a teacher it is important for you to remember that 'empty' praise can have a negative effect on learners' behaviour. If you praise children for everything they do, especially at times when they have applied little or no effort to complete a task, then you run the risk of children either becoming immune to the praise or applying limited or no effort in the future in the knowledge that they will be praised regardless of the effort they have put in.

Praise is most effective when it is richly deserved. That is, when children have persevered with a task despite it being difficult. It is important to reward effort as well as ability. Some very able children might not have to work very hard to produce excellent work and this raises the question of whether or not they should receive praise for their efforts. In this respect, praise is more deceptive than it would initially seem. Vague praise is also ineffective. This is when children are provided with a general comment such as 'brilliant work' but they not know why a piece of work is so good.

IN PRACTICE

Positive descriptive praise communicates to learners specifically why they are being praised. If you observe Abdul helping Fred with a mathematics problem, then you might say '*Thank you Abdul for explaining that problem for Fred. I like how you encouraged him to think it through rather than doing it for him*'. This is an example of positive, descriptive praise.

In your classroom it is important that you praise children for demonstrating good attitudes to learning. You might praise a child for persevering with a problem even though they got the answer wrong. You might praise them for collaborating with their peers. You might notice that they appear to be 'stuck' on a task but they use a specific resource in the classroom to help them overcome the problem. If you praise good learning behaviour then there is more chance that children will repeat it. We sometimes assume that children automatically know how a good learner operates. Often they do not know what good learning looks like. As a teacher you can break this down for them by noticing and praising good learning behaviour.

Rewards

The use of reward systems in classrooms is underpinned by behaviourist theory. You may be in a school which has a policy of not issuing children with tangible rewards. This might arise from the assumption that the use of rewards can promote *extrinsic motivation*. If children are extrinsically motivated by a task, the only reason for their motivation is because they know that they will receive a reward once they have completed the task. However, in contrast, if children are *intrinsically motivated* to complete a task they are motivated not because of an extrinsic reward but because they enjoy the task and they experience a sense of accomplishment when the task has been completed.

You may be in a school that has a clear rewards and sanctions system. This might be a whole-class system for rewarding good behaviour and there are many variations of such a system. However, in addition to whole class reward systems some children benefit from individual reward systems which are understood between the child and the teacher. This model might be used if the child has a behaviour plan or if some specific behaviour targets have been negotiated with the child.

CRITICAL QUESTIONS

* *Some schools have a policy of only implementing praise but not implementing sanctions. Explain your views on this policy.*
* *How effective do you think sanctions are in primary schools? Link your answer to the practice you have observed.*
* *How effective do you think whole class reward systems (eg house points/table points) are? Explain your answer.*
* *Some schools have a policy of not implementing tangible rewards (eg stickers, gold stars and 'goody' bags). What are your views on this policy? Explain your answer.*
* *Should rewards be removed if a child has been previously issued a reward and then subsequently behaved inappropriately. Explain your answer.*
* *Is extrinsic motivation a bad thing? Explain your answer.*
* *Is intrinsic motivation the only acceptable type of motivation?*

Constructivist theories

Vygotsky

Constructivist theories of learning are built on the premise that children construct their own understanding as a result of their interaction with the world. Important constructivist theorists include Vygotsky and Piaget.

Vygotsky is considered to be a socio-constructivist. He was a Russian psychologist and his writings were produced in the early part of the twentieth century. His ideas have been transmitted through translations of his work. Vygotsky believed that children's learning is enhanced through the process of social interaction. He saw the role of social interaction as critical to the development of learning and one of his most widely cited concepts is his *zone of proximal development (ZPD)*. Vygotsky defined the distance between a child's actual level of development and their potential development as the ZPD. When children are operating within this zone they are working at a level of development higher than their actual developmental level. In this zone children are cognitively challenged to achieve a higher level of development. Vygotsky argued that with the support of a more-able other, which could be a peer or an adult, children can move through their own ZPD to achieve their potential level of development. This is often referred to as the *proximal* level. Children are all individual. They have different starting points (actual level of development) and different potential levels of development. Their ZPDs differ but the important point that Vygotsky emphasised is that all children are able to progress with the support of someone who is more knowledgeable and skilled.

IN PRACTICE

Vygotsky's theory and the work of other socio-constructivists has important implications for classroom practice. Much peer-peer learning, group work and collaboration is based on socio-constructivist theories. The ZPD is also an important concept for teachers because it helps you to understand that you need to plan learning experiences at a level above the level at which a child is operating. This will ensure that your learners are challenged and making progress. If the learning is too easy, children will not progress beyond their actual level of development. If the work is too challenging and children are not appropriately supported, then they will not progress through the ZPD. His theory is also useful in relation to informing ways of pairing or grouping children. If children are paired in mixed-ability pairs or work in mixed-ability groups, they can receive support from a more-able peer. In this case, they might not need help from a teacher. If children are paired or grouped in ability pairs or groups, they will require the support of a more-able adult to help them move through their ZPD.

CRITICAL QUESTIONS

- *What are the advantages of mixed-ability pairings or groups?*
- *What are the disadvantages of mixed-ability pairings or groups?*
- *Vygotsky's theory assumes that learning leads to development. Thus, through processes such as interaction with a more-able other and therefore through the process of learning, children's development advances. How is this different from theories which assume that children cannot learn something until they are ready to do so?*

Bruner and scaffolding

Bruner's work on scaffolding theory has been influential in terms of helping teachers and peers to know *how* to support children to move through their zones of proximal development. Bruner was also a socio-constructivist and he developed a framework through which children can be supported to move from their actual level of development to their proximal level. To help you understand the scaffolding process, think of the relationship between physical scaffolding and a building. When the building is developing, the scaffolding holds it up. However, when the building is strong enough to stand up by itself then the scaffolding can be removed. Now translate this to children who are developing new knowledge, skills and understanding. Initially the new learning is challenging for them because they are operating within their ZPD. At this stage they will need support from someone who is more able than them to help them learn the new knowledge, skills or develop the new understanding. After a while they will become confident and they will reach a higher level of development. Eventually the scaffolding (support) can be removed and children can operate on their own.

Critically for teachers (and more able peers), the process of how to provide support (scaffolding) is important to consider. Doing the work for someone will not help that person to reach a higher level of development. If children are to reach a higher level of development they will ultimately need to be able to demonstrate the new knowledge, skill or understanding independently. In order to do this they need opportunities to practise the new learning. There is a real danger that well-meaning more able 'others' may impede development by providing too much help or by doing the work for someone.

It would seem logical that when providing support to enable a child to reach a higher level of development, the process of scaffolding should start with a process of *modelling*. In effect, this means that the knowledge, skill or concept is explained and, where appropriate, demonstrated to the child. After this initial stage the child needs an opportunity to practice the new learning *with* a more-able adult or peer, perhaps through a process of

joint working. The amount of support can then gradually be withdrawn. Eventually, when the child is confident the support can be withdrawn altogether, thus enabling the child to operate independently.

CRITICAL QUESTIONS

* *What are the dangers of over-modelling? Explain your answer.*
* *What are the implications of over-modelling by teaching assistants?*
* *What are the dangers of moving children on too quickly to the next stage of development?*

EXTENDED THINKING

* *There is currently a focus in schools on learners developing 'mastery' in a specific strand of learning before progressing them to the next stage of development. What are the advantages of this approach? What are the disadvantages? Explain your answer.*

Bruner is also well-known for his model of the spiral curriculum. Bruner believed that children learn progressively by revisiting previous learning. His assumption was that learning is like a spiral. Concepts that have previously been taught are re-visited and developed at a higher level to advance learning. The national curriculum resembles a spiral curriculum in that specific concepts are revisited each year but developed at a higher level. The spiral curriculum assumes that there is need to revisit learning before developing learning at the next level.

Piaget

Piaget essentially believed that children actively construct their own understandings through interactions with the environment. He believed that children develop 'schemas' as a result of their learning experience. This is essentially a working theory based on their prior experiences. When children encounter new experiences this results in a state of disequilibrium. This means that children initially cannot make sense of the new experience because it does not fit into their existing schemas. The child has to then adapt the existing schema to accommodate the new learning that has occurred.

EVIDENCE-BASED TEACHING

Piaget is perhaps best known for his ages and stages theory of child development. His model assumes that learning takes place through a set of linear stages. As children develop they move from one stage to another. The stages are summarised below:

Sensorimotor stage: from birth to age two. The children experience the world through movement and their five senses. During the sensorimotor stage children are extremely egocentric.

Preoperational stage: from ages two years to seven. Children cannot conserve or use logical thinking at this stage.

Concrete operational stage: from ages seven to eleven. Children can now conserve and think logically but only with practical aids. Children learn concepts through interacting with physical resources at this stage.

Formal operational stage: from ages eleven to sixteen and onwards (development of abstract reasoning). Children develop abstract thought and can easily conserve and think logically in their mind.The skill of conservation relates to a child's ability to see that some properties are conserved after an object undergoes physical transformation. For example, I can arrange six counters in a line but space them out. I can then arrange six counters on a second line underneath that line but reduce the length of the line by touching the counters. If I have the skill of conservation I know that there are the same number of counters.

EVALUATE

* *What are the strengths and limitations of Piaget's theory?*

CHALLENGE

* *Piaget assumed that children cannot learn until they are ready to do so. Do you agree?*

APPLY

* *Piaget's theory emphasises the importance of children constructing their own understandings. When you next go into school observe children and find examples of children taking responsibility for their own learning. Collect examples of teacher-led learning. Could this have been planned differently to give children greater opportunities to take responsibility for their own learning?*

CRITICAL QUESTIONS

* *Do you agree that children's development is linear?*
* *What are the implications of Piaget's theory for education?*
* *How does Piaget's stage model differ from Bruner's spiral curriculum?*

EXTENDED THINKING

* *Piaget's theory assumes that children cannot learn specific things until they have developed a readiness to learn. Thus, development leads to learning. What are your views on this? What are the implications of this theory for education?*

Current perspectives on development

A lot of the research on child development has been polarised in relation to whether children's development is a product of the environment or a product of their genetic make-up. Current perspectives on child development now adopt a biopsychosocial systems model which acknowledges the inter-relationship and inter-dependence between genes and the environment (Wyse and Rogers, 2016). Thus, the biological make-up and the environmental factors work together and are inter-dependent. In other words, each affects the development of the other. There is always an inter-relationship between the environmental influences which we are exposed to and the biological structure of the brain. Children can be born with developed neuro-systems but environmental influences can affect the structure of the brain. The structures in the brain are malleable. They are susceptible to environmental effects and thus there is an inter-relationship and inter-dependence between genes and the environment.

EXTENDED THINKING

- *To what extent does the education system today, with its focus on attainment, ignore theories of learning?*

Mathematical development

Constructivist and socio-constructivist theories are incredibly useful in informing our understanding about how children learn in mathematics. Piaget's concrete operations stage helps us to understand how children are not capable of learning abstract concepts at this stage in their development. They need to use concrete resources initially to develop their mathematical knowledge and understanding. Children in the early years and Key Stage 1 will need access to a variety of resources to support their mathematical understanding. These include access to counters, number lines, tens and units apparatus, hundred squares, numicon and so on.

In the early stages of their mathematical development children do not understand what ¾ or ½ means. They need to see it represented in a visual way and they need practical opportunities to cut cakes and chocolate bars into various fractions. They need to see a visual representation of equivalent fractions, for example, two quarters is equivalent to one half. When they are exploring money they need to handle and manipulate coins. When they are exploring properties of shapes they need opportunities to see, touch and handle shapes. I am using examples to illustrate a very basic point – children learn from concrete experiences. There is a risk that children's mathematical understanding will not be supported if practical resources are taken away too soon. My view is that if children need to continue using practical equipment to support their mathematical knowledge and understanding into Key Stage 2 they should be allowed to do so. Children cannot move into abstract thinking until they have developed their mathematical understanding using concrete resources.

CRITICAL QUESTION

- *Look at the programmes of study in the mathematics national curriculum, particularly in Years 2, 3 and 4. Can you identify aspects of the curriculum which require abstract thought?*

EVIDENCE-BASED TEACHING

Children's development in learning to count

If you are working in the early years or with children who are struggling to master the skill of counting, a developmental perspective on counting will enable you to support them more effectively. Gelman and Gallistel put forward the following five principles that support counting. You can use this framework to identify the stage of development that children have reached and you can move backwards and forwards to earlier or later stages of development to support the needs of specific children.

The one-one principle

This involves the assigning of one counting word to each of the items to be counted. To follow this principle, a child has to be able to partition and repartition the collection of objects to be counted into two categories: those that have been allocated a number name and those that have not. You will often observe children counting an object twice, thus assigning two number names to the same object. This child cannot have grasped the one-one principle which relies on the child touching one object and assigning one number name to it.

The stable-order principle

The stable-order principle requires children to count a set of objects using a stable set of number names. Thus, a child who repeatedly counts five objects using the number names 1, 2, 3, 4 and 5 has grasped the stable-order principle. They know that there is a set order to the number names and they use this order consistently for different sets of objects. A child who counts five objects using the names 1, 2, 3, 4, 5 and then counts a second set of five objects using 3, 2, 1, 4, 5 has not grasped the stable-order principle.

The cardinal principle

This principle says that, on the condition that the one-one and stable-order principles have been followed, the number name allocated to the final object in a collection represents the total number of items in that collection. When a child has grasped this principle they are able to appreciate that the final number name is different from the earlier ones in that it not only 'names' the final object, signalling the end of the count, but also tells you how many objects have been counted.

The abstraction principle

To understand this principle, children need to appreciate that they can count non-physical things such as sounds. Thus, if they closed their eyes and listened to coins dropping into a jar they would be able to count the coins from the sound of the dropping coin. This is a more advanced stage of counting because prior to this stage young children need to count physical objects. This makes their counting more accurate because they are able to partition a set of objects into two groups, ie those that have been counted and those that are still left to be counted.

The order-irrelevance principle

This principle refers to the knowledge that the order in which items are counted is irrelevant. It does not really matter whether the counting procedure is carried out from left to right, from right to left or from somewhere else, so long as every item in the collection is counted once and only once.

(Thompson, n.d.)

EVALUATE

* *Does this theory of counting seem logical to you? Support your answers.*

CHALLENGE

* *Do children who are mathematically gifted need to progress through each stage of this model?*

APPLY

* *In school observe some children counting. What stage of development are they at in relation to Gelman and Gallistel's model?*

IN PRACTICE

- *Think carefully about the activities you might use to move a child from one stage of this model to another.*

CRITICAL QUESTIONS

- *Look at the mathematics strand of the EYFS framework. Locate the strand on counting. Does it address the principles in this model?*
- *Place value and problem-solving are aspects of mathematics which result in children demonstrating misconceptions, particularly when they start to use column addition and subtraction. Piaget stated that children go through a concrete operational stage up to the age of 11, which would suggest that children need access to mathematical resources to develop their understanding of the value of digits in numbers. However, the national curriculum introduces children to column addition and abstract problem-solving much earlier than the age of 11. Is this appropriate given what we know about child development theory?*

TECHNOLOGY

Technology is changing how children develop. Children now have access to information immediately, both in school and at home. They can access knowledge from anywhere and this fundamentally has implications for the role of the teacher. It is clear that teachers can no longer just deliver knowledge to their classes. Children can access knowledge through the internet and through interacting with software; this is a good example of constructivism in practice. Whether technology has harmful effects on children's development is a matter for debate. Children can certainly develop through their interactions with technology but there may be times when interactions with technology can have a detrimental effect.

CRITICAL QUESTIONS

- *Is there a danger that internet exposure can result in information overload?*
- *Do theories of child development need to be modified to take into account technological advances? Explain your answer.*

Critical reflections

This chapter has introduced you both to theories of child development and practical applications. I have emphasised the need to understand specific stages of development in areas such as reading, writing and mathematics. This practical understanding of child development will help you in the classroom because it enables you to support children through specific misconceptions and to advance development further. However, a theoretical understanding of child development is important because this provides a rationale for your practice in terms of why you teach in the way you do. No one theory of child development can sufficiently explain how children learn. Children are complex beings and learning is a complex process. It is likely that you will draw on all theories at different times in your practice. No one theory is sufficient by itself and therefore no one teaching strategy is appropriate. The theories of learning will provide you with valuable tools to place in your teacher toolkit. You will draw on different tools at different times to support children's learning.

KEY READINGS

Classic:

Keenan, T (2002) *An Introduction to Child Development*. London: Sage.

Contemporary:

Wyse, D and Rogers, S (2016) *A Guide to Early Years and Primary Teaching*. London: Sage.

References

Broomfield, H and Combley, M (2003) *Overcoming Dyslexia: A Practical Handbook for the Classroom*. London: Whurr Publishers.

Carter, A (2015) *Review of Initial Teacher Training*. London: DfE.

Department for Education (DfE) (2012) *Development Matters in the Early Years Foundation Stage*. London: DfE.

Ehri, L C (1995) Phases of development in learning to read words by sight. *Journal of Research in Reading*, 18(2): 116–25.

Gelman, R and Gallistel, C (1978) *The Child's Understanding of Number*. Cambridge, MA: Harvard University Press.

Henderson, E (1985) *Teaching Spelling*. Boston: Houghton Mifflin.

Nicholls, J, Bauers, A, Pettitt, D, Redgwell, V, Seaman, E and Watson, G (1989) *Beginning Writing*. Milton Keynes: Open University Press.

Palaiologou, I (2010) Communication, language and literacy, in Palaiologou, I (ed) *The Early Years Foundation Stage: Theory and Practice*. London: Sage, pp 138–52.

The Communication Trust (n.d.) *Let's Talk About It: What New Teachers Need to Know about Children's Communication Skills*. London: The Communication Trust. [online] Available at: www.thecommunicationtrust.org.uk/media/12285/let_s_talk_about_it_-_final.pdf (accessed 15 May 2016).

Thompson, I (n.d.) *The Principal Counting Principles*. Available at: www.ncetm.org.uk/public/files/712850/The+principal+counting+principles.pdf (accessed 15 May 2016).

6: PLANNING AND DIFFERENTIATION

TEACHERS' STANDARDS

This chapter addresses the following Teachers' Standards:

Teachers' Standard 4: Plan and teach well-structured lessons

Teachers must:

* *impart knowledge and develop understanding through effective use of lesson time;*
* *promote a love of learning and children's intellectual curiosity;*
* *set homework and plan other out-of-class activities to consolidate and extend the knowledge and understanding pupils have acquired;*
* *reflect systematically on the effectiveness of lessons and approaches to teaching;*
* *contribute to the design and provision of an engaging curriculum within the relevant subject area(s).*

Teachers' Standard 5: Adapt teaching to respond to the strengths and needs of all pupils

* *know when and how to differentiate appropriately, using approaches which enable pupils to be taught effectively;*
* *have a clear understanding of the needs of all pupils, including those with special educational needs; those of high ability; those with English as an additional language; those with disabilities; and be able to use and evaluate distinctive teaching approaches to engage and support them.*

PROFESSIONAL LINKS

The *Carter Review of Initial Teacher Training* stated that:

Planning should be treated as a priority and given significant time and emphasis. Trainees should be encouraged to master established and evidence-based approaches. Trainees should be taught how to find, adapt and evaluate resources in their planning.

(Carter, 2015, p 10)

CHAPTER OBJECTIVES

* **What is this chapter about?**

This chapter will help you become more effective at planning lessons and sequences of lessons. Lesson planning is a skill that takes time to develop. At the start of your ITT you may spend a significant proportion of your time planning lessons. As you gain more experience you will be able to produce lesson plans more quickly. Effective lessons are usually those that are well considered and well-structured. They are designed to enable children to make progress in their learning and they build on prior learning so that learners develop their skills, knowledge and understanding.

That said, detailed lesson plans do not always result in learners making very good progress. Overly detailed plans can result in too much lesson content. Prescriptive step-by-step lessons may fail to take account of learners' understanding during a lesson. An effective lesson is usually well thought through. There is a clear lesson structure which enables children to make progress in their learning. It is more important to spend time thinking through your lessons carefully rather than focusing on writing the actual plan. Many teachers will tell you that they have taught highly effective lessons from just a few bullet points on a plan.

In the early stages of your development as a teacher you will need to spend a significant amount of time planning lessons. However, this time invested should not be at the expense of time spent producing resources that will significantly engage children. It is important to keep your planning in proportion. The most effective plans are simple, clear and concise. They are well thought through. This chapter will help you to plan lessons and sequences of lessons more effectively.

✱ Why is it important?

It is important to state that there is no one correct model of how a lesson should be structured. For many years, largely as a result of the Primary National Strategy, trainee teachers have been presented with models of how to plan lessons. Lessons have had three or four parts and often each part has been timed. The National Strategies has left its legacy and many schools still provide teachers with planning templates that divide lessons into specific parts. Ofsted no longer expect to see a model of teaching. Inspectors will not focus on how a lesson is structured but they will focus on the quality of learning taking place in the lesson.

That said, it is really helpful for those new to teaching to provide some sort of model or framework upon which to plan lessons. Trainees in particular benefit from being introduced to models of lesson structures which they can adapt when they become more confident. To meet the Teachers' Standards you will have to demonstrate that you are able to teach sequences of lessons which enable your learners to make progress over time. You will also need to demonstrate that you plan individual lessons which enable learners to make progress within the lesson. This chapter will help you to do this.

Checking on prior learning

At the start of a lesson you need to check that your learners are secure with the prior learning they have been introduced to. This is not the same thing as asking your learners to tell you what they were learning in a previous lesson. This is insufficient because it does not tell you anything about their understanding of the prior learning. Equally, it is not sufficient on its own to ask children to show you if they feel that they have understood the prior learning using a thumbs up/down strategy. Again, this does not indicate if the prior learning has been understood.

The most effective way of checking on prior learning is to build in a connection activity. This is an activity that connects them to their prior learning. It provides you with the information that you need to know in that it tells you whether they have understood the prior learning or whether they need further consolidation of that learning. If it becomes evident at this point in the lesson that the prior learning is not secure then you will need to adapt your lesson to respond to the misconceptions that your learners are demonstrating. In this respect, you might not actually end up teaching the lesson that you planned! This is Assessment for Learning in action.

Connection activities need to be short, sharp and snappy. They need to make visible children's understanding of their prior learning. You can design connection activities which involve children working together in groups or pairs or you could organise them so that they are working individually. You will need to use the outcomes of the connection activity to decide whether you need to abandon the planned lesson and address the misconceptions that are being demonstrated. You might need to do this if a significant proportion of your learners have understood the prior learning. If the misconceptions are with specific learners then the planned lesson might go ahead but you might decide to provide specific pupils with individual or group intervention during the lesson to address these misconceptions.

IN PRACTICE

You teach a lesson on recognising odd and even numbers. At the end of the lesson your learners are able to tell you which numbers are odd and which numbers are even. In the next lesson you want your learners to be able to investigate what happens when: two odd numbers are added together; two even numbers are added; an odd and an even number are added together.

You design a connection activity to check on their prior learning. On the tables you have randomly distributed a pile of numbers. You have provided the more able learners with three-digit numbers. Two tables have been given two-digit numbers and one table have been given single-digit numbers and some Unifix cubes.

You ask each group to go to their table and to work as a group. Their task is to sort the numbers into odd and even using sorting hoops. You give them three minutes to do this. At the end of the three minutes it is evident that all groups are struggling to sort odd and even numbers correctly.

CRITICAL QUESTIONS

* *In this scenario what would you do next?*
* *How did you plan to make the progress visible?*
* *What would you do if all of the groups except one of the groups could accurately sort the numbers into odd and even numbers?*
* *How did you plan to enable all the learners to participate in the connection activity?*

Building on prior learning

Your lessons should aim to build on pupils' prior knowledge, skills and understanding so that children make progress over time. There is little point in you spending three weeks on right angles if your learners were able to identify right angles at the end of the first lesson. Having said that, children do need some time for consolidating their understanding and it is important not to move children on too quickly. This is because they need to master the objective that you have taught them. They need to be able to demonstrate that they have understood the objective and that they can apply that learning in a different context. For example, children do need to be able to know that when water heats up, its volume decreases. They need to recognise this process as 'evaporation'. However, they also need to be able to identify this process in everyday life. For example, the reason why puddles dry up is due to evaporation and the reason washing dries on a line is due to evaporation. If children reach a level of understanding where they are able to apply learning from one context into another, that will result in higher level thinking and better quality learning.

Your prior assessment will give you information about children's current level of development in relation to a specific strand of learning. You will know from your observations of prior learning and the level of understanding that they have demonstrated through their previous work if they are ready to move onto the next steps in learning. You will need good subject knowledge because you need to be able to identify what the next steps are within that strand of learning and, providing that prior learning is secure, this will form the basis of the next lesson that you are planning. In this way you are ensuring that you are providing your learners with an appropriate level of challenge. The learning is neither too easy nor too difficult. It provides them with an appropriate level of challenge. Your role as a teacher is to support them to understand the new learning, thus taking them to a higher stage of development. This is an application of Vygotsky's zone of proximal development. If the prior learning was not secure you will need to revisit that learning, perhaps in a different way. In this instance your learners are still being challenged and they are still operating within their zone of proximal development.

The challenge is for you to be able to identify the sequence of progression within a particular strand of learning. The national curriculum is not laid out in a user-friendly way to facilitate this process. Thus, you will need to research progression sequences by referring to Chapters 3 and 4 in this text.

Modelling new learning

Often in lessons you will be introducing new learning to your pupils. You will need to model this new learning very explicitly. The process of modelling involves demonstrating the new learning. For example, you might model a specific calculation strategy in mathematics. This will involve showing the children a question, talking them through the steps to solve the problem, explaining the mathematical strategies and modelling how to set out the calculation. The process involves a combination of teacher-explanation, teacher-demonstration and teacher-questioning. It is not sufficient to simply tell children what to do. You need to show them how to do it. In English you might model the process of writing using a specific genre. You might model the process of orally rehearsing a sentence by thinking of a sentence, saying the sentence out loud and then writing it. When you model writing the sentence, you will model starting the sentence with a capital letter, using spaces between words and putting a full stop at the end of the sentence.

Modelling in this way is a very visual process. You might model using the interactive whiteboard, on a whiteboard or flip chart. You might want to model something using practical resources, film or computer software. You might model a paired activity with the teaching assistant. You can ask your learners to model their understanding by asking them to demonstrate to their peers how to do something. Models such as worked examples impact significantly on children's learning. You therefore need to think carefully about providing learners with good examples of the outcomes that you expect them to demonstrate. Through seeing worked examples, learners have a clear idea of what is expected of them. Worked examples can be displayed on working walls as a reference point to support learners in lessons.

Checking on understanding

Effective teachers check consistently throughout their lessons that their learners have understood the content that they have been taught. You should not wait until the end of a lesson to discover that your learners have developed misconceptions. You should be checking on their understanding throughout the lesson and addressing misconceptions as they occur so that they make good progress. You can check on understanding in a range of ways including through the use of:

* questioning, eg using questions such as *How did you work that out? How did you know that? Prove it to me*;
* observing;
* marking in the lesson;
* mini-plenaries at specific points during a lesson;
* use of plenaries at the end of lessons.

Effective teachers are skilled at adapting the lesson to respond to misconceptions or the need for additional challenge. When you plan your lesson plans it is a good idea to record all the different ways that you are going to check on your learners' understanding throughout the lesson. There might be specific points where you plan to check on their understanding, for example, immediately after you have modelled the new learning. You might also plan to visit a specific group at a specific time in the lesson. Sometimes you will check on their understanding more fluidly throughout the lesson rather than pinpointing exactly when you are going to check. The critical point is to develop the ability to adapt your teaching in response to children's learning needs within the lesson. This is preferable to waiting until the end of the lesson to realise that a specific group or individual developed a misconception in the lesson.

Application of learning

After you have completed the modelling and checked your learners' understanding, they need time on task to practise the skills that you have taught them. The majority of the lesson should be devoted to time on task. It is only through completing specific tasks that you will really know whether their understanding is secure. You will need to design a task which gives your learners the opportunity to practise the lesson content. You will need to decide whether you want them to work in small-groups, pairs or individually. If you choose for them to work in groups, you will need to decide whether you are going to group them in ability groups, mixed-ability groups or friendship groups. The same decisions will need to be made in relation to paired work.

The aim is for children to demonstrate their learning independently of the teacher. This said, you do have an important role to play. You may decide to move around the room supporting individuals and small groups where appropriate. You may decide to do some focused guided teaching with a specific group. It is good practice to mix up the groups from time to time so that pupils gain experience of working with other children. Groupings should be kept flexible so that when a child's ability changes in a specific aspect then they have the opportunity to move to a different group for additional challenge or support.

Making progress visible

Making progress visible does not happen automatically in teaching. You need to plan strategies that make pupils' progress visible. Ofsted inspectors and senior leaders in schools are focusing increasingly on pupil progress during observed lessons. Essentially, this means that within the timescale of the lesson the children may:

* learn something new, for example, a new skill or aspect of knowledge;
* become more confident with some aspect of prior learning.

When you are planning to make progress visible you need to find ways of establishing pupils' starting points at the start of the lesson. This might involve asking questions or providing them with a short task to complete. If the lesson content is pitched correctly, they will struggle with this because this is the content that you are teaching them in the lesson. You need to explain to your learners that they do not need to worry about this but by the end of the lesson they will be much more confident. You will then model the new learning. Following this, you will develop ways of checking their understanding. Typically you will provide them with time on task to enable them to practise what they are learning. Through the outcomes they produce in the lesson and in the plenary, it should become evident that they have made progress in relation to what you have been teaching them. The progress is evident in their books, and in the plenary there should be a high level of participation. Pupils will be able to answer the questions that you ask them, which are similar to the questions that they could not answer at the start of the lesson.

IN PRACTICE

* *Consider how you might use a class mind map using coloured Post-it notes to make progress visible in a lesson.*
* *Consider how you might use a working wall to make progress visible over the duration of a week.*
* *Consider how you might make progress visible in a 20-minute segment in a lesson.*
* *Consider a range of ways of making progress visible.*

CRITICAL QUESTIONS

* *Do pupils always need to make progress from the start of a lesson to the end of the lesson?*
* *What are your views on measuring pupils' progress within a 20-minute segment of a lesson?*
* *If your pupils learn something different to what you intended them to learn does this mean that your teaching was ineffective? Explain your answer.*
* *Is there too much emphasis on pupil progress? Explain your answer.*

EXTENDED THINKING

* *Is the focus on measuring teaching quality through the indicator of pupil progress fair to all teachers? Explain your answer.*
* *Should school effectiveness be judged on the basis of pupils' progress from their starting points or their attainment, which means what they achieve in relation to national indicators of performance?*

Making effective use of lesson time

During your lessons you need to make the best use of the time available. If children spend too long listening to a teacher, they may disengage from the learning process. It is important to remember that children usually have short concentration spans and time spent listening to a teacher often results in learning being passive. There are no hard and fast rules about how long to talk for in a lesson but it is considered good practice for the majority of the lesson time to be allocated to providing children with opportunities to apply the learning they have been exposed to. This usually means that a significant proportion of the lesson should be allocated to providing learners with time on task.

Often, part of a lesson usually involves introducing some new learning to children. This may be done through *modelling* the new learning, perhaps on a board. This is not the only way of teaching something but it is one way of enabling them to understand what you want them to learn. Modelling often involves demonstrating the new learning rather than simply relying on verbal explanations. However, just because you have just taught something does not mean that your learners have understood it. You will need to build in ways of checking their understanding throughout the lesson and you will need to adapt the teaching accordingly to respond to pupils' misconceptions or their need for additional challenge.

When you are directly instructing your learners you will need to find ways of actively engaging them in the learning process. This can be done using a range of strategies. These might include:

- asking your learners questions;
- giving your learners opportunities to think through responses to questions in pairs or to discuss a question in pairs (talk partners);
- asking pupils to demonstrate their understanding of the learning you have introduced them to.

It is important not to confuse active learning with learning by 'doing'. While some active learning strategies might involve learners in some form of 'doing' activity, learners can be actively engaged in learning if the lesson is promoting active *thinking*. Developing learners' thinking is critical to effective learning and therefore the promotion of active thinking is at the heart of all effective planning.

It is important not to overload children in a lesson by introducing them to too many different activities. You might initially think that the pace of learning would be increased in a lesson if you keep moving your learners onto new activities. However, you will not increase the pace of learning if you keep on racing your learners through the lesson content. It is more important to teach something well and then to build it into your lesson opportunities to check that your learners have understood what you have taught them. When you think about pace, think more carefully about the *pace of learning* rather than thinking of pace in relation to the number of tasks that children complete. Moving children on too quickly from one task to another can interrupt the flow of learning. It can result in learning being superficial and not deeply embedded. Children need time to master the skills that you are teaching them and they need opportunities to practise these skills in a range of contexts. Reducing the amount of time that you talk in lessons and providing opportunities for your learners to practise the skills that you have taught them is critical to effective learning.

IN PRACTICE

A group of learners in Year 4 are learning about class debates. They are learning about animals in science and the teacher uses this topic as a context for developing their skills in English. The teacher poses to the class a question: *Should animals be kept in zoos?* She shows them several video clips of animals in zoos and the children are hooked immediately. She tells them that they are going to have a class debate. One half of the class will take the stance that animals should be kept in zoos and the other half will take the stance that zoos should be banned. The teacher divides them into two groups and gives them thinking time. Each group is given a large sheet of paper and a marker pen and they nominate someone to be the scribe. They spend time generating arguments to support the stance they are taking. They have time to think and talk in groups and to orally rehearse their responses. After 20 minutes the class are brought back together. In turn, each group perform their response. Each group listens to the response made by the other group. They are then given five minutes to think in their groups of a counter-response. After giving their counter-responses the class are asked to decide on a class response by voting for or against the initial question.

CRITICAL QUESTIONS

- *What skills are the children learning in this lesson?*
- *Do you think the pace of learning is good in this lesson? Justify your answer.*
- *How could this lesson form part of a sequence of lessons over a week? What might you teach in the previous and subsequent lessons?*

In this example the teacher has thought carefully about the *pace of learning* rather than thinking about pace in relation to the number of tasks that she gave the children. The children have been asked to do one task but they are learning many different skills.

It is important to strike the correct balance between modelling some new learning and giving your learners opportunities to demonstrate that they can apply this learning. If you over-model then you run the risk of 'spoon-feeding' your learners and they will not get the opportunity to demonstrate independently what they can do. If you under-model then your learners may not have understood what you have just taught them.

Teachers or teaching assistants often support small groups of learners within a lesson to aid them in the completion of specific tasks. If you give them too much help then they will not have the opportunity to demonstrate that they can apply the learning independently. We often think that our role as teachers is to help children to complete tasks. However, there is a real danger that giving children too much help can increase their dependency on an adult. It also reduces the opportunities for children to demonstrate what they can do. Additionally, the focus on *task completion* can also be detrimental to effective learning. There may be times when your learners do not need to complete a whole task in order to demonstrate that they have mastered the new skill that you have taught them. Effective teachers are skilled in knowing when learners have demonstrated their understanding sufficiently and they know when to stop them and move them on to something new. Effective teachers are also skilled at identifying when children have misconceptions, and are able to provide them with the right amount of support at the right time. They know when to re-teach, re-model or re-explain something.

Adapting your lessons

It is important to adapt your lessons to meet the needs of your learners. This process of adapting your teaching should take place both within lessons and across a sequence of lessons. You will become more confident at adapting your lessons as you gain experience. Inexperienced teachers tend to stick slavishly to the lesson plans that they have developed. They often think that it is important to get through the content that they have planned. As you gain in experience, you will gradually realise that it is more important to ensure that your learners are understanding what you are teaching them than getting through the planned lesson content. There is little point in moving onto the next stage of a lesson if your learners have developed misconceptions. Less is sometimes more and the quality of learning is far more important than the quantity of material that you teach children. As you gain in experience, you will realise that teaching does not automatically equate with learning. You may have taught your learners something but it does not automatically follow that they have understood or that they will remember what you have taught them.

Adapting your teaching to meet the needs of your learners in the lesson is a characteristic of outstanding teaching. It also takes confidence because it necessitates the need to depart from the planned content of the lesson. There are many ways of adapting your teaching in lessons. If the majority of learners in your class have not grasped something then this suggests that the teaching has not been effective and that you may need to re-teach it in a different way. It prompts you to reflect on your own teaching. If your learners have developed misconceptions then you need to notice these and respond to them. Your responses to misconceptions might include:

- providing your learners with further worked examples;
- re-teaching a skill or concept in a different way;
- re-explaining something with greater clarity;
- asking pupils who have understood to demonstrate their understanding to the rest of the class;
- further breaking down your instructions step-by-step.

The challenge of this is that you will need to respond to misconceptions in the live moment. This has several implications. Firstly, you need to develop a repertoire of teaching strategies. This will enable you to use a different strategy if one strategy has not proved to be effective. Secondly, you need to have a high level of subject pedagogical knowledge. If your learners have not understood something then you may need to take the learning back a stage in order to ensure that the correct foundations are established. This means that you need to understand progression in the development of children's knowledge, skills and understanding in specific strands of learning. At the planning stage you need to be aware of the prior steps in learning that children need to have mastered in order to grasp the lesson content that you are teaching. This will then enable you to take the learning back a stage if you find that the content of the lesson is pitched too high.

You may realise in the middle of a lesson that the content is too easy for *the whole class* and that they need additional challenge to move their learning forward. You will need to notice and respond to this in the live moment. Therefore, you need to ensure that you understand the progression sequence within the specific strand of learning that you are teaching. At the planning stage you need to be aware of next steps in learning so that you are able to provide learners with additional challenge where necessary.

During a lesson you may notice that a specific *group of learners* has developed misconceptions in their understanding. You might respond to these by re-teaching that specific group of learners in the lesson. You might stop them and provide them with further explanations, additional modelling and further worked examples. If the task is too complex you might need to adapt the lesson for this group by moving the learning back a stage. You might notice that a particular task is too easy for a specific group of learners. In this case you might respond by stopping the group and moving them onto more challenging content by taking them onto the next stage within a strand of learning.

You might notice that *specific individuals* have developed misconceptions or require additional challenges in lessons. You might respond in the lesson by providing an individual intervention or challenge. This might be provided by you or your teaching assistant.

The route to highly effective teaching is to recognise when you need to adapt your teaching for the whole class, groups or individuals. This ability to notice and respond will enable your learners to make further progress. It is too late to wait until the end of a lesson to discover that an individual, group or class has developed misconceptions or that they needed additional challenge. If you leave it until the end of a lesson to notice this then your learners will not have made good progress. You need to be alert to how your learners are responding to your teaching, and your teaching needs to be in tune with their responses. A lesson plan is a guide but it is not set in stone and it may need to be adapted in the live moment of the lesson. In this case, it is considered to be good practice to annotate your lesson in order to demonstrate where changes were made. This demonstrates that you are using assessment to inform your teaching; this is critical to effective learning.

At the start of each week it is normal practice in primary schools to produce weekly plans in addition to lesson plans. Weekly plans show the overview of the lesson content over the course of the week. You may need to adapt the content of your lessons over the week in response to children's misconceptions, their need for additional consolidation and their need for further challenge. In the same way that you have been advised to annotate your lesson plans, you are also advised to annotate your weekly plans to show how you adapted the teaching over the course of a week to respond to the needs of your learners.

IN PRACTICE

You are teaching a unit of work on fractions. On the first day of this strand on learning you are focusing on identifying quarters of numbers. You are teaching the children to find ¼ of a number by dividing a number by 4. In the next lesson you are moving them onto finding two quarters and three quarters of a given number. During the first lesson you are not confident that your learners are able to find ¼ of a number. They found this challenging and when you look at their work many of them have found ½ of a number rather than ¼. You cannot move your learners on to the next stage until they are confident with finding ¼ of a number.

CRITICAL QUESTIONS

* *In this example you decide to re-teach ¼ of a number in a different way. How might you approach this skill differently in the next lesson to address the pupils' misconceptions?*
* *What prior learning did the teacher assume in this lesson?*
* *How might the teacher have checked this prior learning before moving them onto finding ¼ of a number?*

Planning to engage learners

In your lessons you will need to find ways of engaging your learners. Highly effective teachers are able to generate very high levels of engagement so that when the lesson comes to an end the learners do not want to stop learning. The costs of disengagement are significant because disengagement can result in disruptive behaviour and/or poor educational achievement.

You will need to find a way of hooking in your learners at the start of the lesson. You can do this in a variety of ways. These include:

* providing a *context* for the learning so that there is a purpose to the learning;
* introducing them to an unusual or interesting object;
* telling or reading them a story;
* teaching in role as a character;
* showing them a film clip;
* creating a scenario in the classroom (eg the room becomes an island which the pupils have just inhabited);
* using pictures, photographs, poems, works of art;
* using their interests as a context for the tasks that you ask them to complete;
* using immersive technology to take the pupils to other places;
* using a children's story as a context for teaching mathematics;
* taking the lesson outdoors.

You can engage your learners in a range of ways. You might do this by asking them to work collaboratively on a project. You can give them projects that relate to real life and specifically their interests. You can make the learning purposeful by designing cross-curricular projects in which pupils have to demonstrate their skills in a range of curriculum areas to produce an outcome. You can provide them with interesting things to touch, smell, feel, taste and observe so that they start to use their senses in a focused way. You can turn them into scientists by providing them with white coats and goggles. You can tell them that they are authors, historians, mathematicians, geographers, writers and so on. They will enjoy having a 'grown-up' status and it will motivate them to carry out their tasks. You can give them opportunities to take part in competitions and you can use the internet as a forum for publishing their work. Embracing the world of modern technology is another way of engaging your learners. Learning can take place on iPads or on the internet rather than through more traditional approaches. They can make their own films, animations, interactive presentations and use email and mobile phone and tablet technology. They can create their own companies and market their own products. They can write their own websites or produce and record their own musical compositions using the latest musical technology. Older children will respond well to competition approaches such as *X Factor* style competitions. Pupils can engage in video conferencing and use technology to communicate with others around the world. They can contribute to blogs, discussion boards, instant chat features and so on.

You will of course be able to add to these ideas. The critical point to make is that education needs to evolve with the developments around them so that schooling starts to reflect their daily lives.

CRITICAL QUESTIONS

* *What are the risks associated with using technology to support learning?*
* *How might you overcome these risks?*

EXTENDED THINKING

Look through the new primary national curriculum.

* *To what extent does it reflect the developments in modern society?*
* *To what extent does it reflect the past?*
* *Will it provide children with the knowledge and skills to live and work in the twenty-first century?*
* *What would you take out, leave in or add in to the national curriculum if you had the power to design a better curriculum?*

Promoting children's intellectual curiosity

Most children are naturally curious but not all are. You need to encourage the development of children's curiosity using a range of strategies. One way of doing this is to provide children with a curiosity box. Children would be encouraged to think of their own curious questions and they could post them in the curiosity box. The questions might begin with the phrase *I wonder why...* Children should be encouraged to ask questions which promote deep thinking. Examples might include:

* *Why does the sea never dry up?*
* *Why does the earth spin?*
* *Where do the stars come from?*

- *Why do we have a moon?*
- *Why do puddles dry up?*
- *Are we all equal?*

The questions that children generate in the curiosity box could be discussed as part of a class circle time. This approach will encourage children to listen to other people's ideas and they can be taught to challenge these ideas in an appropriate way.

One way of promoting intellectual curiosity in young children is to provide children with a curiosity area in the classroom. You can place interesting objects, materials, plants, animals, historical artefacts, drawings, old and new photographs and so on into this area. The resources can be supplemented with questions which promote intellectual thinking. The children might be provided with magnifying glasses, note paper and pencils to give them opportunities to produce written responses or further questions in relation to the resources that you have provided them with.

Planning sequences of lessons: medium term planning

Medium term plans show what children will learn over a period of several weeks. Usually medium term plans show the learning objectives that will be taught within each subject over the duration of half a term and sometimes an overview of the content is provided. The plans show the intended coverage, and the specified learning objectives and content may change in response to children's needs. The purpose of a medium term plan is to:

- demonstrate progression in children's knowledge, skills and understanding over time;
- demonstrate intended coverage in relation to content over time.

Your school may already have medium term plans drawn up which will outline the content that you are required to teach during your school-based training. In this case you should work with the school's plans but do not be afraid to make adaptations to them as the lessons progress. The lessons that you teach need to be responsive to the needs of your learners and so modifying the planning helps to demonstrate that you are using Assessment for Learning to inform your teaching.

Planning sequences of lessons: weekly planning

You need to have an overview of what you will be teaching over the duration of each week. One way of setting out the lesson content over a sequence of lessons is to produce a weekly plan. Most primary school teachers produce separate weekly plans for English and mathematics. These should be concise documents that provide a skeleton outline of the lesson content without specifying exactly how a lesson is going to be taught. Weekly plans focus on *what* you are teaching rather than *how* you are teaching it. Weekly plans should specify:

- what the children will learn in each lesson;
- what content will be modelled;

* a brief overview of how the learning will be pitched for each ability group;
* a brief overview of how you will check pupils' understanding at the end of the lesson;
* the key vocabulary that children will learn over the week.

Weekly plans work most effectively when they are concise. One page of A4 is usually sufficient. This will enable your mentor to quickly skim down the learning objectives to check that you have planned for pupils to make progress over the week. Additionally, your mentor will be able to see at a glance how the learning is pitched each day or to each group and how that learning will progress over the week for each group. The finer details can go in the lesson plan. You should annotate the weekly plan as you progress through the week to demonstrate how you have adapted your lessons to respond to children's needs. This will help to demonstrate that you are using assessment to inform your teaching.

You should check with your ITT provider about the formats for weekly planning. Some providers will allow trainees to use their school's planning templates. Other providers may prefer trainees to use their own templates and some providers may be happy for trainees to design their own planning templates. There is no single correct model for planning. No planning template is perfect but it should be clear, logical and enable you to do your job.

Planning individual lessons

All trainee teachers are required to produce individual lesson plans for the lessons they are responsible for teaching. These should include:

* the learning objective(s);
* the success criteria;
* specific Teachers' Standards that you intend to focus on in your teaching;
* references to the relevant aspects of the national curriculum or Early Years Foundation Stage Framework;
* a breakdown to show how the lesson will be structured;
* key questions that you will ask the pupils in the lesson;
* details of the specific tasks that your learners will be asked to undertake and how they are going to be differentiated;
* organisational details: how are the children going to be grouped and which adults are supporting which groups;
* details of how you intend to check on learners' understanding at specific points in the lesson;
* details of how you intend to check on pupils' understanding at the end of the lesson;
* key vocabulary that you want the pupils to develop;
* assessment opportunities: what you will assess? who you will assess? how you will assess?

It is important to remember that your lesson plan is a guide to what you intend to teach. You will need to adapt the lesson as you teach in order to address pupils' misconceptions and need for additional challenge. You can annotate your lesson plan to show the adaptations that you made to the planned lesson.

Learning objectives

Learning objectives are statements which specify precisely what children will learn in a lesson. They should focus sharply on the skills, knowledge and understanding that you are trying to develop in the lesson rather than the activities that children are doing. More detail in relation to this is available in Chapter 7.

Learning objectives are identified from curriculum frameworks. However, these are often too broad and are not expressed using child-friendly terminology. They are written for teachers and are not for children. You will need to break down the statements from the curriculum frameworks to make them more focused and you will need to present them to learners using language which is accessible.

CRITICAL QUESTIONS

* *Look at the following learning objectives and consider whether they are good learning objectives. Explain your response. Try to make them better:*

1. Choose and use appropriate standard units to estimate and measure length/height in any direction (m/cm); mass (kg/g); temperature (°C); capacity (litres/ml) to the nearest appropriate unit, using rulers, scales, thermometers and measuring vessels.
2. To learn the 2, 3, 4 and 5 times tables. (Key Stage 1 mathematics)
3. To draw a self-portrait using charcoal. (Key Stage 1 Art)
4. To plan a fair test to find out which material is the strongest. (Key Stage 2 Science)
5. Use mathematical vocabulary to describe position, direction and movement, including movement in a straight line and distinguishing between rotation as a turn and in terms of right angles for quarter, half and three-quarter turns (clockwise and anti-clockwise).
6. To make a vehicle using wood.
7. Measure the perimeter of simple 2-D shapes.
8. Identify right angles, recognise that two right angles make a half-turn, three make three quarters of a turn and four a complete turn; identify whether angles are greater than or less than a right angle.

Success criteria

Success criteria are statements that communicate to learners what they need to do to successfully achieve the learning objective. They are a way of communicating to learners what success looks like. Chapter 7 addresses success criteria in more detail.

Vocabulary development

On your lesson plan you need to identify any subject-specific vocabulary that you want your learners to know and understand. It is often necessary to teach vocabulary in a very explicit way. You should not assume that your learners will understand the vocabulary you use without explaining it to them. It is often a good idea to display vocabulary on large cards or to present it on the interactive whiteboard. When you introduce your learners to specific words, you can show them the visual representation of that word. After you have taught the vocabulary you can check their understanding of the terminology by developing effective questions which assess whether they have understood the word.

Planning questions

On your lesson plan you will need to plan the questions that you intend to ask your learners. Effective questioning can promote learning by helping learners to develop a higher level of understanding. It is also a useful assessment tool because questioning enables you to check your learners' understanding of what you have taught them. Questions can be closed or open. Closed questions require a very specific response. There is usually one correct response to such questions. Open questions promote higher level thinking in children. These questions do not require a specific 'correct' response and there may be several possible responses. Examples include:

- Why do you think that?
- How did you work that out?
- How do you know?
- How did X make you feel? Why did you feel that?
- How did you do that?
- What was your favourite X and why?
- Do you agree or disagree? Why do you think that?
- Can you describe this shape to me?
- What is your opinion and why?

Planning a range of open and closed questions into your lessons will enable you to cater for the needs of children with different abilities. Open questions provide a good level of challenge for the more-able learners while less-able learners might benefit from the use of closed questions.

IN PRACTICE

On the following pages you will see examples of medium term plans, weekly plans and lesson plans. They provide a starting point for discussion but they are not perfect examples. Look at each plan and identify:

- *whether the progression in learning is clear;*
- *similarities and differences between the plans;*
- *what you like;*
- *what you do not like;*
- *what you might change;*
- *how you might change it;*
- *different ways of 'framing' success criteria and learning objectives.*

Unit plan for English

	Ancient Greece	Text Type: Non-Fiction – Non-Chronological Reports		Week beg.: 10 October	Unit Length: 1 week
		Unit 'Hook': Ancient Greece Day		Unit Outcome: To write a non-chronological report	
Day	**Objective**	**Shared/Modelled Learning**	**Independent learning (including differentiation and use of TA)**	**Success Criteria**	**AFL Opportunities (including key questions)**
Mon	We are learning about the features of a non-chronological report	**Shared Reading:** Looking at the features of non-chronological reports: title/sub-heading/present tense/facts/labelled diagrams/opening/summary	Give pupils an example of a non-chronological report. Work in pairs to highlight the features of a non-chronological report	- I can highlight the title in yellow - I can highlight the sub-headings in green - I can highlight a question word in red - I can highlight the opening in pink - I can highlight the summary in blue	Show a WAGOLL of pupils' highlighted text and peer assess against the SC
Tues	We are learning to put a non-chronological report in the right order	On the IWB show them a non-chronological report about bats all in the wrong place. Model how the facts must link with the appropriate sub-heading.	Give out "chopped up" non-chronological reports and ask pupils to work as a group to rearrange the report into the correct order – putting the correct facts with the correct sub-heading	- I can put the title at the beginning of the report - I can put the opening next to the title - I can put the correct facts with the correct sub-heading - I can put the summary at the end	Jumbled up non-chronological report on board – ask them to come out and re-organise it

Wed	We are learning to plan a non-chronological report	Produce mind map together with the class – ask for help in generating sub headings: 1 Greece: clothes, buidlings, transport, food, city-states, theatre, writing, religion Model how to add FACTS to one sub-heading	Give out blank mind maps and ask pupils to work in pairs to add facts to each sub-heading. Pupils need to decide what the title and sub-headings will be. Give them non-fiction books/ iPads etc to research the facts	**Remember to:** Include a title Include five sub-headings Use a question for at least one sub-heading Include three facts with each sub-heading	Visualiser – show a WAGOLL of a mind map and ask class to peer-assess it against the SC
Thurs	We are learning to write a non-chronological report	**Shared Writing**: From the class mind map we did on Wednesday. Model how to write the **opening and one full section** of the report based on the facts we put with the sub-heading	Use their mind maps to write their own non-chronological report about Greece Start reports – complete opening and two sub-headings	**Remember to:** Include a title Include an opening Include two sub-headings Use a question for at least one sub-heading Include facts Write in the present tense	Visualiser – look at an example of a good non-chronological Report (work in progress) and peer-assess against the SC
Fri	We are learning to write a non-chronological report	**Shared Writing:** Model how to write the summary	Continue writing their reports, including the summary	**Remember to:** Include a title Include an opening Include five sub-headings Use a question for at least one sub-heading Include facts Write in the present tense Include a summary	Visualiser – look at an example of a good non-chronological report and peer-assess against the SC

Weekly mathematics plan

Day	Learning Objectives	Success Criteria	Connection	Teach/model	Application	Mastery
Mon	We are learning to name 2D shapes	I can find a triangle I can find a circle I can find a rectangle I can find a square Challenge: I can find a pentagon, hexagon and octagon	Recap on number bonds to 10	Introduce names of shapes – triangle, circle, rectangle, square	HA: Identifying pentagons, hexagons, octagons MA: Identifying triangles, circles, rectangles and squares LA: Identifying circles and triangles	Identifying shapes in the environment – PowerPoint images
Tue	We are learning to describe the properties of 2D shapes	I can count the sides I can count the corners Challenge: I can draw a shape from a description of its properties	Recap on names of shapes – triangle, circle, rectangle, square, pentagons, hexagons, octagons	Introduce properties (sides/corners) of triangle, circle, rectangle, square	HA: Shape visualisation – draw shapes from described properties MA: Sides/corners of triangles, circles, rectangles, squares LA: Sides and corners on triangles	Introduce vertices
Wed	We are learning to sort 2D shapes	Must -I can sort shapes into colours - I can sort shapes into sizes -I can sort shapes into those with right angles and those without	Recap on properties of triangle, circle, rectangle, square	Shape sorting activity – model sorting according to one criterion	HA: Sorting into shapes with and without right angles MA: Sorting into colours and size LA: Sort into colours	Sorting according to properties (sides/corners)

Thu	We are learning to find lines of symmetry in shapes	Remember to: - Fold the shape in half - If the two pieces match, draw the line of symmetry - Find other possible lines of symmetry	Recap on sorting shapes according to one criterion – send to tables to complete a shape sorting task	Model folding a shape to find lines of symmetry	HA: Folding pentagons, hexagons and octagons to find lines of symmetry MA: Folding rectangles and squares to find lines of symmetry LA: Folding squares to find lines of symmetry	Symmetrical shapes in the environment
Fri	We are learning to complete a symmetrical pattern	Remember to: - Look at the pattern - Put a mirror on the line of symmetry - Look in the mirror at the reflection - Copy the pattern of the reflection	Recap on folding shapes to find line of symmetry	Model symmetrical patterns using a peg board	HA: Six-colour patterns MA: Four-colour patterns LA: Two-colour patterns	Symmetrical patterns in the environment

Weekly phonics plan

Prior learning: the children can say the phonemes for the following graphemes: *s, a, t, p*

Week Commencing:	Learning Objectives and Success Criteria ***By the end of the session the children will be able to…***	Revisit and Review ***- Consolidation of previous graphemes taught*** ***- Oral blending/ segmentation using previous graphemes taught***	Teach ***Identify new grapheme(s) and tricky words to be introduced***	Practice ***Identify opportunities for blending and segmenting using the new grapheme***	Apply ***Read or write a caption and a sentence***
Mon	I can say the phoneme for *i* I can read *is*	Revisit *s, a, t, p*	Teach *i* Teach *is*	Blend: *pit / tip / it / sip* Segment: *spit*	*sip it*
Tues	I can say the phoneme for *n* I can read *it*	Revisit *i / is*	Teach *n* Teach *it*	Blend: *pan / nap / snap* Segment: *snip*	*snap a pin*
Wed	I can say the phoneme for *m*	Revisit *n / it*	Teach *m*	Blend: *map / man/ pim* Segment: *stamp*	*tap a man*
Thurs	I can say the phoneme for *d* I can read *in*	Revisit *m*	Teach *d* Teach *in*	Blend: *dap / tad / dint* Segment: *dim*	*It is in a pan.*
Fri	I can read and spell *at*	Revisit *d / in / is*	Teach *at*	Practise writing *at* in glitter	*Is it in a tin?*

Phonics lesson plan

<table>
<tr><td colspan="3">Prior Assessments: The children have previously carried out sessions relating up to phase three. The children have completed all sounds within phase three but require additional consolidation of several phonemes/graphemes.</td></tr>
<tr><td colspan="2">Objectives:
I can say the sound that the letters ai make.
I can read some simple words with ai in them.
I can write and spell words with ai in them.</td><td>Resources/Organisation</td></tr>
<tr><td colspan="3">REVISIT (previously taught phonemes/tricky words/blending and segmentation within existing phonic knowledge)</td></tr>
<tr><td>Two minutes</td><td>* Use brain gym to warm up the children and prepare them for the lesson: The owl/cups/cross crawl etc.
* Introduce the success criteria and learning objective of the session.
<u>Beat the Clock:</u>
* Introduce the children to this new game and inform them of the instructions.
* Start the timer and show the children previously taught phonemes and tricky words.
* Place the grapheme cards in one pile if the children are able to say the phoneme correctly. If incorrect, place these grapheme cards in an alternative pile.
* After one minute count the number of cards that have been correctly recognised.</td><td>* Children are to be sitting on the carpet next to their talk partners.
* Lesson objectives and success criteria to be displayed on the IWB/Flip Chart.
* Graphemes to be displayed on the IWB.
* Children are to show thumbs up/down to self-assess their peers' knowledge of grapheme-phoneme recognition.</td></tr>
<tr><td colspan="3">TEACH (new phoneme/new tricky word)</td></tr>
<tr><td>Five minutes</td><td>* Introduce the children to the new grapheme of ai and say the phoneme.
* Encourage the children to echo the phoneme to their partners and to the staff in the room.
* Model air writing/tracing the phoneme in the air using various parts of their bodies, eg fingers, arms, shoulders, toes.
* Encourage the children to choose a partner and then trace the grapheme on their partners' back.
* Give children the opportunity to write the grapheme in different materials, including sand.</td><td>* Grapheme to be displayed on the IWB.
* Kinaesthetic learning such as tracing and air writing to be modelled before allowing the children to carry it out.
* Reinforce behavioural expectations.
* Trays/plates.
* Sand.</td></tr>
</table>

PRACTICE (Blending and Segmentation)		
Five to ten minutes	* Inform the children that they are going to work in teams for the next activity. * Split the children into two teams that are to sit opposite one another. * Introduce the children to the range of words that are stuck to the flip chart. * Inform the children that you are going to sound talk one of the words that is stuck to the board. * The children are to read the list of words written on the board to attempt to identify the correct word that has been sound talked. * Once the children have identified the correct word they are to collect the word from the whiteboard. * The child who has collected the word must then sound talk the word. * The children are to show thumbs up/down to peer-assess. * The child is to then sit down with their team. * This is to be repeated several times until all of the words have been collected. * A record of scores will kept with each team and the children will be informed of the winner at the end of the activity. **Words to be collected** ***wait, pain, tail, bait, aim, main, rain, sail.***	* Children are to work with their new phonics partners to carry out the activity. * Laminated word cards. * Laminated grapheme cards. * Whiteboards. * Whiteboard pens. * Erasers.
	Application (read/write a caption or a sentence)	
Five minutes	* Inform the children that they are to listen to a sentence being said aloud. * The children are to repeat the sentence and say it aloud using different voices. * After doing this several times the children are to write the sentence down. **Sentence to be written down** ***I am in the rain.***	* Success criteria to be displayed on the IWB/flip chart. * Sentence to be displayed on the IWB. * Whiteboards. * Whiteboard pens. * Erasers. * Provide Harry with a finger space template for writing. * Children to self-assess using thumbs up/thumbs down.

Science medium term plan

MEDIUM TERM PLAN Subject: Science Strand: Electricity			Year Group: Y2	
Learning objectives per lesson	**Activity and organisation** **(include differentiation)**	**Pupil outputs**	**Special resources needed**	**Cross-curricular links inc. ICT**
Children will learn: - To communicate by writing a list - About everyday appliances that use electricity.	* Look at pictures of appliances that do and do not use electricity. * Discuss dangers of electricity. * Ask the pupils to produce a list of appliances that use electricity in their books. * Use DVD on electrical safety to allow children to explore the dangers of electricity.	List	Pictures	Literacy: Writing a list. PSHE: Dangers of electricity. (Keeping Safe) History: Invention of electricity. Comparing life now to life before electricity was invented.
- To communicate what happened through drawings - About simple series circuits involving batteries, wires and bulbs.	* Constructing circuits to make a bulb light. * Ask them to record a circuit diagram in their books and label it. * Children at higher stages of development in **science** to investigate using two batteries and one bulb and two bulbs and one battery in order to vary brightness of the bulb. * Children at lower stages of development to be supported by children at more advanced stages of development.	Diagram/ practical work	Batteries Wires Bulbs	History: Invention of the light bulb; Early forms of lighting in houses.

MEDIUM TERM PLAN **Subject: Science Strand: Electricity**			**Year** **Group: Y2**	
- To communicate what happened through drawings - About simple series circuits involving batteries, wires and buzzers.	* Constructing circuits to make a buzzer sound. * Ask them to record a circuit diagram in their book. * Children at higher stages of development in **science** to investigate using two batteries and one buzzer and two buzzers and one bulb in order to vary the sound of the buzzer. * Children at lower stages of development to be supported by children at more advanced stages of development. * Discuss applications – door bells etc.	Diagram/ practical work	Batteries Wires Buzzers	History: Invention of the door bell.
- To communicate what happened through drawings - About simple series circuits involving batteries, wires and motors.	* Constructing circuits to make a motor spin. * Ask them to record a circuit diagram in their book. * Children at higher stages of development in **science** to investigate using two batteries and one motor and two motors and one battery in order to vary the speed of the motor. * Children at lower stages of development to be supported by children at more advanced stages of development. * Discuss where motors are found in everyday life.	Diagram/ practical work	Batteries Wires Motors	History: Invention of the motor and early motor cars.

MEDIUM TERM PLAN Subject: Science Strand: Electricity			Year Group: Y2	
- To use first-hand experiences to answer questions - How a switch can be used to break a circuit.	* Making circuits which incorporate a switch made out of a paper clip, a rocker switch and a slider switch. * Children at lower stages of development to be supported by children at more advanced stages of development. * Discuss where switches are found in the home.	Practical work only	Batteries Wires Bulbs Paperclips Drawing pins Small wooden boards Rocker switches Slider switches	PSHE: Dangers of touching switches with wet hands. History: Invention of the switch.
Success Criteria: By the end of this teaching unit…			**Strategies for Assessment:** * Questioning * Looking at pupil's work * Observation of children working	
Some children will not have made so much progress and will: - be able to make a simple circuit to make the bulb light.	**Most children will:** - be able to construct a circuit to make a bulb work, a motor turn and a buzzer sound. - identify three ways in which the circuit can be broken. - draw simple labelled diagrams of circuits with no gaps between the wires and the components.	**Some children will have progressed further and will:** - compare the effects of using different numbers of batteries and other components in circuits.		

Topic planning: medium term planning

Year Group: Y1	Term:	Subject: Geography. Identify seasonal and daily weather patterns in the United Kingdom and the location of hot and cold areas of the world in relation to the equator and the North and South Poles. Focus of study: Why Can't A Meercat Live in the North Pole?	Resources/Useful texts/Useful links: *The Snowy Day*, Ezra Jack Keats *Meercat Mail*

National Curriculum Objectives:

Highlight the objectives as they are covered during this unit of work

Geography Knowledge, Skills and Understanding				Art and Design Knowledge, Skills and Understanding			
Geographical Enquiry	Physical Geography	Human Geography	Geographical Knowledge	Drawing	Painting	Collage	Use of IT
* Can they answer some questions using different resources, such as books, the internet and atlases? * Can they think of a few relevant questions to ask about a locality? * Can they answer questions about the weather? * Can they keep a weather chart?	* Can they explain the main features of a hot and cold place? * Can they describe a locality using words and pictures? * Can they explain how the weather changes with each season?	* Can they begin to explain why they would wear different clothes at different times of the year? * Can they say something about the people who live in hot and cold places? * Can they explain what they might wear if they lived in a very hot or a very cold place?	* Can they point out where the Equator, North Pole and South Pole are on a globe or atlas?	* Can they draw lines of different shapes and thickness?	* Can they name the colours they use, including shades? * Can they create moods in their paintings? * Can they use thick and thin brushes? * Can they name the primary and secondary colours?	* Can they cut and tear paper and card for their collages? * Can they gather and sort the materials they will need?	* Can they use a simple painting program to create a picture? * Can they use tools like fill and brushes in a painting package? * Can they go back and change their picture?

Geography Challenge	Dance Knowledge, Skills and Understanding
* Can they answer questions using a weather chart? * Can they make plausible predictions about what the weather may be like later in the day or tomorrow?	* Can they explore and perform basic body actions? * Do they use different parts of the body singly and in combination? * Do they show some sense of dynamic, expressive and rhythmic qualities in their own dance? * Do they choose appropriate movements for different dance ideas? * Can they remember and repeat short dance phrases and simple dances? * Do they move with control? * Do they vary the way they use space? * Can they describe how their lungs and heart work when dancing? * Can they describe basic body actions and simple expressive and dynamic qualities of movement?

Cross-curricular links	Literacy Link:	Numeracy Link:	Additional Geography Link:	Creative Art Link:	Expressive Art Link:
	* Use the book *Meerkat Mail* to link to postcards sent home from holiday destinations. * Exciting Vocabulary: *equator*; *poles*; *centigrade*; *meerkats*; *Kalahari*; *freezing point*, etc.	* Possible graphs of children's holiday destinations. * Consider temperature and how it is measured, create charts from data gathered.	* Keep an ongoing record of the weather in their locality; they could include rainfall, temperature, cloud cover, etc. * In addition, more able pupils could find out the temperature in certain parts of the world.	* LC4: Mixing paint to create hot and cold paintings.	* LC7: Movement work focusing on the way Meerkats move. Parents pick up their children 15 minutes early on the Friday so that the class can perform to them.

Grouping arrangements

You will need to make decisions about how you are going to group your learners. Whether you decide to use ability groups, mixed-ability groups or friendship groups, there is no perfect way of grouping children. Theoretically, mixed-ability groups enable you to target specific learning challenges for specific groups, thus making it easier to differentiate your teaching. However, children in lower-ability groups may develop a low self-concept and be subject to low expectations. The advantages of mixed-ability groups are relatively obvious. It is in these groups that the process of scaffolding can take place because those who are more-able can support those who are less able and the less-able learners are provided with appropriate role-models. They also receive exposure to high expectations as they have opportunities to work at a higher level. You might decide to vary your groups so that sometimes your learners work in ability groups for specific subjects and at other times they work in mixed-ability groups. Mixed-ability grouping arrangements are more common in the foundation subjects and ability grouping is more common in the core subjects.

If you decide to use ability grouping it is important to remember that learners within a group still have individual learning needs. It is also important to remember that ability within a subject is not always uniform. Thus, a child may be very skilled in the area of calculations but they may have less developed spatial skills. A child may be a brilliant reader but have less developed writing skills. The implications of this are that even within a subject you may need to adopt flexible grouping arrangements. It is also important that you do not see children's abilities as 'fixed'. Ability can change during the course of the academic year and therefore it is important to move children to different groups if the work is too easy or too difficult for them.

CRITICAL QUESTIONS

* *What are the advantages and disadvantages of ability groups?*
* *What are the advantages and disadvantages of mixed-ability groups?*

Planning for classroom organisation

With careful consideration of classroom organisation you can help to ensure that your classroom runs smoothly. More guidance is given on this in Chapter 8 but for now it is worth pointing out that excellent teachers make classroom organisation look easy. The reality is that it is quite a complex skill to develop and it may take a while for you to master this.

In some ways the easiest form of classroom organisation is whole-class teaching. This form of organisation enables you to keep tight control of the class, although you still have the challenge of trying to keep a whole class engaged in learning which is appropriate for the needs of individuals. This can be complex in itself. When children work in groups things can quickly go wrong if your classroom organisation is not carefully thought through. How will you move children to tables? You will need to consider where you will position yourself. How will you ensure that each group has access to all the resources they need? Which group will you be working with? If you have a teaching assistant, which group will they be working with? The groups that are not working with an adult will be expected to work more independently. What tasks will you set these groups and how will you ensure that they are challenged and not engaged in low-level activities? How will you ensure that they don't need to keep coming to you for help? How will you avoid queues? It is quite a fine art to get all of this right so that your classroom runs smoothly but eventually this will (or should) become an automatic process. Clearly, you need to give as much consideration to the role of adults within a lesson as you give to the lesson content. If you plan too many activities in which the children all need your support at the same time, this will be a recipe for disaster.

Planning to assess your learners

Assessment in the lesson is a tricky business. It is not always possible (or even desirable) to assess every child in every lesson. You might want to focus on assessing specific pupils. On your lesson plan there will usually be a box for completion which is entitled *assessment*. In this box you will need to decide:

* **what** you will assess;
* **who** you will assess;
* **how** you will assess.

It is perhaps obvious, though nevertheless important, to point out that you are not assessing whether children have or have not completed specific activities. The focus is not on task completion. The focus needs to be on whether children have developed the knowledge or skills or understanding that you intended them to learn. Within a lesson you might want to focus your assessments on a specific group of children rather than the whole class.

If you are working with a teaching assistant it is also important to give consideration to their role in supporting you with assessment. You don't need to do everything alone! Your teaching assistant will also need to be clear on what is being assessed, who is being assessed and how the assessment will be conducted.

In terms of what you are assessing, this is the learning objective that you have specified on your lesson plan. Most of the assessment within a lesson is done informally through processes such as observation or questioning. Questioning will enable you to check children's knowledge and understanding and observation will enable you to identify whether children have developed the specific skills that you intended them to develop. You can also look at children's work but this often only provides you with partial information because they may have received support to complete a specific task. In addition to questioning, observation and scrutiny of children's work, you might decide to plan a specific *assessment task* into a lesson which gives the children an opportunity to show you that they know, understand or can do something. This is an *Assessment for Learning* task and I have expanded on this in Chapter 7. It is worth pointing out now that it is not sufficient to ask children if they have understood something, can do something or know something at the end of a lesson. You will need to develop more robust ways of checking on this learning during a lesson so that you know if they have met the learning objective.

You will need to consider how you record the assessments that you make during the lesson. You might want to make rough notes on Post-it notes or you might want to keep a checklist to record whether or not children have met the learning objective. You might want to consider taking photographs or using video to capture some of the learning that is taking place in lessons. The important thing is to make it manageable.

Once you have made the assessments in the lesson, it is important to adapt the lesson so that misconceptions can be addressed and further challenges can be added where necessary. The purpose of formative assessment is to move learning forward. It is not about making judgements or comparisons between pupils. Noticing and responding within the lesson and adapting the lesson in response to what you notice is a critical aspect of outstanding teaching. What you do with the assessment information you collect is far more important than having pretty assessment records. At the end of the lesson you will need to review the assessments of children's learning and use them to plan the next lesson. This forward-feeding of assessment into planning is excellent practice and it will mean that your planning and therefore your teaching is driven by your assessments of children's learning. This process will enable your learners to make progress over time because it allows you to respond to their immediate learning needs.

Reflecting on and evaluating your teaching

Effective teachers reflect on their teaching all the time. It is not just a process which they engage with at the end of a lesson or the end of the week. Reflection should be taking place throughout a lesson. If a lesson is not going well then reflection within the lesson will enable you to adapt it to make it better.

When you are reflecting on your lessons it is too easy to focus on what you did during the lesson. You need to shift the focus from you to your learners in order to become an effective teacher. When you are reflecting on your teaching you need to know whether all children made progress. If they met the intended learning objective, you will need to decide what they need to learn next. If they did not learn what you intended them to learn, you will need to consider what factors contributed to this. Many factors can get in the way of children's learning. If learning did not take place you might need to consider the following prompts:

- Was my subject knowledge at least good?
- Could I answer children's questions and respond to misconceptions and the need for additional challenge?
- Did I understand the next steps in learning in order to accelerate children's learning?
- Did the modelling of the new learning enable children to work relatively independently? Therefore, was the modelling effective?
- Were my behaviour management skills effective in promoting a good climate for learning?
- Did I make effective use of assessment? Did I notice and respond?
- Did the lesson structure facilitate good pace so that learning moved forward?
- Was the deployment of the teaching assistant effective at every stage of the lesson?
- How effective was my use of questioning in promoting learning?
- Am I checking on pupils' learning within a lesson before moving on to the next stage of the lesson?

Although the focus here is on you, every aspect of your practice in the above prompts is linked to children's learning. On at least a weekly basis you need to reflect on children's learning across the week. The focus on children's learning over time is just as important as the learning which takes place in lessons. If children do not appear to be making good progress over time you will need to reflect on why this is. The following prompts will help you to do this:

* Am I planning for progression in pupils' learning?
* Am I using assessment to adapt planning between lessons?
* Am I checking on prior learning each lesson and adapting lesson content if learning is not secure?
* What provision am I making for children whose learning sequence is interrupted through absence?

Lesson structures

The typical lesson structure in a primary classroom might look like this:

* Class come in and sit down for a whole class input.
* Following this the children work in groups.
* Following this there is a whole class plenary.

There are various problems with this model which are worthy of consideration. During the whole-class teaching input it is difficult, if not impossible, to meet the needs of every child. For some children, the content will be too easy, for others it will be too difficult and for others it will be pitched at the correct level. You can of course try to include some differentiated questions but it is almost impossible to meet the needs of all learners during a whole-class input session. This results in wasted learning time for those children who have to sit through this session and find the content too easy or too difficult. The teaching assistant is usually ineffectively deployed during this part of the lesson. Often they sit at the side of the room, listening to the teacher and if the input lasts for 15/20 minutes this is valuable wasted time when more effective deployment could enable them to have a greater impact on children's learning. Whole-class input sessions often go on too long. This results in far too much teacher-talk and this impacts detrimentally on pupils' learning because they do not get sufficient time on task to apply their learning.

At this point it is worth pointing out that there is no perfect model for a lesson structure and you might use different models in different lessons. Children can often disengage from lessons where the same structure is used all the time. Ofsted does not promote one model of teaching over another. What is more important is whether the lesson structure enables the children to make at least good progress, rather than how the lesson was structured.

There are other models that you could try out and you can even develop lesson structures of your own. Teaching is not a science with right or wrong ways of doing things. You can experiment with different structures at different times.

Another model could look like this:

* The children come into class. One group goes straight to a task to work independently on a challenge and another group goes off to work with the teaching assistant. The teaching assistant teaches this group something new.
* The teacher keeps a group back to work with on the carpet. This group is taught something new.
* The teacher sends away the group s/he has been working with to work independently on a task related to what they have just been taught. At this point the teaching assistant leaves their group to monitor the learning of the group that the teacher has just been working with, thus enabling the group they have just been working with to work independently. The teacher then pulls together the group who have been working on the challenge activity to teach them something new.

- The teacher teaches this group and sends them away to work independently and the teaching assistant now monitors these two groups.
- The teacher then works with the group that initially went out to work with the teaching assistant to provide them with feedback on their learning.

CRITICAL QUESTIONS

- *What are the advantages of this suggested approach over the 'traditional' approach?*
- *What are the disadvantages of this approach?*
- *Can you think of another model for a lesson structure?*

Differentiation

According to the Carter Review (Carter, 2015, p 10):

It is important that new teachers are equipped to teach in ways that enable the large majority of pupils to learn essential curriculum content, build on this and keep up with the taught curriculum. Effective differentiation does not mean having several different lesson plans for one class. New teachers should be skilled in careful design and skilled delivery of teaching so that all pupils can access and secure the concepts being taught. Additionally, new teachers should have a sound grasp of practical strategies to enable lower achieving pupils to address critical gaps, make quick progress and keep up.

Additionally, the review stated:

2.3.37. We believe all pupils in the class, including lower and higher achievers, should make progress and keep pace with the curriculum. It is important that new teachers are equipped to teach in ways that enable the large majority of pupils to secure essential curriculum content, build on this and keep up with the taught curriculum.

2.3.39. Additionally, new teachers should have a sound grasp of practical strategies to enable lower achieving pupils to address critical gaps, make quick progress and keep up. Similarly, they should understand how to deepen and to enrich the understanding of pupils who grasp curriculum concepts quickly. These will include, for example: provision of additional tutorial support and practice outside the lesson for pupils who have not secured the concepts covered; and, for higher attaining pupils, more complex tasks and exercises or outside-lesson enrichment activities on the same topic.

(Carter, 2015, p 34)

Traditionally, children in lower-ability groups have been set less challenging work than other pupils in the class. The danger of this is that this transmits an important message to those learners. They start to feel that their teachers expect less of them than their peers and this can result in disengagement and the formation of a low self-concept. Children perform better when their teachers have high expectations of them and a 'can do' ethos is established in the classroom.

There will be occasions when you need to set different work for your less-able learners. However, this should not become the norm. It is important that you adopt a mindset which is underpinned by high expectations for all children. There will be times when children in lower-ability groups can achieve the same learning objective as their peers providing that you build in strategies to remove any potential barriers to learning. Through implementing some simple 'access' strategies, children will often surprise you in relation to their capabilities. These access strategies might include the following:

* use of practical resources to support learning (for example, number lines, number squares, worked-examples, more clearly defined steps to success);
* use of additional adult support;
* use of technology to support learning;
* pairing less-able and more-able children together so that more-able children can coach less-able children;
* pre-teaching before the lesson;
* use of carefully-designed lesson structures (such as the one listed above) so that all learners have the opportunity to work with the teacher during the lesson;
* varying the deployment of the teaching assistant so that teaching assistants do not always support less able children.

This is not an exhaustive list but it gives you a starting point to developing more inclusive practice which actively works towards removing barriers to participation and achievement. It is important also not to provide less-able children with too much help. If they are going to learn effectively, they need to be able to work with a degree of independence. Thus, it is important to strike a balance between helping children too much and helping them too little. It is critical that you communicate to them that you expect them to work hard, that they are capable of achieving to the same level as the rest of their peers and that you expect them to work with increasing degrees of independence. These learners may already have a low self-concept. This has partly developed though comparisons they make with their peers. They may have been told at home that they are not very good or that they are stupid. It is crucial that you challenge this mindset by saying to them *You might not be able to do it now but you WILL be able to do it soon*. All children are entitled to be taught by an adult who believes in them and instils within them a sense of self-belief.

Often the more-able children in the classroom are the ones who are left to work independently because they are capable, hard-working and motivated. However, if they are not challenged they can start to disengage from the process of learning. Additionally, if they have a high self-concept this can limit them from challenging themselves further because they are not used to failure and they may not want to take risks in their learning. It is critical that you challenge this group of learners. They need to know that you have high expectations of them and that they have not in fact reached their educational limit. They need to understand that they may be bright, but that you expect the same amount of effort from them as from everyone else in the class. You need to manage this carefully because many very bright children have been brought up in an environment where they have been surrounded with positive affirmation. It is your role as a teacher to challenge them and to help them to manage and cope with failure. It is your role to help them to take risks in their learning. It is your responsibility to help them to understand that there is so much more they need to learn.

Providing this group with appropriate learning challenges is the key to success. You need to ensure that your own subject knowledge is strong and you need to know what their next steps in learning are in order to challenge them further. You need to provide them with opportunities to deepen their knowledge, skills and understanding, thus developing mastery in learning. The best way of achieving this is to provide them with plenty of opportunities to apply their learning in different contexts. Problem-solving activities and puzzles which promote thinking are very obvious ways of doing this. Bloom's Taxonomy shows the lowest and highest levels of thinking. The higher-level skills include application, analysis, evaluation and creation. If you design activities around developing these higher-level skills that is a useful starting point. That said, it is important to evaluate theoretical models cautiously. The lowest levels of thinking in Bloom's taxonomy include knowledge recall and understanding. This can be done at a very low level. For example, I might understand that I am hungry because I have not eaten. I might know that iron is magnetic. However, knowledge and understanding can also be done at a very high level. For example, it took me several years of doctoral research to understand the work of Foucault! Some of the supposedly higher-level skills in Bloom's taxonomy can be relatively easy. The point I am making here is that you need to challenge more-able learners in all aspects of the framework, ie knowledge, understanding, application, analysis, evaluation and creation.

It is important that you ensure that more-able learners have frequent opportunities to be taught by you, the teacher. Equally, it is important that teaching assistants take some responsibility for the education of more-able learners, thus enabling you to teach less-able groups. All children, regardless of ability, need opportunities to be taught directly by a qualified teacher.

The recent research on the deployment of teaching assistants by the Education Endowment Foundation suggests that teaching assistants are often ineffectively deployed and often focus on task completion rather than developing children's knowledge, skills and understanding during lessons. The same criticism could also be levelled against some teachers. In order to ensure that all learners make progress it is important that the focus shifts from task completion to a focus on how effectively adults support pupils to think in the classroom. Supporting children to think is a critical factor in moving children's learning forward. The development of thinking demands skilled questioning which promotes thinking. This places responsibility on you to think carefully about the questions which you intend to ask children during lessons in order to promote their thinking. You will also need to support teaching assistants in asking questions which promote thinking.

Supporting second language learners

According to the Carter Review:

2.3.40. It is important that new teachers know how to support the progress of pupils with specific needs, such as those who do not speak English as their first language or those with SEND. Using assessment data and information on pupils' starting points, trainees need to be taught how to establish objectives and design programmes for pupils to enable them to make good progress and access the mainstream curriculum.

(Carter, 2015, p 34)

It is important that you do not automatically assume that children whose first language is not English automatically have special educational needs. Their difficulties in learning subject content usually arise from the fact that English is not their first language.

This affects their comprehension and ability to demonstrate their knowledge and understanding.

Many children who have English as a second or third language are automatically assigned to low-ability groups. This then results in low teacher expectations and the setting of low-level work, which subsequently has a detrimental impact on their progress. It is therefore critical that you demonstrate that you have high expectations of all learners. Learners whose first language is not English might receive bilingual support in the classroom. However, this is not always the case. Many children whose first language is not English do pick up the language rapidly when they assimilate into the environment of an English-speaking classroom and English-speaking school. It is often remarkable how quickly they pick up the language. It is important to remember that their comprehension of the language might develop more rapidly than their ability to actually use the language.

To support children whose second language is not English, you should seek support from colleagues in school who may have more experience of this. You should support your teaching with concrete resources such as objects. Using objects in your teaching will provide children with a reference point so that they learn to associate the vocabulary with something concrete. A systematic programme of language development may be necessary. In language development programmes children are systematically introduced to various levels of vocabulary (for example, nouns, verbs, adjectives, adverbs, prepositions). Children are introduced to the written word and this would be linked with an object, photograph, sign or symbol so that children can begin to make associations. You can introduce pre-teaching before lessons by providing one-to-one support so that pupils have some familiarity with the lesson content prior to the lesson. Where possible, teaching should be supported with visual cues such as objects of reference, photographs, pictures, signs and symbols. You need to keep your instructions and general language short, sharp and concise. Children may benefit from the use of visual instructions to support them through a task and they might benefit from the use of a visual timetable so they know what is happening during the day. The resources in the classroom should be clearly labelled using text and accompanying pictures so that children can start to make associations between print and objects. Technology can be used to support communication. Big switches are useful because when pressed they can produce the language for children to hear.

The examples above are not exhaustive. The important thing to remember when teaching children whose first language is not English is to give them lots of opportunity to develop social interaction skills. Through social interactions they will start to hear language and they will then start to use it. It won't be long before they are speaking fluent English. If they are newly arrived in this country, you need to be patient and show empathy. They may take a while to settle and they may be extremely anxious. You can support them by showing them that you care and by gradually aiding their assimilation into the classroom. Providing them with opportunities to work in pairs before they work in groups is a useful way of developing their confidence. Praise them as often as you can and develop a very structured programme of language development, phonics, reading, writing and mathematics in the first instance. Children whose first language is not English are no different to English-speaking children in that they will respond to praise, encouragement and systematic teaching. You have the skills and knowledge to teach them and they often do not require the support of a specialist teacher.

EVIDENCE-BASED TEACHING

According to the Education Endowment Foundation (Sharples et al, 2015, p 12):

On the other hand, there are concerns that TAs can encourage dependency, because they prioritise task completion rather than encouraging pupils to think for themselves. Taken further, it has been argued that over-reliance on one-to-one TA support leads to a wide range of detrimental effects on pupils, in terms of interference with ownership and responsibility for learning, and separation from classmates.

EVALUATE

* *What are the advantages and disadvantages of teaching assistant support for pupils?*

CHALLENGE

* *When can one-to-one support be really effective?*

APPLY

* *Over-modelling tasks can lead to a lack of independence in learning. What should the balance be between modelling new learning by an adult and independent learning?*

IN PRACTICE

* *In your school observe how teaching assistants are deployed. In particular: how are they deployed at the beginning and end of lessons and which groups do they support?*

EVIDENCE-BASED TEACHING

According to the Education Endowment Foundation (Sharples et al, 2015, p 15):

Communication between teachers and TAs is largely ad hoc, taking place during lesson changeovers and before and after school. As such, conversations rely on the goodwill of TAs. Many TAs report feeling underprepared for the tasks they are given. They 'went into lessons blind' and had to 'tune in' to the teacher's delivery in order to pick up vital subject and pedagogical knowledge, tasks and instructions.

EVALUATE

* *Why do think teaching assistants and teachers rarely get time to communicate?*

CHALLENGE

* *Some highly experienced teaching assistants who are trained in the interventions they are delivering may know more than the teacher they are working with in terms of how to support the pupils in those interventions.*

APPLY

* *In school establish the extent of communication between teachers and teaching assistants prior to lessons.*

TECHNOLOGY

Special schools make fantastic use of technology to support the development of pupils' communication skills. Technology may also be useful for supporting the development of language skills for learners whose first language is not English. If you get the opportunity to visit a special school, look at the range of technology that is used and consider how you might use this to support second language learners.

Critical reflections

This chapter has taken you through some key principles of planning and it has discussed approaches to grouping and differentiation. The critical point made throughout this chapter is the need for teachers to demonstrate high expectations of all children. Children respond to high expectations by trying to meet them, especially in classroom environments which engender a positive 'can-do' culture. It is important that teachers do not fall into the trap of viewing 'ability' as fixed. Terms such as *more-able* and *less-able* encourage a fixed mindset. Children's abilities change as a result of really effective teaching. Viewing children as ever-developing learners is important because fixed views on ability often result in a culture where some learners are perpetually exposed to low teacher expectations.

KEY READINGS

Classic:

Pollard, A with Anderson, J, Maddock, M, Swaffield, S, Warin, J and Warwick, P (2008) *Reflective Teaching: Evidence-informed Professional Practice.* 3rd ed. London: Continuum International Publishing Group Ltd.

Contemporary:

Cremin, T and Arthur, J (2014) (eds) *Learning to Teach in the Primary School*. 3rd ed. Abingdon: Routledge.

References

Carter, A (2015) *Review of Initial Teacher Training*. London: DfE.

Sharples, J, Webster, R and Blatchford, P (2015) *Making Best Use of Teaching Assistants Guidance Report – March 2015.* London: Education Endowment Foundation.

7: ASSESSMENT

TEACHERS' STANDARDS

This chapter addresses the following Teachers' Standard:

Teachers' Standard 6: Make accurate and productive use of assessment

Teachers must:

- *know and understand how to assess the relevant subject and curriculum areas, including statutory assessment requirements;*
- *make use of formative and summative assessment to secure pupils' progress;*
- *use relevant data to monitor progress, set targets, and plan subsequent lessons;*
- *give pupils regular feedback, both orally and through accurate marking, and encourage pupils to respond to the feedback.*

PROFESSIONAL LINKS

The *Carter Review of Initial Teacher Training* made the following recommendations in relation to assessment:

Recommendation 1d: *Assessment, including the theories of assessment and technical aspects of assessment, should be part of a framework for ITT content.*

Recommendation 9: *Alongside a central portal on evidence-based practice, a central repository of resources and guidance on assessment should be developed.*

(Carter, 2015)

CHAPTER OBJECTIVES

- **What is this chapter about?**

This chapter will introduce you to key terminology and key concepts in assessment. Specifically, it addresses both formative and summative assessment and concepts such as validity, reliability, norm and criterion-referencing. This chapter will introduce you to theories of assessment, thus enabling you to understand why you assess, when and how to assess your learners. Finally, this chapter will help you to understand how to analyse pupil assessment data in order to advance learning.

- **Why is it important?**

Assessment is a key professional skill. When used effectively it enables teachers to pinpoint accurately where learners are in their development and where they need to go next. This will enable you to plan for future learning, thus building on what learners already know and can do.

Statutory requirements

Primary schools have a statutory requirement to formally assess children's achievement at the end of the Early Years Foundation Stage against the Foundation Stage Profile. Statutory assessment also takes place at the end of Key Stage 1 and Key Stage 2 through the use of statutory assessment tests (SATs). Schools are formally required to report the outcomes of these assessments to parents, governors, local authorities and to the Department for Education in the case of academies, free schools and independent schools. There are no statutory assessments for pupils in Years 1, 3, 4 and 5 although schools are required to demonstrate that they have internal systems for monitoring pupils' achievement.

Why, when and how to assess

Assessment enables teachers to support learning more effectively in classrooms. Through assessment you will gain an accurate understanding of your learners' current achievements. You can then use this information to plan for pupils' next steps in learning, thus enabling you to support their development. Effective teaching builds on what learners already know, understand and can do. This knowledge enables you to pitch your teaching at a slightly higher level than pupils' current level of development in order to ensure that your learners are appropriately challenged. Regular assessment within and between lessons enables you to identify and address pupils' misconceptions in their learning. Through effective assessment you will be able to identify specific misconceptions and subsequently provide targeted intervention to overcome these.

Effective assessment is about promoting learning. It is not about grading pupils but it is about using assessment outcomes to plan subsequent teaching and learning experiences. Highly effective teachers embed assessment strategies into their lessons. In this way assessment is treated not as a bolt-on to teaching but as an integral part of good classroom practice. It is usually informal and carried out on a day-to-day basis within and between lessons. Assessment strategies are varied and range from planned and unplanned written observations, digital and audio footage, questioning, quizzes and specifically designed formal and informal assessment tasks. This might include, but is not restricted to, the use of tests. The aim of these strategies is to ascertain pupils' current level of understanding so that this can inform teaching and future planning. Much of the practice described above refers to *formative* assessment.

Summative assessment takes place at periodic fixed points in time during a child's educational journey. Its purpose is to enable teachers to summarise pupils' achievements at a fixed point in time. It is usually formal, although not always, and may be conducted through the use of standardised tests or teacher assessment professional judgement. Summative assessment data serves a wider accountability function and this is explored in further detail in this chapter.

Assessment *for* Learning: formative assessment

Assessment for Learning (AfL) is an umbrella term for any kind of assessment which enables you to promote future learning. It is often referred to as *formative* assessment because it informs your future planning and teaching. It can include a range of strategies and modes of assessment and it is usually informal, ongoing and takes place within and between lessons.

Effective AfL is underpinned by some key principles which should guide its implementation in the classroom. It has been stated that:

Assessment for Learning is the process of seeking and interpreting evidence for use by learners and their teachers to decide where the learners are in their learning, where they need to go and how best to get there.

(Assessment Reform Group, 2002)

The Assessment Reform Group identified ten principles of AfL. These state that AfL:

* *is part of effective planning;*
* *focuses on how students learn;*
* *is central to classroom practice;*
* *is a key professional skill;*
* *is sensitive and constructive;*
* *fosters motivation;*
* *promotes understanding of goals and criteria;*
* *helps learners know how to improve;*
* *develops the capacity for self-assessment;*
* *recognises all educational achievement.*

(Assessment Reform Group, 2002)

These principles are underpinned by a set of practices which, when implemented, effectively enable learners to make further progress.

Flexible planning

The primary national curriculum specifies the curriculum content which needs to be taught in each year group. Teachers use this framework to develop medium and short-term plans. In the early years the early learning goals specify the outcomes that children need to achieve by the end of the Early Years Foundation Stage. By keeping this 'big picture' in your mind you will have a clear view of what you learners need to achieve by the end of the year.

While curriculum frameworks are useful in outlining progression in learning, effective teaching is underpinned by planning which is sufficiently flexible and responsive to the needs of your learners. Thus, quality of learning is far more important than curriculum coverage. Highly effective teachers are skilfully able to adapt their planning *within* a lesson if it becomes apparent that learners are developing misconceptions. The skill of checking on learners' understanding at various stages in a lesson before moving onto the next stage is fundamental to securing good pupil progress. You may need to re-teach a concept or skill in a different way or you may need to model the new learning further in order to secure pupils' understanding. It is not sufficient to simply ask your learners if they have understood something. You need to develop strategies which enable you to check that they have understood what you have taught them. It is possible to use these assessment opportunities to identify those individuals and groups of learners who have developed misconceptions. You can then adapt your planning and teaching in the lesson to address these misconceptions in order to secure good pupil progress. This ability to *notice and respond* to misconceptions by addressing them is fundamental to effective teaching and learning.

As well as addressing misconceptions you also need to use assessment to identify those learners who need further challenge within a lesson. Some very able children grasp new learning quickly and need further challenge immediately. You need to notice these learners and quickly respond by giving them opportunities to deepen their understanding of a particular concept or skill that you have taught them by providing them with opportunities to apply the learning to different contexts. This will enable them to gain mastery of their learning.

Although your weekly plans will help you to identify the curriculum content over a sequence of lessons, you may need to adapt the content during the week to respond to pupils' needs. You may need to re-teach a lesson in a different way to secure pupils' understanding of a concept or skill. Additionally, you may be able to accelerate learning at a faster pace than you originally anticipated because your learners have grasped something more quickly than you anticipated. You need to treat your planning as a guide rather than being a slave to it! Highly effective teachers are skilled at planning flexibly so that lessons are pitched at exactly the right level to ensure that learners make progress. Your planning should take account of learners' current level of achievement and build on this. You need to have good subject knowledge in order to be able to identify next steps in learning. With a clear understanding of children's development within strands of learning, you will be able to identify what your pupils need to learn next. You will also be able to take learning back a stage if misconceptions develop. Good subject knowledge is essential in the assessment process because once you have a clear understanding of current achievement you need to know what aspects of learning to move the children onto next.

IN PRACTICE

You now know about the importance of adapting your lesson plans and weekly plans by addressing misconceptions and adding in further challenges where this is needed. This section introduces you to strategies through which you can adapt your teaching within lessons.

You might begin a lesson by modelling some new learning. This could be a skill that you want the children to develop. During the lesson you will need to provide your learners with opportunities to practise this skill. This will enable them to become more confident and it will help them to master the skill. Before you send them off to a task, it is important that you check on their understanding. In a mathematics lesson you might model a mathematical strategy. This means that you will demonstrate the strategy. It is not sufficient to simply explain the strategy. The strategy needs to be demonstrated in a very explicit way, for example, on a board. You might work through several examples with your learners in order to build confidence. You then need to build in an AfL question to enable them to show you that they have understood. You could give them a further question to solve on individual small whiteboards. You might want to organise an opportunity for some paired work at this point. Using the mini whiteboards your learners can show you how they have solved the question, thus enabling you to check which pupils have understood and which pupils have developed misconceptions. You could send those who have understood off to complete their task and you might keep those children back who appear to be struggling with the skill. You might use this as an opportunity for re-teaching the skill and going over further examples with them before sending them off to complete their task. This is one way of adapting your teaching in the lesson.

While your learners are on task, you need to notice and respond to misconceptions during the lesson. You might observe specific children who have developed misconceptions and

are in need of additional support. You can move in and support them to overcome the misconceptions, thus enabling them to make progress in their learning. Additionally, you might observe that some pupils need additional challenges because they have mastered the skill and now require opportunities to deepen their understanding. You might move them onto an extension task to give them an opportunity to apply the skill in a different context. This will deepen their understanding and give them mastery over their learning.

If several children appear to be developing misconceptions during the lesson, you might wish to consider stopping the class and doing a mini-plenary. This will give you an opportunity to re-teach the skill or to share good examples of work produced by children. However, you need to avoid stopping the class too many times because too much teacher talk can have a detrimental effect on children's learning, especially if it is preventing them from practising the skill that you want them to develop.

It might become apparent that specific pupils have demonstrated misconceptions right up to the end of the lesson despite intervention during the lesson. Rather than expecting these learners to sit through a plenary it might be more appropriate to ask the teaching assistant to do some intervention work with these learners on the specific skill or concept away from the rest of the class rather than asking them to sit through the plenary. During some lessons it might become apparent that pupils have mastered a particular skill with relative ease. In these instances, rather than using the plenary to recap on the skill, you might want to use the plenary to deepen children's understanding of that skill, for example, by asking them to use the taught skill to solve a problem. This will provide them with an opportunity to practise applying the skill in a different context.

Assessments of pupils' previous learning might indicate that specific pupils were not secure with an aspect of learning that was taught in a previous lesson. At the start of the next lesson it might be more appropriate for these pupils to work separately with the teaching assistant on the misconceptions rather than asking them to participate in the lesson introduction. These approaches to deploying teaching assistants in lessons will ensure that you maximise their impact on learners by asking them to target specific pupils at specific times with specific misconceptions.

Sharing learning goals

Your learners need to be able to understand and articulate what they are *learning* in a lesson. If they do not know what they are learning then they will not be able to self-assess their own progress. Sometimes both teachers and children find it very difficult to distinguish between what they are *learning* in a lesson (ie the learning objective) and what they are *doing* in a lesson (ie the task). If you are not clear on the distinction between the two then your learners will find it difficult to articulate what they are learning.

Learning objectives need to be expressed in child-friendly language. They are taken from the relevant curriculum frameworks and adapted into a form which children can easily understand. It is important for you to remember that curriculum frameworks are written for teachers rather than for learners. Some of the objectives in the curriculum frameworks are too broad and need to be broken down further. They need to be focused and expressed to learners with clarity. You will need to limit the number of objectives that you choose to focus on in any one lesson and it is usually more effective to focus on one objective rather than having too many.

IN PRACTICE

You might find it helpful to think about learning objectives in relation to the development of knowledge and skills. The task thus provides learners with a context for developing the new knowledge or skill that you are teaching. In an art lesson using powder paints you might want your learners to develop the skill of mixing a secondary colour from two primary colours. You might ask them to produce a painting of a flower in order to give them a context for practising the skill of colour mixing. In this example, the children are learning to mix secondary colours rather than learning to produce a painting of a flower. In a design and technology lesson you might want the children to develop the skill of joining two pieces of wood. You might ask them to make a vehicle out of wood. In this example, the children are learning how to make a joint and the vehicle provides them with a context through which to practise this skill. In a science lesson you might want the children to develop the skill of fair testing. You decide to ask them to carry out an investigation to test which material is the best material for waterproofing. In this example, the children are learning to develop the skill of fair testing and the waterproofing investigation provides the context through which this skill is developed.

Sharing criteria for success

Once learning objectives have been identified, pupils need to know what they need to do in order to successfully achieve that objective. They need to be really clear on what you are looking for so that they can self-assess their own work in order to determine whether they have successfully met the learning objective. Success criteria enable the children to achieve the learning objective. They need to be expressed in child-friendly language. Involving the children in generating the success criteria is a really useful way of giving them some ownership of the learning.

IN PRACTICE

This section presents different ways of framing success criteria. I will use examples to make this really clear.

Learning objective: We are learning to partition and recombine

Steps to Success:

Example $24 + 43 = 67$

1. Add the tens: $20 + 40 = 60$
2. Add the units: $4 + 3 = 7$
3. Add the tens and units together: $60 + 7 = 67$

Learning objective: We are learning to solve word problems

Example: There are <u>3</u> children. They <u>share</u> <u>9</u> sweets. How many sweets do they each get?

Steps to Success:

1. Underline the important parts of the problem
2. Decide whether you need to + – X or ÷
3. Record the calculation
4. Write the answer

Learning objective: We are learning to write in a sentence

Steps to Success:

Use a capital letter at the start of your sentence

T G H A

Use a finger space between each word

Use a full stop at the end of a sentence.

Learning objective: We are learning to describe the properties of 2D shapes

Remember to:

- count the number of sides;
- count the number of corners.

Learning objective: We are learning about the features of a non-chronological report

I can:

- highlight the title in yellow;
- highlight the sub-headings in green;
- highlight a question word in red;
- highlight the opening in pink;
- highlight the summary in blue.

Learning Objective: We are learning to use question words

Success criteria:

Must: everyone must ask questions using *what*

Should: most of you should be able ask questions using *where* and *when*

Could: some of you could ask questions using *how* and *why*

Learning Objective: We are learning to write an instructional text

Success criteria:

Tigers: I can put my instructions in the right order.

Zebras:

- I can include a title.
- I can include a list.
- I can put my instructions in order using numbers.
- I can use imperatives.

Lions:

- I can include a title.
- I can include a list.
- I can put my instructions in order using numbers.
- I can use imperatives.
- I can give additional details with my instructions.

It is essential that you refer to the success criteria when modelling the new learning. If your learners see you using the success criteria they will be more likely to refer to success criteria during their independent learning.

CRITICAL QUESTIONS

Reflect on the above examples of success criteria.

* *What are the advantages and limitations of the various approaches?*
* *What are the benefits of using success criteria?*
* *What are the dangers of over-scaffolding children's learning through the use of success criteria?*

Involving learners in the process of assessment

Involving learners in the assessment process gives them a sense of ownership. Assessment is most effective when it is done *with* learners rather than *to* them. The starting point for involving learners in assessment could involve pupils identifying their own targets. This process could be undertaken periodically such as at the end of each half-term so that learners are involved in setting targets for the next half-term. Targets could relate to aspects of the curriculum such as reading, writing or mathematics or they might relate to aspects of social and emotional development.

Providing learners with an opportunity to identify their own success criteria in lessons is a useful way of making success criteria more meaningful. Regardless of whether learners generate their own success criteria or whether these are prescribed, children cannot reliably make assessments of their own learning until they are clear about what success looks like. Once success criteria are identified, pupils can use these to self-assess their own learning. Additionally, peer-assessment is a useful way of children providing each other with feedback about their work. It is more effective when pupils assess each other's work using success criteria so that they know what to look for and what to comment on.

IN PRACTICE

During your next period of school-based training, research into school approaches for implementing self and peer-assessment. How effective do you think these approaches are?

CRITICAL QUESTION

* *What problems might arise from the implementation of self and peer-assessment in the primary classroom?*

Providing feedback which is sensitive and constructive

As a teacher you need to be aware of the emotional impact that feedback, including marks and grades, can have on your learners. Feedback (either verbal or written) needs to be sensitive and constructive in order to preserve in learners a positive sense of self (self-concept). Feedback which is overly harsh, critical and negative can have a long-lasting detrimental impact on learners' sense of self-worth. It is important to celebrate positive aspects and to celebrate success where it has been demonstrated, even where success is evident through learners taking very small steps. Targets for development need to be expressed in ways which both empower learners, so that they believe they can succeed, and motivate them so that they want to succeed.

Emphasising achievement rather than failure

Effective teachers help their learners to recognise the progress they are making in their learning. You need to make this progress visible to them so that they begin to recognise how they have improved within lessons and over time. It is not helpful to compare the achievements of different learners because such comparisons are often unhelpful and can result in pupils disengaging from the learning process. Finding ways of making achievements visible to pupils will be critical to developing within learners a sense of self-worth. This could include:

* looking through previous work with a child and identifying improvements made over time;
* asking pupils to identify their own achievements in half-termly pupil consultations;
* asking pupils to reflect on digital evidence (photographs or film) of their achievements;
* involving children in progress reviews with parents;
* familiarising children with assessment criteria and enabling them to use this to recognise their own achievements;
* involving peers in disseminating positive feedback.

Children need to understand the progress they have made, their current achievements and next steps in learning. You then need to ensure that you explain to your learners how they can achieve these targets so that they are able to take the steps you want them to achieve.

CRITICAL QUESTION

* *Parents are often concerned about how their child's current achievements compare with peers of the same age. How would you address this with parents?*

Marking and feedback

High quality feedback enables learners to make progress in their learning. Marking is a key professional skill and as such it is something that you will need to get to grips with quite quickly. All schools have policies on marking and feedback, and it is important that you follow the guidelines in the policy. However, there are some general principles of effective marking that should guide your practice. These are covered below:

* **Recognise achievement** and celebrate it: achievements should be linked to the success criteria because these specify what learners need to demonstrate in order to achieve the learning objective. You should avoid vague comments such as *Good work* because this gives a learner no information about why the work is good. It would be more effective to write a comment which describes the desired achievement such as *You have used some brilliant adjectives*. Try to find more than one example of where achievement has been demonstrated.
* **Identify a target:** again, this needs to be focused so you need to avoid vague targets. An example of a vague target would be to *Improve your writing*. This gives a learner no information about what actions they need to take to improve their writing. An example of a more focused target would be: *You need to put an adjective before each noun*. You could then give them an example of this through a worked example. You could then ask pupils to respond to this target either by writing their own sentence which includes an adjective or by writing a sentence with the adjective omitted. Pupils can then complete the missing adjective in the sentence.
* **Provide response time:** give them an opportunity to respond to the target. In the last example this might involve going back through the piece of work and adding in the adjectives using a different coloured pen. This will enable them to improve the piece of work. Alternatively, you could provide them with a worked example, so in this case you might present them with an example of a sentence which includes an adjective in front of a noun. You might then write out two or three sentences with nouns, omitting the adjectives, and ask them to read the sentences and add in the adjectives. For some children you might ask them to generate their own sentences with adjectives and nouns.
* **Check that they are making progress as a result of your feedback:** feedback is designed to move learning forward. If you are writing the same target on different pieces of work then this suggests that your learners are not addressing the target in their subsequent pieces of work. This also suggests that your feedback is not helping your learners to make progress. If this is the case you need to consider whether you are providing your learners with sufficient opportunities to respond to their targets. You might need to plan some focused intervention work with specific pupils to help them achieve specific targets.
* **Make your comments child-friendly:** if children are going to be able to use your feedback to make progress then they need to be able to understand it. Feedback needs to be expressed using child-friendly language and it needs to be legible.
* **Do not overload children's work with comments:** if you write too much on children's work they will not be able to process it all. Keep your feedback brief and clear.
* **Focus your feedback on what you asked them to demonstrate:** too often feedback focuses on generic issues such as presentation or spelling. While these issues are important, it is important to focus your feedback on the success criteria because this is what you asked them to demonstrate in the first place. An over-focus on spelling and presentation will lead to disengagement and it is important to focus on the content of children's work rather than overly focusing on how it looks.
* **The best feedback is instant:** children benefit from swift feedback about a piece of work they have just completed. It is most effective to provide feedback within the lesson because children can remember what they have just done. Feedback can be verbal or written. Where instant verbal or written feedback is not practical then learners should be given feedback the following day so that the feedback is meaningful to them. You cannot expect children to reflect on feedback for work they completed several weeks ago. It is likely that they will have forgotten what the focus of the task was.

* **Use the outcomes of marking to inform planning and teaching:** when you mark children's work you will get a good sense of whether you need to re-teach something or whether you are able to progress the learning to the next stage. You will be able to identify specific learners who have developed misconceptions and you will then be able to plan specific interventions to help them overcome these.

While this section has focused on providing learners with written feedback, it is important not to underestimate the power of verbal feedback in the classroom. You will need to provide your learners with verbal feedback throughout lessons to help them to overcome misconceptions or to challenge them further. This will enable them to make further progress. The advantage of verbal feedback is that it can be given instantly in the lesson. As with written feedback, it needs to be sensitive and constructive and it needs to be focused and specific. It needs to help learners understand their current achievement and next steps and pupils need opportunities to respond to it. Different schools have their own policies on whether verbal feedback needs to be documented. Much of the feedback given to very young learners will be verbal, given that they may not be able to read written feedback.

To provide clarification for teachers in relation to feedback, Ofsted has produced the following statement:

Ofsted recognises that marking and feedback to pupils, both written and oral, are important aspects of assessment. However, Ofsted does not expect to see any specific frequency, type or volume of marking and feedback; these are for the school to decide through its assessment policy. Marking and feedback should be consistent with that policy, which may cater for different subjects and different age groups of pupils in different ways, in order to be effective and efficient in promoting learning.

(Ofsted Handbook, 2015, p 2)

CRITICAL QUESTIONS

* *Why do you think Ofsted has produced this statement of clarification?*
* *Does every piece of work need to be marked?*
* *Should all marking be detailed?*

EVIDENCE-BASED TEACHING

According to Coe et al (2014), teaching which has high impact on outcomes for learners includes elements such as effective questioning and use of assessment by teachers. In addition, specific practices, like reviewing previous learning, providing model responses for students, giving adequate time for practice to embed skills securely and progressively introducing new learning (scaffolding) are also elements of high quality instruction.

EVALUATE

* *What are the advantages and disadvantages of providing learners with models and worked examples?*

CHALLENGE

Teachers frequently scaffold children's learning, particularly when children are learning something new. However, it is often the case that pupils are provided with too much help and this limits opportunities for demonstrating what they know and can do independently.

APPLY

* *When you next observe a lesson, look for these elements in the lesson: reviewing previous learning; presenting models; opportunities to practise newly taught skills; scaffolding and questioning.*
* *Were all the elements present in the lesson or were any elements missing?*
* *What practices might you adopt and what might you do differently?*

Mastery learning

The Report of the Commission of Assessment without levels defines *mastery* learning in the following way:

'Mastery learning' is a specific approach in which learning is broken down into discrete units and presented in logical order. Pupils are required to demonstrate mastery of the learning from each unit before being allowed to move on to the next, with the assumption that all pupils will achieve this level of mastery if they are appropriately supported. Some may take longer and need more help, but all will get there in the end. Assessment is built into this process. Following high-quality instruction, pupils undertake formative assessment that shows what they have learned well and what they still need to work on, and identifies specific 'corrective' activities to help them do this. After undertaking these corrective activities (or alternative enrichment or extension activities for those who have already achieved mastery), pupils retake a parallel assessment...The new national curriculum is premised on this kind of understanding of mastery, as something which every child can aspire to and every teacher should promote. It is about deep, secure learning for all, with extension of able students (more things on the same topic) rather than acceleration (rapidly moving on to new content). Levels were not consistent with this approach because they encouraged undue pace and progression onto more difficult work while pupils still had gaps in their knowledge or understanding. In developing new approaches to assessment, schools have the opportunity to make 'mastery for all' a genuine goal.

(McIntosh, 2015, p 17)

IN PRACTICE

Research how your school is addressing the concept of mastery learning.

CRITICAL QUESTIONS

* *What are the advantages of mastery learning?*
* *Can you think of any limitations of this approach to teaching, learning and assessment?*

EVIDENCE-BASED TEACHING

Ian Black and Dylan Wiliam (Black and Wiliam, 1998) carried out research which demonstrated that Assessment for Learning (AfL) has more effect on learning than any other single factor. They found that the effective implementation of AfL raises standards of achievement across the board, but particularly for low achievers. They discovered that AfL reduced the spread of attainment while raising attainment for everyone. Additionally, they found that where pupils are given better quality feedback, and are encouraged and empowered to take more responsibility, they learn more effectively. They found that giving marks and grades to pieces of work had a negative impact in that grades demotivate low attainers and make higher attainers complacent.

EVALUATE

* *What are the advantages and disadvantages of assigning marks or grades to pieces of work?*

CHALLENGE

* *The researchers found that learners benefit from having clear learning objectives. In what ways might objective-led teaching restrict more creative approaches to learning and teaching?*

APPLY

* *In school collect examples of different types of feedback issued to learners and specific examples of where feedback has enabled learners to make progress.*

Assessment *of* learning: summative assessment

Summative assessment is Assessment *of* Learning rather than Assessment *for* Learning. It is assessment which takes place at periodic points and provides a summary of pupils' current level of achievement at that point. Summative assessment can take place at the end of a term, year or key stage and often it is formal rather than informal. For example, a standardised test can be used to assess pupils' achievement at a fixed point in time.

Summative assessment fulfils largely different purposes to formative assessment. Although it provides pupils with an indication of their level of current achievement it is often used for accountability purposes. Schools, local authorities, school inspectors, parents and the Department for Education all make use of summative assessment data to ascertain whether a school is providing its pupils with good value for money. School inspections in England focus heavily on summative assessment data and in particular pupils' performance at the end of the Early Years Foundation Stage, Key Stage 1 and Key Stage 2. The assessment data is used to determine school effectiveness and headteachers may use summative assessment data to determine teacher effectiveness.

Schools have become increasingly accountable to a range of stakeholders. Summative assessment data helps schools to demonstrate that they are doing an effective job. Over the last three decades since the introduction of standardised testing in primary schools, summative assessment data has become *high-stakes* for schools. Testing of pupils in all year groups has become commonplace and the broad and balanced curriculum that the national curriculum was originally intended to provide has become increasingly narrower with a significant focus on the core areas of English and mathematics. The move towards the narrowing of the curriculum was aided by the introduction of the national literacy and numeracy strategies in the 1990s. These strategies have left their legacy in that most primary-aged children spend over 50 per cent of each day learning reading, writing and mathematics. Additionally, the introduction of high-stakes testing has resulted in primary school pupils being systematically coached to pass the tests.

Research has consistently highlighted the detrimental effects of testing young children. Additionally, narrowing down measures of school and teacher effectiveness to summative assessment scores neglects many important aspects which make schools more or less effective. Examples of broader notions of school effectiveness include aspects such as a school's commitment to promoting inclusion and the provision of enrichment activities. These broader notions of school effectiveness are often disregarded when inspectors make an overall evaluation of a school's effectiveness.

The use of summative assessment data has helped to marketise the education system. Summative assessment data are made freely available on the Ofsted website through the publication of the school's data dashboard. The data also has to be available on the school website. The data are assimilated into league tables and schools are ranked against each other, often with little consideration being taken account of the school context (eg level of social deprivation). The publication of summative assessment data ensures that schools remain accountable to a range of stakeholders (including school governors). School inspectors interrogate the data before a school inspection and parents can use the data to make choices about which schools to send their child to.

The marketisation of education inevitably forces schools to compete for the best students. Pupils who might threaten school performance indicators become risky business for schools who are fighting to maintain their positions in the league tables. Barbara Cole (2005) has emphasised that demonstrating a commitment to the principles of inclusivity places schools in a risky position, especially given that narrow performance indicators are the overriding concern for schools. However, schools, unlike businesses, cannot turn away their 'raw material' (ie their pupils). To comply with the Equality Act (2010) schools cannot discriminate on the basis of protected characteristics (such as disability) in their admissions policies. Despite this, the admission of pupils who might never be able to achieve outcomes in line with national expectations places some schools at greater risk than others.

The education system operates in a climate of performativity (Ball, 2003; Lyotard, 1984) in which highly performing schools survive and thrive and poorly performing schools are at risk of being closed down, while others may be converted into academies and taken over by larger more successful corporations. The climate of performativity has fundamentally altered what it means to be a teacher. It has changed teachers' identities and led to a significant degree of instability in the education system (Ball, 2003).

Although summative assessment data serves an accountability function in that it determines to a large extent school and teacher effectiveness, it is possible to use summative assessment data in a formative way to plan for subsequent teaching and learning experiences. The use of pupil data is addressed later in this chapter.

CRITICAL QUESTIONS

* *What are the benefits of standardised testing?*
* *What are the issues with standardised testing?*

EXTENDED THINKING

* *Do learners in school have access to a socially just education system? Explain your views in this respect.*
* *What could a more socially just curriculum look like?*
* *What could a more socially just assessment system look like?*

EVIDENCE-BASED TEACHING

Rosenshine (2010, 2012) has summarised over 40 years of research on effective teaching to identify ten principles of effective instruction. These are listed below:

1. Begin a lesson with a short review of previous learning.
2. Present new material in small steps, with student practice after each step.
3. Ask a large number of questions and check the responses of all students.
4. Provide models for problem-solving and worked examples.
5. Guide student practice.
6. Check for student understanding.
7. Obtain a high success rate.
8. Provide scaffolds for difficult tasks.
9. Require and monitor independent practice.
10. Engage students in weekly and monthly review.

EVALUATE

* *Which of the above principles demonstrate the application of Assessment for Learning?*
* *The current inspection framework for schools in England does not require teachers to demonstrate any particular model of teaching when they teach. What are the advantages and disadvantages of models such as this one?*

CHALLENGE

* *What are the dangers of using 'steps to success' when introducing new learning? Consider this question in relation to mathematics when teachers provide pupils with steps to help them solve a mathematical problem.*

APPLY

* *During your next period of school-based training, observe skilled teachers teaching lessons. Identify which of the above ten principles of effective teaching are evident in the lessons you observed and comment on the outcomes for learners as a result of the teaching.*

Validity and reliability

A valid form of assessment is one which measures what it is supposed to measure. If a test in English is supposed to test skills in creative writing, it does not assess children's skills in spelling and handwriting. If an assessment is reliable, it produces the same results on re-test, and will produce similar results with a similar cohort of students. It produces consistency.

Criterion and norm referenced assessment

Unlike a criterion-referenced test, a norm-referenced test indicates whether the student did better or worse than other people who took the test. For example, if the criterion is *Students should be able to correctly add two single-digit numbers*, then test questions might include the following: 5 + 4 = or 2 + 5 = [ ]. A criterion-referenced test reports the student's performance strictly according to whether the individual student correctly answered these questions. Criterion-referencing involves arriving at a student's grade by comparing his or her achievements with clearly stated criteria, outcomes and standards for particular levels of performance.

A norm-referenced test reports whether a student correctly answered more questions compared to other students in the group. In norm-referencing, the grade a student achieves depends not only on his or her level of achievement, but also on the achievement of other students. The essential characteristic of norm-referencing is that students are awarded their grades on the basis of their ranking within a particular cohort. A process of moderation and grade-adjustment takes place after the assessment has been taken. The final grade is identified after the test has been taken and after a standardisation process in which all pupils are ranked against each other.

CRITICAL QUESTIONS

- *What are the advantages and disadvantages of norm referencing?*
- *What are the advantages of criterion-referenced assessment?*

Use of pupil data

The use of pupil data in schools is currently undergoing a state of flux with the removal of the national curriculum levels. This section will address the use of pupil data both at the end of the Early Years Foundation Stage and the end of Key Stage 1.

Use of pupil data at the end of the Early Years Foundation Stage

Currently, at the end of the Early Years Foundation Stage pupils are assessed against each of the 17 Early Learning Goals. This is the Early Years Foundation Stage Profile (EYFSP), which remains statutory until July 2016, after which it will become non-statutory. The judgement against each goal must say whether the child's learning and development is:

* best described by the level of development expected at the end of the EYFS (expected);
* not yet at the level of development expected at the end of the EYFS (emerging);
* beyond the level of development expected at the end of the EYFS (exceeding).

The government defines a Good Level of Development (GLD) in the following way: children are defined as having reached a good level of development at the end of the EYFS if they have achieved at least the **expected** level in:

* the Early Learning Goals in the prime areas of learning (personal, social and emotional development; physical development; and communication and language) and;
* the Early Learning Goals in the specific areas of mathematics and literacy.

The assessments are made on the basis of ongoing informal assessment which takes place throughout the birth to age five age-range. Final assessments are internally and externally moderated. The data from the EYFSP can be used by Year 1 teachers to target areas of weakness in a child's development. These areas will specifically be the areas against which the child's development has been assessed as *emerging* (ie the child's learning and development in these areas is not yet at the expected level of development at the end of the EYFS). This will be a priority if aspects of a child's learning and development have been assessed as *emerging* in the prime areas of learning (communication and language, personal, social and emotional development and physical development). Additionally, Year 1 teachers will need to ensure that children who are exceeding expected levels of development in areas of learning are given appropriate learning challenges to meet their needs. These learners are often very able and will benefit from additional challenge.

IN PRACTICE

Children whose learning and development has been assessed as *emerging* (ie not yet at the expected level) in the prime areas of learning at the end of the EYFS will benefit from a play-based approach to learning. This will support them in reaching the expected level during the first term of Year 1. These children should be given further opportunities to achieve the Early Learning Goals at the expected level before assessing them against the national curriculum.

CRITICAL QUESTIONS

* *What are the barriers to continuing the assessment journey from the EYFS into Year 1?*
* *If a child is working below the expected level in communication and language at the end of the EYFS, how might this affect their achievements in literacy?*
* *If a child is working below the expected level in personal, social and emotional development at the end of the EYFS, how might this affect their achievements in other areas?*
* *If a child is working below the expected level in physical development at the end of the EYFS, how might this affect their achievement in writing?*

Use of pupil data at the end of Key Stage 1

Key Stage 1 statutory assessment data is used to inform predicted pupil data for the end of Key Stage 2. It important during Year 3 that pupils receive targeted intervention in subject areas where they performed below expected indicators of attainment at the end of Key Stage 1. Additionally, it is important to identify children at the end of Key Stage 1 who are working above expected indicators of attainment and ensure that they receive appropriate learning challenges in Key Stage 2. These are often very able children who require higher level work in order to meet their needs.

Use of pupil data at fixed review points during the year

Schools are now very efficient in tracking pupils' progress on a very regular basis. When you start to teach a new class you need to look at the latest assessment data for that cohort of pupils. You need to use this data to identify:

* pupils who are working below age-related expectations in particular areas;
* pupils who are working above age-related expectations in particular areas;
* pupils who are working at age-related expectations in particular areas.

The above simple analysis will help you to identify those children who need additional intervention and challenge in specific subjects. You then need to carry out a more detailed analysis of the data by looking at the performance of specific groups of pupils. You might want to analyse the following:

* whether there is an achievement gap between boys and girls in particular areas;
* whether there is an achievement gap between pupils with and without special educational needs and/or disabilities in particular areas;
* whether there is an achievement gap between pupils in receipt of pupil premium funding and those not in receipt of funding in particular areas;
* whether there is an achievement gap between minority ethnic groups and non-minority groups;
* whether there is an achievement gap between pupils who are looked after and those who are not;
* is pupil performance consistent between subject areas?

This analysis will help you target specific groups for specific interventions. Additionally, the analysis might raise interesting questions which cause you to reflect on the quality of teaching pupils have received. For example, if boys are performing less well than girls in reading you need to know why this is. You might need to review the range of texts available in your reading area to check that they are appealing to boys. If your learners with special educational needs are not making good progress, this might prompt you to reflect on aspects of your practice such as teacher expectations, level of challenge in lessons for this group of learners and the impact of teaching assistants on outcomes for learners if these children are receiving in-class support. You might also need to reflect on whether you and your colleagues have adequate levels of knowledge and skills to support the education of these pupils. This might flag up a need for further continuing professional development. If outcomes for looked after pupils are poor, this might prompt you to reflect on aspects such as level of challenge, teacher expectations and levels of pastoral support. If your pupils are making greater progress in mathematics than in English, you will need to ascertain why this is and plan actions to address this issue.

Analysis of assessment data will help you to identify those individuals and groups of learners who need further support and challenge in their learning. The process of

analysing data can alert you to issues that you were not aware of from your day-to-day observations. Statistics cannot replace the rich data gleaned from observations of pupils' learning, discussions with pupils and their parents, photographic, audio and digital footage and scrutiny of pupils' work. Much of this data will emerge from ongoing formative assessment. Summative assessment data can be used to support the formative assessments that you have made of pupils' learning. Statistics can enable you to spot trends in data (eg is pupil achievement in a particular subject increasing or decreasing?). Additionally, through statistical data you can make comparisons of performance between groups or individual pupils and this will help you to identify achievement gaps. Additionally, summative assessment data can be helpful when making overall judgements about the performance of a cohort over a period of time. It provides senior leaders, governors, parents and inspectors with headline information about pupils' achievement and hence the quality of teaching.

The new assessment arrangements in primary schools

Assessment processes in primary schools are currently in a state of transition following the government's decision to abolish national curriculum levels. The National Association of Head Teachers (NAHT) published the following response to this policy decision:

In the summer of 2013 the government announced the end of the official use of National Curriculum levels for assessment, following a recommendation from the expert group on National Curriculum Review. This caused concern across the profession and gave rise to such questions as how inspectors would react to multiple different assessment systems in place in schools, how progress would be demonstrated and judged, and how attainment would be measured. 'Levels' had become the accepted language both of pupil attainment and progress and the prospect of the removal of this language caused widespread consternation. The government has a stated policy of freedom and autonomy for school leaders. NAHT believes strongly that freedom need not mean fragmentation and, if the government wants to transfer ownership of assessment to the profession, then the profession should take that ownership and design a proper replacement. The removal of levels provides an opportunity for the government, its agencies and, most importantly, the profession itself to enhance the professionalism of teachers in the development and use of assessment. In furtherance of this aim, NAHT decided, therefore, to establish an independent commission on 'assessment without levels' to consider what lay behind good assessment and to look for examples of good practice already in place or developing in schools.

(NAHT, 2014, p 11)

CRITICAL QUESTIONS

- What do you think of the government's decision to abolish national curriculum levels?
- What are the arguments for and against the use of levels as a measure of achievement?

The NAHT produced the following principles of assessment to support schools in developing their own assessment policies:

Assessment is at the heart of teaching and learning.

- *Assessment provides evidence to guide teaching and learning.*
- *Assessment provides the opportunity for students to demonstrate and review their progress.*

Assessment is fair.

- *Assessment is inclusive of all abilities.*
- *Assessment is free from bias towards factors that are not relevant to what the assessment intends to address.*

Assessment is honest.

- *Assessment outcomes are used in ways that minimise undesirable effects.*
- *Assessment outcomes are conveyed in an open, honest and transparent way to assist pupils with their learning.*
- *Assessment judgements are moderated by experienced professionals to ensure their accuracy.*

Assessment is ambitious.

- *Assessment places achievement in context against nationally standardised criteria and expected standards.*
- *Assessment embodies, through objective criteria, a pathway of progress and development for every child.*
- *Assessment objectives set high expectations for learners.*

Assessment is appropriate.

- *The purpose of any assessment process should be clearly stated.*
- *Conclusions regarding pupil achievement are valid when the assessment method is appropriate (to age, to the task and to the desired feedback information).*
- *Assessment should draw on a wide range of evidence to provide a complete picture of student achievement.*
- *Assessment should demand no more procedures or records than are practically required to allow pupils, their parents and teachers to plan future learning.*

Assessment is consistent.

- *Judgements are formed according to common principles.*
- *The results are readily understandable by third parties.*
- *A school's results are capable of comparison with other schools, both locally and nationally.*

Assessment outcomes provide meaningful and understandable information for:

- *pupils in developing their learning;*
- *parents in supporting children with their learning;*
- *teachers in planning teaching and learning.*
- *school leaders and governors in planning and allocating resources;*
- *government and agents of government.*

Assessment feedback should inspire greater effort and a belief that, through hard work and practice, more can be achieved.

(NAHT, 2014, p 8)

CRITICAL QUESTIONS

* *Compare these principles of assessment to the ten principles set out by the Assessment Reform Group. What are the similarities and differences between the two sets of principles?*
* *Do you agree with all of the principles?*
* *Are there any principles which are omitted from the above list but are, nevertheless, important?*

Diagnostic assessment

The final report of the Commission on Assessment Without Levels stated:

The new national curriculum is founded on the principle that teachers should ensure pupils have a secure understanding of key ideas and concepts before moving onto the next phase of learning. This is particularly beneficial for pupils with special educational needs. It leads to a much more focused approach where early intervention can be provided promptly to address any concerns about pupils' progress. Teachers become much better informed about pupils' understanding of concepts and ideas and can build a more accurate picture of their individual needs. This is an example of how formative assessment can be used for diagnostic purposes.

(McIntosh, 2015, p 16)

Diagnostic assessment is a process of identifying gaps in pupils' understanding, knowledge and skills. Through early intervention these gaps are then addressed through focused teaching which targets the area(s) of weakness.

IN PRACTICE

* *Research the approach used in your school for use of diagnostic assessment. How are gaps in learning identified and addressed?*

Statutory assessments at the end of Key Stage 1

The statutory assessment arrangements for assessing pupils' attainment at the end of Key Stage 1 have been revised for 2016. The Department for Education website (www.dfe.gov.uk) states that the assessment arrangements for 2016 will include the following:

For 2016, a new set of Key Stage 1 national curriculum tests replaces the previous tests and tasks. Schools should no longer use the 2007 and 2009 Key Stage 1 test and task materials as they relate to the old national curriculum.

The new tests consist of:

* English reading Paper 1: combined reading prompt and answer booklet;
* English reading Paper 2: reading booklet and reading answer booklet;
* English grammar, punctuation and spelling Paper 1: spelling;
* English grammar, punctuation and spelling Paper 2: questions;
* mathematics Paper 1: arithmetic;
* mathematics Paper 2: reasoning.

There is no longer a test for English writing. There won't be any test-based assessment of writing as part of the Key Stage 1 tests. This will be done through teacher assessment. Teachers can use their discretion to decide if pupils require a break during any of the tests or whether, if appropriate, to stop the test early.

Key Stage 1 English reading test

The new reading test has a greater emphasis on the comprehension elements of the new curriculum. There are two reading papers, one with the texts and questions combined and one with more challenging texts with the questions in a separate booklet. Both papers must be administered to all pupils. Each paper will have a selection of unrelated texts of increasing difficulty. There will be a mixture of text genres.

Paper 1 consists of a combined reading prompt and answer booklet. It is expected that the test will take approximately 30 minutes to complete but it is not strictly timed. The paper includes a list of useful words and some practice questions for teachers to use to introduce the contexts and question types to pupils.

Paper 2 consists of a reading answer booklet and a separate reading booklet. It is expected that the test will take approximately 40 minutes to complete but it is not strictly timed. There are no practice questions on this paper.

Key Stage 1 English grammar, punctuation and spelling test

The new grammar, punctuation and spelling test has an emphasis on technical aspects of grammar. There are two papers, Paper 1: spelling and Paper 2: questions. The written task has been removed and writing will instead be assessed through teacher assessment.

Paper 1: spelling consists of an answer booklet for pupils to complete and a test transcript to be read by the test administrator. Pupils will have approximately 15 minutes to complete the test but it is not strictly timed; they will write the 20 missing words in the answer booklet.

Paper 2: questions consists of a single test paper focusing on pupils' knowledge of grammar, punctuation and vocabulary. Pupils will have approximately 20 minutes to complete the questions in the test paper but it is not strictly timed. There will be no contextualised questions in the test (as there were in the initial sample questions).

Key Stage 1 mathematics test

In mathematics at Key Stage 1, an arithmetic test has been introduced. There are two papers, Paper 1: arithmetic and Paper 2: reasoning.

Paper 1: arithmetic assesses pupils' confidence and mathematical fluency with whole numbers, place-value and counting. The test consists of a single test paper. It is expected that the test will take approximately 20 minutes to complete but it is not strictly timed.

Some items in the arithmetic test have grids in the answer spaces or working out spaces. The grids are there for questions where the pupils may benefit from using more formal methods for calculations.

Paper 2: reasoning assesses pupils' mathematical fluency, problem solving and reasoning skills. This test consists of a single test paper. It is expected that the reasoning paper will take approximately 35 minutes to complete but it is not strictly timed. The paper includes a practice question and 5 aural questions. After the aural questions, the time for the remainder of the paper should be approximately 30 minutes.

(DfE, 2016)

Statutory assessments at the end of Key Stage 2

The statutory assessment arrangements for assessing pupils' attainment at the end of Key Stage 2 have been revised for 2016. The Department for Education website (www.dfe.gov.uk) states that the assessment arrangements for 2016 will include the following:

For 2016, a new set of Key Stage 2 national curriculum tests has been introduced consisting of:

* English reading: reading booklet and associated answer booklet;
* English grammar, punctuation and spelling Paper 1: short answer questions;
* English grammar, punctuation and spelling Paper 2: spelling;
* mathematics Paper 1: arithmetic;
* mathematics Paper 2: reasoning;
* mathematics Paper 3: reasoning.

Key Stage 2 English reading test

The English reading test will have a greater focus on fictional texts. There is also a greater emphasis on the comprehension elements of the new curriculum. The test consists of a reading booklet and a separate answer booklet.

Pupils will have a total of one hour to read the three texts in the reading booklet and complete the questions at their own pace. There will be a mixture of genres of text. The least-demanding text will come first with the following texts increasing in level of difficulty.

Pupils can approach the test as they choose: for example, working through one text and answering the questions before moving on to the next. The questions are worth a total of 50 marks.

Key Stage 2 English grammar, punctuation and spelling test

The new grammar, punctuation and spelling test has a greater focus on knowing and applying grammatical terminology, with the full range of punctuation tested.

The new national curriculum sets out clearly which technical terms in grammar are to be learned by pupils and these are explicitly included in the test and detailed in the new test framework. It also defines precise spelling patterns and methodologies to be taught, and these are the basis of spellings in the test. There will be no contextual items in the test. As in previous years, there are two papers, Paper 1: questions and Paper 2: spelling.

Paper 1: questions consists of a single test paper. Pupils will have 45 minutes to complete the test, answering the questions in the test paper. The questions are worth 50 marks in total.

Paper 2: spelling consists of an answer booklet for pupils to complete and a test transcript to be read by the test administrator. Pupils will have approximately 15 minutes to complete the test, but it is not strictly timed. They will write the 20 missing words in the answer booklet. The questions are worth 20 marks in total.

Key Stage 2 mathematics test

There are three papers: Paper 1: arithmetic; Paper 2: reasoning; and Paper 3: reasoning.

Paper 1: arithmetic replaces the mental mathematics test. The arithmetic test assesses basic mathematical calculations. The test consists of a single test paper. Pupils will have 30 minutes to complete the test, answering the questions in the test paper. The paper consists of 36 questions which are worth a total of 40 marks.

The questions will cover straightforward addition and subtraction and more complex calculations with fractions worth 1 mark each, and long divisions and long multiplications worth 2 marks each.

Papers 2 and 3 each consist of a single test paper. Pupils will have 40 minutes to complete each test, answering the questions in the test paper. Each paper will have questions worth a total of 35 marks.

In some answer spaces, where pupils need to show their method, square grids are provided for the questions on the arithmetic paper and some of the questions on Paper 2.

(DfE, 2016)

Statutory assessments for learners with special educational needs

The P-scales are the statutory assessment for reporting on attainment in English, mathematics and science at the end of Key stages 1 and 2 for pupils with special educational needs. Schools may also use the P-levels to report on pupils' progress to parents at other assessment points. The P-levels can be accessed on the Department for Education website. Assessment is carried out through teacher assessment based on ongoing observation, discussions with pupils, parents and other professionals, and scrutiny of the child's recorded work.

The baseline assessment in Reception

From September 2016, reception teachers will be required to carry out a baseline assessment on each child at the start of the reception year. This is currently being piloted and a range of commercial assessment packages have been made available for schools to aid this process during the 2015–16 academic year. The data from the baseline will be used to make predictions about each child's expected development. The data from the baseline assessment can be used to pinpoint areas of strength and weakness across a child's profile. The DfE states that:

The reception baseline will be the only measure used to assess progress for children who start reception in September 2016 and beyond. Key stage 1 assessments will remain statutory but will not

be used for the progress floor standard of all-through primary schools. The progress of pupils starting reception in September 2016 in all-through primary schools will be measured in 2023 when these pupils reach the end of key stage 2. Schools that choose not to use an approved baseline assessment from 2016 will be judged on an attainment floor standard alone ... From September 2016 the Early Years Foundation Stage Profile will no longer be compulsory. The Early Years Foundation Stage itself will continue to be statutory, supporting children to experience a broad and engaging programme of learning in reception.

(DfE, 2014, pp 7–8)

CRITICAL QUESTIONS

- *What are the advantages of introducing a baseline assessment at the start of the Reception year?*
- *What are the arguments against the introduction of a baseline assessment at the beginning of the Reception year?*

The phonics screening check in Year 1

The phonics screening check must be carried out during Year 1. It assesses children's ability to decode both real and pseudo words. Ofsted inspections place significant focus on a school's results in this assessment and the test has become 'high-stakes'. Children who do not meet the standard to 'pass' the check are required to repeat the assessment in Year 2.

CRITICAL QUESTIONS

- *What are the benefits of the introduction of a phonics screening check?*
- *What are the academic debates in relation to this assessment?*
- *What are your views in relation to this assessment?*

The school's floor standard

The floor standard defines the minimum that the government expects schools to meet. This relates to the proportion of pupils who meet the expected standard by the end of Key Stage 2 in both English and mathematics.

The DfE states that:

We will continue to set minimum requirements, known as floor standards, for schools...We will have a new floor standard that holds schools to account both on the progress they make and on how well their pupils achieve. A progress measure is the fairest way to assess many schools. We will use the reception baseline, when taken, to assess the progress children make between starting reception and age 11, compared to other children with the same starting points. The arrangements for different types of schools are set out below. To ensure that children succeed across the curriculum, we are proposing that schools will only meet the progress standard if pupils make sufficient progress in all of reading, writing and mathematics. In addition, we want to celebrate the success of schools that equip the vast majority of their pupils for life at secondary school. For that reason we are including an attainment element in the floor standard. Our expectations are high. We want schools to aim to have 85% of their pupils at this new higher standard for the end of key stage

2 by 2016. Over time, we expect more and more schools to reach this standard as they rise to the challenge of ensuring that almost all children master the basics at the end of their primary schooling.

An all-through primary school will be above the floor standard if:

- *pupils make sufficient progress at key stage 2 from their starting point in the reception baseline; or,*
- *85% or more of pupils meet the new expected standard at the end of key stage 2 (similar to a level 4b under the current system).*
- *A junior or middle school will be above the floor standard if:*
- *pupils make sufficient progress at key stage 2 from their starting point at key stage 1; or,*
- *85% or more of pupils meet the new expected standard at the end of key stage 2 (similar to a level 4b under the current system).*

(DfE, 2014, p 10)

CRITICAL QUESTIONS

- *What are the benefits of the government setting schools a floor standard?*
- *What issues might arise from the new attainment standard?*

Performance descriptors

To support schools in making assessments at the end of Key Stage 1 and Key Stage 2, the government has published a set of interim performance descriptors to demonstrate the knowledge and skills that are expected of pupils if they are meeting the expected standards at the end of each key stage. This guidance is intended to support schools in the summative assessment process at the end of each key stage now that national curriculum levels have been removed.

The Standards and Testing Agency has stated some key principles which should underpin the use of the performance descriptors. These are stated below:

- This statutory interim framework is to be used only to make a teacher assessment judgement at the end of the key stage following the completion of the key stage 1 curriculum. It is not intended to be used to track progress throughout the key stage.
- The interim framework does not include full coverage of the content of the national curriculum and focuses on key aspects for assessment. Pupils achieving the different standards within this interim framework will be able to demonstrate a broader range of skills than those being assessed.
- This interim framework is not intended to guide individual programmes of study, classroom practice or methodology.
- Teachers must base their teacher assessment judgement on a broad range of evidence from across the curriculum for each pupil.
- The evidence used must include the key stage 1 English reading test, which does not focus solely on the key aspects listed in this interim framework.
- Individual pieces of work should be assessed according to a school's assessment policy and not against this interim framework.

(Standards and Testing Agency, 2015a, p 2)

The Standards and Testing Agency provided statutory guidance on pupil performance and Key Stages 1 and 2 (which you can find at www.gov.uk/government/publications/interim-frameworks-for-teacher-assessment-at-the-end-of-key-stage-1, and www.gov.uk/government/publications/interim-frameworks-for-teacher-assessment-at-the-end-of-key-stage-2). The guidance identifies three broad categories of achievement at Key Stages 1 and 2 in reading, writing, mathematics and science. Children's achievement is described as 'working towards the expected standards', 'working at the expected standards' or 'working at greater depth within the expected standards'. Descriptions are then provided to help schools to benchmark children's performance against. This provides a national benchmark which ensures consistency in assessments between schools.

EXTENDED THINKING

There is a significant focus on how well schools enable children to reach age-related expectations in reading, writing and mathematics.

- *What effect does this have on pupils who are not able to demonstrate this level of academic achievement but nevertheless have strengths and talents in the wider curriculum?*
- *What effect does this have on teachers who work in schools with significant proportions of learners with special educational needs?*
- *What effect does this have on teachers who work in schools in areas of social deprivation?*

TECHNOLOGY

In order to address *life after levels* many schools have now purchased new assessment software which helps schools to monitor and track children's progress over time. During your ITT you will spend time in different schools. It is important that you familiarise yourself with the assessment software systems in each of the different schools. As you progress through your training you should start to evaluate the different packages that you see in schools.

Critical reflections

This chapter has provided you with an overview of formative and summative assessment. It has emphasised the significant role that formative assessment can have on learning and the dangers of high-stakes summative assessment. Measuring children's academic achievements is nothing new. Education has for many years sorted and categorised children in different ways and this process is disempowering to those learners who are unable to demonstrate academic achievement. The most important thing to focus on is how you move children on from their starting points. The emphasis on achievement rather than attainment is necessary because this acknowledges the small steps that some children take. While educational policy continues to emphasise attainment rather than achievement, teachers who choose to work with learners who struggle academically will continue to be disadvantaged, as will their pupils, by an education system that labels them as failures. In these circumstances, aim to make a difference to children by enabling them to make progress from their starting points and do your very best to enable your learners to reach their full potential. Use assessment to move learning forward rather than to label, categorise and stigmatise.

KEY READINGS

Classic:

Clarke, S (2001) *Unlocking Formative Assessment: Practical Strategies for Enhancing Pupils' Learning in the Primary Classroom*. London: Hodder and Stoughton.

Contemporary:

DfE (2014) *Reforming Assessment and Accountability for Primary Schools: Government Response to Consultation on Primary School Assessment and Accountability*. London: DfE.

McIntosh, J (2015) *Final Report of the Commission on Assessment without Levels*. [online] Available at: www.gov.uk/government/uploads/system/uploads/attachment_data/file/483058/Commission_on_Assessment_Without_Levels_-_report.pdf (accessed 12 April 2016).

References

Assessment Reform Group (2002), *Research-based Principles to Guide Classroom Practice*. London: Assessment Reform Group. [online] Available at: http://cdn.aaia.org.uk/content/uploads/2010/06/Assessment-for-Learning-10-principles.pdf (accessed 15 May 2016).

Ball, S J (2003) The teacher's soul and the terrors of performativity. *Journal of Education Policy*, 18(2): 215–28.

Black, P and Wiliam, D (1998) *Inside the Black Box: Raising Standards through Classroom Assessment*. London: Kings College London.

Carter, A (2015) *Review of Initial Teacher Training*. London: DfE.

Coe, R, Aloisi, C, Higgins, S T and Major, L E (2014) *What Makes Great Teaching? Review of the Underpinning Research*. London: The Sutton Trust.

Cole, B (2005) Good faith and effort? Perspectives on educational inclusion. *Disability and Society*, 20(3): 331–44.

DfE (2014) *Reforming Assessment and Accountability for Primary Schools: Government Response to Consultation on Primary School Assessment and Accountability*. London: DfE.

Lyotard, J F (1984) *The Postmodern Condition: A Report on Knowledge*, Vol. 10. Manchester: Manchester University Press.

McIntosh, J (2015) *Final Report of the Commission on Assessment without Levels*. [online] Available at: www.gov.uk/government/uploads/system/uploads/attachment_data/file/483058/Commission_on_Assessment_Without_Levels_-_report.pdf (accessed 12 April 2016).

National Association of Head Teachers (NAHT) (2014) *Report of the NAHT Commission on Assessment*. London: NAHT.

Ofsted (2015) *School Inspection Handbook*. London: Ofsted.

Rosenshine, B (2010) *Principles of Instruction*. International Academy of Education, UNESCO. Geneva: International Bureau of Education. [online] Available at: www.ibe.unesco.org/fileadmin/user_upload/Publications/Educational_Practices/EdPractices_21.pdf (accessed 15 May 2016).

Rosenshine, B (2012) *Principles of Instruction: Research Based Principles That All Teachers Should Know*. *American Educator*, Spring 2012. [online] Available at: www.aft.org/pdfs/americaneducator/spring2012/Rosenshine.pdf (accessed 15 May 2016).

Standards and Testing Agency (2015a) *Interim Teacher Assessment Frameworks at the End of Key Stage 1*. Standards and Testing Agency.

Standards and Testing Agency (2015b) *Interim Teacher Assessment Frameworks at the End of Key Stage 2*. Standards and Testing Agency.

8: BEHAVIOUR MANAGEMENT

TEACHERS' STANDARDS

This chapter addresses the following Teaching Standard:

Teachers' Standard 7: Manage behaviour effectively to ensure a good and safe learning environment

Teachers must:

- *have clear rules and routines for behaviour in classrooms, and take responsibility for promoting good and courteous behaviour both in classrooms and around the school, in accordance with the school's behaviour policy;*
- *have high expectations of behaviour, and establish a framework for discipline with a range of strategies, using praise, sanctions and rewards consistently and fairly;*
- *manage classes effectively, using approaches which are appropriate to pupils' needs in order to involve and motivate them;*
- *maintain good relationships with pupils, exercise appropriate authority, and act decisively when necessary.*

PROFESSIONAL LINKS

The *Carter Review of Initial Teacher Training* stated that:

Behaviour management should be prioritised within ITT programmes. ITT providers should build in opportunities for trainees to learn from a range of outstanding teachers, with a specific focus on managing pupil behaviour. We have found that the most effective programmes are practically focussed and underpinned by deeper understanding of behavioural issues. We believe it is crucial that trainees receive practical advice – tangible strategies for new teachers, grounded in evidence. All ITT programmes, for example, should support teachers to develop their own classroom presence and cover use of voice, body language and how to develop classroom routines and defuse situations.

(Carter, 2015, para XXII, p 10)

In our discussions with ITT providers, we have found some reluctance towards practical approaches to training in behaviour management. We feel that in all programmes there is a need for more practical and specific advice on managing behaviour.

(Carter, 2015, para XXIII, p 10)

Additionally, the Carter Review made the following recommendation:

Recommendation 1f: *Managing pupil behaviour should be included in a framework for ITT content, with an emphasis on the importance of prioritising practical advice throughout programmes.*

(Carter, 2015, para XXIII, p 10)

It is not sufficient for trainee teachers to only have a theoretical understanding of behaviour management. While it is important that practices in the classroom are theoretically underpinned, trainees need to know a range of practical strategies which are evidence-based and which they can transfer into the classroom. Understanding theories of behaviour management will not help trainee teachers to manage a challenging pupil or indeed work effectively with a challenging class.

Following the publication of the Carter Review (Carter, 2015), the government White Paper (2016) stated that:

unnecessary workload and poor pupil behaviour frustrate teachers and erode their energy, and are the biggest factors of teachers choosing to leave the profession.

(DfE, 2016a, para 2.48, p 36)

Additionally, the government White Paper also made the following points:

To help teachers crack down on bad behaviour, we have already made it clear that teachers can use reasonable force to maintain behaviour. We have also extended searching powers for banned items and allowed teachers to impose same-day detentions. We are now ensuring that new teachers are trained to deal with low-level disruption that stops pupils learning. As set out above, we have asked behaviour expert Tom Bennett to review behaviour management in ITT and to produce a second report on how to prevent and tackle classroom disruption.

(DfE, 2016a, para 2.50, p 37)

The determination of the government to '*crack down*' and use '*force*' and detentions is deeply worrying. It would appear that the focus largely reflects behaviourist psychology which emphasises the consequences of behaviour rather than the causes of poor behaviour.

CRITICAL QUESTIONS

* *What are the arguments for and against the use of reasonable force for managing classroom behaviour?*
* *Why do you think behaviour management has become a policy priority in Initial Teacher Training?*

CHAPTER OBJECTIVES

* **What is this chapter about?**

In addition to introducing you to practical strategies to help you manage pupils' behaviour, this chapter will introduce you to theories which underpin behaviour management. It will introduce you to behaviourism and humanism as branches of psychology which have relevance to understanding children's behaviour. Case studies will be interwoven throughout the chapter to help you apply theory to practice.

* **Why is it important?**

Nearly all trainee teachers and many qualified teachers worry about behaviour management. Anxieties can range from how to manage the behaviour of an individual pupil with challenging behaviour to the challenges of managing the behaviour of a 'tough' class. Anxieties about behaviour management can result in stress and there is evidence to suggest that this is a common reason why teachers leave the profession (Barmby, 2006).

Code of Practice: challenging behaviour

In the *Special Educational Needs and Disability Code of Practice*, children with challenging and disruptive behaviour fall under the category of those with social, emotional and mental health difficulties. The Code states:

Children and young people may experience a wide range of social and emotional difficulties which manifest themselves in many ways. These may include becoming withdrawn or isolated, as well as displaying challenging, disruptive or disturbing behaviour. These behaviours may reflect underlying mental health difficulties such as anxiety or depression, self-harming, substance misuse, eating disorders or physical symptoms that are medically unexplained. Other children and young people may have disorders such as attention deficit disorder, attention deficit hyperactive disorder or attachment disorder.

(DfE, 2015, para 6.32)

In addition, it states:

Schools and colleges should have clear processes to support children and young people, including how they will manage the effect of any disruptive behaviour so it does not adversely affect other pupils.

(DfE, 2015, para 6.33)

Much of the behaviour that you have to deal with in schools will not fall into the category of challenging behaviour. A great deal of it will be in the form of low-level disruption and this is what most of this chapter focuses on. That said, it is likely at some point during your career that you will have to face challenging behaviour. In managing these cases, it is important that you consult with members of the school leadership team to find ways forward. Blanket strategies are not guaranteed to work for specific pupils, although they will give you a basis from which to develop your own strategies. In supporting children with challenging behaviour you should:

- involve children in all decision-making processes;
- involve children in reviewing their own progress and setting new targets;
- involve parents in all decision-making processes;
- involve parents in reviewing progress and setting new targets;
- set SMART behaviour targets (**s**pecific, **m**easurable, **a**chievable, **r**ealistic, **t**imed);
- break lessons into a series of smaller 15/20-minute tasks;
- ask the child what would help them;
- catch the child demonstrating the desired behaviours and reward them;
- consider whether you need to introduce an individual reward system for specific pupils with behavioural needs;
- find out what the child is interested in and build this into their curriculum;
- diffuse situations, for example, through introducing distractions or removing the child from a situation;
- monitor what triggers the child's behaviour and aim to remove these;
- provide support to parents for managing the child's behaviour at home in order to develop consistency in approaches;

* liaise with and seek advice from other professionals such as educational psychologists;
* separate the behaviour from the child;
* develop the child's self-concept and self-esteem;
* ensure that sanctions are applied fairly and are proportionate;
* address situations in school and wherever possible keep situations in school unless an incident is serious. Issuing a punishment at school before a second punishment is issued at home is not fair on the child;
* be consistent in your approach to behaviour management by having consistent expectations;
* consider whether the child might benefit from the use of a visual timetable;
* pre-empt situations;
* believe in the child by telling them you know they can improve;
* plan tasks which enable the child to successfully achieve the learning outcomes;
* never give up on the child – it is your responsibility to educate them.

A principled approach to behaviour management

Some adults view children who behave inappropriately in negative and disempowering ways. They view them as *difficult* students who have a poor attitude to learning. This mindset is unhelpful because children are quick to pick up on how adults feel about them. If children start to believe that adults do not like them, this can result in further disengagement, confrontations and other negative behaviours. I find the following set of principles useful when working with children with behavioural needs:

* All children are inherently good.
* All behaviour is an attempt to communicate something.
* Adults in the classroom significantly affect the quality of the atmosphere for all students.
* Power and control are not effective ways to shape students' behaviour.

It is important that you are able to separate the child's behaviour from the individual. Essentially, you do not have a problem with the child per se but you do have a problem with their behaviour. The child needs to know that they are valued as much as any other child in the class. If they start to pick up that they are not valued, then this can quickly result in them developing a low self-concept which can then result in further undesired behaviours.

Children are not born being disruptive. They are highly susceptible to environmental effects and these shape their behaviours in positive or negative ways. Children's behaviour is influenced by a range of factors, including, but not restricted to: the effects of parenting; community influences; peer and media influences. Additionally, children's behaviour is influenced by cultural factors, relationships with others and the structures which underpin the education system. What happens after birth can significantly influence children's behaviour and it is important to remember this.

It is perhaps over-simplistic to assume that children have a sense of free-will (agency) and therefore make their own choices about how they wish to behave. Structural influences are influences which they have no control over. The education system is a structural influence that is imposed on children. The structures which then underpin the education system (ie the curriculum and the assessment system) can result in disengagement for those learners

who do not see the relevance or value of education. The growth of standardised testing has resulted in the marginalisation of those learners who are unable to demonstrate the required academic achievements that the schooling system values. Disengagement from curricula or assessment processes can manifest in forms of inappropriate behaviour, which are often attempts to communicate that the education system has excluded them and is failing to meet their needs. For some, they give up on the education system and the education system then gives up on them.

Effective teachers never give up on children. Every child deserves to be taught by an adult who respects them and will 'fight their corner'. As the late Rita Pierson said in her famous Ted Talk *'kids don't learn from people they don't like'*. She emphasised in her talk that every child deserves a champion; an adult who stands up for them and never gives up on them and who insists that they become the best that they can be. She talked about the power of human connection and human relationships in teaching. You should not underestimate the power of effective relationships in the classroom. Children often want to please those teachers they like.

Although it takes time to build relationships, there are several strategies that you can try which help to establish effective relationships. These include:

- seeking to understand children by listening to them;
- being positive with children by pointing out what they can do rather than what they cannot do;
- building a 'winning team' spirit – *'You are the best class'*;
- building a 'can-do' culture – emphasising that perseverance and hard work will pay off and even though learning is difficult they can do it;
- having a sense of humour;
- smiling often;
- giving children the chance to prove how well they can behave and allowing them the chance to have fresh starts;
- rewarding good behaviour by 'catching them being good';
- being consistent;
- treating children as individuals rather than comparing them to others.

This is not an exhaustive list but it provides you with a starting point for building relationships with children. It is important to remember that you are the adult and they are children! In order to manage children's behaviour effectively, we must firstly learn to manage our own behaviour. Getting frustrated or angry are rarely effective strategies and children will imitate your behaviour so it is always more effective to stay calm. Naturally, children will test the boundaries that have been imposed upon them. It is your job to gently remind them of the rules and expectations. Shouting at children and applying sanctions are often ineffective because they serve to reinforce the unequal power between children and adults. Such strategies will not help you to establish effective relationships which are rooted in mutual respect.

Children will often behave in ways which you consider to be childish. That is because they are children! Therefore, their behaviour should come as no surprise to you. Children's behaviour is influenced by their maturity as well as expectations by their parents or expectations in the communities in which they live. Their behaviour is also influenced by peers and the media. When children come into school they have to learn different rules of the game. They cannot behave in the same way in school as they behave at home. For some children, they have to completely unlearn behaviours which have been acceptable in the home or community when they start school. They have to learn to adapt their behaviour in different situations and this process of adaptation can take time.

Circle of intimacy

David Moore's *Circle of Intimacy* captures this process of adaptation really effectively. Essentially, the model assumes that all children initially operate within a circle of intimacy where they learn to live with members of their immediate family (parents, brothers, sisters). As children then start to form friendships, they move into a *circle of friendship* where they might be introduced to different codes of behaviour. Some children then enter into a *circle of participation* where they start to participate in wider social groups and networks. This helps to boost their self-esteem. As they move through these two inner circles, children have to learn to adjust their behaviours because those behaviours which were accepted in the circle of intimacy might not be accepted in the circles of friendship or participation. Participating in clubs and societies helps to develop their confidence but also the skill of adjusting behaviour from one context to another. Finally, children enter into a *circle of exchange*. It is in this circle that they meet people with direct authority over them such as teachers.

Increasingly, there are children who operate within a circle of intimacy but who do not enter into the circles of friendship and participation. These children only interact with people who are closest to them and they may observe aggressive or other inappropriate behaviour within this circle. When they go to school they enter into the circle of exchange but as they do so they bring into this circle the aggressive or inappropriate behaviours that they observed in the circle of intimacy. They have not developed the skill of adjusting their behaviours to different situations because they have not had the opportunity to develop wider friendships or to be part of social groups. These children have not had the opportunity to practise adjusting their behaviour prior to starting school. As a teacher you need to support these children to adjust their behaviour to the school context. You need to model appropriate behaviours and you need to teach desired behaviour in a very explicit way.

You cannot assume that children come to school knowing how to behave. Also, there is little point in blaming ineffective parenting or other factors for the child's behaviour. Although this will help you to understand the cause it does not help you to address the issue of their behaviour. Some children need a structured social and emotional intervention programme where they are introduced to social expectations and feelings in a very systematic way. Children also need to know that just because a specific behavioural trait is acceptable in their home it does not mean that it will be accepted in school. They need to know that there will be consequences if inappropriate behaviour is demonstrated and they need to understand that these will be consistently implemented until there is a change in behaviour.

Observing outstanding teachers

Outstanding teachers make behaviour management look easy. It almost appears that they do not have to think about it. During your school-based ITT you should observe some teachers who are particularly effective at managing the behaviour of challenging classes.

Ask if you can go into their lessons and be clear that you want to learn about behaviour management.

When you are observing a lesson it is easy to get side-tracked and to note down everything you see. Try to focus specifically on how they manage pupils' behaviour by observing the following:

* How do they greet the class?
* How do they engage pupils in the lesson from the start?
* When do they use praise?
* How often do they use praise?
* How do they use praise?
* What impact does praise have on children's behaviour?
* Do they use rewards? What impact do these have on children's behaviour?
* How do they apply sanctions?
* How do they use non-verbal strategies such as eye contact?
* How do they communicate a strong teacher-presence?
* How do they use their voice?
* How do they manage transitions?
* How do they manage conflict?
* How do they de-escalate a problem?
* Were any strategies more effective than others?
* How do they reinforce classroom rules?
* Do the learners demonstrate good attitudes to learning (behaviour for learning)? How do you know?
* How do they address off-task talk?
* How do they manage classroom noise?
* How do they manage challenging behaviour?
* Do they use a whole class reward system? If so, what impact does this have on children's behaviour?
* Do specific children have individual reward systems?

Always try to meet with the teacher after the lesson to ask him/her to explain their specific approaches to behaviour management. It is important to remember that what works for one teacher, one class or even one child will not necessarily work for you and different children respond in different ways to specific strategies. There is no magic cure for addressing behaviour problems but classroom observations will give you a range of strategies to make choices from.

Establishing class rules and routines

Children benefit from clear rules and routines. What are your views on class rules? I have been into schools which have *school rules* displayed in each class and I have been into schools where children are involved in compiling a list of class rules. The benefits of involving children in the formulation of class rules are immediately obvious. This gives children some ownership of the rules and if they choose to 'break' the rules they are essentially breaking their own contract.

It is very easy, with a little care, to 'frame' class rules in positive language. Rather than beginning each rule with a negative command, rules can be expressed in positive ways. Examples of rules could be:

Class Rules

* *We always share.*
* *We always listen to the teacher and to each other.*
* *We try our best at all times.*
* *We look after school property.*
* *We care for our classroom.*
* *We keep each other safe.*

It is a good idea to remind the children of the rules at the start of each lesson. It is also worth pointing out that it can take a while for children to internalise the rules. You need to be patient and you need to keep reminding them of the rules. Until you have established good behaviour management, no significant learning will take place in your classroom. It is therefore important that you invest time into ensuring that your learners are clear about the rules and your expectations. At the start of a period of school-based training, investing time into establishing your expectations is not wasted time. In fact, it is essential to do so. In the early stages of meeting a class it does not matter if you do not get through the lesson content that you have planned. It is more important that your learners understand the boundaries that you have set them and that they start to work within these. Once they are ready to learn they will catch up with any missed content from those early days that you spent establishing your expectations. If you do not establish your expectations early in the process of working with a class, they will spend the rest of the time testing the boundaries and this will impede their learning. It is better to establish your expectations right at the start before you get on with the task of teaching them subject content.

Children quite like clear routines. The sense of routine enables them to predict what will happen next and it provides them with security. When you teach a class you need to decide on simple routines. These include:

* Where will the children store their reading books?
* How do they enter the classroom? Do they line up or come straight in?
* What do they do when they first come into the classroom?
* What are the procedures for moving children from a carpet area to tables?
* What are the procedures for tidying away at the end of lessons?
* What lessons do they have in the morning and afternoon?
* What is the routine for getting ready for break time?
* When is snack/milk time?
* When is story time?
* What days do they do PE?
* What days do they go swimming?
* What day is their spelling test?
* Where should finished work be stored?

Although this list seems prescriptive, establishing clear routines so that things happen in certain ways and on certain days at certain times means that children are not 'thrown off' by a sudden departure from the usual routine. Sudden unexpected changes in routine can cause some children to become extremely anxious and this can affect their behaviour. Although routines frequently change in schools (such as assembly over-running) it is a good idea to try to establish a routine and then to prepare children for any changes to a routine by issuing an advance warning. This is not always possible, but it is good practice in relation to supporting children with autism who often become very distressed by sudden changes to established routines.

Use of voice

Low voices seem to work well to indicate authority. There is no need to use a loud voice. The typical *teaching voice* is just slightly above that of normal conversational level. Talk a little more slowly than you think you should, because we underestimate the speed of our speech, especially if we feel a little nervous ourselves. Let a little space creep in between your words at times, to allow children to reflect on what you have said, as well as to frame the content of your conversation with gravity.

Developing a teacher presence

Developing a teacher-presence is a good starting point for managing children's behaviour. Children will respond to you as a teacher if they perceive you as a teacher. Although this seems obvious, it cannot be overstated. It means that you need to give careful attention to aspects such as your professional dress. Dressing in smart attire helps to create a professional image of yourself, and parents and children will relate better to you as a teacher. If you dress too casually you risk undermining your professional reputation. Fashions have changed a lot over time and many primary school teachers prefer a smart but casual attire. Wearing a suit may not be the best idea when you are exposed to paint, glue, sand and water. All schools should have a dress code and you should comply with this. As a general rule of thumb men should wear trousers and a smart top. The range of clothes for females is more varied than for males because there is a greater choice of casual but smart clothes for women. Generally, denim is not allowed and you should avoid wearing clothes that reveal flesh.

It never ceases to amaze me how differently children respond to their teachers compared to other adults. The next time you go into school observe how children respond to voluntary helpers and teaching assistants/cover supervisors. Children will often ask you if you are a teacher. My policy has always been to reply with a resounding 'yes!' because children tend to behave much better for their teachers. It is not just about the way you dress. It is a lot to do with the confidence you portray. To develop a teacher presence, you need to be prepared to challenge children when you observe inappropriate behaviour. You need to be able to project your voice and stop a class with confidence and authority where this is necessary. You need to have the confidence to wait for silence if you are addressing the class. You need to be able to scan the room and develop the skill of having 'eyes in the back of your head'.

A skilled teacher can relax with a class, develop humour in the classroom or get them excited about something. However, at the same time they also have a strong presence which enables them to calm down a class almost instantly. A strong teacher presence means that you can walk into a classroom and the children respond to you almost instantly. They know you are there and consequently they modify their behaviour appropriately. I am not suggesting here that children should be frightened of you. If they are frightened of you then they will not learn effectively. It is more a case of them respecting you and treating you as a teacher.

Parents will often tell you that their child behaves very differently in school compared to how they behave at home. This is partly due to the fact that children very quickly learn that different rules apply at school and that schooling has a function which is to enable them to learn. Most children learn this almost immediately and for others it takes a little longer. However, children modify their behaviour at school, not just because of the school rules but because the teachers they meet have a strong teacher presence. In developing your teacher presence, the following aspects require consideration.

Stance/posture

Think carefully about how you stand in front of others. Try to be assertive and make good eye contact with your learners. At the same time stay relaxed and try not to be too tense.

When you are in situations where you are resolving conflict between two children, be confident but avoid being aggressive or confrontational. In situations of conflict don't get too close as this can be threatening and also dangerous.

Hands

If you have a tendency to fiddle with your hands, try holding something. A good position is to place your hands behind your back. Avoid placing your hands in front of your face or over your mouth because this can demonstrate a lack of confidence.

Eyes

Maintain eye contact with your learners. Always try to scan the room so that you make eye contact with different people and hold the attention of specific individuals for a little longer.

Use of language

Think carefully about register of speech. Keep your language formal. Informal language such as slang and buzzwords are inappropriate.

Movement

Keep your movements slow and considered. Try not to move around the room too much because this makes it difficult for children to focus on you.

Expression

Remember that you are not there to be a best friend. Keep communication positive, brief and simple. Speaking in shorter sentences is more effective than longer sentences because

it gives children a chance to process what you are saying to them. If you ask a question, wait for an answer – don't fill the space. Humour can be effective in defusing situations.

Tone of voice

Keep calm and confident. Only raise your voice when absolutely necessary and only use this strategy very infrequently.

Working in schools with challenging behaviour

It will be an invaluable experience to visit a pupil referral unit and settings for children with autistic spectrum disorders. You may have no desire to work in these settings. However, it is almost a certainty that you will be required to teach children with autism and/or children with challenging behaviour at some point during your training and your career. By visiting these settings, you will learn valuable strategies for managing pupils' behaviour that you can transfer to mainstream schools.

Additionally, do not fall into the trap of assuming that all children in areas of affluence behave well and that children in areas of social deprivation behave inappropriately. Some of the worst behaviour I have witnessed was in a small rural school in an extremely affluent area. The behavioural characteristics of children may be different in different settings. During your training you should spend as much time as possible in different types of schools. In every school that you visit you should ask to see a copy of the school's behaviour management policy. Behaviour management policies are more effective when there is a whole-school approach towards managing children's behaviour. If there are consistent systems and approaches in all classes, then children are very clear about the expectations.

However, you will not find this consistency of approach in all schools. I have been into schools where teachers are only allowed to praise children and where negative behaviour is ignored. What are your views on this? I have been into other schools where rewards are banned. What are your views on this? I will address some of these issues later in the chapter but the key point to make here is that schools vary dramatically in their approaches. As a teacher you need to develop your own set of beliefs about rewards, praise and sanctions. The more schools and classes you go into, the more opportunity you have of observing 'what works' in practice.

Some simple strategies

The following list is not exhaustive but it provides you with some very simple practical strategies for managing pupils' behaviour.

- Use positive descriptive praise: for example, *'Thank you Charlotte, I like the way you are listening to me'*; *'I like the way that you are persevering with that maths problem, Ellie'*.
- Use assertive language: for example, *'John, **you need** to listen'*; *'Emma **you need** to put your hand up'*.
- Waiting for silence: for example, when you want the class to tidy up ensure they are all listening to your instructions; do not talk over the children; insist on silence, then give them clear instructions about what needs to be done.

* Do not allow low-level disruption to build up. 'Nip it in the bud' immediately as soon as you see it happening. Do not ignore it, especially if it is repeated.
* Use instant rewards when you catch children being good. Instant rewards are better for children with challenging behaviour who benefit from instant gratification.
* When one child is legitimately talking or when an adult is talking, insist that they all listen. Wait for silence if necessary.
* Tell them straight away how to modify their behaviour: for example, *'You need to sit still and look at me or you will have to sit on the thinking chair'*. Then make sure you follow it through if necessary.
* Use a thinking mat/chair for 'time-out'. When they re-join the group ask them to explain to you why they had to sit out.
* Provide a learning environment which is distraction-free. This may be difficult to achieve as primary school classrooms are often overloaded with visual distractions. Some children benefit from working in a distraction-free zone so it might be worthwhile to convert an area of the classroom into a space which has limited distractions to help these children to focus more effectively on their learning.
* Time-out: use a sand timer so that they can see how long they need to sit out for. Then ask them to explain what they have done wrong and how they intend to modify their behaviour before they re-join the group.
* Speed up tidying away or getting changed for PE – use a timer. Give them clear expectations about when you expect them to be ready.
* Ensure they tidy away properly – tidy tables, everything in its place, nothing on the floor, for example, pencils, rulers, erasers. Model being tidy yourself. Use calming music at tidy away time.
* Transitions can be problematic, for example, moving children from the carpet to tables or lining up – send one group at a time.
* Find a working noise level that works for you. If it is too loud stop the class and explain how noise can adversely affect learning. When they achieve a noise level which is acceptable, praise and reward them.
* Cloakrooms – insist that cloakrooms are kept tidy and that they hang their coats and bags up!
* Entering the classroom: be at the door ready to receive them. It creates a powerful message.
* Use clear instructions and don't overload them with instructions.
* Clear classroom rules: continually remind them of the classroom rules, for example, at the start of lessons.
* Whole class reward systems: for example, team points, house points, marbles in a jar are useful strategies for rewarding good behaviour.
* Introduce individual reward systems for pupils with challenging behaviour.
* Do not accept rudeness or direct challenges to your authority – you are in charge and they must accept this. If they are rude to you, explain why the behaviour is not acceptable and give them a warning – *'If you speak to me like that again X will happen'* – follow school policy. Make sure that any 'threats' are followed through.
* Do not get into confrontations with children – do not debate with them about their behaviour – they must accept what you say. Always follow the advice in the previous bullet point if they challenge your authority.
* Sometimes allow children the opportunity to choose their own rewards for good behaviour/good work.

* Always ensure children understand why sanctions are being applied.
* Tactically ignore occasional 'incidents' which are low-level.
* Use non-verbal cueing: eye contact is powerful for low-level disruption and you can stop children from behaving inappropriately simply by giving 'the look'.
* Tactical diversion – ask them to do a 'job' for you to re-focus them or try asking them about their work to re-focus them away from adverse behaviour.
* Ask direct questions – *What is our rule for answering questions*?
* Choice/deferred consequence: stating the consequence of a continued disruptive behaviour in the context of a 'choice': for example, *If you choose to not do your work and waste time, I will need to talk to you at playtime*.
* Commands: *'John, stop that **now**'* [raised voice on *now*]. Use sparingly because commands carry a danger that the child will not comply. This places you in a confrontational situation. However, when used infrequently, commands can be effective.

Charlie Taylor's checklists

Back in 2011 Charlie Taylor advised the government of approaches for managing pupils' behaviour. Taylor produced checklists of strategies which I have listed below. In March 2016, the government asked Tom Bennett to conduct a second review of behaviour in schools.

Key principles for headteachers to help improve school behaviour policy

* Ensure absolute clarity about the expected standard of pupils' behaviour.
* Ensure that behaviour policy is clearly understood by all staff, parents and pupils.
* Display school rules clearly in classes and around the building. Staff and pupils should know what they are.
* Display the tariff of sanctions and rewards in each class.
* Have a system in place for ensuring that children never miss out on sanctions or rewards.

Leadership

* Model the behaviour you want to see from your staff.

Building

* Visit the lunch hall and playground, and be around at the beginning and the end of the school day.
* Ensure that other Senior Leadership Team members are a visible presence around the school.
* Check that pupils come in from the playground and move around the school in an orderly manner.
* Check up on behaviour outside the school.
* Check the building is clean and well-maintained.

Staff

* Know the names of all staff.
* Praise the good performance of staff.
* Take action to deal with poor teaching or staff who fail to follow the behaviour policy.

Children

* Praise good behaviour.
* Celebrate successes.

Teaching

* Monitor the amount of praise, rewards and punishments given by individual staff.
* Ensure that staff praise good behaviour and work.
* Ensure that staff understand special needs of pupils.

Individual pupils

* Have clear plans for pupils likely to misbehave and ensure staff are aware of them.
* Put in place suitable support for pupils with behavioural difficulties.

Parents

* Build positive relationships with the parents of pupils with behaviour difficulties.

Behaviour checklist for teachers

Classroom

* Know the names and roles of any adults in class.
* Meet and greet pupils when they come into the classroom.
* Display rules in the class – and ensure that the pupils and staff know what they are.
* Display the tariff of sanctions in class.
* Have a system in place to follow through with all sanctions.
* Display the tariff of rewards in class.
* Have a system in place to follow through with all rewards.
* Have a visual timetable on the wall.
* Follow the school behaviour policy.

Pupils

* Know the names of children.
* Have a plan for children who are likely to misbehave.
* Ensure other adults in the class know the plan.
* Understand pupils' special needs.

Teaching

* Ensure that all resources are prepared in advance.
* Praise the behaviour you want to see more of.
* Praise children doing the right thing more than criticising those who are doing the wrong thing (parallel praise)
* Differentiate.
* Stay calm.

* Have clear routines for transitions and for stopping the class.
* Teach children the class routines.

Parents

* Give feedback to parents about their child's behaviour – let them know about the good days as well as the bad ones.

(DfE, 2011b)

CRITICAL QUESTION

* *The Code of Practice (DfE, 2015) emphasises the importance of giving children and parents a say in all matters which affect them. To what extent do these checklists address the principle of working in partnership with children and parents?*

Checklist for trainee teachers

Back in 2011 the Teaching Agency produced a checklist for trainee teachers to help them in managing pupils' behaviour. This is listed below:

Personal style

* Trainees should understand that they are responsible for ensuring the highest standards of behaviour from their pupils.
* Trainees should have developed their own personal style for managing behaviour. Knowledge of generic behaviour management systems and techniques is essential; the way they are used depends on the attributes of individual teachers and the context in which they are teaching.
* Trainees should be able to vary the tone and volume of their voice to teach effectively and manage behaviour.
* Trainees should know how to look after their voice.
* Trainees should understand how to stand, move, make use of space and use eye contact in order to be an authoritative presence in the classroom.

Self-management

* Trainees should understand what effect their responses, both verbal and non-verbal, can have on children's behaviour. They should be able to manage their own emotions when they are teaching.

Reflection

* Trainees should be able to reflect on the way they manage behaviour and their classrooms and be prepared to change what isn't working well.

School systems

* Trainees should understand how effective school systems support good behaviour management, and prevent and deal with bullying. They should be able to adapt their practice to fit with the school behaviour policy and should understand that consistency is an essential component of managing behaviour.

Relationships

* Trainees should understand that good relationships are at the heart of good behaviour management. They should be able to form positive, appropriate, professional relationships with their pupils.

Classroom management

* Trainees should be able to use praise effectively.
* Trainees should know how to apply rewards and sanctions to improve behaviour.
* Trainees need to know how to develop and teach routines to pupils so that time is used efficiently.
* Trainees need to be able to manage behaviour in a range of different situations such as whole-class teaching, group work, the corridors and the playground.

More challenging behaviour

* Trainees should have an understanding of why children misbehave and why some children demonstrate more challenging behaviour.
* Trainees should be able to plan and teach lessons that take account of individual children's special needs, so that they are less likely to misbehave.
* Trainees should know how to take appropriate and effective action when they are confronted by more extreme behaviour.

Theoretical knowledge

* Trainees should know about scientific research and developments, and how these can be applied to understanding, managing and changing children's behaviour.

(Teaching Agency, 2012)

CRITICAL QUESTIONS

Trainees are charged with the responsibility of planning lessons to reduce the likelihood of misbehaviour. One of the reasons children misbehave is because they disengage from curriculum content as specified in the national curriculum.

* *To what extent is disengagement a result of a teacher's failure to engage pupils with curriculum content or a result of a specified curriculum which fails to meet the needs of all children?*
* *To what extent is disengagement a result of influences outside school?*

Classroom management

Good teachers make classroom management look easy but will have done preparation behind the scenes to ensure that the classroom runs smoothly. I always used a traffic light system to classroom management, which consistently worked and stopped children from queuing. Activities were broadly divided into *red, amber* and *green* as follows:

* **RED ACTIVITIES:** children cannot progress without adult support, for example, a writing activity in Reception or Year 1. This is a teacher-intensive activity and children need a teacher or an adult working with them in order to complete it.
* **AMBER ACTIVITIES:** these are not as teacher-intensive as red activities but you might need to keep 'dipping in' to check they are on task. Children can generally work on the task with a reasonable amount of independence.
* **GREEN ACTIVITIES:** these are independent activities through which children consolidate prior learning and can progress independently to complete the activity. They do not require adult support to complete the task.

This model of classroom organisation is useful when you are teaching in Key Stage 1 or Key Stage 2 and there is no 'continuous provision' to 'absorb' children who are not doing adult-led tasks. Continuous provision is common in the Early Years Foundation Stage and includes activities such as sand and water play, role play, construction play and outdoor activities. If you are fortunate to work in a classroom which has continuous provision, you can set children off on the provision and keep behind a group to work with.

Too many *red* activities will be disastrous – all the children will need your help at once. The traffic light system enables the classroom to 'flow'. If you have more than one adult in the room, you can deploy additional adults to support *red* activities. If there is only you, then it would be wise to only have one red activity in operation. If you can position the red and amber activities near to each other this will make it easier to 'dip into' the amber group to check on their learning.

IN PRACTICE

Look at the following scenarios:

Antecedent (Trigger)	Behaviour	Consequence
Sam is asked to tidy up	Sam says *'No, I don' t want to'* to Mrs Jones and walks out of the room	Mrs Blogs placed Sam in detention at play time
Sam is asked to finish his work quickly	Sam scribbles all over his book and throws it on the floor	Sam is given 'thinking time' outside of the room. Mrs Jones calls his Mum
Class teacher tells Sam to put his hand up before giving the answer	Sam carries on shouting out answers	Mrs Jones takes Sam out of the classroom and he misses break time
Mrs Jones asks Sam to re-draft a story he has written in scribble	Sam scribbles all over his book and rips up the page	Mrs Jones asks Sam to stay in at break so that he can re-do his work

CRITICAL QUESTIONS

* *What patterns if any do you notice in:*
  - the antecedents/triggers that occur before Sam's behaviours?
  - Sam's behaviours?
  - the consequences that occur after the behaviour?
* *What factors could be strengthening Sam's behaviour?*
* *What factors might help to reduce Sam's behaviour?*

Theories of behaviour management

When you go into a school it is essential that you look at the school's behaviour management policy. This will help you to understand the agreed practices, thus ensuring that you are providing your learners with a consistent approach. Understanding theories of behaviour management will provide a theoretical underpinning for the approaches which you use to manage children's behaviour.

Behaviourism and Skinner

B F Skinner (1904–1990) was a well-known American psychologist. He carried out experiments with rats and pigeons by placing them inside a box which became known as the *Skinner Box*. Skinner observed that he was able to control the behaviour of the animals through introducing rewards and punishments. The box had a lever and the rats quickly learned that when they knocked the lever food pellets were released into the box. The rats quickly learned to go straight to the lever in order to receive the reward of food. This was an example of learned behaviour, also known as positive reinforcement. The principle of positive reinforcement is that certain behaviours are rewarded, which results in the behaviour being repeated.

Skinner trained the pigeons to peck on a coloured disc which was labelled with the word *peck*. Following this, the pigeons were introduced to a disc which was labelled with the word *turn*. The pigeons were trained to respond to the words on the disc. When they saw the word *peck* they pecked the disc to receive the food. When they were introduced to the word *turn* they turned around without receiving a reward. The pigeons did this because they quickly learned the pattern, ie following a turn they would be introduced to the word *peck*, which resulted in them pecking the disc to receive food. Following the reward, they would turn, despite the fact that no reward was issued to this response. This was because the pigeons seemed to know that the next response would be rewarded. Rewarding rats or pigeons with food is an example of *positive reinforcement*. Positive reinforcement is the addition of a stimulus (ie food in this case) which causes desired behaviour to be repeated.

In another experiment Skinner placed rats inside a box and issued them with an electric shock. The rats realised that if they pressed the lever, the electric shock stopped. This caused them to go to the lever more quickly the next time they were placed in the box. This is known as *negative reinforcement*, ie the removal of an unpleasant stimulus to create a desired response.

Skinner introduced the term *reinforcement*. Behaviour which is reinforced is often repeated (ie strengthened); behaviour which is not reinforced tends to die out or be extinguished (ie weakened). Reinforcement can be positive or negative depending on whether a stimulus is added or taken away.

The theory also includes punishment. The aim of punishment is to reduce undesired behaviour and to strengthen desired behaviour. Punishment can be negative if something is taken away (eg loss of a playtime) or it can be positive if something is added to reinforce the desired behaviour. An example of positive punishment would be issuing a child with a report slip which they are required to take to every lesson so that their teacher can comment on their behaviour in that lesson.

Skinner's theory of reinforcement and punishment is known as *operant conditioning*. It is based on rewards and sanctions. Good behaviour is rewarded and negative behaviour is sanctioned. Negative reinforcement is not the same thing as punishment and this will be explored in the practical examples below.

Skinner introduced the term *schedule of rewards*. He realised that behaviour did not have to be rewarded on every single occasion. In another experiment the pigeons were not always rewarded with food every time they pecked a disc. The reward was introduced after a number of attempts at pecking a disc. The pigeons carried on pecking the disc because they seemed to realise that eventually if they carried on pecking they would be rewarded

with food. A good example where scheduling rewards works very effectively is in gambling. Gambling is based on scheduling rewards. The reward of cash is not issued every time a gambler places money into a slot machine. Eventually, after a number of attempts to win money the gambler is rewarded with cash. The schedule can be changed so that the cash is released more or less frequently. The behaviour of gamblers suggests that rewards do not have to be issued every single time that money is placed into a slot machine. Gamblers will keep putting money into the machine until the cash is issued.

Scheduling reinforcements is a strategy which some schools use to reinforce desired behaviour. If a child has to collect ten stamps in a book before they are issued with a tangible reward then the reward is scheduled to be released at certain intervals, not every time the desired behaviour is demonstrated.

CRITICAL QUESTIONS

* *What are the advantages and disadvantages of scheduling rewards?*
* *Do you agree with punishments? Explain your answer.*
* *Do you agree with rewards? Explain your answer.*

Applying theory to practice

In each of the following situations consider whether something is added or something is taken away. Negative reinforcement is often incorrectly associated with punishment. In the example given below under the sub-heading *negative reinforcement*, it is obvious that the child is not being punished by being taken into the booth. It is an example of negative reinforcement because the visual stimuli are being taken away. In both of the examples of punishment the child is being punished. In the case of negative punishment, the child is losing their playtime. This is clearly a punishment because the child will not enjoy being kept in a *thinking room* at playtime. In the case of positive punishment, the child is being given a letter to take home to inform his parents about his behaviour. Hopefully, the child will view this as a punishment and make him think twice before ignoring his warnings on another occasion.

If you are issued with a notice that requires you to attend a speeding course, that would constitute a positive punishment. This is because something is being added. If your driving licence is taken away from you, that would constitute a negative punishment because something is being taken away. If you are trying to study in the dining room and your house mate has the television on loud in the next room, you might decide to stand up and close the door to block out the sound. This is an example of negative reinforcement because you are removing the stimulus of the sound. However, it is not a punishment. These examples illustrate the terms but the following examples apply the terms to behaviour management in schools.

IN PRACTICE: POSITIVE REINFORCEMENT

Jack, who struggles to sit still on the carpet, started the session sitting beautifully. This behaviour was instantly rewarded by verbal praise. This positive reinforcement led to Jack continuing to sit nicely with a big proud beaming smile. Further into the session this continued positive behaviour was positively reinforced by his name being put on the smiley face board. He continued to sit nicely following this positive reinforcement and at the end of the session was rewarded with a sticker and further verbal praise. This positive reinforcement was successful in this instance. It also had a positive effect on other children who were eager to receive praise and rewards, which they did.

IN PRACTICE: NEGATIVE REINFORCEMENT

A child with autism reacts negatively to the visual stimuli in a mainstream classroom. The stimuli cause the child to become distressed. The teaching assistant takes the child into a quiet area which is part of the classroom but screened off. There are no visual stimuli in this area. The child immediately calms down and is able to get on with the task they have been set.

IN PRACTICE: NEGATIVE PUNISHMENT

A small group of Year 2 children repeatedly took toys from Year 1 children during playtime. To them this is just fun and they did not see that this is upsetting other children. After a session of restorative justice with all concerned, most of the children stopped this unwanted behaviour but one child continued. The children who had been harmed by his behaviour decided he needed to go to the *Thinking Room*. The child had to miss the next playtime and think about his behaviour and how it was affecting others. This was an unpleasant consequence for the child. By removing playtime and friends from the child, the behaviour changed. The child no longer takes toys from younger children and they can now enjoy playtime with their friends.

IN PRACTICE: POSITIVE PUNISHMENT

A child who misbehaves despite several warnings is given a letter to take home. The letter informs his parents about his behaviour that day and invites the parents to come into school to make an appointment so that they can discuss the issues with the teacher.

CRITICAL QUESTIONS

* *Behaviourist theories emerged out of experimentation with animals. In view of this, what are the limitations of the theories?*
* *Behaviourism focuses on the consequences of behaviour rather than its causes. What are the benefits and limitations of this?*

IN PRACTICE

* *Look at your school behaviour management policy. Identify examples of reinforcements and punishments specified in the policy. Are there any examples of scheduling reinforcements in the policy?*

Mental health: building resilience and character

Examples of mental health needs include: self-harming; eating disorders; depression; anxiety; conduct disorder; attachment disorder and developmental disorder. According to recent government guidance (DfE, 2016b), *Mental Health and Behaviour in Schools:*

The role that schools play in promoting the resilience of their pupils is important, particularly so for some children where their home life is less supportive. School should be a safe and affirming place for children where they can develop a sense of belonging and feel able to trust and talk openly with adults about their problems.

(DfE, 2016b, para 1.5, p 8)

Schools, teachers and the government are increasingly concerned about the apparent increase of pupils presenting mental health needs in schools. Risk factors include exposure to:

* genetic influences;
* low IQ and learning disabilities;
* specific development delay or neuro-diversity;
* communication difficulties;
* difficult temperament;
* physical illness;
* academic failure;
* low self-esteem;
* overt parental conflict including domestic violence;
* family breakdown (including where children are taken into care or adopted);
* inconsistent or unclear discipline;
* hostile and rejecting relationships;
* failure to adapt to a child's changing needs;
* physical, sexual, neglect or emotional abuse;
* parental psychiatric illness;
* parental criminality, alcoholism or personality disorder;
* death and loss – including loss of friendship;
* bullying;
* discrimination;
* breakdown in or lack of positive friendships;
* deviant peer influences;
* peer pressure;
* poor pupil to teacher relationships;
* socio-economic disadvantage;
* homelessness;
* disaster, accidents, war or other overwhelming events;
* discrimination;
* other significant life events.

(DfE, 2016b, pp 9–10)

Loss of or separation from parents, life-changing and traumatic events can affect pupils' ability to be resilient and reduce the effectiveness of strategies which are implemented to protect the child.

The government guidance states that:

Behavioural difficulties do not necessarily mean that a child or young person has a possible mental health problem or a special educational need (SEN). Negative experiences and distressing life events can affect mental health in a way that brings about temporary change in a young person's behaviour. However, consistent disruptive or withdrawn behaviour can be an indication of an underlying problem, and where there are concerns about behaviour there should be an assessment to determine whether there are any causal factors such as undiagnosed learning difficulties, difficulties with speech and language or mental health issues.

(DfE, 2016b, para 2.1, p 14)

Early identification of mental health needs is essential, although an official diagnosis can only be made by a medical professional. The government recommends an assessment tool which is called the Strengths and Difficulties Questionnaire (SDQ) (www.sdqinfo.com/). Schools should share their concerns with the Child and Adolescent Mental Health Services (CAMHS) if they feel that a child needs specific intervention above and beyond what the school is able to provide.

You should be alert to sudden changes in children's behaviour which may suggest that there is a mental health need. If you have any concerns about specific pupils, then you should always discuss these with a more senior colleague in school. This might be the Special Educational Needs Co-ordinator. Schools with well-developed pastoral provision are in a good position to provide pupils with the individual support they require. One simple way of giving pupils a voice is to provide them with a confidential *post-box* in the classroom where they can post any worries. You should discuss any concerns you have fully with the child's parents and you should involve the child in discussion to ascertain their perspectives. Schools should teach all children directly about physical and mental health. This can be done through activities such as circle time or through choosing appropriate stories to read to children which explore some of the issues associated with mental health.

Children at greater risk of mental health difficulties include, but are not limited to, looked after children, children with learning difficulties, children on the autism spectrum and children from disadvantaged backgrounds (DfE, 2016b). Persistent mental health difficulties may lead to pupils having significantly greater difficulty in learning than the majority of those of the same age (DfE, 2016b) and in these cases schools should consider whether children will benefit from being identified as having special educational needs. However, not all children with special educational needs have mental health needs. It is also important to remember that although specific groups of pupils may be at greater risk of having a mental health need, mental health needs can become apparent in any child, irrespective of age, ability, social background or disability. Children who are very academically able can experience mental health problems.

IN PRACTICE

Nine-year-old Alice walks to school every day and passes a place where a group of older children stand around. When she passes them they call her names, make fun of her and sometimes they try to push her. She has become so frightened she doesn't want to go to school anymore and tells her mother she is sick. Her mother knows she is not ill.

What does Alice need?

* Support in helping her to develop a good self-concept.
* To develop more confidence in her ability to solve problems.
* To build more skills in communicating for help.

What actions could the care-giver take that would increase resilience?

* Help Alice to talk about the situation.
* Demonstrate empathy towards Alice.
* Discuss ways of solving the problem.
* Assure Alice that she is not to blame for other children's behaviour.
* Consult with the school to get help.

What responses would not foster resilience?

* Telling Alice not to be afraid.
* Accompanying Alice to school every day.
* Expecting her to challenge the bullies.

Conflict resolution

Often adults interfere when children are in conflict with each other. The usual response is to separate the children. However, this does not help children to resolve the issue and often they will enter into another conflict with each other when an adult is not there. Teaching children to resolve conflicts helps them to take control over the situation and provides them with valuable skills that they will need in life. Conflict is inevitable and is not necessarily a bad thing. The important thing is for teachers and other adults to give children the skills to resolve issues for themselves.

IN PRACTICE

Consider a situation in which James and Ryan want the same toy or equipment and an argument breaks out.

Your response might be: 'If you can't play with it nicely, then neither of you will have it'

How do you think the children will feel? How strong a response is this?

Angry and confused. Neither of their wants and needs have been met and they have not learned the important skill of sharing. The adult is in full control. The situation is likely to repeat itself.

You might suggest: 'James had this first, Ryan, so let him finish with it then you can have a turn'.

What are the strengths of this response?

Self-esteem is intact for both.

They know it's normal to have conflicts and that these can be resolved.

What are the drawbacks (if any)?

The adult is still in control.

In this situation you might wish to consider using **conflict resolution**. In this case you might respond in the following way:

Help them to solve their own problem by acting as a mediator so that they become independent problem-solvers, for example:

- *Approach calmly and crouch down to their level.*
- *Acknowledge feelings: 'James you look angry and Ryan you sound angry'. I will take this game away until you talk about the problem.*
- *Find out what the problem is from James and Ryan.*
- *Repeat the problem back to James and Ryan.*
- *Ask James and Ryan for their solution ... ask them for suggestions to resolve the conflict.*
- *Guide them into an acceptable solution (win-win).*
- *Offer support/encouragement later – 'You two are working well together – brilliant'.*

CRITICAL QUESTION

- *What are the strengths and limitations of conflict resolution approaches to managing children's behaviour?*

Humanism and Carl Rogers

Carl Rogers (1902–1987) was an influential founder of the humanistic approach to psychology. He saw self-concept as a fluctuating, fluid and differentiated concept which is subject to change. The humanistic approach emphasises *unconditional positive regard* as being critical to the process of self-actualisation. Unconditional positive regard is similar to the unconditional love that parents give to their children. Most parents provide their children with unconditional love, irrespective of how their children behave towards them. Humanistic psychology views all people as essentially good people. Humanists adopt a whole-person approach and in doing so they are interested in how factors such as self-concept, self-esteem, access to food, clothing and shelter can influence the behaviour of an individual.

Rogers believed that the child is central to the learning process. He emphasised the importance of providing a classroom environment which is free of fear. He stressed the importance of teachers establishing effective, supportive, encouraging and positive relationships with their learners. He rejected teacher-directed approaches (transmission of knowledge) and emphasised the importance of the individuality of learning, the teacher as a facilitator of learning and the importance of teachers learning alongside and from their students. Classroom environments such as this are open and friendly and function effectively through the formation of positive relationships. Rogers emphasised both the importance of providing learners with a relevant curriculum and introducing learners to multiple perspectives. He also emphasised the creation of a classroom climate in which learners are able to freely express their opinions.

Rogers' vision has real potential for reducing and indeed eliminating disruptive behaviour from schools. Humanism also places value on self-concept/self-esteem enhancing interventions to address issues of low self-esteem and undesirable behaviour.

Self-concept and self-esteem

Self-concept refers to an individual's sense of how they see themselves. In other words, our self-concept is essentially the knowledge that we have of ourselves. Individuals can have a high or low self-concept. We know that we are good at certain things and bad at others. Additionally, our self-concept can fluctuate depending on what aspect of *self* we are evaluating. Children with low self-concepts may start to demonstrate inappropriate behaviour in order to gain some sort of recognition, even if this is negative recognition.

As a teacher you play a pivotal role in developing the self-concepts of the learners you teach. Effective teachers empower children by establishing a *can-do* culture and instilling self-belief. Some learners simply give up when they find a task difficult. They lack resilience and perseverance and then they start to develop *learned helplessness* (this concept is addressed below) and a low self-concept. Encouraging children to be resilient and persevere even when tasks are difficult is one of the most important things that you can do as a teacher because learning was never meant to be easy. Learning requires effort. Just because they cannot accomplish a task right now does not mean that they won't be able to accomplish it and this is a key message that you can transmit as a teacher.

Self-esteem and self-concept are two words which are often used interchangeably. Self-concept is the view we have of ourselves. We might realise that we are weak or brilliant at statistics, for example. Self-esteem is an evaluation of the view we have of ourselves. It is essentially how we *feel* about our abilities and this is informed by the views of others and the *ideal-self*. The ideal-self includes personal ambitions and goals for the future. If an individual has a low self-concept (ie they know that they are not very 'academic', for example) but their ideal-self is out of reach (they want to be academically successful), this can result in low self-esteem. For these individuals there is too great a discrepancy between the self-concept and what they aim to achieve and the ideal-self is viewed as unachievable. If the ideal-self is within reach of the self-concept, then good self-esteem is usually preserved. If the self-concept is low and the ideal-self is also low, good self-esteem may be preserved. An example of this is an individual who knows that they are not very academic but they do not have aspirations or ambitions to do much better. It does not always follow that a low self-concept automatically results in low self-esteem. It is healthy to have an ideal-self which is higher than the self-concept. Having ambitions, goals and aspirations which are within reach is perfectly healthy. Low self-esteem is usually the result of an ideal-self which is out of reach from the self-concept.

As a teacher you will teach learners with low self-concepts and also those with low self-esteem. This can result in some children demonstrating undesirable behaviour characteristics. Our self-concept and self-esteem are largely shaped by our interactions with other people, for example, peers, teachers, parents and extended family members. Charles Cooley developed the concept of the *Looking Glass Self* in 1902. He stated that a person's self grows out of society's interpersonal interactions and the perceptions of others. In other words, how we see ourselves does not come from who we really are, but rather from how we *believe* others see us. The concept suggests that people in our close environment serve as the 'mirrors' that reflect images of ourselves. Cooley identified three steps to this process. First, we imagine how we *appear* to another person. This may be correct or incorrect because it is based on assumptions. Second, we imagine what *judgements* people make of us based on our appearance. Finally, we *imagine* how the person feels about us, based on the judgements they might have made on us. The result is that we often change our behaviour based on our feelings of how people perceive us. The implications of this theory for you as a teacher is that you should consistently make children feel good about themselves so that they do not start to believe that your perception of them is not very good.

Maslow's hierarchy of needs

Maslow believed that people possess a set of motivation systems unrelated to rewards or unconscious desires. He believed that initially people have to satisfy their basic physiological needs (need for food, clothing and shelter) and safety needs before other needs are met. Individuals progress through the hierarchy to have their other needs met. Children whose social needs are met through love and friendships can then develop good self-esteem through interactions with others and achievements in school. Children who do not feel loved or who do not have friendships may find it difficult to learn at school and this can impact detrimentally on their self-esteem. Eventually, when all needs are met, self-actualisation (personal fulfilment) can be achieved.

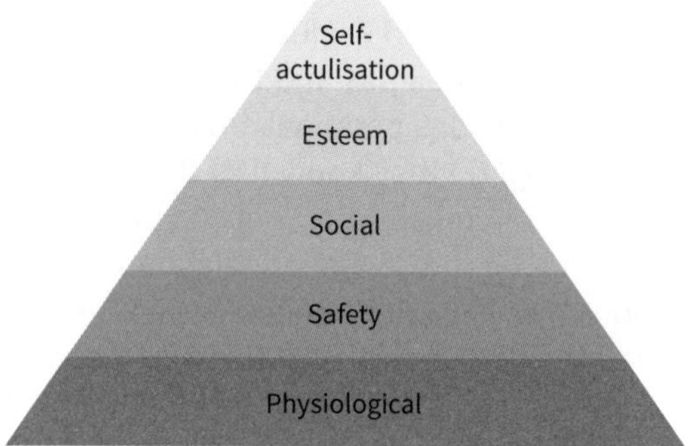

IN PRACTICE

* *Some children come to school tired, hungry and thirsty and this impacts detrimentally on their learning. What provision is available in your school to address these issues?*

Learned helplessness

Learned helplessness is a theory which is attributed to the American psychologist, Martin Seligman. Seligman conducted experiments with three groups of dogs which were placed in harnesses. The dogs in Group 1 were simply put in the harnesses for a period of time and later released. The dogs in Groups 2 and 3 were paired together. The dogs in Group 2 were given electric shocks at random times. The dog could end the shock by pressing a lever. Each dog in Group 3 was then paired with a Group 2 dog. Whenever a Group 2 dog received a shock, its paired dog in Group 3 received a shock of the same intensity and duration, but its lever did not stop the shock. The Group 3 dog quickly realised that it was his paired dog in Group 2 that was causing it to stop. Thus, for Group 3 dogs, the shock could not be avoided.

In the second part of the experiment the same three groups of dogs were tested in a shuttle-box apparatus. All the dogs could escape shocks on one side of the box by jumping over a low partition to the other side. The dogs in Groups 1 and 2 quickly learned this task and jumped over the partition to escape the shock. Most of the Group 3 dogs, which had previously learned that nothing they did had any effect on shocks, simply lay down passively and whined when they were shocked.

Although Seligman's experiments were clearly unethical the theory has been applied to humans in a similar way to Skinner's experiments with rats and pigeons. The theory of learned helplessness assumes that repeated exposure to uncomfortable or painful situations can result in individuals giving up. Children who are repeatedly assessed and told that they are underachieving may start to give up. They may literally stop trying to improve because they have become so used to failure. Children who are repeatedly bullied may start to blame themselves for being bullied rather than attempting to seek help. Children who give up and demonstrate passivity do not demonstrate resilience. They may start to hate themselves and they might start to self-abuse, become anxious and avoid social contact. In most cases of learned helplessness self-concept and self-esteem will be low and children may start to demonstrate a range of behaviours. These might include;

- a lack of willingness to make an effort;
- passivity;
- disruptive behaviour;
- self-harm;
- avoidance of social contact;
- lethargy;
- self 'put downs'.

Children who demonstrate signs of learned helplessness may benefit from a self-esteem boosting intervention programme such as *Circle of Friends* (CoF). Research by Frederickson et al (2005) has shown that this small-group intervention strategy can lead to increased social acceptance of children experiencing difficulties by their peers and increased global self-esteem of the focus child. In this intervention, a group of volunteers form a support group (CoF) and the focus child joins the group. This group meets on a weekly basis. The meetings are managed carefully to ensure that they are a positive and supportive experience for the focus child. The group set the child targets and support the child in meeting them. Successes are celebrated in the group and new targets are set for the following week. Whitaker et al (1998) found that this strategy was successful in increasing the social acceptance of pupils with autistic spectrum disorders in mainstream classes. The researchers found that there was a reduced tendency to blame *the child* for specific behavioural traits and an increased tendency to attribute the behaviour to the impairment. This led to a greater understanding of specific developmental disorders. This intervention is a variation of circle time, but would appear to be useful for children with persistent difficulties.

CRITICAL QUESTIONS

- *To what extent might the curriculum be responsible for learned helplessness?*
- *How might the introduction of standardised testing have contributed to learned helplessness?*

Locus of control

Children with an internal locus of control believe that they are responsible for their own destiny. They accept that they have responsibility for their actions and their achievements and they therefore have a sense of agency. Children with an internal locus of control will accept responsibility for situations that occur which are their fault. They will take responsibility for their future actions to ensure that similar situations are not repeated.

Children with an external locus of control tend to abdicate responsibility for situations to other people. They might locate the cause of their poor behaviour on another pupil for making them angry or they might shift the blame to a teacher for not making the lesson interesting.

Now apply this situation to yourself. If you are late for an appointment, do you take responsibility for this by admitting that you should have left home earlier to get to the appointment in time? Or do you blame the traffic, trains or buses for being late? How you perceive this situation will determine whether you have an internal or an external locus of control. If you failed an exam or scored a low mark in an assessment at school or university, did you blame yourself for not working hard enough? Or did you blame your teacher for not teaching you properly or not supporting you? Perhaps you might blame the library for not giving you access to the right books to support you? Or do you blame your friends for distracting you and making you go out when you should have been working or revising?

Perhaps you consistently take responsibility for situations that you felt you were able to control or perhaps you consistently blame other people for your own failures. Or perhaps you switch from having an internal to an external locus of control depending on the situation.

An interesting fact is that if you have an external locus of control your self-concept is likely to be kept in-tact. This is because you do not take responsibility for situations which occur. It is always someone else's fault. If you have an internal locus of control your self-concept might be damaged because you take responsibility for situations and admit that you could have taken an alternative course of action. This can result in you feeling bad about yourself and can damage your self-concept.

IN PRACTICE

When you are in school try to ascertain whether children with behaviour problems have an internal or an external locus of control. Do they take responsibility for their own behaviour or do they blame other people or imposed structures for their behaviour? Supporting a child to take greater responsibility for their actions is the first step towards addressing poor behaviour. If we can help children to realise that they are in charge of their actions, emotions and words then we can start to help them to take greater control. Some children with challenging behaviour might need some very explicit teaching about this. We can help them by introducing them to fictional scenarios which involve fictional characters making specific choices about the actions they choose to take. The scenarios can be played out in two ways to demonstrate both desirable and undesirable effects.

Introducing children to choices is a powerful way of enabling them to understand that they are in charge of how they behave. If they make the wrong choice, then we can introduce

a sanction which then results in an undesirable effect (eg missing a playtime). If they make a correct choice, this will result in a desired effect (eg going out to play). Children soon realise that they can make a choice about how they behave but some choices result in negative effects while other choices result in positive effects. Getting children to take greater responsibility for their own actions and shifting the blame away from others is the starting point for this type of work.

IN PRACTICE

Read the following case study:

Mrs Johnson, the headteacher of a small primary school, argues that the school cannot meet the needs of Jess who is in Year 2. Mrs Johnson thinks Jess would be better supported in a special school for children with behavioural problems and says that if something is not done soon she will be forced to exclude her.

Jess has been violent towards teaching support staff on a daily basis since she arrived at school last term. Jess is verbally aggressive towards peers, calling them 'stupid' and often 'picks' on vulnerable members of the class. Peers are afraid of Jess and tend to avoid her. She also frequently refuses or ignores instructions from the classroom support assistant. She will engage with her work sometimes but often scribbles over it or rips it up.

Staff say that Jess is often tired during lessons and they think she has a television in her room at home. Jess frequently comes to school hungry and her clothes are often dirty. Teachers say they think the problem is at home but that parents won't engage so there's nothing they can do. Jess's class teacher says that she is not surprised, that she taught Jess's elder brother who was just the same. She says that she's had enough of Jess's behaviour and cannot cope. She says that unless Jess learns to 'toe the line' she will refuse to teach her!

* What factors might have contributed to Jess's behaviour?
* What do you think about the response of Jess's teacher?
* Can you suggest any ways forward in relation to supporting Jess?

CRITICAL QUESTIONS

* *Humanism helps us to understand some of the causes of children's behaviour but it does not help us to apply consequences quickly when incidents occur in the classroom. Are interventions which focus on causation more effective than interventions which focus on consequences?*

Social learning theory and Bandura

Albert Bandura suggested that children imitate behaviours that they have observed in the environment. In his famous Bobo Doll experiment, children observed a male or female model behaving both aggressively and non-aggressively towards a doll. The adults attacked the doll with a hammer in the aggressive play and in the non-aggressive play the adults played in a calm manner with other toys while ignoring the doll. The results of the study were astounding: Boys were more likely to imitate same-sex models than girls and boys imitated more physically aggressive acts than girls. Children in groups which observed the aggressive acts demonstrated more aggressive responses than children in groups which had observed non-aggressive acts.

The implications of this research are that it is likely that children will imitate the aggressive behaviours they observe around them and the likelihood of this occurring increases for boys. Children who observe acts of aggression in their homes are at risk of imitating this behaviour. As a teacher, you are a role model. If you model acts of aggression and are disrespectful towards others there is a risk that children will imitate your behaviour.

Rudolf Dreikurs

Rudolph Dreikurs (1897–1972) believed that children have four unconscious and conscious goals in mind when they misbehave: attention, power, revenge, and avoidance of failure (helplessness).

IN PRACTICE

Read the following case studies. Apply Dreikur's explanations to each of these case studies to explain each child's behaviour.

Sally is constantly unable to comprehend instructions and directions. She nearly always asks for clarification before getting on with things. You have just slowly and carefully explained to everyone what they are to do but Sally, as usual, looks confused whereas the others all get on with it. She often fails to complete tasks claiming that they are too hard.

You have to repeatedly halt a group discussion to stop Holly and Megan from talking noisily about a television programme they watched last night. You ask them to be quiet but a little later they're at it again.

You are in the middle of some group work when Abbie comes to you and complains that Jas, a member of a different group, pushed her without justification. When you approach Jas she says that Abbie broke her pencil. In her defence, Abbie argues that other people have been unkind to her.

You are in the middle of talking to a group when you realise that Mohsan is clicking his fingers constantly. You are aware that he has often done it before and you have already commented twice on it today.

You're coming towards the back end of the day. You are having difficulty keeping the group together/ in order particularly as there are a few trouble-makers. The worst is Jane who, when you try to stop her throwing things, can be heard to mutter, 'Who the hell do you think you are?'

Attachment theory

Attachment theory in psychology originates with the seminal work of John Bowlby. Bowlby observed that children experienced significant distress when separated from their mothers. Even when such children were fed by other caregivers, their anxiety did not diminish. Attachment is characterised by specific behaviours in children. These include seeking proximity with the attachment figure when upset or threatened. Different types of attachment are shown in Table 9.1.

Table 9.1 Types of attachment

Attachment Type	Causes	Common Features
Secure	'Sound' parenting	* Feeling safe * The child develops meaningful connections * The child is able to deal with stress * The child's emotions are balanced.
Insecure (General)	* Caregiver unable to provide for the child – parents. Caregiver doesn't know how to provide. They may have a history of neglect themselves –depression, abuse and neglect, drugs/ alcohol * Constantly changing caregivers * Child in local authority care * Child illness or disability. eg in hospital	* The child has emotional problems and low self-esteem; the child is clingy and is not able to deal with stress; the child shows signs of depression; the child is unresponsive and resists comforting * The child may demonstrate physical problems such as chronic illness * The child may demonstrate social problems. The child may demonstrate a lack of self-control; be overly friendly with strangers; be aggressive and violent; the child may lack trust, affection, empathy and compassion and demonstrate a pessimistic view on life * The child may have learning difficulties.
Insecure Avoidant	* Parent emotionally unavailable, rejecting or prematurely forcing independence	* The child may avoid closeness and emotional connections * The child may be insecure * May have difficulty forming relationships by being aggressive or bullying others.
Insecure Anxious (Ambivalent)	* Parents' communication inconsistent	* Insecure and anxious * Excessive and dependency on caregivers.
Insecure Disorganised	* Parental behaviour a source of disorientation or terror	* The child may be extremely disengaged, passive and aggressive towards others.

Attachment disorder can result from early experiences of abuse, neglect or abrupt separation from parents. The disorder can result in emotional and behavioural problems including the following:

* destructive to self, others and material things ('accident prone');
* cruelty to animals;
* lying;
* stealing;
* lack of conscience;
* poor peer relationships;
* poor relationships with adults.

EVIDENCE-BASED TEACHING

The latest research on use of praise is summarised in Coe et al (2014):

Praise for students may be seen as affirming and positive, but a number of studies suggest that the wrong kinds of praise can be very harmful to learning. For example, Dweck (1999), Hattie & Timperley (2007). Stipek (2010) argues that praise that is meant to be encouraging and protective of low attaining students actually conveys a message of the teacher's low expectations. Children whose failure was responded to with sympathy were more likely to attribute their failure to lack of ability than those who were presented with anger. Praise for successful performance on an easy task can be interpreted by a student as evidence that the teacher has a low perception of his or her ability. As a consequence, it can actually lower rather than enhance self-confidence. Criticism following poor performance can, under some circumstances, be interpreted as an indication of the teacher's high perception of the student's ability.

(Coe et al, 2014. pp 22–23)

EVALUATE

* *What are the advantages and disadvantages of teacher praise?*

CHALLENGE

* *Think of a time when you used praise in the classroom to good effect. How did you use the praise and why was it successful?*

APPLY

* *What are the implications of this research for the following aspects of professional practice?*
  - *task setting;*
  - *use of praise;*
  - *use of criticism in response to failure in a task;*
  - *teacher responses to failure in a task;*

- *use of sympathy when a child fails a task;*
- *teacher expectations.*

EXTENDED THINKING

* *Consider the following two perspectives. Which perspective would you adopt and why?*

I encourage all those affected by an incident to consider the way forward if at all possible.

Or...

The person who misbehaves is the focus of my attention. I do not involve those affected by the misbehaviour in deciding the way forward.

EVIDENCE-BASED TEACHING

According to the Education Endowment Foundation (EEF) website:

Evidence suggests that behaviour interventions can produce large improvements in academic performance along with a decrease in problematic behaviours, though estimated benefits vary widely across programmes. Effect sizes are larger for targeted interventions matched to specific students with particular needs or behavioural issues, than for universal interventions or whole school strategies ... The majority of studies report higher impact with older pupils. Different treatment approaches, such as behavioural, cognitive and social skills for aggressive and disruptive behaviour, seem to be equally effective.

Additionally, a study by Wilson and Lipsey (2007) synthesised the outcomes from 249 experimental studies on behavioural intervention programmes. Positive overall intervention effects were found, especially where interventions were targeted at specific children. The mean effect sizes for these interventions represent a decrease in aggressive/disruptive behaviour that is likely to be of practical significance to schools.

EVALUATE

Targeted individual interventions to address pupils' behaviour often result in pupils being withdrawn from their classroom for a period of time while the intervention is taking place.

* *What are the advantages and disadvantages of this approach to intervention?*

CHALLENGE

The research suggests that targeted interventions for specific pupils are more effective than whole-school interventions which aim to create a positive climate for learning. However, approaches such as *Building Learning Power* by Guy Claxton focus on creating a positive whole-school climate for learning through focusing on the development of appropriate learning behaviours.

* *What are the advantages and disadvantages of whole-school approaches that aim to promote behaviour for learning?*

APPLY

- *Many schools now use social skills intervention programmes for developing appropriate social skills in children where these are lacking. Visit a school which uses a social skills intervention programme and observe a session.*
- *In your current school ascertain if any children are following specific interventions to reduce aggressive or other undesired behaviour. If this is the case, arrange to meet with the person who administers the intervention. Find out about how the intervention programme is structured and arrange to observe an intervention session if this is possible.*

EXTENDED THINKING

- *Consider the following two perspectives. Which perspective would you adopt and why?*

Misbehaviour is often a symptom of, or a reaction to, interpersonal conflict from which all sides can learn to do things differently. Therefore, every situation needs considering separately.

Or...

The behaviour management policy of the setting sets out the appropriate responses to misbehaviour and they need to be applied consistently.

TECHNOLOGY

Many children now enjoy learning with and through technology. For children who disengage with subject content, research into available software and other applications which offer the potential for increasing their engagement with learning. iPads, computers, laptops and mobile phones are technological devices which open up new possibilities for learning aspects of the curriculum. It is very easy nowadays for children to use technology to produce presentations, films, animations and to communicate with others. Embracing technology in learning and teaching offers opportunities to increase student engagement. Teachers should consider the use of technology both for learning and teaching and as a reward.

Critical reflections

This chapter has introduced you to key theories of behaviour management. It has also introduced you to some practical strategies to support children's behavioural needs. It is important to remember that strategies will vary in terms of their effectiveness when applied to different individuals, and even specific children can respond in different ways to a strategy at different times. The most important thing you can do to support your professional development is to keep talking to colleagues when you are addressing a specific case. They might not be able to provide you with a solution that works but they can provide you with strategies that you can implement and evaluate. If strategies do not work, try something else. However, in the process of trying things out never give up on children. There is always a reason why children misbehave and often their behavioural characteristics represent a desire to communicate something.

KEY READINGS

Classic:

Petty, G (2014) *Evidence-Based Teaching: A Practical Approach*. 2nd ed. Oxford: Oxford University Press.

Contemporary:

Bennett, T (2010) *The Behaviour Guru: Behaviour Management Solutions for Teachers*. New York: Continuum.

Delaney, M (2008) *Teaching the Unteachable: Practical Ideas to Give Teachers Hope and Help When Behaviour Management Strategies Fail: What Teachers Can Do When All Else Fails*. London: Worth Publishing.

References

Barmby, P W (2006) Improving teacher recruitment and retention: The importance of workload and pupil behaviour. *Educational Research*, 48(3): 247–65.

Carter, A (2015) *Review of Initial Teacher Training*. London: DfE.

Coe, R, Aloisi, C, Higgins, S T and Major, L E (2014) *What Makes Great Teaching? Review of the Underpinning Research*. London: The Sutton Trust.

DfE (2011a) *Teachers' Standards*. London: DFE.

DfE (2011b) *Getting the Simple Things Right: Charlie Taylor's Behaviour Checklists*. London: DfE.

DfE (2015) *Special Educational Needs and Disability Code of Practice: 0 to 25 Years. Statutory Guidance for Organisations Which Work With and Support Children and Young People Who Have Special Educational Needs or Disabilities*. London: DfE.

DfE (2016a) *Educational Excellence Everywhere: Assessment of Impact*. London: DfE.

DfE (2016b) *Mental Health and Behaviour in Schools: Departmental Advice for School Staff*. London: DfE.

Education Endowment Foundation (n.d.) Behaviour Interventions. [online] Available at: https://educationendowmentfoundation.org.uk/pdf/toolkit/?i=151&u=https://educationendowmentfoundation.org.uk/evidence/teaching-learning-toolkit/behaviour-interventions&t=Behaviour%20interventions&c=toolkit&d=30th%20March,%202016 (accessed 15 May 2016).

Frederickson, N, Warren, L and Turner, J (2005) Circle of friends: An exploration of impact over time. *Educational Psychology in Practice*, 21(3): 197–217.

Moore, D (n.d.) [online] Available at: www.bing.com/videos/search?q=circle+of+intimacy&&view=detail&mid=71D822CDF079731D605F71D822CDF079731D605F&FORM=VRDGAR (accessed 26 March 2016).

Pierson, R (n.d.) [online] Available at: www.bing.com/videos/search?q=Rita+pierson&&view=detail&mid=937FFD13E5AB23319662937FFD13E5AB23319662&FORM=VRDGAR (accessed 26 March 2016).

Teaching Agency (2012) *Improving Teacher Training for Behaviour*. London: Teaching Agency.

Whitaker, P, Barratt, P, Joy, H, Potter, M and Thomas, G (1998) Children with autism and peer group support: Using 'circles of friends'. *British Journal of Special Education*, 25: 60–64.

Wilson, S J and Lipsey, M W (2007) School-based interventions for aggressive and disruptive behaviour: Update of a meta-analysis. *American Journal of Preventive Medicine*, 33: 130–43.

9: SPECIAL EDUCATIONAL NEEDS AND DISABILITY

TEACHERS' STANDARDS

This chapter addresses the following Teachers' Standards:

Teachers' Standard 5: Adapt teaching to respond to the strengths and needs of all pupils

Teachers must:

* *develop approaches which enable pupils to be taught effectively;*
* *have a secure understanding of how a range of factors can inhibit pupils' ability to learn, and how best to overcome these;*
* *demonstrate an awareness of the physical, social and intellectual development of children, and know how to adapt teaching to support pupils' education at different stages of development;*
* *have a clear understanding of the needs of all pupils, including those with special educational needs; those of high ability; those with English as an additional language; those with disabilities; and be able to use and evaluate distinctive teaching approaches to engage and support them.*

Teachers' Standard 1: Set high expectations which inspire, motivate and challenge pupils

Teachers must

* *set goals that stretch and challenge pupils of all backgrounds, abilities and dispositions.*

PROFESSIONAL LINKS

The *Carter Review of Initial Teacher Training* made the following recommendations:

Recommendation 1g: *Special educational needs and disabilities should be included in a framework for ITT content.*

Recommendation 10: *Wherever possible, all ITT partnerships should build in structured and assessed placements for trainees in special schools or mainstream schools with specialist resourced provision.*

(Carter, 2015, p 11)

This chapter should also be read in conjunction with the revised *Special Educational Needs and Disability Code of Practice* (DfE, 2015). It will not tell you everything you need to know about supporting learners with special educational needs and disabilities because this is a vast area and cannot be addressed in its entirety in one chapter. However, it provides you with the key information that you need to know during your Initial Teacher Training.

CHAPTER OBJECTIVES

* **What is this chapter about?**

This chapter helps you to understand the key principles of the *Special Educational Needs and Disability Code of Practice* (DfE, 2015) which relates to learners from birth to the age of 25. In addition, the chapter examines the nature of specific impairments and suggest ways of overcoming barriers to learning. Theories of disability and theoretical perspectives are addressed throughout.

Why is it important?

The *Code of Practice* states that:

The leaders of early years settings, schools and colleges should establish and maintain a culture of high expectations that expects those working with children and young people with SEN or disabilities to include them in all the opportunities available to other children and young people so they can achieve.

(DfE, 2015, para 1.31, p 27)

The code makes it clear that the accountability for the progress of learners with Special Educational Needs and Disability (SEND) rests with the teacher. Thus, all teachers need to have the confidence, knowledge and skills needed to be able to plan effectively to meet the needs of all learners, including those who are the most vulnerable. During your Initial Teacher Training and your career, you will be responsible for the education of learners with diverse needs. Evidence suggests that these learners achieve less than learners without SEND and that too often they have been exposed to a culture of low expectations throughout their education (DfE, 2010; Ofsted, 2010).

Underachievement in primary and secondary education has far-reaching implications for access to further and higher education, employment and general life chances. Addressing this culture of low expectations and providing teachers with knowledge, skills and confidence in this area will significantly improve outcomes for learners with SEND.

What do we mean by Special Educational Needs and Disability?

The *Code of Practice* states that:

- *a child or young person has SEN if they have a learning difficulty or disability which calls for special educational provision to be made for him or her;*
- *a child of compulsory school age or a young person has a learning difficulty or disability if he or she: has a significantly greater difficulty in learning than the majority of others of the same age, or has a disability which prevents or hinders him or her from making use of facilities of a kind generally provided for others of the same age in mainstream schools or mainstream post-16 institutions.*

(DfE, 2015, pp 15–16)

Legislation

The Equality Act 2010 (HM Government, p 5) defines a disability as *'...a physical or mental impairment which has a long-term and substantial adverse effect on their ability to carry out normal day-to-day activities'*. The Equality Act provides learners with disabilities in schools, further and higher education with protection from direct or indirect discrimination. The Act stipulates that educational providers:

- **must not** directly or indirectly discriminate against, harass or victimise disabled children and young people;
- **must not** discriminate for a reason arising in consequence of a child or young person's disability;

* **must** make reasonable adjustments to ensure that disabled children and young people are not at a substantial disadvantage compared with their peers;
* **must** have regard to the need to eliminate discrimination, promote equality of opportunity and foster good relations between disabled and nondisabled children and young people;
* **must** publish information to demonstrate their compliance with the Equality Act including publishing accessibility plans setting out how they plan to increase access for disabled pupils to the curriculum, the physical environment and to information about their policies for the admission of disabled pupils.

(DfE, 2015, pp 16–17)

This legislation has direct implications for schools as a whole and for your role as a classroom teacher. The legislation places a duty on schools to both promote good relationships between disabled and non-disabled pupils and to address directly all forms of bullying, harassment and discrimination in order to safeguard pupils with disabilities. Additionally, schools and teachers are required to make reasonable adjustments to ensure that disabled pupils are able to access the curriculum and achieve highly. These might include adjustments to teaching, learning and assessment strategies to ensure that pupils with disabilities are not placed at a disadvantage. Adjustments might also need to be made to the physical layout of the classroom or to the structure of the school building to ensure that learners with disabilities can access the physical space in which they will learn.

The nature of the adjustments will largely depend on the needs of the child. Some learners with specific needs may need a slightly adjusted timetable in order to maximise their potential for learning and achieving. Many learners with SEND can access the same learning opportunities as their peers with some small adjustments in place. This might include additional in-class support in specific lessons. It is crucial that you have high expectations of all learners, including those with SEND. Too often, pupils with SEND are subjected to a culture of low teacher expectations and provided with insufficient challenge in lessons. Low teacher expectations can result in both underachievement and disengagement. It is critical that you ensure there is a good level of challenge for all learners in your lessons.

IN PRACTICE

* *In the schools you go into find out what adjustments are provided to ensure equality of opportunity for learners with disabilities.*

The Code of Practice

The *Special Educational Needs and Disability Code of Practice* states that local authorities and schools must have regard to:

* *the views, wishes and feelings of the child or young person, and the child's parents;*
* *the importance of the child or young person, and the child's parents, participating as fully as possible in decisions, and being provided with the information and support necessary to enable participation in those decisions;*
* *the need to support the child or young person, and the child's parents, in order to facilitate the development of the child or young person and to help them achieve the best possible educational and other outcomes, preparing them effectively for adulthood.*

(DfE, 2015, p 19)

These principles are designed to ensure high quality provision for learners with special educational needs and/or disabilities through the early identification of needs, effective early intervention to address these needs and more effective collaboration between education, health and social care services. The principles are also designed to ensure that children, young people and their parents take an increased role in decision-making processes and that they have greater choice.

The *Code of Practice* (DfE, 2015) replaces its predecessor Code (DfES, 2001). The revised code provides:

* a much clearer focus on the participation of children, young people and parents;
* a 0–25 framework for supporting children and young people into adulthood;
* an increased emphasis on the need for schools and teachers to have high aspirations for all learners, including those with SEND;
* an increased emphasis on outcomes (including achievement/attainment/levels of independence/ employment/access to further education) for learners with SEND;
* an increased emphasis on collaboration between services through the introduction of 0–25 Education and Health Care (EHC) plans which replace statements of special educational needs;
* increased choice in decision-making for parents through the introduction of personal budgets for learners with EHC plans.

For those learners who are formally identified as needing SEN support, schools are required to operate a four-part cycle. This is known as a *graduated approach*. As part of this process schools should:

* ***assess** learners' needs through the analysis of assessment data and consultation with pupils, parents and other services where applicable;*
* ***plan** appropriate interventions to address the child's needs both in school and at home;*
* ***do** interventions to address the child's needs;*
* ***review** the effectiveness of interventions on the child's progress in a timely manner.*

(DfE, 2015, pp 86–87)

Parents, carers, children and young people should be involved fully at each stage of the graduated approach. Effective interventions improve outcomes for learners. Thus, it is vital that teachers monitor the impact that specific interventions have on children's progress. This can only be achieved if there is a clear baseline assessment prior to the child being placed on an intervention. If an intervention appears not to be impacting on outcomes for learners, then the intervention should be discontinued and a more effective intervention should be implemented. Regular review of children's progress and other outcomes throughout the duration of an intervention should ensure that teachers are able to identify whether or not that intervention is effective.

According to the *Code of Practice*:

The class or subject teacher should remain responsible for working with the child on a daily basis. Where the interventions involve group or one-to-one teaching away from the main class or subject teacher, they should still retain responsibility for the pupil. They should work closely with any teaching assistants or specialist staff involved, to plan and assess the impact of support and interventions and how they can be linked to classroom teaching.

(DfE, 2015, p 101)

In this respect the code communicates a clear message that teachers must not abdicate their responsibilities for the education of learners with SEND to teaching assistants. As a teacher you are ultimately accountable for the progress and attainment of every child and you have a duty to take this seriously.

CRITICAL QUESTIONS

* *What is your response to the principles of the code?*
* *The increased emphasis on outcomes over the emphasis on provision places greater accountability on schools. What is your response to this?*

IN PRACTICE

* *In school meet with the Special Education Needs Co-ordinator (SENCO) to find out how the school is addressing the principles in the Code of Practice.*

Identifying needs

The *Code of Practice* states:

> *It is particularly important in the early years that there is no delay in making any necessary special educational provision. Delay at this stage can give rise to learning difficulty and subsequently to loss of self-esteem, frustration in learning and to behaviour difficulties. Early action to address identified needs is critical to the future progress and improved outcomes that are essential in helping the child to prepare for adult life.*
>
> **(DfE, 2015, para 5.36, p 86)**

It is important that all schools have a clear and systematic approach towards identifying SEND. This is the responsibility of the SENCO who works in conjunction with the senior leadership team. It is also important to recognise that exposure to high quality teaching will result in fewer pupils being identified with SEND. Schools should establish the entitlement to high quality teaching as the minimum entitlement for all pupils. Before identifying pupils as requiring *SEN support*, schools need to be able to demonstrate that those pupils have received their entitlement to high quality teaching. In cases where teaching is less than good, schools should take action to remedy this. The Code clearly states that '*slow progress and low attainment do not necessarily mean that a child has SEN and should not automatically lead to a pupil being recorded as having SEN*' (DfE, 2015, para 6.23, p 96).

There are a range of possible indicators which might point to a child requiring *SEN support*. These include:

* the pupil is making less than expected progress given their age and individual circumstances;
* progress is significantly slower than their peers starting from the same baseline;
* the child's progress fails to match their previous rate of progress;
* the child's progress fails to close the attainment gap between them and their peers;
* the child's progress results in a widening of the attainment gap.

(DfE, 2015, p 95)

There is a clear expectation in the Code that:

The first response ... should be high quality teaching targeted at their areas of weakness. Where progress continues to be less than expected the class or subject teacher, working with the SENCO, should assess whether the child has SEN. While informally gathering evidence (including the views of the pupil and their parents) schools should not delay in putting in place extra teaching or other rigorous interventions designed to secure better progress, where required. The pupil's response to such support can help identify their particular needs.

(DfE, 2015, para 6.19, p 95)

It is important that you listen to and take seriously any parental concerns about a child, given that research has drawn attention to the fact that some teachers often dismiss these concerns without investigating them fully.

It is significant to emphasise that the purpose of identification of special educational needs is not to fit children into categories. In many instances, children's needs cut across several categories of need rather than falling neatly into one. Additionally, diagnosis of specific needs is an area of specialist and often medical expertise. The purpose of identifying SEND is to enable teachers to provide the right kinds of interventions in a timely manner. This ensures that children do not fall further behind and enables them to catch up with their peers. It is also important to understand that attainment in line with chronological age does not necessarily mean that a child does not have special educational needs. The Code of Practice states that *'Some learning difficulties and disabilities occur across the range of cognitive ability and, left unaddressed may lead to frustration, which may manifest itself as disaffection, emotional or behavioural difficulties'* (DfE, 2015, p 96).

The Code of Practice (DfE, 2015) explicitly emphasises the importance of teachers identifying special educational needs early on. However, it is important that the formal identification of SEND does not result in teachers lowering their expectations or making excuses for lower rates of progress (NASEN, 2014). Before special needs can be formally identified it is necessary to ask critical questions about whether pupils have received their entitlement to high quality, differentiated teaching. If a child is making less than expected progress this does not automatically mean that the child has special needs. This section will introduce you to the process of identifying needs and the graduated response which follows on from the identification process.

The Code of Practice (DfE, 2015) emphasises the importance of:

- the early identification of needs;
- the importance of maintaining high expectations of all learners;
- the importance of establishing high aspirations for children and young people;
- integrated planning and intervention with a focus on outcomes;
- integrated assessment processes;
- high quality, differentiated and individual provision to meet the specific needs of pupils.

You have a responsibility to adapt your teaching to meet the specific needs of individual learners. This accountability is embedded within the Teachers' Standards (specifically Teachers' Standard 5). In addition, the Teachers' Standards make all teachers accountable for the progress and outcomes of their learners (see Teachers' Standard 2). Thus, the accountability for identifying SEND and meeting the individual needs of learners does not solely rest on the SENCO.

CRITICAL QUESTIONS

* *What are the advantages of identifying needs early?*
* *Are there any disadvantages of early identification?*

IN PRACTICE

* *In school meet with the SENCO to find out what processes are in place to enable early identification of SEND.*

Children with English as an additional language

Particular attention should also be given to the identification of special educational needs within groups of learners whose first language is not English. It is important to establish whether a child's development in a specific area is as a result of special educational needs or as a result of the fact that their primary language is not English. Research has found that there is an over-representation of second language learners with a diagnosis of special educational needs. It is critical that you do not assume that behavioural issues are a result of special educational needs without a thorough investigation of the factors that may be contributing to the child's behaviour. In these cases, it is important to establish the cause of the behaviour and to rule out any external factors including housing, family and domestic circumstances.

Improving outcomes for learners with special educational needs and disability

According to the Code of Practice:

High quality teaching that is differentiated and personalised will meet the individual needs of the majority of children and young people. Some children and young people need educational provision that is additional to or different from this ... Special educational provision is underpinned by high quality teaching and is compromised by anything less.

(DfE, 2015, para 1.24, p 25)

It is important to consider the principles which underpin high quality teaching. While the following characteristics are not exhaustive, it could be considered that high quality teaching:

* is specifically targeted at the area(s) of need that need to be addressed;
* ensures that pupils are provided with exactly the right level of challenge based on an accurate assessment of pupils' starting points to enable them to make further progress;
* is characterised by enabling pupils to become increasingly independent and confident in their learning so that they are not afraid to challenge themselves and take risks in their learning;

* focuses relentlessly on identifying and removing barriers to learning so that learners can participate and achieve their full educational potential;
* is underpinned by a culture of high expectations for learners and a *can-do* attitude by both teachers and learners;
* is underpinned by strong subject and pedagogical knowledge;
* is underpinned by the principles of Assessment for Learning.

The principles which underpin high quality teaching for learners with SEND apply to high quality teaching for all learners. Some teachers hold the view that they lack the knowledge or expertise needed to teach pupils with SEND. To some extent it might be argued that the special educational needs 'system' which is supported by a range of professionals working within specialist fields (such as educational psychology or speech and language therapy) has resulted in some teachers feeling that they are not sufficiently qualified to support pupils with specific needs. This can result in teachers feeling disempowered in classrooms.

However, while children with specific needs might require additional or different interventions to address their needs, it is important for you to recognise that the principles which underpin high quality teaching for learners without SEND can be applied effectively to ensure high quality teaching for all learners. While it is invaluable and indeed essential to seek advice from external professionals about specific interventions, it is important for you to recognise that the majority of learners with SEND do not require any form of 'specialist' teaching. They need exactly the same high quality teaching as that which you provide for learners without SEND. Some pupils may be working at a lower stage of development and they may need to learn at a slower pace. However, high quality teaching through targeted intervention will enable the vast majority of learners with SEND to make good progress from their starting points. Undoubtedly, through applying the principles of high quality teaching some learners with SEND will be able to catch up with their peers.

Even where pupils are working at a lower stage of development, it is important that effective, personalised and targeted interventions are enabling children to make good progress from their starting points. Children with highly complex needs might require some forms of specialist teaching and these learners will be supported by Education and Health Care plans. However, the majority of learners who are identified as requiring *SEN support* will make progress if they are provided with high quality teaching which targets the area(s) of need.

IN PRACTICE

* *In school find out how the progress of learners with SEND is monitored. How is children's progress on interventions monitored?*

There may be times when pupils with SEND do not appear to be making progress or times when progress appears to be slow. Try not to be despondent in these situations. They might require a different intervention to address their specific needs. In these circumstances it might be useful to consider the following questions.

* Is the intervention appropriate? Does it specifically target the area of need or are there any other interventions which might be more effective?
* Is the intervention being delivered as it is intended to be delivered (eg frequency of intervention, use of resources)?

* Is the teaching delivery underpinned by the principles of high quality teaching?
* Do you have systematic evidence that the intervention has been effective with pupils with similar needs?
* What are the child's views about the intervention?
* What are the parent's views about the intervention?
* What are the views of specialist professionals about the intervention?
* What might make the intervention more effective?

Having considered these questions, you will ultimately need to make a decision about whether you continue or discontinue with the intervention. You do not need to make this decision in isolation. Talk to colleagues, parents, pupils and then together decide on the best course of action. Avoid the temptation of feeling that you have failed the child if you discontinue an intervention! The same intervention may well have been effective for a different pupil. Adapting your classroom practice in response to pupils' needs demonstrates that you are a reflective classroom practitioner. The most effective teachers are inclusive teachers. They continually review and refine their practice on a regular basis and their teaching is responsive to the needs of learners. There is no hard and fast rule about how long to leave children on an intervention. This largely depends on the area of need being addressed and the specific intervention. However, what is significant is that you need to review pupils' progress on the intervention on a regular basis. It makes sense to do this in line with the assessment points during the annual school calendar so that you can then discuss pupils' progress on interventions with more senior colleagues in school. Lack of progress should trigger a process of review and reflection followed by an appropriate course of action. You cannot justify keeping a child on an intervention for a whole school year only to find that the child has made no progress if you knew at the end of the autumn term that the child was not making progress.

The Code of Practice states that:

All children and young people are entitled to an appropriate education, one that is appropriate to their needs, promotes high standards and the fulfilment of potential. This should enable them to:

* *achieve their best;*
* *become confident individuals living fulfilling lives, and*
* *make a successful transition into adulthood, whether into employment, further or higher education or training.*

(DfE, 2015, para 6.1, p 92)

The Green Paper on Special Educational Needs and Disability (DfE, 2011) stated that *'children's support needs can be identified late; families are made to put up with a culture of low expectations about what their child can achieve at school'* (p 6). As a teacher it is therefore critical that you have high expectations of all pupils, including those with SEND. You need to ensure that you communicate these expectations to your learners by what you say to them and by the work you set them. Learning outcomes need to be challenging but achievable. Tasks should be cognitively demanding in order to stretch pupils. You need to ensure that pupils are offered the appropriate amount of support but this needs to be gradually reduced so that children are able to work with increasing independence. You should communicate an expectation that pupils will demonstrate increasing independence in learning. This has implications for the way in which you set expectations not only with learners but also with support staff.

IN PRACTICE

* *In school talk to the SENCO to find out what interventions are available for specific needs.*

It is important that learners with SEND are not excluded from activities which are available to those without SEND. Under the Equality Act (2010) this could be viewed as a form of direct discrimination. As a class teacher you will need to consider practical aspects such as the timing of interventions so that pupils do not miss out on other opportunities from which they could potentially benefit. When planning educational visits, you will need to plan to remove barriers so that learners with SEND can participate in these experiences. If you are supporting learners with physical disabilities or with visual impairment, you will need to give serious consideration to ways of enabling their participation in physical education. Schools need to ensure that pupils with SEND can benefit from being fully included in the life of the school. This includes opportunities for pupils with SEND to benefit from peer/social interaction at break times or lunchtimes and opportunities to participate in extra-curricular activities.

It is important to recognise that inevitably you will make some mistakes along the way. There is a great deal to consider as a teacher and it is impossible to think of everything. The most important thing is to learn from these experiences and to talk to parents and pupils honestly about the most and least successful aspects of implementing the process of inclusion. The path to inclusive education is often winding rather than straight. Accept that you are working in partnership and that by working together you can find solutions to problems. Too often teachers feel a sense of accountability and are afraid of making mistakes. However, teaching is not an exact science. You cannot always get it right and inclusion is a complex business. Parents will generally accept that you have made a mistake if they recognise that you are willing to try to do your very best for their child.

CRITICAL QUESTIONS

* *What are the advantages of interventions?*
* *What are the disadvantages of interventions?*

Removing barriers to achievement

Access to coloured acetates to lay over black print on a white background, coloured backgrounds on computer screens, and printing worksheets and other handouts on coloured paper may also reduce glare for learners with dyslexia. Pupils with visual impairment may benefit from access to enlarged text or raised print. Learners with autistic spectrum conditions may find it helpful to access a visual timetable to create a sense of structure and routine.

These suggestions are not intended to be exhaustive. I have included them to illustrate that *reasonable adjustments* can sometimes be very small, minor adaptations to classroom practice to enable pupils to access the curriculum. They do not have to be expensive, although this is dependent upon the nature of the adjustment and the needs that are being addressed. It is also important not to assume that all learners with a specific need will benefit from a specific type of adjustment. I have worked with pupils with a diagnosis of autism who have not needed visual timetables and I have taught pupils with dyslexia who have not required coloured overlays.

It is important to recognise that each learner is an individual. They may well share a diagnosis but their needs are not necessarily the same. They may not respond equally effectively to a specific teaching strategy even if that strategy has been recommended for that specific group of learners. The best way of finding out what adjustments learners might require to help them access the curriculum is to consult them. Children often have unique insights into what helps them to learn and even very young children are capable of expressing their views. You should also take the opportunity to consult with the child's parents to ascertain what reasonable adjustments you might be able to make in the classroom. Parents know their child better than you do and they will appreciate being consulted about their education.

The role of the SENCO

It is important that the SENCO establishes a whole-school agreed approach to the identification of SEND. It is not sufficient to assume that just because a pupil has received tailored interventions then their needs have been met and that lack of progress must mean that the pupil has SEND. The SENCO will need to check that:

* pupils' progress during an intervention has been carefully monitored;
* class teachers have been informed of pupils' progress during interventions and these assessments of pupils' learning have been used to inform planning for the child when the child is not undertaking the intervention;
* the knowledge and skills that the intervention addresses are further addressed during times when the child is not undertaking the intervention.

SENCOs will need to ensure that a record-keeping system is established so that teachers can record any concerns in relation to those pupils who appear to make little or no progress despite high quality teaching and targeted intervention. The use of an initial concern form is recommended. This form can be used to collate evidence of formative and summative assessments undertaken with the child and observational assessments undertaken by teaching assistants and teachers.

Sources of evidence

Evidence to support the identification of a pupil's needs may be drawn from:

* *teachers' assessment and experience of the pupil;*
* *pupil progress, attainment and behaviour;*
* *the individual's development in comparison with their peers;*
* *advice from external support services;*
* *the pupil's own views;*
* *the views and experience of parents.*

(NASEN, 2014, p 4)

The most effective identification processes result in a complete evaluation of needs. Sources of evidence should be collated from key stakeholders and the child's own views should be captured to inform the assessment process.

Range of assessment tools

The SENCO will need to make decisions about which assessment tools to use to identify whether or not a pupil has SEND. There are a range of commercial resources available on the market including:

- *criterion-referenced assessments and checklists;*
- *observation schedules and prompt sheets;*
- *profiling tools, for example, for behaviour and speech, language and communication needs;*
- *questionnaires for parents;*
- *questionnaires for pupils;*
- *screening assessments, for example, for dyslexia;*
- *standardised tests.*

(NASEN, 2014, pp 4–5)

Once a pupil has been identified as requiring SEN support, a graduated approach should be followed. This is summarised below.

IN PRACTICE

- *In school meet with the SENCO to find out what assessment tools are used.*

The graduated approach

Plan

Schools should ensure:

- that expectations of the child remain high;
- that they have high aspirations for the child and the child shares these;
- access to high quality differentiated teaching for individual pupils;
- that the SENCO supports class or subject teachers in planning to meet the needs of the pupil;
- that all colleagues who work with the child are aware of their specific needs;
- that parents are consulted and included in the planning process;
- that pupils are consulted and included in the planning process;
- that class and subject teachers remain accountable for planning to meet the needs of the child;
- that skills and knowledge developed during intervention sessions are subsequently applied in the classroom when the intervention is not taking place;
- that class and subject teachers are fully aware of the progress a child is making during an intervention and take account of this in their daily planning;
- that those interventions are fully evaluated on the basis of the extent to which they address the needs of the child and accelerate achievement.

There is no expectation that schools will plan in a particular way to meet the needs of individual pupils. Some schools will continue to use individual education plans but there is no legal requirement for schools to do so and schools should adopt innovative approaches that best meet the needs of specific pupils.

Do

It is important that the planned actions to address the specific need are implemented. The SENCO will play an important role in ensuring that planned interventions take place and that the impact of these interventions is evaluated. All pupils deserve to be taught by a qualified teacher and it is important that class and subject teachers continue to teach pupils with SEND. You remain accountable for pupils' progress, and teachers' involvement in teaching pupils with SEND is critical to successful outcomes.

In cases where teaching assistants are responsible for delivering interventions for addressing specific areas of need, the teaching assistant:

- must have the knowledge, skills and training to deliver the intervention;
- should have received up-to-date training in the intervention;
- should know how to use an intervention flexibly to meet the specific needs of pupils.

Review

It is important that schools do not wait for formal reviews to evaluate the impact of the provision offered for pupils with SEND. The provision should be reviewed regularly and adaptations should be made to the teaching to ensure that pupils get the opportunity to catch up. When reviewing the quality of provision, SENCOs, class and subject teachers need to consider the following points.

- Are the pupils on track to achieve their targets?
- Is the gap narrowing between pupils with and without SEN?
- Is the provision enabling learners with SEND to make progress?
- What are the views of support staff?
- What are the views of the child?
- What are the views of the parent?

Interventions which are not successful and are not having a desired impact on pupil progress should be discontinued and replaced with more effective interventions. Additionally, interventions need to be time-limited rather than permanent. The aim of an intervention is to enable pupils to catch up with their peers as quickly as possible so that they can continue with the differentiated work in the classroom.

Supporting learners with communication and interaction needs

It is important to recognise that many learners with communication and interaction needs do not have cognitive delay. In fact, they might be very able. You cannot automatically group them with other learners with cognitive delay for this very reason.

Speech, language and communication needs

You are likely to meet children with speech, language and communication needs during your teaching career. However, it is important to distinguish between these terms:

> ***Speech*** *is the skill of speaking clearly, without repetition or hesitation and with correct pronunciation.*
>
> ***Language*** *is the ability to join words together to make sentences that are grammatically correct using correct word choices.*
>
> ***Communication*** *is both verbal and non-verbal. It is the ability to sustain a conversation, to respond to other people's ideas by challenging them, developing them or showing empathy and it includes the use of gesture.*
>
> **(The Communication Trust, 2011)**

Children might have deficits in all three areas or in one or more area. The nature of the deficit will largely determine the nature of the intervention that is used to support the child. Some children will already have been referred to speech and language therapy services and the therapist may visit the school on a regular basis to carry out assessments and interventions. The therapist will suggest ways in which you might support the child in the classroom. It is essential that you listen to them, value their advice and implement the recommendations that they suggest as they are experts within this area.

You may be responsible for teaching children who you suspect have speech, language and communication impairments but have not yet been referred to a speech and language therapy team. You need to take advice from the SENCO in these cases and referrals always have to be made with the full co-operation of parents and carers. Some parents may be reluctant to admit that their child has a need, while others will have recognised this but not discussed it with you. In all cases you should be sensitive and conversations should be framed around how best to support the child.

Identification

Children with specific language impairments have a primary deficit in the area of speech, language or communication. Their cognitive and physical development may be unaffected. For others, the speech, language and/or communication impairment may be part of another impairment such as autism, learning difficulties or hearing impairment. Schools will need to establish a clear process through which speech, language and communication needs can be identified. The following characteristics are a useful starting point but the list is not exhaustive. Children with speech, language and communication needs may:

- have underdeveloped social skills;
- struggle to listen and concentrate;
- have a limited vocabulary;
- talk in shorter sentences or not in sentences;
- struggle to understand language;
- have some problems with accessing the curriculum, for example, following instructions, answering questions, processing verbal information and following everyday conversations;
- have low-level difficulties in the acquisition/use of language;

- have difficulties in expressing themselves clearly through incorrect pronunciation, inability to construct sentences or incorrect grammar;
- stammer;
- have language difficulties which have an impact on social inclusion;
- struggle with some aspects of phonics work;
- have speech sound production which may be delayed or muddled.

(Glazzard et al, 2015, p 119)

Removing barriers to learning

One of the most effective ways of enhancing speech, language and communication is to immerse children in a talk-rich, communication-friendly environment. Children will learn to develop their speech, language and communication skills through being exposed to it. It is amazing to observe how quickly those learners whose first language is not English pick up the language in a very short time just through exposure to English. Although some one-to-one work will inevitably be required to support learners with speech, language and communication needs, it is important that they spend the majority of their time in the classroom so that they are exposed to the skills they need to develop. The following suggestions may be helpful in developing inclusive practice.

- Reduce background noise.
- Face the child when speaking to him/ her.
- Provide them with thinking time so they can process what you have said.
- Simplify your language – use short, clear statements.
- Slow down your speech.
- Show them what you want them to do as well as explaining what they have to do.
- Be patient.
- Praise them.
- Build on what they have said.
- Do not finish their sentences.
- Model the correct speech, language or communication.
- Rephrase what they say using the correct language.
- Teach new vocabulary explicitly and in a structured way using a vocabulary programme.
- Provide opportunities for paired talk.
- Provide opportunities for collaborative group work and discussion.

(Glazzard et al, 2015, pp 109–10)

IN PRACTICE

- *In school ask if there are children with speech, language and communication needs.*
- *If so, shadow one child for one lesson.*
- *What are the barriers to learning?*
- *How is the school addressing these barriers?*

Autistic spectrum conditions

Autism is a neurodevelopmental condition which is more common in boys than girls. It is characterised by language, communication and social difficulties and lack of flexibility in thought. It is important to recognise that children with autistic spectrum conditions (ASC) form a diverse group of individuals. They fall along a spectrum which ranges from mild to severe, and individuals with a diagnosis do not necessarily demonstrate identical characteristics. Leo Kanner first defined *infantile autism* in 1943 to describe individuals who demonstrated specific traits which are now associated with classic autism. Asperger syndrome is sometimes referred to as *high-functioning autism*. It was first described by Hans Asperger in 1944. Individuals who fall within this group generally have average or above average abilities, good spoken language and no language delay. They may demonstrate a high level of ability in a specific area but their difficulties in other areas can be severe.

Autism is a lifelong condition that affects individuals in various ways. There is a need for teachers to respect the ways in which these individuals think and learn and to understand that no two individuals with autism will behave or think in the same way (Jordan and Powell, 1995). There is no one single identifiable cause of autism.

Identification

The work of Lorna Wing and Judy Gould (1979) and Wing (1996) has been influential in identifying children with ASC. They describe a cluster of characteristics which are common in all individuals with ASC and these have commonly been referred to as Wing's *Triad of Impairments*. The term *autistic spectrum disorders* was first used by Wing in 1996 (Wing, 1996) and this has more recently started to be replaced by the term ASC. Wing claims that all children in this group are affected by a triad of impairments.

1. **Social language and communication:** language can be impaired or delayed, verbal or non-verbal. Some children with ASD have highly developed grammar and pronunciation (Jordan and Powell, 1995). However, regardless of the level of spoken language, communication remains a fundamental problem (Jordan and Powell, 1995). For example, individuals may have difficulties in understanding gesture, facial expression, body postures and positioning and they may struggle with the semantic and pragmatic aspects of language (Jordan and Powell, 1995).
2. **Social interaction:** social development is impaired, deviant or delayed and children may have difficulty in understanding social conventions and rules such as turn-taking. They may be solitary and withdrawn and express themselves and interpret instructions literally.
3. **Flexibility and thought:** rigidity of thought, ritualistic behaviour, reliance on routines and absence of imaginative play may be evident in individuals with ASC. Some individuals with autism may demonstrate imagination but they may have difficulty in distinguishing imagination from reality. They may develop special interests or obsessions.

(Wing, 1988)

Possible indicators of autism

As a teacher you are not qualified to diagnose autism. However, having a basic knowledge of some of the characteristics of autism will be helpful in initiating discussions with other professionals. The following indicators are a starting point to frame these discussions but the list is not exhaustive. Additionally, individuals may demonstrate all or some of these characteristics and not have autism. A child with autism may:

* have difficulties with social relationships and communication, and this may affect functioning as a member of a group;
* have difficulties in understanding that s/he is part of a group;
* show signs of poor hand/eye co-ordination;
* have unusual responses to sensory stimuli, eg bright lights, loud noises;
* show signs of stress and anxiety particularly at times of transition;
* have difficulties understanding whole class instructions and general information;
* only understand spoken language which is literal, and speech may be delayed or unusual;
* find abstract concepts difficult;
* prefer their own agenda and may be reluctant to follow directions or accept a change in routine;
* not have a diagnosis of autism by an appropriately qualified professional;
* have difficulties with fine and gross motor skills;
* have difficulties with reciprocal social interaction with peers;
* have a poor concept of time and sequencing of events.

(Glazzard et al, 2015, pp 117–18)

Removing barriers to learning

This section provides some helpful practical advice on ways of supporting learners with ASC in the classroom. You should ensure that you talk to other professionals who may be supporting children in the classroom. You should maintain daily communication with parents and carers through the use of written, telephone or electronic communication. Finding ways to listen to the voice of the child with autism may be more challenging but it is not impossible. If oral language and verbal communication skills are developing, then it should be relatively simple to involve pupils in decisions about their own learning. If the child does not communicate verbally then you can use augmentative and alternative communication (AAC) to enable the child to express their views and select choices.

Visual strategies

Many adults with high-functioning autism have described how they tend to *think in pictures* (Grandin, 1996). Visual strategies are therefore an important way of helping children to learn. Visual support systems can make use of objects, photographs, drawings, symbols and text to represent activities. Progressing from objects to text can be considered as a developmental sequence so that you start with objects first as an approach to visual learning.

The starting point for developing an inclusive classroom is to label classroom resources using words and pictures. Learners can then easily locate specific resources that they need and return them to their correct place when they have finished using them. The use of a visual timetable will support children to develop a sense of routine. This will enable them to identify what they are learning first, second, third and so on, so they know what is happening next, thus reducing any anxiety. Many individuals with ASC benefit from clear predictable systems and routines. It is important to establish a clear timetable during the week and to establish clear, consistent routines during the day to aid predictability. The

daily tasks can be denoted using pictures and captions and each task can be removed as an activity is completed. You might want to build in some time during the day for children to work on their own interests. However, children with ASC need to understand that tasks on the daily timetable should be completed in order and if they refuse to engage with a task or complete a task they will be unable to progress to the next activity. In this way, it is useful to position their favourite activity further down on the visual timetable.

Where possible, the order and timing of the daily tasks should remain consistent with the visual timetable. However, all children need to understand that sometimes, for reasons which are often outside the teacher's control, the timing and order of the activities may need to change. In this instance it is helpful to warn children in advance of changes which will affect them. Sudden changes from the timetable can invoke anxiety and this can lead to outbursts of unwanted behaviour. The pictures should be clear and you need to ensure that the child understands them. If tasks or resources become unavailable to children, then the picture can be removed from the timetable or a cross can be drawn over the picture.

The length of an activity can be represented visually using a moving arrow which moves across a line with the words START and STOP on the left and right-hand sides of the line, respectively. As the task progresses the arrow can be moved across the line from left to right so that the child can see how much longer they will spend on the specific task.

The *Picture Exchange Communication System* (PECS) developed by Bondy and Frost (1994) is a system which facilitates communication. The child gives a picture of an object to another person in exchange for the object. In this way, the child is able to initiate the conversation and the approach enables children with limited or no language to communicate with others. It is always useful to discuss whether any of these approaches are being used in the home so that you can establish consistency between home and school.

When you plan your lessons, identify opportunities to use visual cues in your teaching at different stages of a lesson. This will benefit all learners. Consider how you might explain knowledge, skills and concepts using objects, pictures, diagrams, flow charts and digital footage to enhance understanding. Try to reduce the amount of teacher talk in your lessons.

Sensory stimuli

Children with ASC are often easily distracted by sensory overload (colour, patterns, background noise, smells etc). This can be problematic within the context of a mainstream primary school because environments are often brightly coloured, highly visual and noisy. Children with ASC may demonstrate an aversion to specific smells, textures and tastes. Through communicating with parents and other professionals you will be able to ascertain whether children have specific problems with receiving sensory information. Some children may dislike the smell of perfume and others may dislike being touched. Others may have an aversion to the texture of specific materials such as sand or jelly. While it is impossible to eliminate sensory information, it is worth considering how you can reduce it. Some children with ASC benefit from being taught separately in a study zone which has bare white walls. This might reduce distractions and the space could be created within the classroom. Some children with ASC prefer to block out background noise with the use of ear mufflers. Consider developing strategies to reduce the amount of noise in your classroom. This will benefit all learners and keep you sane at the same time!

Social stories

Social Stories were developed by Carol Gray (Gray, 1994) in America. Some children with ASD may find particular situations or experiences difficult. A social story is built around this experience and aims to describe the events that happen and the feelings of the 'characters' in the story. They can help children learn to cope with new social situations, such as going into assembly, participating in lunch time or play time and going on a school trip. Children can read these stories prior to an event (or have them read out) to help them rehearse the experience.

Developing emotional literacy

Individuals with autism may have difficulty in understanding how others think and feel. They may demonstrate a lack of empathy and poor emotional expression. They may demonstrate limited or no awareness of how their words or actions might affect other people. They may express no desire to please others. Due to their social communication difficulties, they may lack an understanding of social conventions such as nodding, eye contact and turn-taking and they may switch the topic midway through a conversation (Jordan and Powell, 1995). These difficulties need to be addressed through a very structured teaching programme which focuses on developing emotional literacy. They may benefit from structured teaching on feelings, social behaviour and relationship-building with others.

Providing a communication curriculum

Teaching the skill of communication is the most important aspect of educating children with autism (Jordan and Powell, 1995). There is some debate about whether children with autism can receive information from more than one channel at the same time (Jordan and Powell, 1995). This raises questions about whether teachers should use spoken language alongside alternative forms of communication such as sign language. However, the general consensus seems to be that spoken language should be used in conjunction with alternative forms of communication. Picture-exchange communication systems have been discussed above as an approach to facilitate helping children to make requests.

However, in teaching communication it is important that the non-verbal skills of communication are taught in a structured way. These include turn-taking, politeness, use of gesture, proxemics, body posture, body contact and maintaining attention. These skills may be best taught discretely in one-to-one situations before they are applied in social situations with peers.

Managing behaviours

It is important that you understand the triggers for unwanted behaviour. If the triggers are identified, then potentially they can be removed or minimised in order to reduce the behavioural response. In identifying triggers, it is important to identify patterns in behaviour such as specific times of the day or specific lessons when behavioural incidents occur. It is possible that poor behaviour may arise from anxiety. Children with autism can become stressed in certain situations and particularly when there are sudden changes to the planned routine. It is important to minimise changes to daily routines and to try to

keep routines consistent where possible. In situations where routines have to change, it is important to prepare children in advance for these changes. Sometimes this may not be possible and children may respond negatively to these situations.

Ascertain whether unwanted behavioural responses occur as a result of specific stimuli (exposure to light, noise, temperature, smells, textures, colours etc). Consider whether it is possible to reduce the stimuli in order to minimise the unwanted behaviour. Children can become anxious if they do not understand what they need to do to complete specific tasks. To reduce this, it is possible to provide children with written and/or visual instructions which break down the task into a series of steps. In cases of extreme behaviour, it is important to ensure the safety of both the child who is demonstrating the behaviour and their peers. Sometimes it is better to remove the child to a calm space. However, it is important to point out that children with autism may not view this as a punishment but as a reward for their poor behaviour. The most effective approach to managing behaviour is to use positive reinforcers to reward desirable behaviour. These can operate on a hierarchy as follows.

* **Primary reinforcers:** these are related to satisfying physical needs and sensations and may include music, vibratory massage or vestibular stimulation (rocking, twirling and swinging).
* **Secondary reinforcers:** these include reward systems (eg a star chart or points chart) which can subsequently be exchanged for a tangible reward.
* **Intrinsic reinforcers:** these are forms of reward which arise from academic success/performance and result in increased self-concept and self-esteem, which then produces positive learning behaviours.
* **Postponed gratification reinforcers:** these are mediated by setting long-term goals which when achieved are subsequently rewarded.

(Jordan and Powell, 1995, p 138)

You will need to check that there are sufficient accessible positive reinforcers available to reward desirable behaviour. Some children with autism will only respond to reinforcers at the primary level. It is important to communicate with parents and carers to ascertain what reinforcers are successfully used at home. Behaviour management is always more effective when there is consistency in approaches between home and school. Agreeing on the same reinforcers is one way of increasing this consistency.

Developing social skills

When you are teaching children with autism a new skill or helping them to understand a new concept, this is usually best achieved through teaching the child individually in one-to-one teaching sessions. If you are using group work to develop children's subject-specific knowledge, skills or understanding then you are asking them to focus on developing subject-specific learning as well as developing the skill of working in groups. The new learning for the child with autism is how to relate to others, so if you are focusing on this skill it makes sense for the subject-specific learning to be secure. Thus, you need to be very clear about the teaching focus when children with autism are learning in social situations. The focus might be different from that which you have identified for their peers.

It might be effective to start the process of collaborative learning by using pairs or very small groups before progressing to larger groups. The skills of group work (turn-taking, sharing, listening, helping etc) can be taught in one-to-one sessions with an adult before you ask children to apply these with their peers. Many children with autism require very explicit and structured teaching of these skills. This can be accompanied by the use of positive reinforcers to reward desired behaviour. They might also need very structured learning in order to teach them friendship behaviours. Additionally, it is important to teach their peers how to respond appropriately to them so that responses do not invoke anxiety, fear or distress.

IN PRACTICE

* *In school ask if there are children with autistic spectrum conditions.*
* *If so, shadow one child for one lesson.*
* *What are the barriers to learning?*
* *How is the school addressing these barriers?*

Supporting learners with cognition and learning needs

The Code of Practice states:

Support for learning difficulties may be required when children and young people learn at a slower pace than their peers, even with appropriate differentiation. Learning difficulties cover a wide range of needs, including moderate learning difficulties (MLD), severe learning difficulties (SLD), where children are likely to need support in all areas of the curriculum and associated difficulties with mobility and communication, through to profound and multiple learning difficulties (PMLD), where children are likely to have severe and complex learning difficulties as well as a physical disability or sensory impairment.

(DfE, 2015, para 6.30, pp 97–98)

When supporting learners with cognition and learning needs, you will need to make decisions about the curriculum. Specifically, it will be up to you to decide whether children with these needs are able to undertake the same learning as their peers with additional support or resources in lessons. Depending on what you are teaching, it is sometimes possible for everyone to be working on the same learning objective. Sometimes this is not appropriate and you will need to identify different learning objectives for this group of learners within a lesson. Where possible, most learners should be taught the same content, even though some might learn it at a slower pace. For children with severe learning difficulties it might be more appropriate to focus on specific content which is more appropriate in order to address their needs.

Supporting learners with specific learning difficulties

Children with specific learning difficulties may typically demonstrate difficulties in one or more areas of the curriculum, despite demonstrating average or above average ability in other areas. To support you in identifying children with specific learning difficulties look out for the following characteristics:

* low level difficulties in the acquisition and use of language/literacy/numeracy/motor/memory/organisational skills;

* evidence of unexpected/inconsistent/unusual patterns of strengths and specific weaknesses in skills development;
* access only to specific curriculum areas is affected while high cognitive abilities may be demonstrated in other areas.

(Glazzard et al, 2015, p 119)

Dyslexia

Developmental dyslexia was first described in the *British Medical Journal* in 1896 (Pringle-Morgan, 1896). The article cited a case report of a boy named Percy who, despite adequate intelligence, was unable to learn to read. Early explanations of dyslexia attributed the difficulty to a visual deficit, and dyslexia was described as *congenital word blindness* (Hinshelwood, 1917). In 1968 the World Federation of Neurology described dyslexia as:

A disorder manifested by difficulty in learning to read despite conventional instruction, adequate intelligence and sociocultural opportunity. It is dependent upon fundamental cognitive disabilities which are frequently of constitutional origin.

(cited in Snowling, 2000, p 15)

This definition was problematic on several levels. Firstly, it fails to explain what is meant by terms such as *conventional* instruction or *adequate* intelligence (Snowling, 2000). In addition, the definition adopts a medical model of disability by locating the source of the problem within a person's biological make-up. It fails to acknowledge that environmental factors and access to poor teaching can cause difficulties. Finally, the definition fails to provide any criteria to aid the positive diagnosis of dyslexia in that it fails to identify the specific difficulties that people with dyslexia may experience (Snowling, 2000). In contrast, the definition offered by the British Psychological Society describes the characteristics which are typically evident in poor readers with dyslexia:

Dyslexia is evident when accurate and fluent word reading and/or spelling develops very incompletely or with great difficulty. This focuses on literacy learning at the 'word' level and implies that the problem is severe and persistent despite appropriate learning opportunities.

(British Psychological Society, 1999, p 64)

Traditionally, dyslexia has been identified through a discrepancy model. Thus, individuals with average or above average intelligence who struggle with literacy are viewed as characteristically different from those who have below average intelligence but struggle to master the skills of reading. In the case of the former, there is a discrepancy between the individual's predicted potential based on their IQ and their literacy skills. This has warranted the need for a positive diagnosis due to the unexpected and specific nature of the literacy difficulty. In the case of the latter, it has tended to be assumed that the child's reading skills are not significantly out of line with their cognitive ability and thus there is no evidence of a specific learning difficulty.

The use of IQ as a measure of learning potential is problematic given both the contested nature of IQ and research findings which have indicated that reading difficulties exist largely independently of intellectual functioning (Stanovich and Stanovich, 1997). These debates have resulted in modifications to the definition provided by the World Federation of

Neurology, with more recent definitions acknowledging that dyslexia is evident across the full spectrum of intellectual ability.

Distinguishing between two groups of poor readers is problematic given that a positive diagnosis of dyslexia can lead to access to funding and additional resources for those individuals whose profiles demonstrate evidence of a discrepancy. The non-discrepant poor readers are then left without access to the same resources. This is despite the fact that research has indicated that the information processing operations underlying word recognition are the same for both discrepant and non-discrepant poor readers. Additionally, research also suggests that both groups of poor readers respond equally well to reading intervention. These research findings have led Elliott and Gibbs (2008) to conclude that:

There appears to be no clear-cut scientific basis for differential diagnosis of dyslexia versus poor reader. At various times and for various reasons it has been a social convenience to label some people as dyslexic but consequences of labelling include stigma, disenfranchisement and inequitable use of resources.

(Elliott and Gibbs, 2008, p 488)

Whether you agree or disagree with this argument, it is important to draw some practical implications from the research. Thus, you need to ensure that all poor readers receive appropriate intervention to enable them to become skilled readers.

Although earlier explanations of dyslexia focused on deficits in the visual system, recent research has emphasised the important role of phonological awareness in reading development (Bradley and Bryant, 1983, 1985; Snowling, 2000). Most cognitive psychologists now view reading as a linguistic rather than a visual skill (Elliott and Gibbs, 2008) and the ability to identify the sounds of speech and reflect on them is critical to reading development. Thus, reading deficits are now usually attributed to impairments in the part of the brain that processes language rather than the part of the brain that controls the visual system. This research has important implications for the way in which teachers provide intervention for pupils with literacy difficulties.

If reading difficulties are attributed to deficits in phonological awareness skills, this would suggest the need for a phonological awareness programme and the gradual introduction of a multi-sensory programme to develop phonemic awareness. However, many interventions focus on correcting perceived deficits in the visual system. These include the use of coloured overlays to lay over text, tinted lenses and printing text on coloured paper. While these might alleviate eye-strain and build confidence, it is questionable whether such interventions improve reading because they do not target the core deficit in phonological awareness. Some commercial intervention programmes have also focused on improving balance and hand-eye coordination through simple exercises such as throwing a beanbag into a hoop. However, there is no scientific evidence that these interventions improve reading because they do not address the primary cause of the reading problem.

Dyslexia is best considered as a *learning difference*. Learners with dyslexia demonstrate a profile of strengths and weaknesses. Weaknesses may be evident in reading, spelling and writing and sometimes in number and calculation (TDA, 2008). Learners with dyslexia may also have associated weaknesses in sequencing, short-term memory and speed of processing. The difficulties that they experience are often both unexpected and persistent. Difficulties in spelling are often persistent and extend into adulthood even when the skill of reading has been mastered. It is important that teachers recognise

what learners with dyslexia can do well and celebrate these strengths. Although many learners with dyslexia experience specific difficulties in aspects of literacy, they may well demonstrate strengths in aspects such as group work and oral communication. It is critical that areas of strength are recognised and that you draw on these to maximise access and participation.

IN PRACTICE

- *In school ask if there are children with dyslexia.*
- *If so, shadow one child for one lesson.*
- *What are the barriers to learning?*
- *How is the school addressing these barriers?*

Identification

Although your ITT programme does not qualify you to diagnose dyslexia, it is helpful as a starting point to be able to identify potential indicators so that you are able to start planning appropriate intervention. The following list is not exhaustive but learners at risk of dyslexia may demonstrate the following characteristics:

- slow processing speeds;
- limited concentration, frequently tired and poor short-term memory;
- difficulty following instructions;
- sequencing difficulties;
- poor standard of written work;
- poor letter formation, including letter reversals and poor pencil grip;
- spells a word several ways in one piece of writing;
- bizarre spelling;
- makes anagrams of words (eg writes *tired* instead of *tried*);
- unusual sequencing of letters and words;
- poor reading skills;
- difficulty in blending phonemes;
- difficulty in identifying syllable divisions in words;
- poor reading comprehension;
- symbol confusion in mathematics;
- difficulty in learning multiplication tables, days of the week, months of the year, alphabetic order, understanding left and right and other direction;
- difficulty in telling the time;
- poor personal organization;
- poor motor control;
- easily distracted.

(TDA, 2008, pp 29–30)

Some schools now purchase computer screening software to support the identification of dyslexia. A range of software is available and children are asked to complete specific tasks on a computer. It is important to emphasise that these programs cannot be used to diagnose dyslexia. They can, however, be used to indicate the likelihood of a child having dyslexia and thus to indicate whether further referral and official diagnosis is necessary. It is particularly important that you do not tell parents that their child has dyslexia because an official diagnosis can only be made by an appropriately qualified professional such as an educational psychologist.

Many children with dyslexia demonstrate poor phonological awareness. Thus, they may struggle to detect and generate rhyme and they may struggle to divide words into syllables. They may find it difficult to split compound words into their two constituent words. They often have specific difficulty with phonemic awareness. Thus, they struggle to identify the individual phonemes in a spoken word and they may struggle specifically with the skill of blending phonemes for reading. Their specific difficulties with phonemic awareness often mean that children with dyslexia have considerable difficulty with phonemic deletion and phonemic addition tasks. They may also struggle with phoneme substitution tasks. These are briefly summarised below:

* **Phonemic deletion:** removing a phoneme from a word, for example, say the word *cat* without the /c/.
* **Phonemic addition:** adding a phoneme onto a word, for example, if you put the sound /m/ at the front of the word *at*, what word do you get?
* **Phoneme substitution:** substituting one phoneme for another, for example, in the word *dog*, if I change the /d/ to a /f/ what word do I get?

Devising some simple tasks in relation to these three skills targets the core phonological deficit that is often evident in learners with dyslexia. They can be completed quickly and the skills that are being targeted are independent of measures of IQ. Deficit skills in phonemic deletion, phonemic addition and phonemic substitution are very reliable indicators of dyslexia, especially if a child has been exposed to quality teaching in these areas and has failed to master the skills.

Removing barriers to learning

The ground-breaking work of Keith Stanovich has indicated that poor readers with both high and low intelligence demonstrate deficits in phonemic addition, deletion and substitution. We know from his work that both groups of poor readers respond equally well to intervention. Identification of the deficit skills informs the intervention process. Thus, poor readers may benefit from *multisensory interventions* which focus specifically on developing the skills of phonemic addition, deletion and substitution. In order to master these skills, there is a need for frequent opportunities for over-learning in these areas in order to embed the skills. Effective intervention targets the core problem rather than the symptoms. Thus, intervention programmes which address accompanying weaknesses (such as poor balance and co-ordination) are likely to be less effective than those interventions which focus on the deficient skills.

Phonological awareness is the skill of detecting the sounds within a spoken word. It includes phonemes but also includes the ability to detect larger sound units within words such as syllables and rimes. Children with dyslexia may have specific difficulties in developing the skill of phonological awareness. Thus, intervention at the level of the

syllable and the rime as well as intervention at the level of the phoneme (smallest units of sound) may also be required.

It is important to recognise that learners with dyslexia are not homogenous. They may not demonstrate the same characteristics and they may not respond equally well to the same interventions. Despite this, it is useful to have a bank of strategies at your fingertips as a starting point to develop inclusive practice. As a reflective teacher, you will need to implement the interventions and evaluate their effectiveness on a regular basis. If an intervention appears to be having a limited impact on pupils' outcomes then you will need to modify or change the intervention in order to accelerate pupil achievement.

The following suggestions will provide you with a useful starting point for developing inclusive pedagogy for learners with dyslexia:

- Educate all pupils about dyslexia.
- Share examples of famous personalities with dyslexia.
- Never ask learners with dyslexia to read aloud.
- Provide a multi-sensory phonic intervention that provides opportunities for over-learning.
- Allow children to learn through, and represent their ideas in, pictures, diagrams and mind maps.
- Copy worksheets onto cream or buff coloured paper.
- Provide children with multiplication squares, number lines and word mats.
- Display letters of the alphabet to aid correct formation.
- Provide learners with alternative ways of recording their ideas rather than writing, for example, making a poster; voice recording; making a presentation; recording through pictures, diagrams and mind maps.
- Provide learners with a *reading buddy* or a scribe sometimes to help them with recording ideas in writing.
- Keep oral and written sentence length to a minimum.
- Break up text.
- Use bold text to highlight rather than italics or underlining and use size 14 font and a clear font style (eg Arial or Tahoma).
- Use portable electronic writing aids, for example, tablets or laptops.
- Mark written work sensitively and focus on the content of written work rather than the spelling or presentation.
- Help children to organise their writing through the use of writing frames.
- Use pre-teaching in advance of literacy lessons.
- Give pupils clear steps to success through a specific task so that pupils understand what to do first, second and third.
- Break learning into smaller chunks.
- Give pupils a chance to show their abilities in areas they are better at.

The suggestions offered here are useful for developing inclusive pedagogy for all learners, including learners with dyslexia. However, you should always develop inclusive approaches to learning and teaching in collaboration with the learner and his/her parents or carers. Including the views of children and parents in curriculum planning will ensure that they feel that you are working with them and that you respect their ideas.

Dyspraxia

Identification

There are no formal diagnostic criteria for dyspraxia. The term is made up of *dys*, which means 'difficulty', and *praxis*, which means the ability to organise and carry out a sequence of movements. Difficulties include:

* reduced muscle strength;
* impaired coordination and movement;
* poor balance;
* difficulty in combining movements into a sequence;
* poor fine motor skills;
* poor spatial awareness;
* poor visual-spatial memory;
* problems with hand-eye coordination;
* problems with sense of direction (left/right);
* difficulties with organising and sequencing tasks;
* poor attention and concentration;
* social and behavioural difficulties.

(Abdullah, 2012, pp 98–111)

Removing barriers to learning

You should plan lessons which provide pupils with opportunities for active, multi-sensory learning with clear instructions so that pupils are clear about what they need to do in a task. Visual timetables may help pupils with dyspraxia to understand the sequence of tasks which need to be completed. Learners with dyspraxia might benefit from completing a series of shorter tasks in a lesson rather than trying to concentrate on one task for an extended period of time. A range of activities to develop finger strength, hand-eye coordination and sequencing may need to be planned into the daily timetable.

Supporting learners with social, emotional and health difficulties

The Code of Practice states:

Children and young people may experience a wide range of social and emotional difficulties which manifest themselves in many ways. These may include becoming withdrawn or isolated, as well as displaying challenging, disruptive or disturbing behaviour. These behaviours may reflect underlying mental health difficulties such as anxiety or depression, self-harming, substance misuse, eating disorders or physical symptoms that are medically unexplained. Other children and young people may have disorders such as attention deficit disorder, attention deficit hyperactive disorder or attachment disorder.

(DfE, 2015, para 6.32, p 98)

This is a broad group of learners and characteristics will be different in each case. However, children belonging to this group may:

* be withdrawn or isolated;
* display some occasional stress or anxiety;
* have immature social skills;
* demonstrate occasional disruptive and disturbing behaviours;
* demonstrate low-level hyperactivity and lack of concentration;
* demonstrate following most but not all routines in the learning environment;
* demonstrate difficulties with social relationships;
* demonstrate difficulties with complying with the structure of a group;
* demonstrate difficulties joining in group/whole class work;
* show signs of stress and anxiety;
* demonstrate difficulty following whole class instructions.

(Glazzard et al, 2015, p 118)

It is important to identify the triggers which cause disruptive behaviour and try to remove these with a view to alleviating the behaviour. The use of positive, descriptive praise is important for reinforcing good behaviour. Additionally, the use of an individual reward system may aid motivation, although this does promote extrinsic rather than intrinsic motivation. Providing opportunities for active learning and breaking learning up into smaller chunks will help to reduce disengagement. Some learners in this group may benefit from specific interventions to promote self-esteem and to develop social skills. You need to establish positive, supportive relationships with learners and their parents and carers so that they feel valued and respected.

Some children will need a behaviour plan which identifies very specific but achievable targets. In identifying potential solutions, it is important to deal with each child on a case by case basis rather than identifying generic strategies which might be adopted, because each child is different. Many schools now employ teaching assistants with a pastoral commitment so that pupils with social and emotional difficulties have a point of contact. Involving the pupils in setting targets for self-improvement and reviewing progress are important steps to take to demonstrate that you value the child's perspectives and show that you are working with them to find solutions. Separating the behaviour from the person is critical to help maintain positive relationships. Children in this group will benefit from clear rules and routines and appropriate sanctions which are proportionate to their behaviour. If children have specific health/medical needs, it is important to be aware of these and to communicate with health care professionals and parents. Children within this group may not have any cognitive delay and may demonstrate high ability. These learners cannot therefore be automatically grouped with learners with cognitive delay.

IN PRACTICE

* *In school ask if there are children with mental health needs.*
* *If so, find out what the specific mental health needs are.*
* *What provision is the school implementing to address these needs?*

Supporting learners with sensory and/or physical needs

Children may have been identified with visual or hearing impairment or a combination of the two. This is known as multi-sensory impairment. The term is broad because within each group there can be varying degrees of severity. Children with visual impairment may benefit from exposure to a larger text size, enlarged teaching resources and the use of a multi-sensory approach to teaching and learning. The use of tactile or textured letters and numbers may support the early teaching of mathematics and reading. Consider the layout of your classroom and try to keep it predictable. Children can have varying degrees of hearing impairment. It is important to face the child directly when speaking to them and to speak clearly and slowly. The use of sign language may aid communication. Again, a multi-sensory approach to teaching and learning will support development and the use of visual strategies in particular may be beneficial. It is important to reduce background noise so that children with hearing impairment can concentrate on what you are saying to them.

Children with physical difficulties may demonstrate:

* problems with fine motor skills, pencil/pen control, scissor skills, dressing and undressing/self-care skills;
* difficulties with written recording;
* problems with gross motor skills often seen in PE/outside environment;
* lack of co-ordination, eg difficulty carrying a tray at meal times;
* unsteadiness in crowded areas or on uneven surfaces;
* possible low levels of self-esteem.

(Glazzard et al, 2015, p 118)

The nature of the intervention will largely be dependent on the underlying difficulties that the child is experiencing. Specially adapted resources can be purchased to support the development of gross and fine motor skills. In some schools, environments are adapted to support the movement of pupils from one area to another. The occupational therapist will be able to offer you invaluable advice to support the development of inclusive practice. It is important to recognise that pupils with sensory or physical difficulties may not have any underlying cognitive difficulties. These learners may be very able and therefore cannot automatically be grouped with pupils who have cognitive delay.

IN PRACTICE

* *In school ask if there are children with sensory or physical needs.*
* *If so, shadow one child for one lesson.*
* *What are the barriers to learning?*
* *How is the school addressing these barriers?*

Labelling

The Code of Practice (DfE, 2015) refers to specific categories of SEND. It is interesting to consider how the terminology used to describe disability has changed over the years.

Terms such as *sub-normal, backward, retarded and handicapped* were common terms throughout the twentieth century yet no-one would dare to use this terminology in schools today. The terms are offensive and place the 'blame' directly on the individuals who have specific needs. They reflect a medical model of disability in which disability is located or situated within a person's biological make-up.

Since the 1980s, moves towards the social model of disability have emphasised the distinction between impairment and disability. Thus, within a social model, disability refers to access to goods, services or opportunities. The model acknowledges that impairments exist but emphasises that impairments do not need to become disabling if society makes the correct adaptations. Adaptations can be physical, financial, attitudinal and pedagogical. The model therefore views disability as a social construction rather than being rooted within a person's biology.

As the social model has evolved, the term *impairment* has gained increasing credibility because although impairments may have a biological origin it is not inevitable that impairments result in disability. Thus, through effective high-quality teaching and a culture of high expectations, learners with specific needs can access education and employment.

Despite the benefits that the social model has brought to the lives of so many disabled people, it is interesting how the terminology constantly evolves. Mary Warnock in her influential Warnock Report (DES, 1978) replaced the term *handicapped* with the term *special educational needs*. However, this term is not without criticism. For example, the term *special* can create a sense of *othering* which marginalises those who own the label. Thomas and Loxley (2007) have critically interrogated the term *need*. In relation to learners with behavioural needs, they argue that the needs of the education system to create order and control and the need of schools to demonstrate high standards are placed onto learners so that they are viewed as having the problem. This shifts the emphasis away from the education system (curricula/assessment system) which is fundamentally 'faulty' and contributes to learner disengagement in the first place. It is also interesting to note that the term *disorder* is being replaced with the term *condition* in some fields (eg autism), and the term *disability* is sometimes now being expressed as *differently abled*.

CRITICAL QUESTIONS

- *What do you consider are the benefits of labels?*
- *What are the disadvantages of labelling?*
- *Why do you think labels change?*

EXTENDED THINKING

- *The medical model of disability effectively locates the source of the disablement within a person's biological make-up. To what extent does the existence of specialists such as educational psychologists reflect a medical model of disability?*
- *The social model of disability separates impairment from disability by viewing disability as a social construction. Can you think of instances where biological impairments might become profoundly disabling in their own right? Is the social model therefore ideological?*

Working in partnership

Working in partnership with parents and carers

The Code of Practice for Special Educational Needs and Disability (DfE, 2015) emphasises the importance of schools working in partnership with parents and carers to support the needs of children who have been formally identified as having SEND. Parents should be involved in all decisions which affect their child. They should be consulted at all stages, including the initial identification of needs and the graduated approach (plan, do, review) discussed earlier in this chapter. It is important that initial discussion about the needs of the child should involve parents so that any formal identification of SEND does not come as a surprise to them. In your role as a teacher you will need to involve parents in setting targets/goals for their child. Target setting should be carried out in consultation with parents so that agreement can be reached about which goals the parent will work on with their child outside school and the strategies they might employ to help their child achieve these specific goals. Parents should be involved in all reviews of the child's progress and involvement in reviews should not be limited to annual reviews.

The SEND policy in the school should outline very clearly the ways in which parents and carers will be involved in the process of identifying, supporting and reviewing their child's needs. The SENCO will need to consider how parents of pupils with SEND are involved in developing and reviewing the SEND policy and the school information report. This is a statutory document which must be published on the school website. It outlines the provision that is available in the school to meet the needs of learners with SEND. Involving parents in policy formulation is one way of schools demonstrating that parents have a strategic as well as operational involvement in the provision which is offered to pupils.

CRITICAL QUESTIONS

* *How might you support a parent who refuses to accept that their child has a specific need which has to be addressed?*
* *How could you develop parent partnerships for parents who are reluctant to come into school?*

Working in partnership with children and young people

Too often the views of children and young people have been excluded from decision-making processes. Article 12 of the United Nations Convention on the rights of the Child states that:

1. *States Parties shall assure to the child who is capable of forming his or her own views the right to express those views freely in all matters affecting the child, the views of the child being given due weight in accordance with the age and maturity of the child.*
2. *For this purpose, the child shall in particular be provided the opportunity to be heard in any judicial and administrative proceedings affecting the child, either directly, or through a representative or an appropriate body, in a manner consistent with the procedural rules of national law.*

(United Nations, 1989)

Sociological perspectives on childhood now emphasise the role of children as social agents in their own lives. This perspective adopts the view that children are confident and capable of articulating their views and making decisions which affect them. This is a shift from historical perspectives on childhood which positioned children as inferior beings to adults. Throughout history, children have been exploited by adults and have not been given a voice. Historically, children with SEND have been marginalised through being excluded from mainstream society. Current perspectives on childhood now emphasise the vulnerability of children and the need to protect them as well as the need to give them a voice.

The SEND policy in the school will need to set out how the participation of children will be increased in the initial process of identification of needs and the subsequent graduated process. As a teacher you will need to involve children in initial discussion about their needs. You will also need to involve them in setting long and short-term goals or targets to aid their development. You will need to consider how you will involve them in reviews of their progress.

Schools need to make sure that the most vulnerable pupils are included in school decision-making bodies such as school councils. These pupils are often excluded from having a say in whole-school decisions and it is important to ensure that such bodies are fully representative of the whole-school community. You will need to consider how you will give a voice to children who have limited or no verbal communication as a means of expression. One way of achieving this is to consult with colleagues in special schools to learn about strategies for facilitating pupil voice for learners without verbal communication. The SENCO will need to consider how pupils with SEND are involved in developing and reviewing the SEND policy and the school information report.

CRITICAL QUESTIONS

* *What are the challenges associated with working in partnership with pupils?*
* *How might these challenges be addressed?*

Working in partnership with colleagues

Effective inter-agency collaboration will help to improve outcomes for learners with SEND. Many children with SEND are supported by colleagues from external services. These services may include but are not limited to educational psychology, speech and language therapy, occupational therapy, nurses, behaviour support teams and mental health services. The SENCO will take responsibility for co-ordinating support from these services in schools. Colleagues working in these services may be involved in the initial identification of needs. They usually come into school regularly to carry out assessments and interventions with the child and they communicate with teachers, teaching assistants and parents. They often write reports and make recommendations to help support the development of inclusive practice. They are a valuable source of specialist knowledge for teachers who have often only received general training in special educational needs.

The Code of Practice states that:

If children and young people with SEN or disabilities are to achieve their ambitions and the best possible educational and other outcomes, including getting a job and living as independently as possible, local education, health and social care services should work together to ensure they get the right support.

(DfE, 2015, para 1.22, p 24)

However, while the principle of collaboration is laudable, it is not always easy to implement in practice. Organising a time to meet colleagues from different services can be difficult, especially given your heavy teaching commitments. Information sharing between different services (education, health and social care) is not always straightforward. Making contact with services can be problematic. Additionally, you have the needs of a whole class to consider as well as the needs of one child. Balancing the needs of one child against the needs of a whole class is never an easy task. Increasingly, external colleagues now make recommendations which support the development of inclusive pedagogy for all learners. Thus, implementation of the recommendations will benefit all learners as well as the child with SEND. It is important to recognise that the principle of effective teaching applies to all learners. Therefore, you should focus on developing inclusive approaches to learning and teaching for all learners rather than developing individual approaches for one learner with specific needs.

CRITICAL QUESTIONS

- *What are the challenges associated with working in partnership with other teachers?*
- *How might these challenges be addressed?*

Working with teaching assistants

If teaching assistants are effectively deployed they can have a striking impact on supporting learners to make progress. However, it is important that they do not provide learners with too much help and it is important that they focus on learning rather than task completion. Too often, the ineffective deployment of support staff in classrooms can result in a culture of dependency where pupils become over-reliant on in-class support. Effective teachers support and enable all learners to work with increasing levels of independence. The outcome of good and outstanding teaching is that pupils are able to demonstrate independently the skills and knowledge that they have been taught. It is essential that pupils with SEND do not become over-dependent on others to do the work for them, even if learning opportunities have to be structured differently to enable them to achieve.

Teaching assistants need to be trained both in how to model new learning to pupils and how to assess understanding before asking pupils to demonstrate their understanding. Teaching assistants also need to be supported in developing their skills at 'checking-in' on pupils' understanding throughout a task and adjusting the task where necessary if the challenge is too easy or too difficult. These are high level teaching skills and it is important to remember that while many teaching assistants are excellent in their role, they have often not experienced rigorous training on aspects such as Assessment for Learning that you will have experienced as part of an Initial Teacher Education programme.

As the classroom teacher you remain accountable for the achievement of all learners in your class. This includes learners with SEND. It is vital that you retain responsibility for planning the learning experiences of these children. This will enable you to maintain an overview of pupils' progress both within lessons and over time. Many trainee teachers have

found it useful to provide teaching assistants with a separate plan for the child or group of learners they will be supporting in lessons. This might include:

* a statement of the learning objectives;
* assessment outcomes identified for specific pupils;
* a brief description of how to model the new learning broken down into steps;
* key questions to ask to check on pupils' understanding;
* subject knowledge which includes information about developmental progression within the strand of learning so that additional challenge can be added or misconceptions addressed by taking learning back a stage;
* a space for the teaching assistant to record assessment information about each pupil in relation to the assessment outcomes.

It is also helpful to provide teaching assistants with an overview of the progression sequence for a specific strand of learning. This will enable them to understand how the learning will develop over a sequence of lessons. Providing your teaching assistant with separate planning for specific pupils is one way that you can demonstrate that you have made reasonable adjustments.

CRITICAL QUESTIONS

* *What are the challenges associated with working in partnership with teaching assistants?*
* *How might these challenges be addressed?*

EVIDENCE-BASED TEACHING

Sharples et al (2015) found that the typical deployment and use of teaching assistants (TAs), under everyday conditions, is not leading to improvements in academic outcomes for pupils. Additionally, they found that TAs tend to be more concerned with task completion and less concerned with developing pupils' understanding. TAs spend the majority of their time in an informal instructional role supporting pupils with the most need (Sharples et al, 2015).

READ

* *Read: Webster, R, Blatchford, P and Russell, A (2013) Challenging and changing how schools use teaching assistants: Findings from the Effective Deployment of Teaching Assistants project. School Leadership and Management, 33(1): 78–96.*

The research outlines the positive effects that TA deployment can have on school and classroom processes.

EVALUATE

* *Evaluate these research outcomes from your professional experience.*
* *Identify examples of effective TA deployment where deployment led to improved outcomes for learners.*
* *Identify examples of less effective TA deployment where deployment was more concerned with task completion.*

APPLY

During your school-based training, conduct a learning walk around the school to observe how TAs are deployed in supporting learning. In particular notice:

* *which groups of learners they are supporting;*
* *whether learners are being supported individually or as part of a group;*
* *what type of questioning they use;*
* *whether the TA provides opportunities for pupils to work independently;*
* *whether they encourage learners to think independently;*
* *how the learning is differentiated for the pupils they are supporting;*
* *whether they demonstrate high expectations of their learners.*

IN PRACTICE

Your ITT provider might provide you with some structured school experience in a special school. If you do not get this opportunity, try to organise your own professional development time by spending some of it in a special school. In particular, you should research:

* *the curriculum that the school is using;*
* *the approach towards assessing learners' progress;*
* *ways in which the school environment has been adapted to support learners with SEND;*
* *the use of systems to support children's communication development;*
* *the use of multi-sensory approaches to learning and teaching;*
* *the use of systems and strategies to support behaviour management;*
* *the deployment of teaching assistants in lessons.*

Common issues and ways to address them

This section addresses common challenges that you might face in the classroom and makes practical suggestions for addressing these. However, it is important to emphasise that there are no 'magic' solutions. You will need to implement strategies and evaluate them to identify what works and what does not. The best approach is to consult the SENCO or your mentor/line manager for initial advice, but do remember that the role of the SENCO is not to fix your problems with individual cases. They have a strategic role in the school. You need to research into the specific issues you are facing through reading, research and visiting other schools. Build your own networks and be prepared to try things out, evaluate them and modify your practice.

How do I support children with difficulties in mathematics?

Provide:

* access to number lines;
* access to counting squares on tables/hundred squares;
* access to concrete apparatus, eg counters, multilink cubes, counting rods, beads;

* pre-teaching of mathematical skills/concepts;
* clear modelling of new mathematics skills;
* a multi-sensory approach to number recognition/number formation, eg writing numbers in sand and tracing over sandpaper numbers;
* a developmental approach, eg knowing the stages of progression through a topic;
* active teaching to provide hands-on learning;
* paired support – pairing a less-able child with a more-able child;
* visual representation where possible.

How do I support children with reading difficulties?

Provide:

* pre-teaching: reading a story to a child before a shared reading experience with the whole class;
* an individualised multi-sensory phonics programme but at a slower pace (using magnetic letters for word building; writing graphemes and words in sand, salt, sugar, glitter etc). Focus on grapheme-phoneme correspondence first and reinforce this in a multi-sensory way, then focus on blending and segmenting;
* daily one-to-one reading;
* opportunities for paired reading: pairing an able/less-able reader;
* opportunities for adults and children to read together in pairs;
* pause, prompt, praise (PPP) as a strategy when attempting to read an unknown word;
* opportunities for developing rhyme awareness, auditory discrimination and awareness of syllables prior to teaching phonics;
* opportunities to develop a love of stories: share 'real' books with them together.

How do I support children with writing difficulties?

Provide:

* alphabet mats on tables;
* key word mats on tables;
* jumbled sentences: put a separate word in each card and ask the child to read the words and arrange the cards together to make a sentence – use when the child is attempting to write a sentence by asking them to think of and say the sentence out loud. The teacher writes each word on a separate card and then the child orders the cards to make a sentence and then copies the sentence;
* dictation: dictate sentences within the child's phonic knowledge (daily);
* opportunities for paired writing: less-able and more-able writers work together to compose a story. The more-able child collects ideas from the other child and notes them down. Then the more-able child starts the writing process and gradually hands responsibility over to the other child;
* opportunities for patterned/repetitive writing – child follows a simple repetitive structure (as in the story of *The Little Red Hen*);
* writing frames help children to structure their writing: use planning frameworks, eg story boards, story maps, mind maps, flow charts and give them prompts: eg *first*, *next*, *then*, *after that*;
* opportunities to use word processers.

How do I support children with dyslexia?

Provide:

* handouts on coloured paper;
* access to simple dictionaries and spell checkers;
* access to key word mats;
* access to alphabet strips;
* access to mind maps;
* writing frames to help them structure their writing;
* daily dictation;
* sensitive marking not over-focusing on spelling;
* clear success criteria: *'This is what I am looking for in your work'* rather than asking them to think about too much at once;
* access to a word processer so they can think about the content rather than the technical skills of writing;
* pre-teaching;
* a multi-sensory approach to reading/phonics;
* visual strategies to support teaching: show them as well as tell them what to do;
* short focused tasks with breaks;
* active learning.

How do I support children with behavioural needs?

Provide:

* opportunities for promoting active engagement;
* short, focused tasks rather than one long task;
* plenty of praise.

Ensure that you:

* find their strengths and capitalise on these;
* separate the behaviour from the person;
* give them achievable and focused clear behaviour targets which you negotiate with them;
* use a reward system (this might be individualised for the child);
* involve the parents in setting targets and reviewing progress;
* apply sanctions fairly: make them reasonable and proportionate to the issue.

Try to:

* build the curriculum around their interests;
* ignore minor behaviour incidents;
* use a solution-focused approach: *'John, you need to ...'* rather than focusing on what they have done wrong;
* deal with issues in school: you do not always need to tell parents about every single issue unless it is serious;

- not to get into confrontations: think before you speak;
- always think: what is wrong with my teaching rather than the child.

EVIDENCE-BASED TEACHING

According to the latest research:

Although the majority of TA-delivered interventions showing positive effects involve one-to-one instruction, small group approaches also show promise, with similar impacts observed compared to one-to-one interventions. Although further research is needed, this suggests it may be worth exploring small group interventions as a cost-effective alternative to delivery on a one-to-one basis.

(Sharples et al, 2015, p 25)

EVALUATE

Consider the above research finding.

- *What are the advantages of small group interventions?*
- *Think of examples of where interventions are best delivered individually to specific pupils.*

CHALLENGE

- *To what extent might group interventions lead to labelling or generate a sense of 'othering'?*
- *How might group interventions lead to a culture of low expectations?*

APPLY

- *During your school-based training, review the intervention programmes used across the school. Find out how the impact of the interventions is measured and specifically whether the impact is measured in a systematic and quantifiable way in relation to pupil achievement.*

EXTENDED THINKING

Julie Allan (2008) has drawn on the work of the famous philosopher, Foucault, to demonstrate how children with special educational needs become objects of power and surveillance in school. Foucault wrote extensively about power and surveillance within institutions and the effects of this on individuals. Linda Dunne (2009) has also drawn on Foucault's work to illustrate the *othering* effects of inclusion for children with SEND.

- *Critically interrogate the Code of Practice for Special Educational Needs and Disabilities. Can you find examples of processes which situate children with SEND as objects of power, surveillance and intense scrutiny?*

TECHNOLOGY

Immersive space technology enables different environments to be created for pupils to explore through the use of projected images, music and other sounds. Whole rooms can suddenly become deserts, forests, oceans, cities or space at the touch of a button. Smaller *pop-up* immersive spaces can also be purchased which resemble tents. When pupils go inside these, they can change the environment and then explore it through role-play and drama. This technology offers real potential for engaging learners and providing them with opportunities to explore environments that they would otherwise not get to experience. The immersive space can be used to develop pupils' knowledge of a specific aspect of the curriculum. The selected environment can link to a class theme or topic and the potential for vocabulary development is extensive.

Some learners may need different resources to enable them to access the same learning opportunities as their peers. Technology can play an important role in breaking down barriers to learning. Examples of this include the use of digital spell checkers, tablet technology and laptop computers for learners with dyslexia.

Critical reflections

This chapter has introduced you to the fundamental principles of the Code of Practice for Special Educational Needs and Disability. It has emphasised the need to establish a culture of high expectations for learners with SEND and the need to ensure that the children who are underachieving receive their entitlement to high quality teaching as the first response. The chapter has stressed that underachievement is not synonymous with SEND. Additionally, it has reiterated the critical importance of retaining a focus on outcomes for learners with SEND. While the above assertions are laudable, it is essential to bear in mind that not all learners will attain the national age-related standards, irrespective of exposure to high quality teaching. However, all learners should make good progress from their starting points.

As a critical and reflective educator it is important to question the relevance of the national curriculum and the appropriateness of the assessment systems which measure attainment for some learners with SEND. While this has not been debated in this chapter, critical academic debates continue to circulate about the extent to which the education system meets the needs of all learners. It is important to question the extent to which the curriculum and the assessment system create learner disengagement and underachievement. While the national curriculum is intended for all learners, it is important to reflect critically on the extent to which one curriculum and one model of assessment can effectively meet the needs of all learners. Policy texts such as the Code of Practice continue to emphasise the relevance of the curriculum and measures of assessment but academic literature remains divided on this issue.

KEY READINGS

Classic:

Department for Education and Science (DES) (1978) *Special Educational Needs: Report of the Committee of Enquiry into the Education of Handicapped Children and Young People (The Warnock Report)*. London: HMSO.

Oliver, M (1990) *The Politics of Disablement*. Basingstoke: Macmillan.

Oliver, M (1996) *Understanding Disability*. Basingstoke, Macmillan.

Contemporary:

DfE (2015) *Special Educational Needs and Disability Code of Practice: 0 to 25 Years: Statutory Guidance for Organisations Who Work with and Support Children and Young People with Special Educational Needs and Disabilities*. London: DfE.

Slee, R (2011) *The Irregular School: Exclusion, Schooling and Inclusive Education*. London: Routledge.

Thomas, G and Loxley, A (2007) *Deconstructing Special Education and Constructing Inclusion*. Berkshire: Open University Press.

References

Abdullah, J (2012) Developmental coordination disorder and dyspraxia from an occupational therapist's perspective, in Peer, L and Reid, G (eds) *Special Educational Needs: A Guide for Inclusive Practice*. London: Sage, pp 98–111.

Allan, J (2008) *Rethinking Inclusive Education: The Philosophers of Difference in Practice*. Dordrecht: Springer.

Bondy, A and Frost, L (1994) The Picture Exchange Communication System. *Focus on Autistic Behavior*, 9(3): 1–19.

Bradley, L and Bryant, P (1983) Categorising sounds and learning to read: A causal connection. *Nature*, 301: 419–21.

Bradley, L and Bryant, P (1985) *Children's Reading Problems*. Oxford: Basic Blackwell.

British Psychological Society (1999) cited in Hall, W (2009) *Dyslexia in the Primary Classroom*. Exeter: Learning Matters.

Carter, A (2015) *Review of Initial Teacher Training*. London: DfE.

DeS/Warnock, M (1978) *Special Educational Needs: Report of the Committee of Enquiry into the Education of Handicapped Children and Young People*. London: HMSO.

DfE (2010) *The Importance of Teaching: The Schools White Paper 2010*. London: DfE.

DfE (2011) *Support and Aspiration: A New Approach to Special Educational Needs and Disability: A Consultation*. London: DfE.

DfE (2015) *Special Educational Needs and Disability Code of Practice: 0 to 25 years: Statutory Guidance for Organisations Who Work With and Support Children and Young People with Special Educational Needs and Disabilities*. London: DfE.

Department for Education and Skills (DfES) (2001) *Special Educational Needs Code of Practice*. Nottinghamshire: DfES.

Dunne, L (2009) Discourses of inclusion: A critique. *Power and Education*, 1(1): 42–56.

Elliott, J and Gibbs, S (2008) Does dyslexia exist? *Journal of Philosophy of Education*, 42 (3–4), 475–91.

Glazzard, J, Stokoe, J, Hughes, A, Netherwood, A and Neve, L (eds) (2015) *Teaching and Supporting Children with Special Educational Needs and Disabilities in Primary Schools*. 2nd ed. Sage: London.

Grandin, T (1996) *Thinking in Pictures*. Vancouver, WA: Vintage Books.

Gray, C (1994) *The Social Storybook*. Arlington, TX: Future Horizons.

Hinshelwood, J (1917) *Congenital Word Blindness*. London: Lewis.

HM Government (2010) *Equality Act 2010 Guidance on Matters to be Taken into Account in Determining Questions Relating to the Definition of Disability*. London: Office for Disability Issues.

Jordan, R and Powell, S (1995) *Understanding and Teaching Children with Autism*. Chichester: John Wiley and Sons.

Kanner, L (1943) Autistic disturbances of affective contact. *Nervous Child*, 2: 217–250.

Kanner, L and Eisenberg, L (1956) Early infantile autism, 1943–1955. *American Journal of Orthopsychiatry*, 26: 55–65.

NASEN (2014), *SEN Support and the Graduated Approach: A Quick Guide to Ensuring That Every Child or Young Person Gets the Support They Require to Meet Their Needs*. Tamworth, Staffordshire: NASEN.

Ofsted (2010) *The Special Educational Needs and Disability Review: A Statement is Not Enough*. London: Ofsted.

Pringle Morgan, W (1896) A case study of congenital word blindness. *British Medical Journal*, 2: 1378.

Sharples, J, Webster, R and Blatchford, P (2015) *Making Best Use of Teaching Assistants Guidance Report – March 2015*. London: Education Endowment Foundation.

Snowling, M (2000) *Dyslexia*. Oxford: Blackwell.

Stanovich, K E and Stanovich P J (1997) Further thoughts on aptitude/achievement discrepancy. *Educational Psychology in Practice*, 13(1): 3–8.

The Communication Trust (2011) *Let's Talk About It: What New Teachers Need to Know about Children's Communication Skills*. London: The Communication Trust [online] Available at: www.thecommunicationtrust.org.uk/media/12285/let_s_talk_about_it_-_final.pdf (accessed 15 May 2016).

Thomas, G and Loxley, A (2007) *Deconstructing Special Education and Constructing Inclusion*. Berkshire: Open University Press.

Training and Development Agency for Schools (TDA) (2008), *Special Educational Needs and/or Disabilities: A Training Resource for Initial Teacher Training Providers: Primary Undergraduate Courses*. London: TDA.

United Nations (1989) *The UN Convention on the Rights of the Child*. London: UNICEF.

Wing, L (1988) The continuum of autistic characteristics, in Schopler, E and Mesibov, G (eds) *Diagnosis and Assessment in Autism*. New York: Plenum Press, pp 91–110.

Wing, L (1996) *The Autistic Spectrum: A Guide for Parents and Professionals*. London: Constable.

Wing, L and Gould, J (1979) Severe impairments of social interaction and associated abnormalities in children: Epidemiology and classification. *Journal of Autism and Developmental Disorders*, 9(1): 11–29.

10: PROFESSIONALISM

TEACHERS' STANDARDS

This chapter addresses the following Teachers' Standards:

Part Two

A teacher is expected to demonstrate consistently high standards of personal and professional conduct. The following statements define the behaviour and attitudes which set the required standard for conduct throughout a teacher's career:

- *Teachers uphold public trust in the profession and maintain high standards of ethics and behaviour, within and outside school, by:*
  - *treating pupils with dignity, building relationships rooted in mutual respect, and at all times observing proper boundaries appropriate to a teacher's professional position;*
  - *having regard for the need to safeguard pupils' well-being, in accordance with statutory provisions;*
  - *showing tolerance of and respect for the rights of others;*
  - *not undermining fundamental British values, including democracy, the rule of law, individual liberty and mutual respect, and tolerance of those with different faiths and beliefs;*
  - *ensuring that personal beliefs are not expressed in ways which exploit pupils' vulnerability or might lead them to break the law.*

In addition:

- *teachers must have proper and professional regard for the ethos, policies and practices of the school in which they teach, and maintain high standards in their own attendance and punctuality;*
- *teachers must have an understanding of, and always act within, the statutory frameworks which set out their professional duties and responsibilities.*

PROFESSIONAL LINKS

The *Carter Review of Initial Teacher Training* (Carter, 2015) stated that:

As implied by the Teachers' Standards, ITT should cover the professional role of the teacher explicitly, covering the wider responsibilities of a teacher, including important issues such as working with parents and carers as well as other professionals. We believe it is also important that ITT includes explicit content on resilience and time management.

(Carter, 2015, p 71)

CHAPTER OBJECTIVES

- **What is this chapter about?**

This chapter covers the essential aspects of teacher professionalism that you need to know and understand. It covers key aspects of professional conduct and explores theories of professionalism. In addition, it addresses your statutory responsibilities as a teacher.

✱ Why is it important?

Right from the very start of your ITT, it is essential that you recognise that teaching is a profession. However, being treated as a professional is not an automatic right. You will have to earn the right to be viewed as a professional by your colleagues, the parents and carers, and more importantly your learners. If you want to be respected as a teacher, and given the professional recognition that is associated with the status of being a teacher, then you need to behave in an appropriate professional manner. Your behaviour both inside and outside of school are critical in this respect. Additionally, you need to ensure that your behaviour, attitudes, values and beliefs do not bring your school or the teaching profession into disrepute.

In recent decades teachers in England have been largely de-professionalised. Their performance is now monitored frequently by school leaders and external professionals such as inspectors and consultants. To some extent, a culture of professional mistrust has developed. It would seem that teachers are not trusted to do their jobs. A culture of surveillance is prevalent in the profession and teacher performance is monitored both directly in the classroom and indirectly through pupil achievement and attainment data. This professional mistrust of teachers is not characteristic in all countries around the world. It is time for teachers to reclaim their professionalism. The most effective way of doing this is for all teachers to ensure that they take their role seriously and enact it in a highly professional way. This chapter covers the key elements of teacher professionalism that you need to know and understand.

Personal and professional conduct

Learning to conduct oneself in an appropriate professional manner does not always come easy to some trainees and indeed some teachers. Many trainees begin their professional training having just left school, college or university while others will begin their training after having spent time in different careers. Some of these careers will have been spent in education, perhaps as teaching assistants, while others will come from diverse careers in other sectors. All of these scenarios can cause problems.

Trainees beginning their training having come straight from school, college or university will suddenly be expected to make the transition from being a student to being a teacher. This transition may not be smooth but it needs to be swift in order to survive the professional training. Others who enter the profession having spent several years building careers in other sectors outside education may well have been enculturated by the profession they have just left. They may have become used to particular ways of working, managing and leading colleagues in previous careers, which are not acceptable and not transferable to school contexts. Those who have worked in education previously in roles such as teaching assistants may find aspects of professionalism challenging.

Essentially, whatever your background you need to quickly learn the 'rules' of being a teacher if you want to be treated as an equal and valued member of the profession. Often these 'rules' are unspoken and not written down. They are simply expected and this makes it all the more challenging when you are trying to navigate your way into the profession. The starting point is your initial teacher education provider's Code of Professional

Conduct. You will be expected to read this Code, sign it and abide by it. If you view the expectations of the Code as non-negotiable, this is probably the best way of learning the rules of professionalism in teaching. An example of a Code of Professional Conduct is stated below.

IN PRACTICE

The following example of a Code of Professional Conduct is taken from a university provider of initial teacher education:

Trainee teachers are expected to work within a framework of legislation, statutory guidance and school policies. There is an emphasis on promoting equality of opportunity, challenging stereotypes, opposing prejudice and respecting individuals regardless of age, gender, disability, race, ethnicity, class, religion, marital status or sexual orientation. The opportunity for undertaking school-based training depends on the co-operation and support of the Head Teachers and staff of the schools. We expect trainee teachers to adhere strictly to the Code of Professional Conduct listed below. The Code has been designed to align with the professional code of professional conduct set out in the Teachers' Standards (DfE, 2012). All trainees are provisionally registered with the National College for Teaching and Leadership. Trainees who fail to comply with the following Code of Professional Conduct risk failure of the placement. In extreme cases the University will apply its Fitness to Practise policy and the trainee will be withdrawn from the course and the University.

All trainees have a personal responsibility to reflect on their own professional behaviour. As such, all trainees are accountable for their own actions. In addition to the Code of Professional Conduct, the Head Teacher and other staff in school will also have their own expectations about professional conduct. All trainees are required to comply with school policies in relation to punctuality, courtesy and consideration for others. It is essential that the highest standards of professional conduct are maintained at all times and trainees are reminded of their status both as a representative of the University and a guest in school.

The University expects trainees to dress professionally on placement. We stipulate that jeans, trousers with low waistlines and low cut tops are unacceptable. Bare skin, in the main, should be covered. Male trainees should wear trousers and a smart top. Clothing with offensive slogans is unacceptable. Trainees must remember that they are a role model at all times and this should be reflected in their dress. Nails must be an appropriate length for health and safety purposes. All trainees should check if the school has a policy on dress code on their first day. Mentors and Head Teachers should take appropriate action if trainees are inappropriately dressed. Schools must be respectful towards trainees' religious beliefs and cultural dress codes.

The University will take any breaches of the Code of Professional.Conduct extremely seriously. The Code covers school and University-based training.

Trainee teachers in the ITE primary partnership are expected to:

1. *demonstrate respect for all staff employed by the school, Local Authority, University and external agencies;*
2. *demonstrate respect for all children;*

3. *demonstrate respect for all parents and carers;*
4. *demonstrate respect for other trainee teachers and students from other institutions;*
5. *be a role model for children and demonstrate the highest professional standards through appropriate personal values;*
6. *carry out their duties in line with school policies. This will vary from school to school and as such trainees are required to be fully informed of the school's expectations;*
7. *comply with equal opportunities legislation and follow school policies in relation to safeguarding and protecting the welfare of children and young people;*
8. *declare any disabilities to the school so that reasonable adjustments can be made to school-based training programmes;*
9. *maintain appropriate professional boundaries with children, parents, carers and all staff working in the school;*
10. *maintain good attendance (in University and in school);*
11. *carry out procedures for notifying absence as stipulated in the school-based training handbook. Unauthorised absence may result in the termination of the placement;*
12. *keep in daily contact with schools during initial absence and forward lesson planning to the school to cover planned teaching;*
13. *obtain medical certification for absences exceeding seven working days;*
14. *firstly seek the permission of the Head Teacher followed by the Head of ITE should absence be required for reasons other than illness;*
15. *attend a progress review following periods of sickness and attend a meeting with the University Occupational Health department following extensive periods of illness;*
16. *attend progress reviews;*
17. *be punctual;*
18. *maintain professional standards of dress and appearance in line with school policy – no jeans, no low cut tops or low waist lines, no unnecessary bare flesh, no long nails;*
19. *demonstrate appropriate use of internet facilities in line with University and school policies;*
20. *listen to and act on advice from mentors and University tutors;*
21. *work effectively as part of teams and demonstrate a commitment to collaborative and co-operative working;*
22. *reflect on and improve their practice;*
23. *carry out their professional duties in line with the code of professional conduct drawn up by the ITE partnership;*
24. *take responsibility for their own learning including self-evaluation, action planning and appropriate use of Professional Development time;*
25. *self-declare any cautions, convictions, reprimands and final warnings from the Police, irrespective of the nature of these;*
26. *demonstrate appropriate professional behaviour towards children and young people in all formal and informal settings;*

27. demonstrate appropriate professional behaviour towards all staff, parents and carers;
28. carry out all school-based tasks as stipulated in specific school-based training handbooks;
29. adhere to ethical codes of conduct in relation to Child Protection. Photographic images of children must not be taken. All mobile phones must be switched off in the classroom and on school premises;
30. maintain confidentiality in relation to school resources, staff and children;
31. comply with all University policies, particularly in relation to equal opportunities and race relations policies;
32. comply with health and safety legislation and policies when working in school and in the University;
33. keep all paper work relating to school placements up to date throughout the entire duration of the placement, including planning, evaluations, assessment and record keeping;
34. ensure that adequate planning and preparation has been completed prior to starting a block placement;
35. ensure that social networking sites are used responsibly and usage does not bring either the school or University into disrepute. There must be no contact with children or parents via such sites;
36. ensure that confidential information about pupils is kept safe and secure and not left in public places;
37. maintain honesty at all times;
38. complete University evaluations of all aspects of the provision;
39. respond to communications promptly;
40. refrain from smoking on school premises (inside or outside);
41. ensure that any activity in one's personal life does not bring the teaching profession or the ITE partnership into disrepute;
42. all interactions with children must only be undertaken on a professional basis;
43. comply with all elements of the Teachers' Standards (part 2).

Unacceptable Professional Conduct is conduct which falls short of the standard expected of a registered teacher...and is behaviour which involves a breach of the standards of propriety expected of the profession.

Examples of unacceptable conduct include:

* *demeaning or undermining pupils, parents, carers or colleagues (for example – swearing at them or damaging their self-esteem);*
* *acting in a discriminatory manner towards pupils, parents, carers or colleagues in relation to gender, marital status, religion, belief, colour, race, ethnicity, social class, sexual orientation, disability or age (for example –making racist or sexist remarks towards them);*
* *failing to safeguard and protect the welfare of children;*
* *failing to observe confidentiality;*

* *failing to maintain standards of honesty and integrity (for example – theft of school property; abuse of ICT facilities);*
* *demonstrating standards of behaviour that bring the reputation and standing of the profession into serious disrepute.*

Serious professional incompetence could constitute:

* *inadequate subject knowledge;*
* *failure to establish appropriate learning objectives;*
* *failure to meet the needs of pupils through the provision of inappropriate activities;*
* *inability to manage pupil behaviour;*
* *inability to safeguard and protect the welfare of children;*
* *inability to work effectively with colleagues;*
* *inability to follow school policies and procedures.*

If a trainee teacher fails to follow the Code of Professional Conduct the Head Teacher should contact the Head of Primary ITE. The issues will be investigated and the trainee teacher will be required to attend a progress review with senior partnership colleagues. The trainee can bring a representative to this meeting. In extreme cases of inappropriate behaviour the Head Teacher has the discretion to suspend the trainee from the school and in this situation the Course Leader should be immediately notified. The issues will be thoroughly investigated. In all cases of professional conduct the University reserves the right to instigate the fitness to practise policy.

CRITICAL QUESTIONS

* *Do you agree that providers should regulate the professional conduct of trainee teachers in this way? Give reasons to support your answer.*
* *Are there any points in the above Code that you wish to challenge?*
* *Is anything missing from the above Code?*

Building resilience

Teaching is a challenging career and you will need to develop your resilience to help you cope with day-to-day situations in school. Being resilient in the face of challenging situations will help you to survive but it will not eliminate stress from your working life. Teaching is undoubtedly a stressful career and to some extent a certain amount of stress is inevitable when you are working with many different people who all have the highest expectations of you.

One of the most exciting aspects of teaching is that you cannot predict exactly what events will unfold on each day. From the very beginning of your ITT and beyond you will experience stressful situations which you will be required to deal with. These may include the following:

* dealing with challenging pupil behaviour, including direct defiance;
* responding to parental complaints in relation to your teaching;
* periods of heavy workload (hot spots);

* being professionally undermined by colleagues;
* receiving negative feedback on aspects of your work from colleagues in more senior positions;
* lesson observations which did not go as well as expected;
* being challenged by colleagues;
* the introduction of changes to policies or practices;
* bullying, harassment or victimisation against you by colleagues;
* not feeling valued or feeling marginalised in the workplace.

This is not an exhaustive list but there is a very high chance that you will experience at least one of these situations during your teaching career. You may find that you are protected from some of these issues during your initial training. For example, parental complaints may be addressed by your mentor rather than yourself during your training. When you subsequently begin your teaching career, you then become accountable for the progress of your learners. This level of responsibility means that complaints will often be directed directly at you. Over a period of time this can become mentally exhausting and it can start to erode your confidence.

To help you cope with challenging situations, you need to develop resilience. You will teach lessons that do not go according to plan. You will experience days where colleagues, parents and children upset you. The key point is not to over-dwell on these situations, to learn from them and move on. You will need to quickly develop the ability to 'bounce back' from challenging situations. Tomorrow is another day and you will have new priorities to focus on. Try not to let challenging situations get you down. When people challenge you and criticise you, hopefully this will be done in a positive, constructive way. Listen to their concerns and respond to these in a calm, professional manner. If you find that someone directly challenges something that you have done, then listen to their views. Explain why you did what you did and stay calm. If you are in the wrong then do not be afraid to admit this. In this case you should apologise for your actions. You will find that people give you greater respect if you accept your mistakes. Sometimes you might need some time to step away from a situation and to think it over before giving an immediate response. In these instances it might be necessary to go back to someone at a later time to discuss a situation. If you are sure that you took the correct course of action, you should explain this to people but at the same time demonstrate that you value their comments.

Learning to be resilient can take time and experience. It is something that you will get better at. We all make mistakes and no-one is perfect. People will forgive you for making mistakes during your ITT and during the early stages of your teaching career. After all, you are learning to be a teacher. When you experience challenges in your daily professional life it is important to remember why you went into teaching in the first place. You want to inspire your learners, help them to achieve and make a positive difference in their lives. Your learners will respect you more if you apologise to them when you get things wrong. They will learn that you are a human being and that all people make mistakes at some point. Learn from the day-to-day challenges and use these experiences to make you a more effective teacher.

Time management

Right from the start of your ITT you will be told that good teachers are very skilled at managing their time. You will learn that teaching is a challenging job. There is a great deal of work to do and you know that you are going to be busy balancing the conflicting demands of your professional and personal lives. Although you know these things, you will not begin to understand them until you actually have to put the skill of time management in practice.

As a trainee teacher it is highly likely that you are a perfectionist! As a perfectionist you like to do a thorough job and consequently you spend many hours planning and resourcing your lessons. On top of planning and making resources, you need to keep up-to-date with your marking and other assessments. You need to create a stimulating learning environment which changes frequently. You will be required to attend meetings with colleagues and parents and you will be required to participate in professional development opportunities. On top of all these professional responsibilities, you may have commitments outside of school. You may have caring responsibilities to other members of your family. You may have pets that you need to look after and you will certainly have commitments to your friendships.

Initially, balancing all of your professional commitments might be a significant challenge. There are simply too many tasks to complete and not enough time to complete them in. You need to plan your time carefully. Tasks such as planning and assessment always take longer initially but you need to learn to complete these tasks much more quickly if you are going to survive. When you first start teaching during your initial training you will be on a reduced teaching timetable. While it may be possible at this stage to spend several hours planning and resourcing a single lesson, you will not have the luxury of this amount of time when your teaching commitment increases to 80 per cent. The purpose of effective planning is to help you do your job more effectively. There is no point in spending several hours writing a detailed lesson plan if a more concise plan helps you to teach the lesson just as effectively. Your planning is for you and it should enable you to be a more effective teacher. There is little point in spending several hours making a resource that you are only going to use once for a very short period of time. If you are going to invest time making a resource, try to make sure that you will be able to use the resource on different occasions so that you get the maximum use out of it.

As your teaching commitments grow you will need to allocate specific timescales to specific jobs. When you are responsible for teaching 80 per cent of the weekly timetable, then you will have to prepare your lesson plans and resources much more quickly. It is easy to forget to look around in the school to see what resources are already available. There is little point in making a resource if that same resource is already available in school. It is a useful exercise to look in resource rooms to see what is already available. A great deal of time can be saved by asking your colleagues in school if they have a specific resource that you might be able to use. Your colleagues will generally be happy to support you and they will be grateful that you have approached them. The internet is a valuable way of collecting resources to support your teaching. Resources can be sourced quickly and cheaply using the internet. However, do check that the resources are suitable for your class before you use them.

Teaching assistants in school are one of your most valuable resources. If you establish effective relationships with them they will often happily do things for you. Tasks that you delegate could include the creation of displays, resource production or marking/ assessment tasks. You are not expected to do everything yourself. Remember that you are working as part of a team and you need to make the very best use of people's skills.

Trying to do everything by yourself is not sustainable long term so you need to find ways of working more efficiently.

Keeping up-to-date with marking is often a significant challenge for trainees. You need to approach this in ways that make the task manageable and sustainable. One way of doing this is to strategically plan your lessons so that pupils are not always producing 'work' that needs to be marked in every single lesson. It is quite overwhelming at the end of a day to face four piles of thirty books, all of which need to be marked. Think carefully about the *outputs* that children can generate in a lesson. These could include:

* recorded work;
* tangible artefacts, eg making a product;
* oral discussions, debates and presentations;
* visual outputs, eg drawings, paintings, posters, diagrams, mind maps;
* performances, eg musical compositions, dance, drama, physical activity.

By planning different outputs across a day or week, this will make the marking load easier to manage. Additionally, feedback is more effective when it is given instantly. Therefore, you need to consider ways of enabling you to provide your learners with instant written feedback in the lesson so that feedback is more immediate. One way of doing this is to organise your lesson so that different groups of learners produce different kinds of outputs. Limiting the number of groups producing recorded/written work makes the task of marking that work in the lesson more manageable. You might work with a group while the teaching assistant works with another group. Both groups could be producing recorded outputs which are subsequently marked by each of you in the lesson. The other groups might be asked to generate different kinds of output which do not need to be marked in the same way.

Try to ensure that you use all your time efficiently during the school day. This might involve using parts of break times and lunch times to mark children's work or to get resources ready for the following day's lessons. Although it is advisable to spend some time socialising with your colleagues, this can result in wasted time if you do not use your time in a focused way. It is a good idea to start each day with a list of priorities which need to be completed. As you complete the various tasks that you have set yourself, you can tick each one off on the list. This is quite a rewarding experience as it enables you to see what you have achieved and what tasks are outstanding. If you do not complete all the tasks that you have allocated yourself on a specific day then do not panic. Simply move them forward onto the next day. Give yourself a specific amount of time to complete each task and work hard to ensure that the task is completed in that time-frame.

At the end of each school day, focus on resourcing your lessons for the following day. Aim to get your resources prepared for the next day's lessons before you leave school at the end of the day. This will mean that you do not have to panic too much the following morning about getting your lessons ready. If you know that you have a staff meeting or a course to attend straight after school then attempt to plan and resource the following day's lessons during the day so that you are always one step ahead. Do not spend time laminating resources if you are only going to use a resource once. High quality resources do not automatically result in high quality learning and detailed step-by-step planning does not automatically result in high quality teaching.

Balancing personal commitments against your teaching commitments is never an easy task. During intensive periods of school-based training your friends and family will need to give you the space to complete the work that you need to do to succeed. People around you will hopefully understand that teaching is important to you and they may relieve you of other responsibilities such as domestic chores. However, it is important that you find a work-life balance. Without a work-life balance you may start to become resentful of the amount of work you are doing. While most teachers take work home with them in the evenings, most do try to identify specific slots of time during the week when they will not be working. You should not feel guilty about going shopping, visiting the theatre or cinema or participating in personal interests and hobbies. While teaching is often, for many people, a vocation, it is important to ensure that it does not become all-encompassing. You will do your job more effectively if you have given yourself some space away from it to unwind. If you are well-organised and you use your time efficiently during the week then you should be able to take one day off at the weekend to do other things.

There is also the issue of prioritising your roles and responsibilities. Some tasks are more important than others and need to be completed first. Other tasks, while still important, may not be urgent and can be completed after the urgent tasks have been completed. You will need to decide, often on a daily basis, which tasks are urgent and need immediate attention. You may have a daily list of jobs which need to be completed but other more urgent priorities may arise when you go into school on a particular morning. For example, if a safeguarding issue arises with a child it is more urgent to address that issue than to complete your lesson plan for the following day. As you become more experienced, you will become skilled in prioritising tasks and you will become more efficient at allocating specific time-frames to specific tasks.

There may be occasions when you are asked to do things by your mentor or other colleagues in school. During your ITT it is wise to deal with such requests as priorities. When you start employment as a full qualified teacher, you will largely be responsible for managing your own workload. Sometimes your colleagues may request certain things from you and you will need to establish whether such requests are priorities or whether they can be addressed later. In the case of the latter it is beneficial to give colleagues an indication of when you can get the work completed. You might find it helpful to carry around a notebook to add 'jobs' that have been requested of you to your list of actions that need to be completed. This will prevent you from forgetting important actions that you need to undertake.

Sometimes the best ideas in teaching will come into your head at times when you least expect. You might have a brilliant idea while you are travelling on a bus or train. You might think of something while you are dropping to sleep or waking up or you might wake up in the middle of the night with an idea. If you keep a notebook with you or near to you then you can jot down the idea. The process of taking it out of your head and onto the page means that you do not need to remember the idea because you have now recorded it. This will help to keep you organised.

IN PRACTICE

The following extract is taken from an initial teacher education provider's partnership handbook:

Schools are requested to regard trainees as a member of staff and as such they are therefore subject to the same rules and regulations as the rest of the staff. Trainees are expected to arrive at school

punctually at the time indicated by the Head Teacher and not to leave prior to the end of the school day even if this is part of their non-contact time. The course expectations require trainees to arrive by 8.00 am by the very latest and not leave before 17.00 pm without permission of the school. Trainees with responsibility for children should make childcare arrangements during periods of school-based training.

CRITICAL QUESTIONS

* *A trainee is a parent of young children but is unable to afford after-school or before-school childcare. Friends and family are unable to help with childcare arrangements. How might the trainee manage this situation during periods of school-based training?*
* *A trainee is in a school in which staff normally arrive at 8.30 am and they leave at 4.15 pm. What should the trainee do in this situation?*

Use of social media

You need to consider carefully your personal use of social media. Parents may try to search for you on social media and add you as 'friends' to their accounts. Additionally, children may try to search for you too, particularly if you are teaching older children. It is crucial that you set your privacy settings so that parents and children cannot see your profile. Requests by parents and children to add you as social media 'friends' should never be accepted because this breaches professional boundaries. Additionally, please consider carefully what you write on your social media profile, blogs and websites. What you write online stays online and it may come back to haunt you! You need to ensure that you avoid using the names of children, parents or schools online. You may have been criticised by a parent or had a challenging day with a child in school. In these situations it is not appropriate to go online and vent your frustrations to the world! Events that happen in school need to stay in school and you should not breach confidentiality by sharing these situations potentially with the rest of the world.

Increasingly, teachers sadly are becoming victims of abuse on social media. Parents may sometimes use social media sites and other electronic forums to publicly criticise teachers. In this instance you should never respond to any comments that you see. Unfortunately there are people who enjoy criticising people in public in order to elicit a reaction. The best response that you can make is to give no reaction. You are the professional and you need to ensure that your own behaviour does not place the school or teaching profession into disrepute. Always try to rise above these situations. Although you want everyone to like you and respect you as a teacher, you will never be able to keep everyone happy. Accept this and try to build up your resilience so that you are not damaged personally by unfounded criticism.

Many schools now have strict policies on staff use of social media. Unfortunately there have been cases where teachers have faced disciplinary action for posting inappropriate comments online. It is a good idea to 'clean' your social media profiles by deleting any comments or photographs which are inappropriate. Your social media profiles may have been in existence for several years prior to you making the decision to train to become a teacher. You may well have made comments previously that could potentially bring your school or the teaching profession into disrepute. In these instances these comments should be deleted from your profiles if you are able to do so. If you are not able to delete comments it may be appropriate to delete your profile and start a new profile. Some headteachers may try to discourage you from having a social media profile. However, this is contentious as it restricts personal freedom. If you do decide to have social media profiles then use them cautiously and adopt a common-sense approach. If you think that a comment or image might potentially bring your reputation into disrepute then it is probably better to avoid uploading it in the first place. You inevitably leave your footprint on the web and you are accountable for it, so think carefully about how you use it.

Your life outside school

You have a right to a life outside school. However, issues can arise when personal situations impact detrimentally on your reputation as a teacher, the reputation of the school and the teaching profession as a whole. It is important that you do not bring the reputation of your school into disrepute. You do not suddenly stop being a teacher at the end of the school day. You have a professional identity as a teacher and you should always aim to conduct yourself in an appropriate professional manner in order to protect your reputation, the reputation of the school and the reputation of the profession.

A useful starting point for this discussion is to consider where you live. Obviously the choice of where you live is yours and you retain the right to decide where to reside. Some teachers choose to live outside the school catchment area. Others choose to live in the community immediately surrounding the school or in the nearest town. If you choose to live away from the catchment area then there are fewer possibilities of meeting parents and children outside of school. However, do not take this for granted! Consider carefully where you do your shopping and the places you go for cultural or social stimulation. Meeting parents during a social outing with friends and family should not, at least in theory, be a problem. You expect parents to understand that you have a right to a life outside school. However, the boundaries between a personal and professional life can become blurred when you are their child's teacher. Parents will still relate to you as a teacher and they may be observing your behaviour outside of school. They still need to be reassured that they are leaving their child in safe and capable hands and they will not respect you if you appear to be contravening the values you teach in school. If you do meet parents or children outside of school then it is important to relate to them just as you would do in school – be courteous, friendly and professional.

Safeguarding children

Legislation and Guidance

Education Act 2002

- Section 175 of the Education Act 2002 requires local education authorities and the governors of maintained schools and further education (FE) colleges to make arrangements to ensure that their functions are carried out with a view to safeguarding and promoting the welfare of children.
- Section 157 of the same Act and the Education (Independent Schools Standards) (England) Regulations 2003 require proprietors of independent schools (including academies and city technology colleges) to have arrangements to safeguard and promote the welfare of children who are pupils at the school.

Counter Terrorism and Security Act 2015

Section 26 of this Act applies to schools and other providers. It states that providers must have due regard to the need to prevent people being drawn into terrorism.

Working Together to Safeguard Children (DfE, 2015a)

This document covers the legislative requirements and expectations on individual services (including schools and colleges) to safeguard and promote the welfare of children. It also provides the framework for Local Safeguarding Children Boards (LSCBs) to monitor the effectiveness of local services, including safeguarding arrangements in schools.

Keeping Children Safe in Education (DfE, 2015b)

This guidance document was issued under Section 175 of the Education Act 2002, the Education (Independent School Standards) (England) Regulations 2014 and the Education (Non-Maintained Special Schools) (England) Regulations 2011. Schools and colleges must have regard to this guidance when carrying out their duties to safeguard and promote the welfare of children.

Unless otherwise stated, *school* in this guidance means all schools, whether maintained, non-maintained or independent, including academies and free schools, alternative provision academies, pupil referral units and maintained nursery schools.

College means further education and sixth form colleges under the Further and Higher Education Act 1992 and relates to under 18s, but excludes 16–19 academies and free schools.

Prevent Duty Guidance – England and Wales

This guidance covers the duty of schools and other providers in relation to Section 29 of the Counter Terrorism and Security Act 2015. All educational providers must have due regard to the need to prevent people being drawn into terrorism. The document can be located using the following link: www.gov.uk/government/publications/prevent-duty-guidance.

EXTENDED THINKING

* *Is it the role of schools or parents to keep children safe? Explain your answer.*

Teachers' Standards

The Teachers' Standards 2012 state that teachers, including headteachers, should safeguard children's well-being and maintain public trust in the teaching profession as part of their professional duties.

Good safeguarding practice

Good safeguarding practice includes the following:

* treating all pupils with respect;
* being alert to changes in pupils' behaviour and to signs of abuse and neglect;

* recognising that challenging behaviour may be an indicator of abuse;
* setting a good example through appropriate personal conduct, including behaviour online;
* involving pupils in decisions that affect them;
* encouraging positive, respectful and safe behaviour among pupils, including challenging inappropriate or discriminatory language or behaviour;
* avoiding behaviour or language which could be seen as favouring pupils;
* avoiding any behaviour which could lead to suspicions of anything other than a professional relationship with pupils;
* reading and understanding the school's child protection policy and guidance documents on wider safeguarding issues, for example, bullying, behaviour, and appropriate IT/social media use;
* asking the pupil's permission before initiating physical contact, such as assisting with dressing, physical support during PE or administering first aid;
* maintaining appropriate standards of conversation and interaction with and between pupils. Avoiding the use of sexualised or derogatory language, even in joke;
* being clear on professional boundaries and conduct with other staff when pupils are present;
* being aware that the personal, family circumstances and lifestyles of some pupils lead to an increased risk of abuse;
* applying the use of reasonable force only as a last resort and in compliance with school procedures;
* dealing with student infatuations in an open and transparent way, for example, informing the correct managers and managing the situation in a way which is sensitive to the feelings of the student;
* referring all concerns about a pupil's safety and welfare to the Designated Safeguarding Lead, or, if necessary, directly to police or children's social care;
* following the school's rules with regard to communication with pupils and use of social media and online networking;
* avoiding unnecessary time alone with pupils and risk manage any time alone or 1:1 working;
* avoiding sharing excessive personal information with pupils.

Abuse of a position of trust

All staff who work in school should be aware that inappropriate behaviour towards pupils is unacceptable and that their conduct towards pupils must be beyond reproach. In addition, staff should understand that, under the Sexual Offences Act 2003, it is an offence for a person over the age of 18 to have a sexual relationship with a person under the age of 18, where that person is in a position of trust, even if the relationship is consensual. This means that any sexual activity between a member of the school staff and a pupil under 18 may be a criminal offence, even if that pupil is over the age of consent.

Vulnerable children

Some children may have an increased risk of abuse. It is important to understand that this increase in risk is due more to societal attitudes and assumptions, and child protection procedures that fail to acknowledge children's diverse circumstances, rather than the

individual child's personality, impairment or circumstances. Many factors can contribute to an increase in risk, including prejudice and discrimination, isolation, social exclusion, communication issues and reluctance on the part of some adults to accept that abuse can occur.

Children who may be particularly vulnerable include those who are:

* missing education/missing from education;
* disabled or have special educational needs;
* young carers;
* looked after children;
* privately fostered children;
* affected by domestic abuse;
* affected by substance misuse/drug use;
* affected by mental health issues, including self-harm and eating disorders;
* affected by poor parenting;
* at risk of Fabricated or Induced Illness;
* at risk of gang and youth violence;
* asylum seekers;
* living away from home;
* vulnerable to being bullied, or engaging in bullying, including cyber, homophobic, and racist bullying;
* living transient lifestyles;
* LGBT (lesbian, gay, bisexual, transgender);
* missing from home or care;
* living in chaotic and unsupportive home situations;
* vulnerable to discrimination and maltreatment on the grounds of race, ethnicity, religion, disability or sexuality;
* vulnerable to extremism or radicalisation;
* vulnerable to faith abuse;
* involved directly or indirectly in child sexual exploitation CSE or trafficking;
* identified as not having English as a first language;
* at risk of female genital mutilation (FGM);
* at risk of forced marriage.

This list provides examples of additional vulnerable groups and is not exhaustive.

EXTENDED THINKING

* *To what extent does grouping children as vulnerable lead to the formation of stereotypes?*

Child Sexual Exploitation (CSE)

This involves exploitative situations where a child, male or female, receives something from an adult as a result of engaging in sexual activity. This can range from seemingly 'consensual' relationships to serious organised crime gangs. There will be an imbalance of power where the perpetrator holds power over the victim. This is a serious crime.

Female Genital Mutilation (FGM)

This is illegal and a form of child abuse. It involves a procedure to remove all or some of the female genitalia or any other injury to these organs. You will be required to undertake training in school or training organised by your provider to identify the signs of FGM.

Preventing radicalisation

This is part of the wider safeguarding duty. Schools must intervene where possible to prevent vulnerable children being radicalised. The internet has become a major factor in radicalisation and recruitment. As with all other forms of abuse, you should be confident in identifying pupils at risk and act proportionately. You will receive training on this by your provider. Schools must ensure safe internet filters are in place and provide pupils with an e-safety curriculum.

Photography and images

The vast majority of people who take or view photographs or videos of children do so for entirely innocent and acceptable reasons. Sadly, some people abuse children through taking or using images, so schools must ensure that they have some safeguards in place.

To protect pupils schools should:

- seek their consent for photographs to be taken or published (for example, on the website or in newspapers or publications);
- seek parental consent;
- not use pupils' full names with an image;
- ensure pupils are appropriately dressed;
- ensure that personal data is not shared;
- store images appropriately, securely and for no longer than necessary;
- only use school equipment, ie not personal devices;
- encourage pupils to speak up if they are worried about any photographs that are taken of them.

Physical intervention and use of reasonable force

All teachers should attempt to use de-escalation techniques and creative alternative strategies that are specific to the child. Restraint should only be used as a last resort and all incidents of restraint should be reviewed, recorded and monitored. Reasonable force must be used in accordance with government guidance.

Intimate care

If a child requires regular intimate care in school, this is likely to be written into a care plan which staff will adhere to. If an accident occurs and a child needs assistance with intimate care this will be risk managed to afford dignity to the child as well as security to the

staff member. Staff should behave in an open and transparent way by informing another member of staff and having the child's consent to help. Parents should be informed and incidents recorded.

E-safeguarding

Pupils increasingly use mobile phones, tablets and computers on a daily basis. They are a source of fun, entertainment, communication and education. However, unfortunately some adults and young people will use these technologies to harm children. The harm might range from sending hurtful or abusive communications, to enticing children to engage in sexually harmful conversations, webcam photography, encouraging radicalisation or face-to-face meetings. The school's e-safeguarding policy will explain how to keep pupils safe in school. Cyberbullying and sexting by pupils, via texts and emails, should be treated as seriously as any other type of bullying. In the absence of a child protection concern, these should be managed through the school's anti-bullying and confiscation procedures.

Chatrooms and some social networking sites are the more obvious sources of inappropriate and harmful behaviour and schools will have policies about usage of these. Some pupils will undoubtedly be 'chatting' outside school and are informed of the risks of this through the taught curriculum. Acceptable use of technology by staff and pupils should be enforced by schools.

Categories and definitions of abuse

To ensure that pupils are protected from harm, teachers need to understand what types of behaviour constitute abuse and neglect. Abuse and neglect are forms of maltreatment. Somebody may abuse or neglect a child by inflicting harm, for example, by hitting them, or by failing to act to prevent harm, for example, by leaving a small child home alone, or leaving knives or matches within reach of an unattended toddler. Abuse may be committed by adult men or women and by other children and young people. There are four categories of abuse: physical abuse, emotional abuse, sexual abuse and neglect.

Physical abuse

Physical abuse may involve hitting, shaking, throwing, poisoning, burning or scalding, drowning, suffocating or otherwise causing physical harm to a child. Physical harm may also be caused when a parent or carer fabricates the symptoms of, or deliberately induces, illness in a child. This used to be called Munchausen's Syndrome by Proxy, but is now more usually referred to as fabricated or induced illness.

Emotional abuse

Emotional abuse is the persistent emotional maltreatment of a child such as to cause severe and persistent adverse effects on the child's emotional development. It may involve conveying to a child that they are worthless or unloved, inadequate, or valued only insofar as they meet the needs of another person. It may include not giving the child opportunities to express their views, deliberately silencing them or 'making fun' of what they say or how they communicate. It may feature age or developmentally inappropriate expectations being imposed on children. These may include interactions that are beyond a child's developmental capability, as well as overprotection and limitation of exploration and learning, or preventing the child participating in normal social interaction. It may involve seeing or hearing the ill-treatment of another. It may involve serious bullying (including cyberbullying), causing children frequently to feel frightened or in danger, or the exploitation or corruption of children. Some level of emotional abuse is involved in all types of maltreatment of a child, although it may occur alone.

Sexual abuse

Sexual abuse involves forcing or enticing a child or young person to take part in sexual activities, not necessarily involving a high level of violence, whether or not the child is aware of what is happening. The activities may involve physical contact, including assault by penetration (for example, rape or oral sex) or non-penetrative acts such as masturbation, kissing, rubbing and touching outside of clothing. They may also include non-contact activities, such as involving children in looking at, or in the production of, sexual images, watching sexual activities, encouraging children to behave in sexually inappropriate ways, or grooming a child in preparation for abuse (including via the internet). Sexual abuse is not solely perpetrated by adult males. Women can also commit acts of sexual abuse, as can other children.

Neglect

Neglect is the persistent failure to meet a child's basic physical and/or psychological needs, which is likely to result in the serious impairment of the child's health or development. Neglect may occur during pregnancy as a result of maternal substance abuse. Once a child is born, neglect may involve a parent or carer failing to:

* provide adequate food, clothing and shelter (including exclusion from home or abandonment);
* protect a child from physical and emotional harm or danger;
* ensure adequate supervision (including the use of inadequate caregivers);
* ensure access to appropriate medical care or treatment. It may also include neglect of, or unresponsiveness to, a child's basic emotional needs.

Bullying

While bullying between children is not a separate category of abuse and neglect, it is a very serious issue that can cause considerable anxiety and distress. At its most serious level, bullying can have a disastrous effect on a child's well-being and in very rare cases has been a feature in the suicide of some young people. All incidences of bullying, including cyberbullying and prejudice-based bullying, should be reported and will be managed through the school's anti-bullying procedures. If the bullying is particularly serious, or the procedures used by the school to address the bullying are deemed to be ineffective, the headteacher and the Designated Safeguarding Lead should consider implementing child protection procedures.

There will be occasions when a pupil's behaviour warrants a response under child protection rather than anti-bullying procedures.

Children with sexually harmful behaviour

A lot of child sexual abuse is committed by someone under the age of 18. The management of children and young people with sexually harmful behaviour is complex and the school

will work with other agencies to maintain the safety of the whole school community. Young people who display such behaviour may be victims of abuse themselves and the child protection procedures will be followed for both victim and perpetrator. If you become concerned about a pupil's sexual behaviour you should speak to the Designated Safeguarding Lead as soon as possible.

Indicators of abuse

Physical signs define some types of abuse, for example, bruising, bleeding or broken bones resulting from physical or sexual abuse, or injuries sustained while a child has been inadequately supervised. The identification of physical signs is complicated, as children may go to great lengths to hide injuries, often because they are ashamed or embarrassed, or their abuser has threatened further violence or trauma if they 'tell' someone. It is also quite difficult for anyone without medical training to categorise injuries into accidental or deliberate with any degree of certainty. However, children may have no physical signs or they may be harder to see (for example, bruising on black skin) and therefore staff need to also be alert to behavioural indicators of abuse.

A child who is being abused or neglected may:

- have bruises, bleeding, burns, fractures or other injuries;
- show signs of pain or discomfort;
- keep arms and legs covered, even in warm weather;
- be concerned about changing for PE or swimming;
- look unkempt and uncared for;
- change their eating habits;
- have difficulty in making or sustaining friendships;
- appear fearful;
- be reckless with regard to their own or other's safety;
- self-harm;
- frequently miss school or arrive late;
- show signs of not wanting to go home;
- display a change in behaviour – from quiet to aggressive, or happy-go-lucky to withdrawn;
- challenge authority;
- become disinterested in their school work;
- be constantly tired or preoccupied;
- be wary of physical contact;
- be involved in, or particularly knowledgeable about, drugs or alcohol;
- display sexual knowledge or behaviour beyond that normally expected for their age.

Individual indicators will rarely, in isolation, provide conclusive evidence of abuse. They should be viewed as part of a jigsaw, and each small piece of information will help the Designated Safeguarding Lead to decide how to proceed. It is very important that you report and record your concerns. You do not need 'absolute proof' that the child is at risk.

Impact of abuse

The impact of child abuse should not be underestimated. Many children do recover well and go on to lead healthy, happy and productive lives, although most adult survivors agree that the emotional scars remain, however well buried. For some, full recovery is beyond their reach, and research shows that abuse can have an impact on the brain and its development. The rest of their childhood and their adulthood may be characterised by anxiety or depression, self-harm, eating disorders, alcohol and substance misuse, unequal and destructive relationships and long-term medical or psychiatric difficulties.

Taking action

It is the responsibility of staff to report and record their concerns as soon as possible. The best attitude to adopt is *never do nothing* if you have a concern about a child. It is your responsibility to initiate a discussion with the Designated Safeguarding Lead if in any doubt. As a teacher it is not your responsibility to investigate or decide whether a child has been abused. Any child, in any family in any school, could become a victim of abuse. In any school you should always maintain an attitude of "it could happen here".

Key points to remember for taking action are:

- report your concern to the Designated Safeguarding Lead as soon as possible;
- follow the school procedures for recording information;
- do not start your own investigation;
- share information on a need-to-know basis only – do not discuss the issue unnecessarily with colleagues, friends or family;
- seek support for yourself if you are distressed.

There will be occasions when staff may suspect that a pupil may be at risk, but have no 'real' evidence. The pupil's behaviour may have changed, their artwork could be bizarre, and they may write stories or poetry that reveal confusion or distress, or physical but inconclusive signs may have been noticed. In these circumstances, you should give the pupil the opportunity to talk. The signs that you have noticed may be due to a variety of factors, for example, a parent has moved out, a pet has died, a grandparent is very ill and so on. It is fine for staff to ask the pupil if they are OK or if you can help in any way. You should record these early concerns. If the pupil does begin to reveal that they are being harmed, you should follow the advice below. Following an initial conversation with the pupil, if you remain concerned, you should discuss your concerns with the Designated Safeguarding Lead.

Dealing with a disclosure from a pupil

It takes a lot of courage for a child to disclose that they are being abused. They may feel ashamed, particularly if the abuse is sexual; their abuser may have threatened what will happen if they tell; they may have lost all trust in adults; or they may believe, or have been told, that the abuse is their own fault.

If a pupil talks to you about any risks to their safety or well-being, you will need to let the pupil know that you will have to pass the information on. They need to know that staff are not allowed to keep secrets. The point at which you tell the pupil this is a matter for professional judgement. If you jump in immediately, the pupil may think that you do not

want to listen. If you leave it until the very end of the conversation, the pupil may feel that they have been misled into revealing more than they would have otherwise.

During their conversations with the pupils it is best practice to:

* allow pupils to speak freely;
* remain calm and not overreact – the pupil may stop talking if they feel they are upsetting their listener;
* give reassuring nods or words of comfort – *'I want to help'*; *'This isn't your fault'*; *'You are doing the right thing in talking to me'*;
* give the pupil space and time to express themselves;
* clarify or repeat back to check what you have heard if needed but do not lead the discussion in any way and do not ask direct or leading questions – such as whether it happens to siblings too, or what does the pupil's mother think about it;
* use questions such as *'Tell me...?' or 'Is there anything else?'*;
* at an appropriate time tell the pupil that in order to help them, then you will need to pass the information on;
* not automatically offer any physical touch as comfort. It may be anything but comforting to a child who has been abused;
* remember professional boundaries and do not share personal experiences such as *'That happened to me'*;
* avoid admonishing the child for not disclosing earlier. Saying things such as *'I do wish you had told me about this when it started'* or *'I can't believe what I'm hearing'* may be one way of being supportive but may be interpreted by the child to mean that they have done something wrong;
* tell the pupil what will happen next. The pupil may agree to go with you to see the Designated Safeguarding Lead. Otherwise let them know that you will be consulting them;
* write up their conversation as soon as possible on the record of concern form and hand it to the designated lead;
* seek support if they feel distressed.

Allegations against staff

When an allegation is made against a member of staff, set procedures must be followed. It is important to have a culture of openness and transparency and a consultation with the Designated Officer will happen if staff have: behaved in a way which has harmed, or may have harmed a child; possibly committed a criminal offence against or related to a child; or behaved towards a child or children in a way that indicates they would pose a risk of harm to children. It is rare for a child to make an entirely false or malicious allegation, although misunderstandings and misinterpretations of events do happen. Children may also make an allegation against an innocent party because they are too afraid to name the real perpetrator. However, if a child is found to continually make false allegations this may be a sign of mental health issues and a referral to services such as CAMHS (Child and Adolescent Mental Health Services) may be required.

An uncomfortable fact is that some professionals do pose a serious risk to pupils and schools must act on every allegation. However, staff who are the subject of an allegation have the right to have their case dealt with fairly, quickly and consistently and to be kept informed of its progress. Suspension is not the default option and alternatives to suspension will always be considered. In some cases, staff may be suspended where this is deemed to be the best way to ensure that children are protected. Staff will be advised to contact their trade union and will also be given access to a named representative.

Allegations against staff should be reported to the headteacher. Allegations against the headteacher should be reported to the Chair of Governors. Staff may also report their concerns directly to the police or Designated Officer if they believe direct reporting is necessary to secure action.

Staff, parents and governors must be reminded that publication of material that may lead to the identification of a teacher who is the subject of an allegation is prohibited by law. Publication includes verbal conversations or writing, including content placed on social media sites. Schools should communicate this to all parties.

Establishing effective relationships with pupils

Children do not learn from people they do not like. A fundamental part of your role as a teacher is to establish positive relationships with your learners. This involves a range of aspects including the following:

- empowering children to believe that they can achieve to the best of their abilities;
- praising children and catching them when they are good or when they do something well and celebrating their achievements;
- showing an interest in your learners as people by being interested in what they have to say, their views, beliefs and their lives outside of school;
- supporting them to overcome misconceptions in learning;
- being kind to your learners;
- being friendly to your learners;
- providing your learners with clear boundaries;
- engendering a sense of belonging;
- helping them to feel valued;
- issuing sanctions when appropriate but re-building relationships with them following incidents where sanctions are required;
- respecting the families and communities that support your learners;
- being willing to apologise to children when you need to do so;
- treating children fairly;
- empowering your learners by giving them a voice.

It is easy to focus on developing high-level subject knowledge so that you become an expert in teaching the curriculum. While this is crucial to teacher effectiveness, children remember good teachers not by their subject knowledge but by the quality of the relationships they established with them. This aspect of teacher effectiveness is often assumed and rarely addressed in teacher training courses. Courses of ITT often focus almost exclusively on developing trainees' subject knowledge, and aspects such as establishing relationships are often neglected. Children like teachers who are kind, friendly and happy to be with them.

You may be addressing stressful or traumatic issues in your personal life and this can impact detrimentally on your teaching ability and on your relationships with your learners. While it is difficult to leave these issues outside of school, this is something that you will need to learn very quickly. The ability to leave behind personal problems and focus on the learning and teaching is part and parcel of being a professional. Some children have to also contend with traumatic home lives and in these cases school becomes their sanctuary. They deserve consistency in your approach and whether or not they enjoy their day will largely depend on how you have made them feel. This is a great responsibility but also a privilege. If you feel like you cannot demonstrate these positive attributes because of personal issues then it is probably better to report your absence.

You need to ensure that you provide all of your learners with equal opportunities to achieve what they are capable of achieving. It is important that you do not demonstrate favouritism towards particular pupils and you give every child the right amount of support so that they can make progress. You will like some children more than others. This is natural. However, it is vital that you do not communicate this to your learners through your words and interactions with them. Children will very quickly pick up on whether you like them and thus it is important that they know that you do.

Professional boundaries

You need to work within the professional boundaries of being a teacher. To a large extent this means abiding by the code of professional conduct of your school and Part Two of the Teachers' Standards. Working within professional boundaries includes:

- not entering into relationships with pupils;
- not providing children with your personal contact details (eg mobile phone number or your personal email address);
- not arranging to meet with pupils outside of the school premises when this is not connected with their education;
- not enabling children to break the law (eg by purchasing cigarettes for them outside school);
- not accepting requests for friendship from pupils on social media sites;
- not using inappropriate language in front of children;
- not making discriminatory, hurtful or offensive comments against groups or individuals who have a protected characteristic under the Equality Act (2010);
- not abusing your position through subjecting children to any type of abuse;
- not abusing your position through stealing property or other resources from your school;
- breaching confidentiality by sharing information which should not be shared to others inside and outside of school;
- ensuring that you work within the statutory guidelines.

CRITICAL QUESTIONS

- *The above list is not exhaustive. Can you add any more 'rules' of professional conduct?*
- *Can you think of ways that pupils might encourage you to breach the professional boundaries of being a teacher?*

Fundamental British Values

Part Two of the Teachers' Standards defines Fundamental British Values (FBV). These include:

* democracy;
* the rule of law;
* individual liberty and mutual respect;
* tolerance of those with different faiths and beliefs.

To promote these values, particularly in the early years, you might:

* challenge stereotypes against groups with protected characteristics using stories;
* teach tolerant behaviour, for example, sharing, patience, queuing, listening to others;
* teach children to respect different cultures, faiths, beliefs and traditions through teaching cultural and social diversity;
* provide resources which expose children to diversity, for example, use of stories, puppets, posters, computer software;
* teach children that their views are important by asking them to decide on the class rules;
* introduce the idea of voting, for example, when making decisions as a class;
* teach children to listen to other people's ideas and how to respect them;
* teach children appropriate ways of challenging other people's perspectives;
* use circle time or stories to teach children about morals in order to help them become ethical people;
* build links with the local police force and ask them to come into school to teach children about illegal behaviour;
* promote the use of the student council as a way of developing children's understanding of democracy.

CRITICAL QUESTIONS

* *Are the values identified in the Teachers' Standards fundamentally British?*
* *Whose role is it to teach children values? Is it the role of the school or is it the role of the parent?*
* *Is the inclusion of FBV in the curriculum a way of controlling people's behaviour?*

Personal beliefs

Part Two of the Teachers' Standards states that teachers must ensure '*that personal beliefs are not expressed in ways which exploit pupils' vulnerability or might lead them to break the law*'. We all have personal beliefs on a range of topics including religion, sexuality, gender, marriage, war/conflict, politics and so on. These beliefs are formed largely by influences from our families, the media, friends, social media and engagement with literature. Your personal beliefs in relation to these issues should be kept private and not shared with your learners. This is because, as a teacher or even as a trainee teacher, you are in a strong position of influence. It is better to remain impartial on these issues so that you do not exploit the vulnerability of your pupils.

Working within school policies

All schools have their own policies. These will include learning and teaching policies in relation to specific national curriculum subjects. There will be policies on general themes, including assessment, safeguarding, bullying and behaviour management. This is not an exhaustive list and increasingly schools are developing an extensive bank of policies. You should be able to locate these easily on the school website and they will also be available on the school's intranet. Policies may also be available in hard copy in the staffroom.

Each policy should set out clearly and concisely a set of principles which underpin the practices of the school. The operationalisation of these principles should also be stated in the policy so that all staff know what they need to do to meet the principles. Working within the frameworks of the school policies will enable you to carry out your duties in a professional manner. It is important that all staff adhere to the policy frameworks in order to ensure consistency of approaches across the school. This sense of consistency provides children with security because the operationalisation of each policy should be similar in each class.

CRITICAL QUESTIONS

- *To what extent do school policies restrict teachers' personal sense of agency?*
- *What are the advantages and disadvantages of school policies?*

Attendance and punctuality

Teachers who are absent are costly to schools and society and disruptive to children's education. Additionally, trainee teachers have a limited amount of time in schools to demonstrate that they have achieved the Teachers' Standards to the minimum level. If you are absent from school then you cannot demonstrate that you are achieving the Standards. As a teacher you expect your learners to demonstrate good attendance and punctuality. It is therefore obvious that your own attendance and punctuality should be excellent because you are a role model. The fact that attendance and punctuality are now part of the Teachers' Standards means that you are at risk of not achieving Qualified Teacher Status if your attendance and punctuality are erratic. Additionally, once qualified you can be dismissed on the grounds of ill health if there are concerns about your attendance and punctuality.

This is a relatively easy issue to solve. Make sure that you get sufficient sleep by going to bed at a reasonable time. Make sure that you have a good alarm to wake you up in the morning. Keep yourself healthy by making sure that you eat healthily regularly and keep yourself hydrated by drinking plenty of water. Everyone is prone to catching coughs, colds and other infections. When you first work in school you are more susceptible to picking these up because your immunity takes a while to build up. Newly Qualified Teachers, for example, often get ill in their first year of teaching but by their second year they have built up their immunity to many infections. In the case of minor illnesses then you should not take time off work. Only take time off if you literally are unable to teach and if your illness is more serious. In the case of sickness and diarrhoea you should follow the school policy on absence and return to work. In all cases you should contact the school early on the first day of absence. This is usually by 8 am. You should forward your planning to the school. You should give the school an indication of when you are likely to return to work. You should keep in contact with the school on a daily basis during the initial five days to inform them of your intentions for the following day. If your absence exceeds one week then you will need medical certification to cover you for further absence.

IN PRACTICE

The following guidance is taken from an Initial Teacher Education (ITE) provider's handbook:

In all cases of absence trainees are reminded that they have to demonstrate their capability to pass the placement within the given time frame for that placement. Extensive absence may make it impossible for a judgement to be made. Trainees must not start a teaching placement unless they are medically fit. Parents, spouses or partners of trainees should not be asked to inform the school or University about a trainee's absence during school-based training unless the situation is unavoidable.

Trainees must ask their class mentor to sign the attendance register to certify attendance in school. This form must be placed at the front of the placement file. All absences from school placement must be made up. If there is considerable absence from school, without medical proof, the University reserves the right to terminate the placement. In such instances the trainee will not be granted Extenuating Circumstances (ECs) and will not pass the placement. In such instances the University may consider whether the absence constitutes a breach of the Code of Professional Conduct and may apply the Fitness to Practise policy.

If medical evidence is available the University still reserves the right to terminate the placement and the student can apply for ECs to be taken into consideration. In such instances the placement will be deferred and the trainee will undertake an additional placement during the re-sit period. Placements cannot be extended into periods when trainees are University-based.

Trainees should attend training days (even if off-site), staff meetings, twilight meetings and parents' consultation meetings unless otherwise advised.

Procedures for reporting absence from school:

On the first day of absence the trainee must:

- *contact the school by telephone and speak to the Head Teacher or available member of staff;*
- *ensure that the absence is reported to the school by 8.15 am at the latest;*
- *forward lesson planning to the school and resources via e-mail by 8 am if the trainee was due to teach a lesson that day;*
- *report the absence to their link tutor and Head of Primary ITE;*
- *the student must telephone the school on each day of an absence so that the school can plan accordingly.*

It is not acceptable for a trainee to send a text message to the class/senior mentor to notify them of an absence from school. It is not acceptable for a trainee to email the school with notification of an absence as emails may not be checked regularly. If a trainee teacher fails to attend a school placement without contacting the school the school should contact the University immediately. In this situation it is better to contact the administration staff who will pass on the message to the relevant tutor. Unexplained absence may lead to the start of disciplinary procedures as the University takes this extremely seriously. If absences from school placement exceed one week the University reserves the right to terminate the placement. In the case of requests for absence due to attendance at religious festivals, trainees can expect schools to be sensitive and grant leave of absence for such purposes. However, there is an expectation that trainees will inform the school well in advance of the dates so that arrangements can be made to cover the absence. The notification of absence form for religious observance must be used in this instance. Trainees will be granted a maximum of two days leave of absence for religious observance. Trainees can only take leave of absence with the written permission of the Head Teacher.

The only reasons that are accepted for absence are as follows:

1. *illness;*
2. *urgent compassionate reasons eg bereavement; family illness;*
3. *interviews for teaching posts [arrangements to visit schools must be made either during PPA time, Professional Development time or after school, not during planned teaching time].*

Trainees will not be granted leave of absence to attend weddings or for holidays. Trainee teachers must remember that absence from school placements places colleagues in school under additional pressure. If you have lessons planned for the day of an absence you must ensure that any necessary planning and resources are forwarded to the school. The permission of the Head Teacher and the Head of Primary ITE must be sought for any absence under (ii) and (iii). You should inform any person affected by your absence as well in advance as possible.

CRITICAL QUESTION

* *Are there any points in the extract above that you wish to challenge? Give reasons for your response.*

Discipline and physical contact

It is illegal in the United Kingdom to carry out any form of corporal punishment on children. This was outlawed by parliament in 1987. Your school should have a policy on physical contact with children. This might be part of the safeguarding policy. In most instances it is better to avoid physical contact with children. This includes touching them, sitting them on your lap or holding their hands. If you limit the amount of physical touch then your actions cannot be misconstrued. In some cases children need and expect some form of physical contact from adults. This might happen if they hurt themselves or if another person hurts them and they seek comfort from you. In cases where physical contact is necessary it is better if you can do this in a public place where other adults can witness what is happening. You should try to avoid being left alone with children in classrooms. Your motives might be innocent but actions can easily be misconstrued.

IN PRACTICE

The following guidance is taken from an ITE provider's handbook:

At the commencement of the placement trainees should discuss with the Head Teacher or Senior Mentor what disciplinary strategies are regarded as appropriate for use. Trainees should follow the advice they are given. In no circumstances should trainees use any form of corporal punishment. It is a criminal offence and will result in failing the placements and possible suspension from the University. Trainees must follow school discipline policies and make sure they are not left alone with children. In cases where they need to speak to pupils individually, trainees must ask another member of staff to be present. Our view is that trainees must not have any physical contact with any pupil. This is difficult when working with young children, as there may be times when children approach adults for reassurance. Trainees are advised to discuss the boundaries of acceptable/unacceptable physical contact with class and senior mentors. Trainees should follow the guidance on physical contact in the school's safeguarding policy. The Senior Mentor must ensure that the trainee has been given all relevant information regarding child protection and safeguarding. If trainees are supervising pupils while they are changing for PE they should ask for the support of another adult to be present. We believe that any form of behaviour management must be positive and take into account pupils' self-esteem. Trainee teachers will risk failing a placement if strategies for behaviour management are negative.

CRITICAL QUESTIONS

- *Does children's need for physical contact change as they get older?*
- *What are the limitations of positive behaviour management strategies?*
- *What might constitute negative behaviour management strategies?*
- *Are there any times when negative behaviour management strategies might be appropriate?*

Equal opportunities

The following characteristics are protected characteristics under the Equality Act (2010).

- age;
- disability;
- gender reassignment;
- marriage and civil partnership;
- pregnancy and maternity;
- race;

* religion or belief;
* sex;
* sexual orientation.

Direct discrimination is where a person or organisation treats a person less favourably because of a protected characteristic. Indirect discrimination occurs when a person or organisation implements a rule, policy, criterion or practice which disadvantages a person with a protected characteristic. It is both unprofessional and illegal to directly or indirectly discriminate against any individual who has a protected characteristic. You therefore need to consider carefully your words, attitudes and actions towards your learners, colleagues, parents, carers and the wider community.

CRITICAL QUESTIONS

* *Can you think of some examples of direct discrimination in the context of schools?*
* *Can you think of some examples of indirect discrimination in the context of schools?*

IN PRACTICE

The following guidance is taken from an ITE provider's handbook:

We are all different but we all deserve to be treated fairly. The University will not tolerate discrimination of any kind. This includes discrimination on the basis of:

* *disability (including mental illness);*
* *sexual orientation;*
* *race, ethnicity, colour and religious/cultural beliefs;*
* *age;*
* *gender (including gender reassignment);*
* *social class;*
* *marital status.*

Please note – this is not an exhaustive list. Any form of discrimination will not be tolerated.

Schools must comply with the Equality Act (2010). The ITE partnership will challenge all forms of discrimination, bullying and harassment. Discrimination against trainees with disabilities is unlawful and partnership schools and initial teacher training providers are required by law to make reasonable adjustments in order to remove barriers to participation and achievement.

If trainees feel they are being discriminated against by a member of staff in school, a pupil or by a parent, they are advised to discuss their concerns with the Senior Mentor and/or the University Link Tutor. Link tutors routinely monitor harassment and discrimination during visits to school. However trainees are advised to contact Link Tutors immediately if a problem arises. In all cases of prejudice and discrimination against trainee teachers, Link Tutors must be informed. Link Tutors will make a full report to the Head of Primary ITE and the case will be investigated.

CRITICAL QUESTIONS

- *Is the above equal opportunities statement compliant with the Equality Act (2010)?*
- *Can you think of an example of both direct and indirect discrimination in the context of a primary school?*

Working with parents and carers

Developing effective professional relationships with parents and carers is critical in the context of teaching. Most parents want the very best quality educational experience for their child. Most parents will support you if they know that you are working in their child's best interests.

Current policy frameworks (such as the *2015 SEND Code of Practice and the Early Years Foundation Stage framework*) emphasise the role of parents as partners in the process of their child's education. Children achieve better when the partnership between parents and the school is strong. You need to adopt a professional and supportive approach when working with parents. Some parents may have had negative personal experiences of education and for this reason they may be less willing to engage with teachers than those who had a more positive experience. It is important that parents view you as approachable and friendly. If they feel like you are judging them in negative ways this can disempower them and result in them disengaging from the education process. Some parents experience challenging personal situations in their daily lives. They will appreciate you if you show them empathy and support and they may be more willing to seek your advice if they know that you are not going to judge them. As a teacher it is crucial that you keep an open mind. It is critical that you do not form negative judgements against parents on the basis of any of the protected characteristics in the Equality Act (2010) as this might be viewed as discrimination.

Parents and carers should be included in decision-making processes which affect their child. It is important that you provide them with a clear view of how their child is progressing in the national curriculum subjects in relation to nationally expected indicators of achievement. It is best to avoid the use of educational jargon in discussions so that there is clarity in communication. You need to create a dialogue with parents which essentially enables them to understand what they can do with their child at home to accelerate their child's educational achievement. For children with SEND it is crucial that there is regular on-going dialogue between parents and teachers and that they are involved in reviewing their child's progress and setting targets for their future development.

Regular communication with parents will help parents to understand what their child is learning in school, what they need to learn next and how they can support the school to help their child achieve their targets. Communication can be enacted in a variety of ways. Examples include:

- regular telephone calls, emails or text messages to parents;
- a parents' section on the school website;
- the use of a daily home-school diary;
- weekly newsletters.

Communications should always be positive and professional, at least on your part. Sometimes there may be occasions when a parent is very upset and/or angry with you. It is helpful to consider here how you might address this.

IN PRACTICE

A parent comes into school one morning to tell you that they are upset because you issued a sanction to their child on the previous day due to disruptive behaviour.

- *Explain to the parent that you understand that they are upset – show empathy.*
- *Explain that you cannot speak to them immediately because you have a teaching commitment. Ask them to come back to see you at 3.45pm – buy yourself some time to consider how to respond.*
- *At 3.45pm meet the parent in a space where you can be seen by your colleagues – be visible to others.*
- *Sit down – avoid hierarchies.*
- *Give them an opportunity to state their concerns – give them ownership of the meeting.*
- *Make eye contact, nod, smile, listen – show interest in what they have to say;*
- *Respond to their comments by explaining why the sanction was issued – offer an explanation.*
- *Ask them how they might have dealt with the situation – give them ownership.*
- *Respond to the points they make. Reiterate why you responded in the way you did.*
- *Reiterate that the sanction was issued because of the child's behaviour and that the behaviour is problematic, not the child.*
- *Agree how both school and home can work together to resolve the child's behaviour.*
- *Note down the actions, thank them for their time and reiterate that they can talk to you at any time and you will listen to them.*

Sometimes you will need to admit to parents that you took the wrong course of action against their child. In these situations, parents may respect you for being honest with them and they will appreciate the fact that you have listened to their concerns.

There may be challenging situations to address where you have specific concerns about the child's safety in the home. In these situations you should follow the school's policy on safeguarding which will emphasise the need for you to refer information on to the named Safeguarding Officer in school rather than addressing concerns directly to the parents.

Working with colleagues and other professionals

You will be working with colleagues with a range of roles in school. These will include teaching, non-teaching, clerical/administrative and ancillary/domestic roles. Schools need a range of people in order to be able to function. It is important that you respect all of your colleagues in school and treat them as you would expect to be treated. It is also important that you do not view your role as more important than anyone else's role. Everyone has a role to play in enabling the school to function.

You will spend a lot of time developing working relationships with teaching assistants. As a trainee you will go into classes where teaching assistants already have clearly defined roles and responsibilities. It is important that you find an opportunity to talk to them about their roles and responsibilities. Try to find out what their strengths are and use this knowledge to inform how you deploy them. One of the most significant skills that you will need to develop is the skill of communication. You might be really busy organising yourself but if you are going to get maximum impact from the teaching assistant they need to be clearly briefed on their roles and responsibilities in the lessons in which they are supporting. This is most effective when it is done in advance so that when they enter the classroom they know exactly what is expected of them. Your teaching assistant will need to be clear on what you want the children to learn in a lesson and the support that they need to provide to enable the children to achieve this. It is critical that you clearly distinguish between the learning objective (ie *what* you want the children to learn) and the task (*how* they will learn it). The teaching assistant will need to have clarity on exactly what level of support they are expected to provide their learners with during the lesson and when to withdraw support, thus enabling independence in learning. They will also need to have clarity on how to extend the learning for those children who demonstrate a good level of understanding and how to support learners to overcome misconceptions in their learning. They will need to know the specific vocabulary that you want the children to learn. Teaching assistants will need to have clarity in relation to how they model the new learning and the types of questions they need to ask their learners.

It is good practice to provide teaching assistants with a sheet which summarises all of the above information. However, you need to find the time to discuss this with them and if necessary you might need to 'walk them through' the steps.

Working with teaching assistants can be hugely rewarding. They can provide your learners with additional support that you are not able to provide. If they are confident and highly skilled in their roles they will know how to challenge children further and they will be able to ensure depth of learning as well as coverage. However, it is not without its challenges. They might be reluctant to take instructions from you, either because they do not know you very well or because they feel that you lack the appropriate experience to undertake the teaching role. They may not agree with your plans for the content of a session and they may wish to change the content or the way in which you have suggested something is taught.

In the above situations it might be helpful to talk some of these challenges through with your school-based mentor. Many of these issues can be overcome by establishing an effective relationship with your teaching assistant right from the beginning. Tell them that you are there to learn and that you can learn from them as well as from your mentor. Demonstrate to them that you value the work they do. Try to involve them as much as possible in planning for the learners they will be supporting. Involve them in discussions about assessments and together formulate next steps/actions for learners which then inform your future planning. If they perceive that you are treating them as a professional and that you respect them, they will more than likely go above and beyond the call of duty to help you. If you observe them doing something incorrect, consider carefully how you might address this immediately in the lesson without undermining their sense of professionalism. This is not an easy task but intervention is necessary in these situations to prevent learners from developing misconceptions.

Consider carefully how you can develop positive relationships with the cleaners or caretaker. At the end of the teaching day they may well need to move into your classroom to clean it. You need to think carefully about where you do your work after school and where you hold private meetings. You do not want to make the cleaners feel like they should not be there. They have a job to do and they need to be able to do it. It is very easy to upset cleaners by leaving an untidy classroom at the end of the day. Their role is to clean but not to tidy. In relation to this, you need to ensure that your learners take greater responsibility for the general tidiness of the classroom at the end of each school day. Make sure that their tables are tidy and that learning resources are not scattered around on the floor for cleaners to pick up. Putting resources away in the correct place and looking after resources is all part of the learning process. If you need to stay late into the evening or to come into school during a holiday then make sure that you discuss this with the site manager/caretaker. Do not simply assume that you can do this without permission. Even if you are given a key, you may still need to alert the caretaker that you will be on the premises.

Developing effective relationships with clerical staff is also important. Remember to complete the registers on time and to distribute letters to pupils when you are required to do so. If you arrange a meeting with an external professional or parent, remember to notify the clerical staff so that this can be added into the school diary. Make sure that you are familiar with all the necessary processes for ordering resources or reclaiming expenses. Take the time to get to know these processes.

Developing effective relationships with external professionals is critical to securing successful outcomes for learners. You will inevitably at some point during your teaching career have to liaise with a range of external professionals. These include but are not restricted to the following:

* educational psychologists;
* speech and language therapists;
* physiotherapists;
* behaviour support workers;
* learning support teachers;
* occupational therapists;
* social care;
* nurses and health care practitioners;
* doctors.

In cases where children have an Education and Health Care Plan, external professionals may come into school periodically to carry out assessments on individual children. They may also come into school to carry out focused, regular intervention work with pupils. They may provide you with recommendations to you to help you remove barriers to learning. It is important that you recognise that these professionals have knowledge and skills as a result of highly specialised training. It is important that you value this expertise and implement the actions that they have recommended to you. It is a good idea to try to 'shadow' these colleagues when they support specific pupils. Work shadowing is a valuable form of professional development and this will provide you with knowledge, skills and expertise which is impossible to learn through reading a book. This is because children are unique and respond differently to strategies and interventions which are applied to them. Use this as an opportunity to observe the effectiveness of a strategy or intervention on a specific child.

EVIDENCE-BASED TEACHING

Studies have shown an association between parental substance misuse and neglect, for children's basic needs for food, warmth and hygiene may go unnoticed or unmet. Additionally, widespread poverty, housing stress and drug and alcohol availability are all known to add to the stresses of living in a particular neighbourhood, and increase the likelihood of abuse and neglect (Davies and Ward, 2012).

EVALUATE

* *Why might some of these issues result in neglect?*

CHALLENGE

* *Is it inevitable that parents living in poverty neglect their children?*

APPLY

* *In school identify some children who you think might be neglected. What characteristics lead you to this assumption?*

EVIDENCE-BASED TEACHING

Children are twice as likely to have neglect confirmed within their first five years if there is domestic abuse in the household (Davies and Ward, 2012).

EVALUATE

* *Why might domestic violence lead to neglect?*

CHALLENGE

* *Is it inevitable that parents living in domestic violence neglect their children?*

APPLY

* *In school identify the provision that is available to support children who are neglected.*

TECHNOLOGY

Webonauts Internet Academy is a game developed by PBS Kids in which players are taken through an intergalactic world where they must navigate key topics relating to safe and responsible Internet usage. It is best used with younger children to introduce them to internet safety in a fun but informative way. The link is http://pbskids.org/webonauts/.

Critical reflections

This chapter has emphasised the role of the teacher as a professional and the role of teachers in safeguarding the welfare of children and young people. The extent to which schooling can compensate for multiple societal issues is debatable. As issues occur within society, it would seem that the responsibility to address such issues is placed at the doors of schools and ITT institutions. However, schools need to do all they can to keep children safe and children have a right to be taught by a teacher who takes their professionalism very seriously. If the profession is to be respected then one way of facilitating this is for teachers to be excellent role models. Being a teacher is a privilege, not a right, and that privilege means that the expectations on you are high. However, they are not insurmountable.

KEY READINGS

Classic:

Tomlinson, S (2001) *Education in a Post-Welfare Society*. Buckingham: Open University Press.

Whitty, G, Power, S and Halpin, D (1998) *Devolution and Choice in Education: The School, the State and the Market*. Buckingham: Open University Press.

Contemporary:

Carter, A (2015) *Review of Initial Teacher Training*. London: DfE.

DfE (2015a) *Working Together to Safeguard Children: A Guide to Inter-agency Working to Safeguard and Promote the Welfare of Children*. London: DfE.

DfE (2015b) *Keeping Children Safe in Education: Statutory Guidance for Schools and Colleges*. London: DfE.

References

Carter, A (2015) *Review of Initial Teacher Training*. London: DfE.

Davies, C and Ward, H (2012) *Safeguarding Children across Services*. London: Jessica Kingsley.

INDEX